Options

Theory, Strategy, and Applications

Robert S. Hamada
Series in Finance

Options

Theory, Strategy, and Applications

Peter Ritchken

Weatherhead School of Management
Case Western Reserve University

Scott, Foresman and Company
Glenview, Illinois
London, England

To the memory of my parents

Library of Congress Cataloging-in-Publication Data

Ritchken, Peter.
  Options : theory, strategy, and applications.

  Includes bibliographies and index.
  1. Put and call transactions—Mathematical
models.   I. Title.
HG6042.R57   1987   332.64′52   86-29721
ISBN 0-673-18307-6

1 2 3 4 5 6-EBI-92 91 90 89 88 87

Preface

Options: Theory, Strategy, and Applications is an introductory text for advanced undergraduate students in the fields of business, finance, and economics, as well as for MBA students. It provides a comprehensive introduction to the management of portfolios using options in financial markets. Stock, index, debt, and foreign currency options are discussed, as well as forward and futures contracts and options on these instruments. Insights are offered into why such contracts are useful, especially as risk-transferring devices. The process of valuing options within an efficient market is closely examined. Although this theory has immediate applications in option markets, it also finds exciting applications in many other areas of finance because almost all corporate securities can be viewed as portfolios of options.

Interesting applications, including the valuation of treasury and corporate bonds, convertibles, warrants, and operating leases, are discussed. This book emphasizes throughout the central risk-management feature associated with the intelligent use of option contracts.

This text differs from other options texts in that it provides considerable breadth of coverage. It consists of sixteen modularized chapters, each of which covers a particular aspect of options and includes exercises and references. Some chapters contain appendices, which provide additional details relevant to those chapters. For example, the appendix to Chapter 3 describes the new margin regulations, while the appendix to Chapter 9 provides a computer program for valuing stock options. All advanced material, indicated by asterisks, can be omitted without creating difficulties in comprehending later material. Some chapters are self-contained and can be skipped without loss of continuity. For example, Chapter 5, which deals with the economic role of options, can be omitted.

This modularity allows instructors to select chapter sequences that best reflect the needs of their classes. For example, a course in speculative markets might focus on existing option markets and emphasize the role of particular option strategies in portfolio management, while a course in corporate finance might focus on the application of option theory in valuing corporate securities.

The first part of the text introduces the reader to option contracts, to the stock option markets, and to some pricing relationships. *Chapter 1* provides a broad overview and history of the option markets. In *Chapter 2,* put and call options are defined and the operation of the current option markets is examined. *Chapter 3* discusses stock option strategies and illustrates how stock option contracts can be meshed, possibly with the underlying security, to produce payouts that are consistent with the investor's desire for security and willingness to take risks. *Chapter 4* is concerned with pricing relationships that must exist between a particular option and its underlying security and between options on the same stock. Since investors naturally want to make more money, some very powerful pricing relationships can be established.

The next three chapters are self-contained. *Chapter 5* emphasizes the economic role of options and examines conditions under which exact option prices can be computed using the arbitrage principles discussed in Chapter 4. Students taking speculative market courses could skip this chapter. *Chapter 6* discusses the statistical behavior of the prices of both common stock and portfolios of common stock. The characterization of the statistical process driving stock and portfolio prices is important, since it allows exact option-pricing models to be established. (These models are presented in Chapter 8.) Through portfolio diversification, nonmarket-related risks can be reduced, although market-related risks still exist. *Chapter 7* investigates index options, which can provide effective hedges against market-related risk. Index options account for over 40 percent of all trading in options. Advantages of index options and stock options are compared.

Chapters 8, 9, and 10 are concerned with the pricing of stock options. In *Chapter 8,* the Black-Scholes model is presented and properties of the option prices are investigated. *Chapter 9* carefully develops the binomial option-pricing model, which contains the Black-Scholes model as a special case. The model is developed in such a way that the key assumptions of the Black-Scholes model become quite clear. *Chapter 10* presents several applications of option-pricing models in speculative markets. In addition, empirical support for option-pricing models is examined.

Chapter 11 examines alternative financial instruments useful in transferring risk associated with price uncertainty. Forward and futures contracts are defined and their relationships to put and call options are investigated. Options on forward and futures contracts are also examined.

Chapter 12 and 13 are concerned with interest rate risk management. *Chapter 12* provides some background information on debt instruments issued by the Treasury. Properties of bonds are summarized and theories of the term structure of interest rates are reviewed. *Chapter 13* investigates ways financial contracts such as debt options and debt futures can be used to manage the risk exposure of interest-rate-sensitive securities. Swaps and options on swaps are discussed as alternative hedging devices.

Chapter 14 illustrates how option theory can be used to value corporate liabilities. Risky bonds, equity, subordinated debt, warrants, convertibles, foreign currency bonds, and other types of claims on firms are discussed. Compound options, options on the greater or lesser of two prices, and exchange options are discussed as well.

Chapter 15 investigates the foreign currency option market and risk management of exchange rates. *Chapter 16* provides an introduction to continuous time mathematics that is useful for financial economists who use arbitrage arguments to price securities. Illustrations of its use in solving a variety of problems discussed in earlier chapters are provided.

A basic introductory course in options would cover Chapters 1 through 4, review Chapter 6, and include Chapters 7, 8, and 9. A more complete treatment would include a discussion of forward and futures contracts together with their options (Chapter 11). Chapters 12, 13, and 15 are relevant if interest rate risk management and currency risk management can be covered. Chapter 14 is important to students of corporate finance who are interested in valuation, while Chapter 16 is important to students who want to follow the mathematics in journal articles that apply option theory to value financial claims.

This book has evolved from lecture notes that I used in teaching speculative market classes in the MBA program at the Weatherhead School of Management at Case Western Reserve. I would like to thank the MBA students of my 1983 and 1984 classes, especially George Marko, John Currier, Colleen Boland, Lisa Brockett, Richard Adler, Terrance Kelley, John Cook, and Wen Kuei Chen. I would also like to thank Greg Getts and Shyanjaw Kuo for developing the computer programs in this book. I have benefited from discussions with Charles Tapiero, Harvey Salkin, J. B. Silvers, Arnie Reisman, Danny Solow, Mike Ferri, Sarkis Koury, Laurent Jacques, Robin Symes, and C. F. Lee. My thanks also go to the following reviewers:

Warren Bailey, The Ohio State University;
Georges Courtadon, New York University;
A. James Ifflander, Arizona State University;
Ravi Jagannathan, Northwestern University;
Robert W. Kolb, University of Miami;
Carl F. Luft, DePaul University; and
Alan Marcus, Boston University.

A very special thanks goes to George Lobell, Senior Acquisitions Editor at Scott, Foresman, for his continuous help, enthusiasm, and encouragement throughout all phases of this project. Thanks, too, to Diane Culhane for editing the final manuscript and to Frances McKinney for editing earlier drafts.

Finally, I would like to thank the Department of Operations Research and the Banking and Finance Division of the Weatherhead School of Management for their support of this project.

Peter Ritchken
Department of Operations Research
Weatherhead School of Management
Case Western Reserve University
Cleveland, Ohio

Contents

14   VALUATION OF CORPORATE SECURITIES   328

15   FOREIGN CURRENCY OPTIONS   366

16   AN INTRODUCTION TO CONTINUOUS TIME MATHEMATICS   382

1

Introduction

In April 1973 the Chicago Board Options Exchange began trading stock options. The exchange initially traded call options on sixteen common stocks. The success was remarkable and led to a series of expansions. In 1975 and 1976 the American, Philadelphia, and Pacific Stock Exchanges began trading call options on common stock and in 1977 put options were listed on all the exchanges. The volume of contracts traded continued to grow and the number of securities upon which options were traded increased from the original sixteen securities to nearly four hundred. By the early 1980s the daily volume of trading in stock options grew to a point where the number of shares underlying the options exceeded the daily volume of shares traded on the New York Stock Exchange.

The 1980s have seen the expansion of option contracts onto other securities, such as fixed-income securities, a variety of stock and bond indexes, foreign currencies, and onto a range of futures contracts including commodity and financial futures. By 1985 options on indexes accounted for almost 50 percent of total option trading. Indeed, the most active option contract, a contract on the Standard and Poor's 100 index, had an average daily volume of 350,000 contracts, which made it by far the most active contract ever issued.

The innovation and proliferation of new contracts have been remarkable and have had major effects in the financial markets. Of course, not all the new contracts were successful. Occasionally, due to a lack of market interest and low liquidity, an exchange withdrew a contract. Nonetheless, innovative products continue to be designed and the various exchanges continue to vie for regulatory permission to introduce new products.

OPTIONS FOR RISK MANAGEMENT

The success of the option markets must be attributable to the fact that they do fulfill definite needs. Some of these needs can be traced back to the very uncertain financial environment of the last two decades, which saw dramatic

1

changes in the behavior of prices in the labor, financial, and commodity markets. Foreign currency exchange rates and interest rates—both long- and short-term—together with stock prices have displayed unprecedented volatility. At the macroeconomic level, the early 1980s saw increasing bank failures, high unemployment, and large deficits. All these factors led investors to demand financial products that could be used to manage price risks in a more precise fashion. The exchanges eagerly responded to these needs by designing and seeking approval of new financial products in futures and options. Although these instruments have increased the complexities of the financial markets, they have also created new opportunities for investors. Indeed, with these instruments readily available, decision makers can do a much more effective job of pricing and choosing which risks to maintain and which risks to hedge. One of the primary objectives of this text is to highlight the relevance of options as risk management devices and to illustrate how different investors, faced with different investment objectives, can intelligently use options in their investment strategies.

Options are used by speculators and hedgers. *Speculators* are typically individual investors who trade for their own accounts and who are prepared to commit funds into ventures whose outcomes are highly uncertain. *Hedgers,* on the other hand, attempt to invest funds as judiciously as possible. Their goals are to protect capital from adverse consequences. Hedgers are often private investors or professional money managers employed by corporations and financial institutions such as banks, pension funds, and savings and loans. Although the objectives of speculators and hedgers are contrary in that one group desires risk while the other group seeks to avoid it, both groups operate in the same marketplace and have access to the same prices. Indeed, the two types of investors complement each other. We shall see that a hedger can use options to repackage risk in such a way that any unwanted risk can be transferred to speculators willing to bear it. Of course this transference of risk does not take place without cost. The size of the cost depends on the risk that is transferred and is embedded into the premiums of the option contracts. In this regard, options can be viewed similarly to insurance policies, whose price depends on the risk transferred.

OPTIONS IN FINANCE

The prices of option contracts are established by competitive bidding in free, centralized marketplaces. The establishment of theoretical fair prices for these contracts has attracted considerable attention by academic researchers. However, prior to the 1970s no satisfactory theory had emerged. In 1973, the same year that the Chicago Board Options Exchange opened, two professors by the names of Black and Scholes published a theoretical paper on option pricing that provided a major breakthrough in the field of finance. Although conceived in theory, their paper had an immediate and significant impact on the financial markets. Indeed, the Black-Scholes option pricing model has been adopted as the standard model for both theoretical and applied studies in option markets. The model is so useful that it is often included as a hard-wired function in financial hand-held calculators. Discussion of this model and its applications in financial markets is essential in any text on options.

The importance of the Black and Scholes article, however, extends beyond the arena of listed option markets. Black and Scholes were the first to recognize that all corporate liabilities could be viewed as combinations of option contracts. Their insight was profound in that it provided a unifying framework for the valuation of corporate liabilities. Within the last decade, the basic option theory that they provided has been extended and used to value all types of corporate liabilities, including convertible bonds, warrants, coupon bonds, and common stock. The application of option theory to valuation problems in corporate finance is referred to as *contingent claims analysis*. Application of contingent claims analysis to a variety of problems in finance is rapidly increasing in importance.

In the next section a brief history of option markets is presented. Then some of the primary uses of options in the investment arena are introduced. A few investment problems are considered to illustrate situations where the intelligent use of options would be beneficial. Most of the problems involve hedgers, who are keen to avoid risks such as declining stock markets, rising interest rates, adverse changes in foreign exchange rates, or uncertainty in future commodity prices. The primary purpose of investigating potential uses of options at this stage is to provide a foundation for the chapters that follow. The actual solutions to the problems discussed require an understanding of option strategies and option pricing. While the theory of option pricing is crucial for this analysis, as discussed earlier, these theories are also of importance to financial problems outside the speculative markets area. Some applications of option pricing to problems in corporate finance are mentioned.

THE HISTORY OF STOCK OPTION MARKETS

Although options have been traded for centuries, until recently they were relatively obscure financial instruments. The first extensive use of option contracts occurred during the Dutch tulip bulb mania in the seventeenth century. At that time, tulip bulbs were fetching extremely high prices. To avoid volatile prices, growers would often purchase put options on their crops that would, in essence, guarantee them a minimum price. If the market price fell below this minimum price, the grower would exercise the option and deliver the crop to the put option seller for the contracted minimum price. The sellers of put options were speculators who anticipated that the price of tulips would continue to increase. They hoped this would occur, since the growers would then not exercise their contracts and the sellers would be wealthier by the size of the original premiums paid to them. The risk they bore, of course, was that prices would fall below the agreed-upon floor price. If this occurred, the speculators would be forced to pay the contracted price for tulip bulbs whose market prices were lower.

Unfortunately, the tulip market was undisciplined, and many of the speculators who sold put contracts to the growers did not have the financial backing to fulfill their side of the bargain. Indeed, at that time there were no margin requirements to keep speculators from ruining themselves and the people with whom they did business. Of course the tulip market eventually broke, the speculators could not deliver on their obligations, and an enormous debt crisis followed that caused severe disruptions in the Dutch economy. Moreover, the episode gave options a bad name throughout Europe.

Organized trading in puts and calls began in London in the eighteenth century. However, such trading was banned on several occasions, including 1931 and the period from the Second World War to 1958. Option trading in the United States began in the late eighteenth century. Before the 1930s there were several large-scale abuses of stock options that added to their bad reputations. Many of these abuses involved investors who issued options on certain stocks to their brokers, in return for which the brokers actively recommended their stocks to their clients.

In the 1930s lawmakers established a regulatory framework that dealt effectively with the misuse of options. Option sellers were required to post margins to ensure they would honor their contracts. Granting options to induce investment advisors to recommend a particular stock was banned, and buying options to take advantage of inside information was prohibited.

Prior to 1973, the option market in the United States was an over-the-counter market dominated by about thirty firms that belonged to the Put and Call Broker and Dealers Association. Its function was to bring buyers and sellers of option contracts together. Occasionally some firms would make markets in options on particular stocks. Usually, however, the buyer of a contract was directly connected to a seller, and it would be impossible for the buyer to resell or transfer the contract to a third party. In specific cases a broker wanting to close out a position might try to resell the option contract of a client to a third party. These types of sales would be listed in the newspapers as "specials." For providing this service, the broker would charge a fee.

The over-the-counter market was extremely fragmented, matching trades was difficult, transaction costs were high, and liquidity was virtually nonexistent. In 1973 the Chicago Board Options Exchange began trading completely standardized call option contracts. The organized market overcame many of the problems of the over-the-counter market, and from the start, trading was heavier than expected. The operation of these organized option markets is discussed in the next chapter.

In the 1980s listed stock option trading was expanded to include options on debt instruments, stock and bond indexes, and foreign currencies. All these contracts are regulated by the Securities and Exchange Commission (SEC).

The History of the Commodity Option Markets

Like stock options, options on agricultural commodities were introduced in the United States in the eighteenth century. During the early 1900s the markets went through several periods of suspension. The first significant growth occurred after the First World War, when speculators started to enter the market, which until then had been dominated by commercial interests alone. By the 1930s market manipulations and fraud were common occurrences. Under the Department of Agriculture, a regulatory body was established to investigate the commodities that were then being offered. The body concluded that commodity options served no economic role, and it banned trading on all commodity options it regulated. However, the commodity industry continued to expand into new areas over which the regulatory body had no authority, such as coffee, cocoa, platinum, silver, and copper. Options on these unregulated commodities continued to be traded. In addition to these contracts, there were no restrictions on trading commodity options issued in London. Indeed, during the 1970s a new type of commodity firm became popular. These firms would essentially buy London options and then sell them to American investors at higher prices. Some of these firms decided to grant options themselves, rather than to buy the London options. Such option contracts were called *dealer options,* since they were issued by a dealer rather than regulated on an exchange.

In 1974 Congress created a new regulatory agency, the Commodity Futures Trading Commission (CFTC). The commission's responsibility was to regulate all commodity futures transactions carried out in the United States, including options on futures. One of the first tasks of the CFTC was to establish a committee to review all the market instruments that were currently being traded. This committee concluded that commodity options served an important role; however, since commodity options were such a small part of its business, the CFTC did not give them much attention.

During the 1970s there were several cases of fraud in the commodity option industry. Much of this fraud involved dealers who were buying commodity options in London and reselling them to American investors at absurdly inflated prices. Partially as a result of the bad publicity created by these fraudulent activities, the CFTC decided to ban the sale of all London options by American firms and to ban all dealer options on commodities. In addition, all domestic-exchange-traded commodity options were banned. Subsequently, the CFTC introduced regulations under which a commodity option dealer could qualify for an exemption to the ban. In 1981 the CFTC also proposed rules that provided regulations under which exchange-traded options on commodity futures could be traded. A pilot program that allowed each exchange regulated by the CFTC to introduce one option contract was successfully introduced in 1982. In that year options began trading on gold futures, heating oil futures, sugar futures, long-term U.S. Treasury bond futures, and some stock index futures. Since then, a variety of other new contracts have been introduced.

The Current Option Markets

The current option markets are regulated by the SEC and the CFTC. Jurisdictional problems between these two commissions have always existed, but they intensified in 1976 and 1977 when disputes arose over which agency should regulate financial futures and options. In 1981 the two agencies published an accord whereby the CFTC would retain exclusive jurisdiction over financial futures and options on financial futures while the SEC would have exclusive jurisdiction over options on the instruments underlying the financial futures. Minor adjustments in this accord were finally enacted into law by Congress.

Today listed option contracts are traded in exchanges regulated by SEC and the CFTC. The exchanges are responsible for providing the investment community with educational material on all their products. The quality of these publications is quite high, and it is recommended that potential investors obtain this market literature. The U.S. options and futures exchanges and their current addresses are listed at the end of this chapter.

OPTIONS IN INVESTMENTS

The next several chapters are concerned with defining option contracts, discussing option strategies, and investigating how option prices are determined. To begin the discussion, this section describes some of the most common reasons investors use options.

Molding Payoff Patterns to Reflect Investment Outlooks

Stock options provide payoff patterns that cannot be provided by stocks. As an example, consider an investor who believes that a news announcement to be released will have major positive or negative ramifications on the stock price. Without option contracts, the investor cannot establish a position on the stock that profits from this knowledge. If, for example, the investor buys the stock and the announcement is negative, large losses could result. With stock options available, the investor could establish a position that would be profitable if the stock price increased or decreased by significant amounts. The investor would lose money only if such a stock price change did not occur.

This example illustrates that, with options available, investors have more flexibility in designing positions on a stock that best reflect their outlooks for the stock.

The Insurance Feature of Options

Closely related to the first use of options, but worthy of special attention, is the insurance feature of option contracts. The next several examples illustrate situations in which investors would consider using option contracts.

Stock Options for Price Protection   Consider an investor who would like to purchase a particular stock but is afraid that the losses could be substantial. With options available, the investor could purchase the stock and buy option contracts that would effectively insure against the stock's declining below a particular floor price. The option contract purchased would depend on the degree of price protection demanded. Clearly, greater price protection could be achieved only at greater cost.

Hedging Against Stock Market Declines Investors who hold diversified portfolios of stocks generally experience wealth increases as the stock market increases and wealth declines as the stock market declines. Managers of well-diversified portfolios must either contend with this market risk or "time" the market. This latter strategy involves selecting times to enter and withdraw from the stock market and can result in large transaction costs. Using index options, investors can hedge their portfolios against market-related declines. Essentially, investors can buy contracts that profit if the market as a whole declines. If the market does decline, dragging their portfolio values down, then the losses on investors' portfolios can be partially (or totally) offset by the gains on the contracts. Strategies involving meshing index options with portfolios can be established to smooth out returns in volatile markets.

Hedging Against Stock Market Increases Option contracts can also be used as devices that allow investors to minimize regrets of incorrect decisions. As an example, consider an investor who, believing the stock market is about to drop, withdraws funds from the market and places them into government treasuries. To insure against making the wrong decision, the investor could purchase option contracts that, for a small fraction of the costs of the diversified portfolio, would provide the opportunity of participating in any bull market, should it arise.

Hedging Industry-Related Risks Consider an investor who chooses stocks in the computer industry. The investor believes that his or her portfolio will outperform the computer industry market as a whole. However, the investor is not certain that, over the short term, the computer industry itself will perform well. The investor is keen to maintain the current portfolio, but would like some insurance in the event of a short-term downturn in the computer industry. By means of index options, investment strategies with these goals can be achieved.

Hedging Against Falling Interest Rates Consider an investment manager who expects to receive $5 million in three months time for investments in the bond market. The investor is concerned about falling yields that will require investment at a much lower rate in the future than presently could be achieved. In order to lock into higher rates, the investor could consider eliminating interest rate uncertainty by entering into a futures contract. However, if the investor is wrong about rates falling, or if the $5 million does not materialize, the strategy of buying futures contracts may not be as appropriate as purchasing debt options. With debt options, insurance against falling rates can be obtained.

Hedging Against Rising Interest Rates   Similarly, consider a bond portfolio manager who anticipates an abnormal increase in interest rates. The manager could consider adjusting the maturities of bonds to minimize the impact of price declines. However, this strategy could be expensive, since liquidation of certain bond positions may be impractical. Ideally, the manager would like to purchase insurance against interest rates increasing beyond a critical point. By using debt options, the investor can protect the portfolio with predefined risk exposures.

Hedging Foreign Currency Exchange Risks   Consider an American company that is competing in a bid for the delivery of a turnkey plant to the Japanese government. The bid is in Japanese yen. If the firm wins the bid, profits could be eroded by an unfavorable change in foreign exchange rates. The company is keen to establish ways in which the exchange rate risks can be better managed. By means of foreign currency option contracts, the risk of the Japanese yen's declining in value against the American dollar can be hedged. Similarly, exporters of foreign goods can use foreign currency markets to hedge against the likelihood of the dollar's weakening dramatically against the currency of the country in which they trade.

Hedging Commodity Prices   Consider a farmer who is concerned that the prices of next year's wheat could drop further than anticipated. Ideally, the farmer would like to establish a floor price for his or her crop. If pessimistic forecasts are incorrect, the farmer would like to sell wheat at the higher prices. However, if the worst forecasts are realized, the farmer would like to be guaranteed the floor price. Such a farmer has "safety first" objectives, which can be met by using options on wheat futures.

Options for Speculation

Options provide a way for investors to participate in financial markets for a fraction of the price of the underlying securities. Rather than purchasing a stock, the investor could purchase a call option on the stock. The call option appreciates if the stock price increases. If the stock price decreases, the loss is limited to the initial premium paid for the contract, which typically is a small fraction of the stock price.

Other Applications

In future chapters we shall explore other uses of options. For example, we shall see that options may allow investors to take a position on a stock under more favorable margin restrictions than would be available directly in the stock market. Options also may offer opportunities to reduce costs of borrowing. They may provide ways to hedge against events such as unanticipated changes in dividend policies and unanticipated changes in the volatility of securities, exchange rates, and short-term interest rates.

OPTIONS IN CORPORATE FINANCE

As discussed earlier, the analysis of option strategies and option pricing has application outside speculative markets. Research on broadening the original Black-Scholes model to value more complex contingent claims than simple stock options has mushroomed in the last decade. Option theory has been used to value risky corporate debt, coupon bonds, warrants, convertibles, loan guarantees, subordinated debt, operating leases, equity, and a variety of other claims on the value of a firm.

The option approach to pricing of corporate liabilities considers the firm's total capital structure and uses a single methodology to simultaneously price each of the individual components of that structure. The methodology differs from other approaches, which tend to ignore the interactive effects among all the securities in a firm. Empirical testing of the accuracy of these new models in pricing complex capital structures is just beginning. With increased knowledge in this area, contingent claims analysis is fast becoming an increasingly useful tool for analyzing corporate liability strategy and planning.

Whenever managers make choices, there is a chance that their decisions are incorrect. Choosing, then, has costs—namely, the costs of error. Yet not choosing, or delaying decisions, can also have costs in terms of missed opportunities. Managers like to keep available as many options as possible. Retaining options increases flexibility, making a firm more responsive to change. However, options can only be retained at an increased cost.

As an example, consider the management of an electric utility that has to choose between building a power plant that burns only oil and one that burns either oil or coal. Although the latter plant costs more, it provides management with greater flexibility because it allows management a choice of fuels along with the ability to switch back and forth in response to changing energy market conditions. In choosing between plants, management has to weigh increased flexibility against cost. Traditional project selection and capital budgeting methods pay little attention to valuing these option features. By means of option pricing theory, however, the value of this increased flexibility can be established. This example illustrates just one of hundreds of possible applications of option pricing theory to problems in corporate finance. The increasing application of contingent claims analysis to problems in corporate finance makes the theory of option pricing very useful and relevant.

CONCLUSION

Although the trading of option contracts dates back many centuries, the real development of organized option markets is quite recent. The option market has flourished in the last decade and many innovative contracts have successfully been introduced. The next few chapters provide a broad introduction to option contracts and to their role as risk management devices. In addition, the theory of option pricing is developed and the role of this theory in corporate finance is discussed.

References

The Chicago Board Options Exchange, together with the American Stock Exchange, New York Stock Exchange, Pacific Stock Exchange, Philadelphia Stock Exchange, and Options Clearing Corporation, publishes a series of very informative pamphlets that describe option contracts. In addition, the other exchanges publish their own educational documents. The pamphlets published by the Chicago Board Options Exchange are excellent. The addresses of the above exchanges, together with other option and futures exchanges, are provided below. The history of option trading is discussed by Gastineau. A description of option markets in Canada, Europe, and the Far East, together with the history of commodity options, is provided by Mayer.

American Stock Exchange, Inc.
86 Trinity Place
New York, NY 10006

Chicago Board of Trade
141 West Jackson Blvd.
Chicago, IL 60604

Chicago Board Options Exchange, Inc.
141 West Jackson Blvd.
Chicago, IL 60604

Chicago Mercantile Exchange
30 S. Wacker Drive
Chicago, IL 60606

Citrus Associates of the
New York Cotton Exchange, Inc.
4 World Trade Center
New York, NY 10048

Coffee, Sugar, and Cocoa Exchange
4 World Trade Center
New York, NY 10048

Commodity Exchange, Inc.
4 World Trade Center
New York, NY 10048

Kansas City Board of Trade
4800 Main Street
Kansas City, MO 64112

Mid America Commodity Exchange
444 West Jackson Blvd.
Chicago, IL 60606

Minneapolis Grain Exchange
400 S. 4th Avenue
Minneapolis, MN 55803

New York Cotton Exchange, Inc.
4 World Trade Center
New York, NY 10048

New York Futures Exchange
20 Broad Street
New York, NY 10005

New York Mercantile Exchange
4 World Trade Center
New York, NY 10048

New York Stock Exchange, Inc.
11 Wall Street
New York, NY 10005

Options Clearing Corporation
200 S. Wacker Drive
Chicago, IL 60606

Pacific Stock Exchange, Inc.
301 Pine Street
San Francisco, CA 94104

Petroleum Associates of the
  New York Cotton Exchange, Inc.
4 World Trade Center
New York, NY 10048

Philadelphia Stock Exchange, Inc.
1900 Market Street
Philadelphia, PA 19103

Gastineau, G. *The Stock Options Manual.* New York: McGraw-Hill, 1979.
Mayer, T. *Commodity Options: A User's Guide to Speculating and Hedging.* New York: New York Institute of Finance, 1983.

2

Stock Option Contracts

Options are financial instruments that can be used to achieve a variety of investment objectives.[1] For example, we shall see that ownership of a call (put) option allows an investor to profit from an increase (decrease) in the price of a security for a fraction of the price of the security. Furthermore, since losses are limited by the size of the initial investment, the holder of the call is protected against large losses that stock ownership may involve.

Options also allow shareholders to transfer unwanted risk associated with stock ownership to speculators willing to bear it. The necessity for transferring this risk generally reflects the shareholders' reluctance to sustain large losses. Option writers are investors who accept these risks. They are enticed into selling options by the size of the premium that compensates them for these risks. The size of the premium is related to the size of possible losses, the time of coverage, and other factors to be discussed. Option writers may be in a better situation to sustain such losses, or they may be more speculative. In many cases, option writers may be able to pool these risks with other risks in such a way that, in aggregate, the potential losses in their portfolios are more manageable.

In order to understand how options add another dimension to portfolio risk management, it is first necessary to understand how these contracts trade in an organized market. In this chapter we shall describe listed call and put stock options and present the basic terminology used in this market. The prices of these standardized contracts are determined in a competitive marketplace, and we shall discuss some of the factors that determine their prices. The appendix to this chapter describes the option exchanges and illustrates how option contracts are actually traded.

---

[1]In this chapter all options we discuss are of the American variety. European options are discussed in Chapter 4. The terminology of these contracts is unfortunate in that it has no geographic meaning. Most options contracts traded throughout the world are American. However, a few contracts traded in America and Europe are of the European variety.

CALL OPTIONS

An American call option is a contract that gives the owner the right to purchase a given number of shares of a specific security at a specific price at any point in time prior to a predetermined date. Usually the number of shares per contract is one hundred.

To completely characterize a call contract, it is necessary to know the following:

1. The name of the underlying security,
2. The specified purchase price or strike price, and
3. The duration of the contract or time to expiration.

Strike Prices

Strike prices are available at values surrounding the current stock price. Usually the prices are spaced at $5 intervals for stocks priced below $70 and $10 intervals for stocks priced above $70. As the stock price changes, new contracts are introduced in a well-defined way, to be discussed later.

Call options with strike prices less than the stock price are termed *in the money*. Options with strike prices equal to the stock price are called *at the money*. Finally, calls whose strike prices exceed the stock price are said to be *out of the money*.

Expiration Dates

At any point in time, each underlying stock has option contracts available with three possible expiration dates. Each date is separated by three months. The first option to expire is called the *near series*, the second one the *middle series*, and the option with the longest time to expiration is called the *far series*. Options expire on the Saturday following the third Friday in their stated month. When the near series expires, a new nine-month series is introduced.

As an example, consider a stock that has January, April, and July options. When the January options expire, new nine-month October options are introduced. There are two other possible expiration cycles for an option. These are the February/May/August/November cycle and the March/June/September/December cycle. The three particular expiration month contracts that are traded depend, of course, on the current date.

The above expiration date rules applied until 1985. In an effort to bring additional liquidity into the stock option market, the option exchanges instigated a program whereby stocks belonging to a select group could trade an additional near-term contract. As a result, some stocks have four expiration dates. Each has the nearest two months and the next two months of its normal 3–6–9-month cycle trading at one time. Exhibit 2.1 illustrates the option contracts that are available at each possible expiration month.

EXHIBIT 2.1
Option Contracts Available by Expiration Month

Expiration Month	Option Contracts Available
November	December, January, April, July
December	January, February, April, July
January	February, March, April, July
February	March, April, July, October
March	April, May, July, October
April	May, June, July, October
May	June, July, October, January
June	July, August, October, January
July	August, September, October, January
August	September, October, January, April
September	October, November, January, April
October	November, December, January, April

As an example, consider a stock in this select group that has an option contract expiring in January. After the expiration date, February and March contracts will trade as well as the usual April and July contracts.

Creation of Options with New Strike Prices

As already mentioned, when one option expires, a new series is introduced with strike prices surrounding the current stock price. As the stock price changes in value, new strike prices are added. In particular, if a stock price closes above (below) the highest (lowest) existing strike price for a certain number of days (usually two), a new strike price is created. Newly created contracts usually have a time to expiration exceeding thirty days. This often means that new contracts at the near series are not introduced.

As a result of this method of introducing new strike prices, securities that have experienced significant price fluctuations over the past nine months could have a significant number of different strike prices available. The most actively traded option contracts, however, tend to be those contracts trading near the money and with the closest expiration date.

Example 2.1

To illustrate the concepts, Exhibit 2.2 shows the class of all XYZ call options that were available on February 1st, when the stock price was 40. The 40 strike price options are at the money, the 45s are out of the money, the 30s and 35s are in the money, and the 20s and 25s are said to be deep in the money.

EXHIBIT 2.2
Available Contracts on XYZ

Strike	April	July	October
25	√	X	X
30	√	√	X
35	√	√	X
40	√	√	√
45	√	√	√
50	√	√	√

Note that the July 25 and October 25, 30, and 35 options are not trading. The reason for this is that when the July series was introduced (in the previous October), the stock price was above 30 and only options surrounding 30 were introduced. Also, when the January options expired and the new nine-month October series was introduced, the stock price was above 35 and has remained above 35 since then, so that only strike prices above 35 were introduced. The April 35, 40, and 45 options will probably be the most liquid options at this point in time.

PRICING OF OPTIONS

The price of a call option is determined in a competitive marketplace. The largest exchange is the Chicago Board Options Exchange. Other exchanges include the American, Philadelphia, Pacific, and New York Stock Exchanges.

Exhibit 2.3 illustrates the option price information as reported in the *Wall Street Journal*. First the name of the underlying security is presented with the closing stock price beneath. The strike price is in column two. The remaining columns indicate the closing prices for the options. Option prices are reported on a per share basis, so the actual price is obtained by multiplying the quoted price by the number of shares per contract (usually 100). Due to space constraints, the option tables listed in newspapers display only the three nearest-term monthly contracts. The six columns in Exhibit 2.3 are arranged with call prices first, and then puts, ordered by maturity. Option prices under $3 trade in sixteenths of a point, while those over $3 trade in eighths of a point. A lowercase *r* indicates that the option is available for trading but did not trade during that day. A lowercase *s* indicates that no option is offered. A lowercase *o* next to the name of the stock indicates certain options that have nonstandard terms resulting from stock splits, stock dividends, spin-offs, or other special circumstances.

EXHIBIT 2.3

Option Price Quotations from the Wall Street Journal

CHICAGO BOARD

Option & NY Close	Strike Price	Calls–Last Jul	Calls–Last Aug	Calls–Last Oct	Puts–Last Jul	Puts–Last Aug	Puts–Last Oct
Amrtch 130	130	1 1/2	r	5	1/2	r	r
131 3/4	135	3/8	r	r	4 3/4	r	6 1/2
131 3/4	140	r	1/4	2	r	r	r
Atl R	45	r	r	4	1/16	7/8	1 1/2
47 5/8	50	3/16	11/16	1 1/2	2 1/4	3 1/4	4
47 5/8	55	r	r	1/2	7	r	7 3/4
47 5/8	60	r	r	3/16	r	r	r
BankAm	12 1/2	2 1/4	r	2 5/8	r	1/8	5/16
14 3/4	15	1/4	1/2	1 1/16	7/16	3/4	1 1/8
14 3/4	17 1/2	1/16	3/16	3/8	2 3/4	2 7/8	3
14 3/4	20	1/16	s	3/16	r	s	r
BellAtl	60	r	s	r	r	s	1/8
69 5/8	62 1/2	7 1/2	s	r	r	s	r
69 5/8	65	4 1/2	r	r	r	r	7/8
69 5/8	70	3/4	1 1/4	2 1/2	3/4	r	r
69 5/8	75	r	r	13/16	r	r	r
Citicp	45	13 5/8	s	r	r	s	r
58 5/8	50	8 5/8	s	9 1/2	r	s	3/8
58 5/8	55	3 3/4	r	5 1/2	1/16	3/4	1 1/4
58 5/8	60	1/4	1 1/8	2 1/4	1 3/4	r	3 1/4
58 5/8	65	1/16	r	1	r	r	r
Cullin	10	r	r	2	r	r	r
11	12 1/2	1/16	r	1/2	1 5/8	r	1 3/4
11	15	1/16	1/8	5/16	4 1/4	r	4
Delta	35	4 1/2	r	6	r	1/4	1/2
39 1/2	40	1/4	1 3/8	2 3/8	3/4	1 3/4	2 5/8
39 1/2	45	1/16	1/8	7/8	5 1/2	r	5 1/4
39 1/2	50	r	s	5/16	r	s	10 1/2
EKodak	50	3 7/8	5	5 1/8	r	1/4	1 1/8
53 3/4	55	1/4	1 3/8	2 1/2	1 1/4	1 7/8	3 1/4
53 3/4	60	1/16	3/16	1 1/8	6 1/2	6	7
53 3/4	65	1/16	r	7/16	11	r	r
Exxon	50	8 3/8	s	8 5/8	r	s	3/16
58 1/8	55	3 3/8	3 3/4	4	r	1/4	11/16
58 1/8	60	1/8	1/2	1 3/8	1 7/8	2 1/2	3
58 1/8	65	r	1/16	3/8	6 1/8	r	r
FedExp	45	8 1/8	s	s	r	s	s
52 7/8	50	3 1/4	4	5 3/8	5/16	7/8	1 7/8
52 7/8	55	1/4	1 3/8	2 7/8	2 1/8	3 1/8	3 3/8
52 7/8	60	1/16	1/2	1 3/8	7	7	7 1/2
52 7/8	65	1/16	r	11/16	12	r	r
52 7/8	70	r	s	r	16 3/4	s	r
52 7/8	75	r	s	1/8	r	s	r
Grumm	25	3	r	r	r	r	r
28	30	1/16	r	1 1/4	2 1/8	r	r
Halbtn	20	r	r	1 3/4	1/8	1/2	3/4
20 3/4	25	1/16	r	r	4 1/2	r	r
20 3/4	22 1/2	1/16	1/4	1/2	1 7/8	r	2 1/4
20 3/4	30	r	s	s	9 3/4	s	s
Homstk	17 1/2	r	s	r	r	s	5/16
20 3/4	20	1 1/8	1 3/8	2	1/8	3/4	1 1/8
20 3/4	22 1/2	1/16	r	1	1 11/16	r	2 3/8
20 3/4	25	r	1/8	7/16	4 1/4	r	4 1/4
20 3/4	30	r	s	1/16	r	s	r
I B M	130	10 1/2	s	s	r	s	s
139 1/2	135	4 1/2	7	9 1/4	3/16	1 5/8	3
139 1/2	140	1 1/4	3 3/8	6 3/8	1 15/16	4	5
139 1/2	145	3/16	1 9/16	4	6	7 1/4	8 1/4
139 1/2	150	1/16	11/16	2 1/2	11 1/4	10 1/2	12
139 1/2	155	1/16	1/4	1 1/2	14 3/4	r	16
139 1/2	160	1/16	s	13/16	19 1/4	s	r
139 1/2	165	1/16	s	7/16	24 7/8	s	r
In Pap	55	12 1/4	s	13 3/8	r	s	3/8
66 5/8	60	7 1/2	r	7 3/8	r	1/4	1 1/4
66 5/8	65	2	3 1/2	4 1/2	5/16	r	2 3/4
66 5/8	70	5/16	1 1/2	2 3/4	3 1/2	4 1/4	6
LAC	15	1/4	s	r	r	s	r
LorTel	25	r	r	3 1/4	r	1/2	r
26 1/8	30	1/16	3/8	1 5/16	r	3 1/4	r
26 1/8	35	r	r	3/4	r	r	8
M M M	85	22 1/4	s	s	r	s	s
106 1/2	90	16 3/8	s	r	r	s	r
106 1/2	95	11 1/2	s	r	r	s	r
106 1/2	100	7 1/2	s	10	1/16	s	1 5/8
106 1/2	105	2 3/4	3 7/8	5 3/8	3/4	2	3 3/8
106 1/2	110	1/4	2 3/8	3 1/2	3 1/4	4 3/8	6
106 1/2	115	1/16	3/4	2	8 1/8	r	r
106 1/2	120	r	1/4	1 1/4	r	r	r
Pepsi	23 3/8	7 1/2	s	r	r	s	r
30 1/2	25	r	s	6 1/8	r	s	r
30 1/2	26 5/8	4	s	4 7/8	r	s	1/2
30 1/2	28 3/8	2 1/8	s	3 5/8	1/16	s	7/8
30 1/2	30	1 1/8	2	2 7/8	3/8	1	1 3/4
30 1/2	31 5/8	1/4	s	2 1/4	1 1/8	s	r
30 1/2	33 3/8	1/8	s	1 7/8	3	s	3 1/2
30 1/2	35	1/16	7/16	1 3/16	4 3/4	r	5
30 1/2	40	r	1/8	7/16	r	r	r

Option & NY Close	Strike Price	Calls–Last Jul	Calls–Last Oct	Calls–Last Jan	Puts–Last Jul	Puts–Last Oct	Puts–Last Jan
41 1/2	35	6	r	r	1/16	1/2	r
41 1/2	37 1/2	4 1/8	r	s	r	1 1/8	s
41 1/2	40	2	4 1/2	r	3/16	1 3/4	r
41 1/2	45	1/16	2 1/4	3 3/4	3 1/4	5 1/4	r
41 1/2	50	r	1 1/2	r	r	r	r
Loral	35	r	11 1/2	r	r	r	1/2
45	40	5 5/8	r	8 5/8	r	7/8	1 3/8
45	45	1	3 3/4	5 3/4	3/4	3 1/8	r
45	50	1/8	1 5/8	3 1/2	r	r	r
Lotus	35	r	r	r	2 7/8	r	r
M C I	10	1/16	3/4	1 1/16	3/8	3/4	15/16
9 3/4	12 1/2	1/16	1/4	1/2	3 1/8	r	r
9 3/4	15	r	1/16	s	r	5 1/2	s
Merck	65	r	36	s	r	r	s
98 1/2	90	8 3/4	11 1/2	r	1/16	1 1/2	2 9/16
98 1/2	92 1/2	7 1/8	9 7/8	r	r	r	r
98 1/2	95	4	8 1/4	10 1/8	1/2	3	r
98 1/2	100	15/16	5 1/4	7 3/8	2	5 1/4	6 1/2
98 1/2	105	3/8	3 1/8	6	r	r	r
98 1/2	110	r	2	4 1/2	r	r	r
Monsan	55	13	13	r	r	r	r
67 3/4	60	7 5/8	r	r	r	r	1 1/2
67 3/4	65	2 5/8	5 5/8	r	3/16	r	r
67 3/4	70	1/4	3 1/8	r	2 1/2	r	r
67 3/4	75	r	1 9/16	r	r	r	8 3/4
N W A	45	7/16	2 1/2	3 1/4	1 3/8	2 1/2	r
43 7/8	50	1/16	1	r	6	r	r
43 7/8	55	r	7/16	r	r	r	r
PaineW	30	r	r	r	1/16	5/8	r
34 1/2	35	5/16	2 3/8	3 1/2	1 1/8	2 1/4	3 3/8
34 1/2	40	1/16	3/4	1 3/4	r	r	r
34 1/2	45	1/16	5/16	3/4	r	r	r
Pennz	45	8 3/4	9 1/2	11	r	r	1 3/4
53	50	3 3/8	6	7 3/4	1/8	2 1/4	3 5/8
53	55	7/16	3 1/2	5	2 5/8	4 3/4	r
53	60	1/16	2	s	r	r	s
53	65	1/16	1 1/8	r	11 3/8	r	r
53	70	r	3/4	r	r	r	r
53	75	r	5/8	s	r	r	s
Squibb	95	19	21 3/4	r	r	3/4	r
114 3/8	100	14 3/4	16 3/4	r	r	1 3/4	r
114 3/8	105	9	12 3/4	16	1/16	2	r
114 3/8	110	4	9 1/4	r	3/8	4 1/4	r
114 3/8	115	1 1/4	7 1/4	10 1/8	1 3/4	6 1/2	r
114 3/8	120	s	4 3/4	r	s	r	r
Upjohn	70	18 1/2	r	s	r	r	s
85	72 1/2	r	r	s	r	3/4	s
85	75	r	r	r	r	7/8	r
85	77 1/2	r	r	r	r	r	2 1/2
85	80	5 1/2	r	r	1/8	3	3 1/2
85	82 1/2	4 1/4	9	r	3/8	4	r
85	85	1 1/2	7 1/2	r	1 1/8	5 1/2	6 1/2
85	87 1/2	1	7 1/4	r	3	r	r
85	90	3/8	5 1/8	7 3/4	5	7 3/4	9
85	95	1/16	3 1/8	6 1/4	10	12	r
85	100	1/16	2 1/2	5	14 1/2	14 1/2	r
85	110	1/16	1	2 1/2	r	r	r
Weyerh	30	3 5/8	4	r	r	r	r
33 1/2	35	1/16	1 1/16	r	1 1/4	2 1/8	r
33 1/2	40	1/16	r	r	r	r	r
		Aug	**Nov**	**Feb**	**Aug**	**Nov**	**Feb**
AlexAl	40	1	2 3/8	r	r	r	r
Amdahl	15	1 5/8	r	r	3/8	r	r
16 1/2	17 1/2	1/2	r	r	1 5/8	r	r
A E P	25	3 3/4	3 3/8	4	1/8	r	r
28 3/4	30	3/16	5/8	3/4	r	2 11/16	r
AlnGrp	115	9 3/4	r	r	r	r	r
123 5/8	120	r	12 5/8	r	r	r	r
123 5/8	125	4	r	r	5	r	r
123 5/8	130	2 1/8	r	r	8 1/2	r	r
123 5/8	140	1/4	r	s	r	r	s
Amoco	50	6 1/2	r	s	1/16	1/2	s
55 3/4	55	1 3/4	3	r	1 1/2	2 1/4	3 1/8
55 3/4	60	5/16	1 1/4	r	5	r	r
55 3/4	65	1/16	9/16	r	8 3/4	r	r
55 3/4	70	r	3/16	r	r	r	r
A M P	35	r	r	r	7/8	1 3/8	r
37 1/8	40	1/2	1 9/16	r	3 1/2	r	r
37 1/8	45	r	15/16	r	8	r	8 1/4
37 1/8	50	1/16	r	s	r	r	s
Baxter	15	r	r	4	1/16	1/4	r
17 7/8	17 1/2	15/16	1 7/8	2 3/8	7/16	7/8	1
17 7/8	20	1/4	13/16	1 1/4	2 1/4	2 5/8	r
17 7/8	22 1/2	1/16	5/16	11/16	4 3/4	r	r
Blk Dk	17 1/2	1 1/4	2 1/4	2 3/4	1/2	r	1 5/8
18	20	7/16	1 3/16	1 5/8	2 1/8	2 5/8	3
18	22 1/2	1/4	3/4	r	4 3/4	r	r
18	25	1/8	r	3/4	r	r	r
Boeing	45	16 1/4	r	s	r	r	s

Option & NY Close	Strike Price	Calls–Last Sep	Calls–Last Dec	Calls–Last Mar	Puts–Last Sep	Puts–Last Dec	Puts–Last Mar
AlldSt	37 1/2	r	10	s	r	3/8	s
46 3/8	40	7	r	r	r	r	r
46 3/8	45	3	r	r	1 1/4	r	r
46 3/8	50	1 1/4	2 3/4	r	r	r	r
46 3/8	55	1/2	r	r	r	r	r
Apache	7 1/2	r	1 1/4	r	r	r	r
8 3/8	10	1/8	3/8	r	r	1 7/8	r
BrisMy	60	r	s	s	1/8	s	s
79 1/2	65	15 1/2	17 1/2	s	r	r	s
79 1/2	70	10 1/4	12	s	1/4	1/2	s
79 1/2	75	7	9 1/2	s	7/8	2	s
79 1/2	80	3 3/4	6 3/4	r	2 7/8	4 1/2	r
79 1/2	85	1 5/8	4 1/4	5 7/8	6	6	r
79 1/2	90	3/4	2	3 1/4	r	r	r
Bruns	30	7 7/8	r	r	r	3/8	r
38	35	3 1/4	4 1/2	r	7/8	r	2
38	40	1 1/4	2	3 1/2	r	r	r
Celan	170	r	s	s	1/2	s	s
204	190	22 1/2	r	s	r	6	s
204	195	r	23	s	4 1/2	r	s
204	200	13 5/8	21 1/2	r	6 3/4	10 1/2	r
204	210	9	r	r	r	r	17
204	220	6	12	r	r	r	23 1/2
204	230	2 1/4	9	r	r	r	r
204	240	1 1/2	5 3/4	9	r	r	r
Chamin	22 1/2	1 1/2	r	3	1/2	3/4	1 1/8
23 1/2	25	5/8	1 5/16	r	1 3/4	2 3/8	2 1/2
23 1/2	30	1/8	1/2	r	r	r	r
Chryslr	30	5 1/2	r	7 1/2	7/16	3/4	1 5/16
34 5/8	35	2	3 1/4	4 1/4	2	2 7/8	3 3/8
34 5/8	40	9/16	1 9/16	2 5/8	5 7/8	6 1/4	6
34 5/8	45	1/8	5/8	s	10 1/8	r	s
34 5/8	50	1/16	r	s	r	r	s
Chrys o	30	5 1/2	s	s	3/8	s	s
34 5/8	33 3/8	r	s	s	1 1/4	s	s
34 5/8	36 5/8	r	s	s	2 7/8	s	s
CompSc	30	5 1/4	r	s	r	1	s
34 1/4	35	2 3/4	4	r	2 3/4	2 1/2	r
34 1/4	40	7/8	1 7/8	r	5 1/4	r	r
Dow Ch	40	13 1/4	s	s	r	s	s
53	45	9	r	s	1/8	3/8	s
53	50	4 5/8	5 1/2	6 1/4	13/16	1 1/2	r
53	55	2	3	r	3 1/4	4 1/4	r
53	60	5/8	1 1/2	2 5/8	6 1/4	7	r
53	65	1/8	3/4	1 1/2	r	r	r
FBost	50	2 1/2	r	r	2 7/8	3 1/2	r
49 5/8	55	1	r	r	6 1/2	r	r
49 5/8	60	3/8	1 1/4	s	r	r	s
49 5/8	65	1/8	r	s	r	r	s
Ford	50	4 1/2	6 1/4	r	1	2 1/4	3
53	55	1 3/4	3 1/8	4 1/4	r	r	r
53	60	1/2	1 1/2	2 3/8	r	r	r
Ford o	36 5/8	16 1/2	s	s	r	s	s
53	43 3/8	10 3/4	s	s	r	s	s
53	46 5/8	7 3/8	8 1/4	s	1/4	r	s
53	50	4 3/8	r	s	r	r	s
53	53 3/8	2 5/8	4	s	2 3/4	r	s
53	56 5/8	1 1/4	2 1/4	s	r	r	s
53	60	3/8	1 1/4	s	r	r	s
GenCp	70	r	r	r	2 1/4	r	r
69	75	1	r	r	r	r	r
Gen El	65	12	s	s	r	s	s
75 7/8	70	7	8 3/4	r	9/16	1 1/2	2
75 7/8	75	3 3/4	5 3/4	r	2	3 3/8	4
75 7/8	80	1 11/16	3 1/8	4 1/2	5	6 1/8	r
75 7/8	85	5/8	1 7/8	3 1/8	9 1/4	r	r
G M	70	4 3/4	6 1/4	r	11/16	1 5/8	2 1/2
74	75	1 13/16	3 1/4	4	3	4	4 1/2
74	80	11/16	1 5/8	2 5/8	6 1/2	7 1/4	7 3/4
74	85	3/16	3/4	2	11 1/4	r	r
74	90	1/16	3/8	s	r	r	s
Glf Wn	45	22 1/2	s	s	r	s	s
66 5/8	55	13 1/4	r	s	r	r	s
66 5/8	60	8 1/2	10 1/2	11 1/4	3/4	r	r
66 5/8	65	5	6 3/8	r	2	r	r
66 5/8	70	2 5/8	4 1/4	r	r	r	r
66 5/8	75	1	2	r	r	r	r
Heinz	35	9 1/2	10 1/4	s	r	r	s
43 1/2	40	5	6	r	5/8	1 1/2	r
43 1/2	45	1 3/4	3 3/8	4 1/4	r	3 1/2	4
43 1/2	50	3/4	1 1/2	r	r	r	r
HughTl	7 1/2	r	r	r	1/8	r	r
9 1/4	10	1/4	9/16	13/16	7/8	1 1/16	r
9 1/4	12 1/2	r	r	5/16	r	r	r
9 1/4	15	1/16	s	s	r	s	s
ICX Ind	20	4 1/2	r	r	r	r	r
23 1/2	22 1/2	2 1/8	r	r	r	r	r
23 1/2	25	3/4	1 5/8	r	r	r	r
I T T	35	20 3/4	s	s	r	s	s
54 3/4	40	15 1/4	r	r	r	r	r
54 3/4	45	10 1/4	12 1/8	12 1/2	3/16	5/8	r
54 3/4	50	6 1/4	8 1/8	r	1 1/8	2	2 3/4

Exhibit 2.4 shows the closing prices, in dollars, of the XYZ call options. The prices are recorded on a per share basis. Thus, the actual prices per contract are obtained by multiplying the price by the number of shares per contract, which in this case is 100. The actual price of an April 35 call contract, for example, is $700.

EXHIBIT 2.4
Call Option Prices
Stock Price = $40, Time to Expiration of Near Series = 12 Weeks

Strike	April	July	October
25	15.06	—	—
30	10.88	12.12	—
35	7.00	8.62	—
40	4.00	5.75	7.38
45	2.00	3.69	5.39
50	0.88	2.38	3.75

Notation

In order to distinguish among call contracts, their price will often be written as an explicit function of key parameters.

Let S_0 = Current stock price at time 0,
S_T = Stock price at the expiration date, T,
C_0 = Current call price,
C_T = Call price at expiration,
X = Strike price,
T = Initial time to expiration.

Then, at time t, with $T - t$ years to expiration, the call price will be represented by the following:

$$C_t = C(S_t, T - t, X).$$

The call price initially is given by

$$C_0 = C(S_0, T, X)$$

and at expiration is

$$C_T = C(S_T, 0, X).$$

The Intrinsic Value of Call Options

The *intrinsic value* of a call option is defined as the difference between the stock price and strike price or zero, whichever is greatest.

$$\text{Intrinsic Value} = \text{Max}(S_0 - X, 0)$$

All in-the-money call options have positive intrinsic value. Options trading at their intrinsic value are said to be trading *at parity*. Theoretically, an option should never trade below parity. If it did, an investor wanting to purchase the stock would find it cheaper to buy the stock by purchasing the option and exercising it immediately. For example, with XYZ trading at $40, the value of all 35 options should exceed the intrinsic value of $5.

Property 2.1

Call prices should equal or exceed their intrinsic values.

$$C(S_0, T, X) \geq \text{Max}(S_0 - X, 0)$$

At expiration the option holder has the choice of buying the stock for the strike price or allowing the option to expire. The option should be exercised if it is in the money. If it is out of the money, the option is worthless.

Property 2.2

At the expiration date, the value of an option equals its intrinsic value.

$$C(S_T, 0, X) = \text{Max}(S_T - X, 0)$$

Time Premiums

The difference between the observed call price and its intrinsic value is called the *time premium*. If the time premium is zero, the call is trading at parity. Exhibit 2.5 illustrates the time premiums of XYZ call options. Note that all options are trading above parity.

Since an option with a longer time to expiration has all the characteristics of an option with a shorter duration but lasts longer, it should carry a higher price. The time premium reflects this value.

Property 2.3

The value of call options with the same strike price increases as time to expiration increases.

$$C(S_0, T_1, X) \leq C(S_0, T_2, X) \quad \text{if } T_1 \leq T_2$$

The call value can be represented as the sum of two components:

Call Premium = Intrinsic Value + Time Premium

EXHIBIT 2.5
Time Premiums of XYZ Call Options

Strike	April	July	October
25	0.06	—	—
30	0.88	2.12	—
35	2.00	3.62	—
40	4.00	5.75	7.38
45	2.00	3.69	5.39
50	0.88	2.38	3.75

As the expiration date nears, the time premium shrinks to zero. Prior to expiration, the size of the time premium depends on the time remaining and the intrinsic value. From Exhibit 2.5 it can be seen that the time premiums of at-the-money options are relatively larger than time premiums of in-the-money or out-of-the-money options. This phenomenon will be discussed in more detail in later chapters.

CALL OPTION TRANSACTIONS

A call buyer's opening transaction consists of the initial call purchase. Since the time premium shrinks as the expiration date approaches, call buyers hope that this decay is more than offset by an increase in the intrinsic value.

At any time, the call holder can do one of three things:

1. Exercise the call by paying the strike price in return for shares.
2. Cancel the position by selling the call option at the current market price.
3. Hold onto the call and take no immediate action.

Exercising Call Options

If an option is exercised and the acquired stock is immediately sold at market price, then ignoring commission costs, the option holder will profit only from the intrinsic value.

Example 2.2

Suppose an investor owns an April 40 call option on a stock that is priced at $42. By exercising the call option, the investor pays $40 for a stock whose market value is $42. If the stock is sold at its market value of $42, then ignoring commission costs, the net profit to the option holder will be $2 less the initial cost of the option.

Property 2.4

By exercising a call option, the investor forfeits the time premium.

Rather than exercising the call option, the investor could have cancelled his or her position by selling the option at its current market price. In this way, the time premium would not be forfeited.

Although it appears that early exercise of a call option is not a sound strategy, there are circumstances in which it is appropriate. These include the following situations:

1. If the investor wants to own the stock and the option is trading at parity, exercising the call rather than selling the option and buying the stock may be advantageous, once transaction costs are considered.
2. Immediately before an ex-dividend date, the holder of an in-the-money call option may find it profitable to exercise the call early. This strategy would be desirable if the dividend paid on the stock is greater than the time premium.

Example 2.3

With six months to expiration, the owner of an XYZ 40 call option decides whether to exercise the call. The stock price is $40, the call price is $2, and a $1.50 quarterly dividend is due.

By exercising the call early, the investor gains $150 in dividends but forfeits the time premium of $200. Hence, in this case early exercise is not appropriate.

The optimal timing of exercising options is discussed more fully in Chapter 4.

Selling Call Options

For every opening transaction involving an option purchase, there is an opening transaction involving an option sale. The seller (or writer) of an option is *obliged* to deliver 100 shares of the underlying stock for the agreed strike price in the event that the option is exercised. The writer of the call receives the call premium for this obligation. The writer anticipates that the stock price will decline in value or increase at a rate slower than the decrease of the time value of the option.

Unlike the call purchaser, who has a voluntary right to exercise the call, the writer has a legal obligation to deliver 100 shares at the strike price in the event that the option is exercised.

Example 2.4

An XYZ April 45 call option initially sold for a premium of $2. In March, with the stock price at 52, the option is exercised. The writer, in this case, is obligated to deliver 100 shares of the security for $45 per share.

At any point in time the writer of a call option can do one of two things:

1. Close out the position by buying the call back at the current market price, or
2. Do nothing.

The call writer should be particularly aware of conditions that will encourage the buyer to exercise the call. As discussed, exercise can occur if the call trades at parity and an ex-dividend date is near.

The maximum loss an option buyer can experience is limited to his or her initial investment. However, the maximum loss in selling options is unlimited. To guarantee that the writer can meet obligations, brokerage firms require certain margin requirements to be met. These requirements may be stricter than the minimum set of requirements set by law. In addition, the initial call premiums taken in are held by the brokerage firm as collateral.

PROFIT DIAGRAMS FOR CALL OPTIONS

The profit obtained by holding a call option to expiration depends on the stock price at expiration. The solid line in Exhibit 2.6 illustrates the potential profit of an April 40 call option initially purchased for $4 and held to expiration.

The profit from selling the call is the mirror image of the profit from buying the call and is represented by the dashed line. The profit functions clearly illustrate that the profit (loss) of the buyer equals the loss (profit) of the writer. Notwithstanding commission costs, options are zero sum games.

LISTED PUT OPTIONS

A put option is a contract that gives the owner the right to sell a given number of shares of a specified security at a specified strike price at any point in time prior to a specified date. The writer of a put is legally obliged to accept delivery of the shares for the strike price in the event that the put holder exercises his or her right.

EXHIBIT 2.6
Profit Table for Purchasing a Call

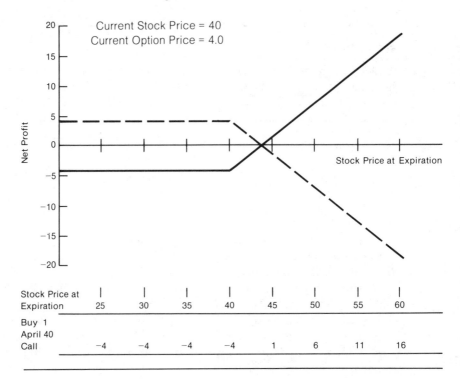

Current Stock Price = 40
Current Option Price = 4.0

Stock Price at Expiration	25	30	35	40	45	50	55	60
Buy 1 April 40 Call	−4	−4	−4	−4	1	6	11	16

PRICING OF PUT OPTIONS

Exhibit 2.4 illustrated the prices of all call options available on XYZ when the stock price was $40. Exhibit 2.7 shows the prices of all put options on a per share basis. Note that the available strike prices and times to expiration are the same as for the call options.

An owner of an April 40 XYZ put option has the right to sell 100 shares of XYZ at $40 per share, regardless of the market value of the security. The ability to do this extends to the third Friday in April.

A buyer may purchase a put in anticipation of a stock price decline. The buyer need not own the underlying security. If it is owned, then the put provides insurance against stock price declines below the strike. This is more fully explained in the next chapter.

The put options with strike 40 are trading at the money. Since their strike price equals the stock price, their full premium is a time premium. Put options have intrinsic value if the strike price is higher than the stock price. For example, the 45 put options have intrinsic value, since the put holder could buy 100 shares of XYZ at the market price of $40 per share, and then "put" the shares onto the option seller for the strike price of $45 per share.

EXHIBIT 2.7
Put Option Prices
Stock Price = $40, Time to Expiration of Near Series = 12 Weeks

Strike	April	July	October
25	0.06	—	—
30	0.25	0.75	—
35	1.00	1.95	—
40	3.00	3.88	4.50
45	5.88	6.62	7.12
50	10.00	10.06	10.25

Thus, for put options, the intrinsic value is given by the following equation:

$$\text{Intrinsic Value} = \text{Max}(X - S_0, 0)$$

Options with positive intrinsic value are called *in-the-money options*. Thus, the 45 and 50 strike priced options are in the money.

Exhibit 2.8 (page 24) illustrates the dollar time premiums of the put prices in Exhibit 2.7. Note that the April 50 put option is trading at parity.

As with call options, if put options traded below parity, arbitrage opportunities would exist. For example, if the 45 put was priced below the parity value of $5, say at $3, then an arbitrager would buy the put and the stock for an initial investment, excluding transaction costs, of $43. By exercising the put immediately, the investor would obtain a $2 profit.

PUT OPTION TRANSACTIONS

At any point in time a put holder, like a call holder, can exercise or cancel his or her position or do nothing. If the put holder exercises his or her right, then any positive time premium is lost. However, early exercising of put options can be advantageous. For example, immediately after an ex-dividend date, the holder of an in-the-money put option who also owns the stock may decide to exercise even though several months may remain to expiration. This is especially likely if the put is deep in the money. By not exercising the option, the investor is foregoing receiving the higher strike price on which interest could be earned.

The following example illustrates that if there are no dividends prior to expiration, put holders who own the stock may correctly exercise their right prior to expiration. If the stock pays a dividend, then the investor may decide to wait until after the last ex-dividend date before exercising. However, if the put is deep in the money, early exercise may still be appropriate. In this case, the size of the interest income received by early exercise should exceed the foregone dividend.

EXHIBIT 2.8
Time Premium of Put Options

Strike	April	July	October
25	0.06	—	—
30	0.25	0.75	—
35	1.00	1.95	—
40	3.00	3.88	4.50
45	0.88	1.62	2.12
50	0	0.06	0.25

Example 2.5

The owner of the three-month XYZ 50 put option and 100 shares of XYZ may exercise early. The stock is at $40, and the put option is at its parity value of $10. No further dividends are due prior to expiration. The interest rate is 8 percent.

By exercising early, the investor receives $5000 immediately. This money will generate $100 in interest over the three-month period. If the investor delays exercising, then he or she is sacrificing potential interest income.

Property 2.5

1. For stocks paying no dividends, early exercise of calls is not optimal, but early exercise of puts may be optimal.
2. For stocks paying dividends, early exercise of calls and puts may be appropriate. As dividend sizes increase, early exercise of call options becomes more likely and early exercise of put options before the last ex-dividend date becomes less likely.

The decision to exercise a call or put option early depends on trade-offs between dividend and interest income and is discussed in more detail in Chapter 4.

PROFIT FUNCTIONS FOR PUT OPTIONS

The profit from holding a put option to expiration is represented graphically by the solid line in Exhibit 2.9. In this exhibit, the profit diagram of the three-month 40 put option is presented. The initial cost is $3 and it is assumed that the put is held to maturity. The sale of a put option is the mirror image and is indicated by the dashed line.

EXHIBIT 2.9
Profit Table for Purchasing a Put

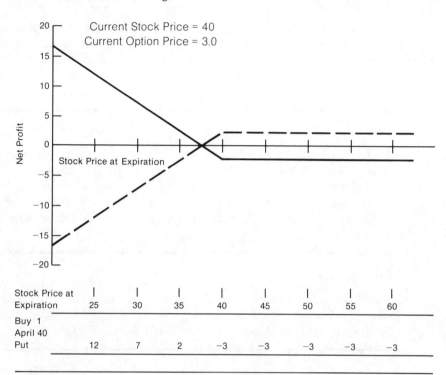

Stock Price at Expiration	25	30	35	40	45	50	55	60
Buy 1 April 40 Put	12	7	2	−3	−3	−3	−3	−3

The relationship between put and call prices together with the effects of dividends and interest rates will be explored in the next chapters.

ADJUSTMENT OF OPTION CONTRACTS FOR STOCK SPLITS AND STOCK DIVIDENDS

Listed call options are not adjusted for cash dividends. However, strike price adjustments are made if the stock splits or if stock dividends occur.

Example 2.6

Suppose a stock declares a two-for-one split. If the stock were trading at $60, then after the split the price would be $30. A call option with strike 50 would, in this case, split into two call options with strike 25 each. A 55 call option would split into two 27.5 strike-priced calls.

If the split ratio were not an integer, the adjustment would be more complex. For example, consider a three-for-two split. In this case, not only would the strike price be adjusted, but also the number of shares per contract.

Example 2.7

For a three-for-two split, new strike prices are established by dividing the old strike price by 1.5 and rounding off to the nearest 1/8th of a point. If the strike price were 85, then the new strike price would be near 85/1.5, or 56 2/3. The investor would not hold one option contract with strike 56 5/8. If the option were exercised, 150 shares (rather than 100 shares) would be delivered.

Example 2.8

XYZ Corporation "spins off" its subsidiary, ABC Inc., by distributing to its stockholders 1.5 shares of ABC for every share of XYZ stock. In this case, outstanding XYZ options might be adjusted to require delivery of 100 shares of XYZ plus 150 shares of ABC stock. Alternatively, the strike prices of XYZ might be reduced by the value, on a per share basis, of the distributed property.

Example 2.9

XYZ is acquired by a corporation in a cash merger. Each holder of XYZ stock receives $50 per share. In this case, XYZ options might be adjusted to call for the delivery of $5000 in cash, rather than 100 shares of XYZ.

THE DETERMINANTS OF OPTION VALUE

We have seen that the stock price, strike price, time to expiration, and dividend policy are factors that influence option prices. There are only two other primary determinants of option prices—the volatility of the underlying stock price and interest rates. In future chapters the exact relationship of option prices to each of these variables will be analyzed. Nonetheless, we have already seen that American option prices increase as time to expiration increases and as the stock price moves deeper into the money. Moreover, we have seen that as dividend size increases, early exercise of call options becomes more likely and early exercise of puts before the ex-dividend date becomes less likely. In this section we shall provide intuitive explanations of the impact volatility and interest rates have on option prices.

The Role of Volatility

The *volatility* of a stock is a measure of its potential dispersion over future possible stock prices. A stock with high volatility would have a high degree of dispersion in future values and could thus increase or decrease by significant amounts. In contrast, a stock with no volatility would be riskless since future prices would be certain.

As volatility increases, call prices also increase. To see this, note that buying a call option provides an alternative to purchasing stock in anticipation of capturing gains from the stock price advance. As volatility increases, the future dispersion of possible stock prices expands. While this increases the likelihood of large profits from the stock, it also increases the chances of large losses. However, the call holders will obtain all the benefits from expanded dispersion without the drawbacks. Specifically, by exercising the call option, call holders can participate dollar for dollar in favorable outcomes. If unfavorable outcomes occur, however, call holders merely do not exercise their contracts. Consequently, call holders will prefer more volatility to less. As a result, the higher the volatility of the stock over the lifetime of the call option, the higher its value relative to the stock.

Note that the same argument holds true for put options. The greater the dispersion of future potential stock prices, the greater the chance the stock price will end up in the money (below the strike). Since it is not necessary for put holders to exercise their option, their losses are limited, should the stock price appreciate. Thus, put premiums should expand as volatility increases.

The Role of Interest Rates

As interest rates increase, call prices also increase. To see this, recall that buying a call option provides an alternative to purchasing stock in anticipation of capturing gains from an increasing stock price. As interest rates rise, the cost of carrying the underlying security rises and the call option will appear more attractive vis-à-vis the stock.

An alternative way of illustrating the impact of interest rates on option prices is provided by considering an investor who buys the call option and invests sufficient funds (at the riskless rate) to ensure that, at expiration, the account will have grown to the strike price. The effective strike price at expiration is really the present value of the strike. As interest rates increase, this effective strike price decreases. Hence, an increasing interest rate has the same impact on option prices as a decreasing strike price.

This simple analysis has assumed that interest rates do not affect the stock price. Clearly, if interest rate increases reduced the volatility of the stock, for example, then the analysis would be more complex. Note, too, that with interest rates rising, the effective strike prices are reduced, and hence put premiums fall. Thus, put prices will move in an opposite direction to call prices when interest rates change.

Exhibit 2.10 illustrates the direction option premiums will move as each variable increases.

EXHIBIT 2.10
Effects of Variables on Option Premiums

| | Effect of Increases | |
Variable	Call Premiums	Put Premiums
Stock price	Increase	Decrease
Strike price	Decrease	Increase
Time to expiration	Increase	Increase
Cash dividends	Decrease	Increase
Stock volatility	Increase	Increase
Interest rates	Increase	Decrease

CONCLUSION

Standardized stock option contracts are introduced into the marketplace in a well-defined way. At any point in time, a variety of option contracts that differ in strike price and time to maturity can trade. Option prices are set so that in-the-money contracts are more valuable than out-of-the-money contracts, and the far series are more valuable than the near series. Although the strike price and expiration date are key ingredients in determining the price of an option, we have seen that interest rates and dividends are factors that must be considered. The volatility of the stock also affects the value of an option contract.

Options are highly leveraged financial instruments that allow speculators to participate in the stock market without owning stock and allow shareholders to hedge against unwanted risk. Options can be bought or sold. The maximum loss associated with the purchase of an option is the initial investment. On the other hand, the sale of an option can expose the writer to unlimited losses. The purchase of an option provides the investor with a right. In contrast, an option writer is obligated to fulfill the terms of the option contract if it is exercised.

Options are zero sum games. That is, ignoring transaction costs, the profit (loss) obtained by the buyer of an option is equal to the loss (profit) incurred by the seller. In the next few chapters we shall see that the primary economic role of options is to provide a financial mechanism of transferring risk among investors.

References

There are numerous books and brochures that define put and call stock options and describe the institutional structure of the option markets. The Options Clearing Corporation and the option exchanges publish many booklets that describe the risks and rewards of trading options. These pamphlets can be obtained directly from the exchanges or through a stock broker. The Cox-Rubinstein textbook provides an in-depth study of the actual operations of the Chicago Board Options Exchange.

Bookstaber, R. *Option Pricing and Strategies in Investing.* Reading, Mass.: Addison Wesley, 1981.

Cox, J. C., and M. Rubinstein. *Option Markets.* Englewood Cliffs, N.J.: Prentice-Hall, 1985.

Gastineau, G. *The Stock Options Manual.* New York: McGraw-Hill, 1979.

Khoury, S. *Speculative Markets.* New York: Macmillan, 1984.

McMillan, L. G. *Options as a Strategic Investment.* New York: New York Institute of Finance, 1980.

Exercises

1. The January 18, 1985, issue of the *Wall Street Journal* gave the following option prices on IBM:

		Calls			*Puts*		
		Jan.	**April**	**July**	**Jan.**	**April**	**July**
123 1/2	95	29 3/8	*s*	*s*	*r*	*s*	*s*
123 1/2	100	23 3/4	26	*s*	1/16	1/8	*s*
123 1/2	110	13 1/2	15 1/2	17 1/4	*r*	9/16	1 7/16
123 1/2	120	3 1/2	7 1/2	10 3/8	1/16	2 9/16	3 7/8
123 1/2	130	1/16	2 7/8	5 5/8	6 3/8	8 1/8	8 1/2
123 1/2	140	*r*	13/16	2 1/2	*r*	*r*	16 1/2

   a. Which call options are in the money, and which contracts are out of the money?

   b. Which put options are in the money, and which are out of the money?

   c. Compute the time premiums of all contracts.

   d. Based on the contracts trading, can you deduce whether the prices of IBM have been rising or falling over the past several months? Explain.

2. A three-month call option with strike price $50 is currently trading at $5. The stock price is $50. An investor has $5000 to invest and is considering buying 100 shares or 10 options.

   a. For both strategies, compute the three-month return on investment if at the expiration date the stock price is $40, $50, or $60.

   b. Repeat (a) if the option is a put option.

   c. Based on (a) and (b), can you conclude that options are highly leveraged financial instruments?

3. Mr. Vestor knows that his certificate of deposit matures in two months, at which time cash will be released, which he will invest in the stock market. However, he would like to buy stock now, for he feels a rally is imminent. Would you recommend that Mr. Vestor buy call or put options in the interim? What type of contracts (strike price and maturity) would you recommend?

4. XYZ trades at $50. The $45 put option trades at 1 1/2, and the $50 put option trades at $3.

    a. Compute the profit (and return) from buying the $45 put and the $50 put if the stock price at expiration is $40 and $45.

    b. Does the out-of-the-money put option offer a higher reward (and higher risk) potential?

5. XYZ is trading at $50. Ms. Vestor feels it would be a good buy at $45. Rather than place a limit order to buy at $45, she decides to sell a $50 put option that is currently trading at $5. Discuss the benefits of this strategy by considering what happens if at the expiration date the stock trades above $50 and below $50.

6. Consider the following information:

    Price of XYZ = $50   Price of ABC = $50

    XYZ April 50 Call = 3   ABC April 50 Call = 5

    Based on this information alone, can an investor determine which option contract is overpriced? If not, what other factors should be considered?

7. XYZ is selling at $50 and a four-month call option with strike 45 is selling at $9.

    a. What is the maximum profit obtained if the call option is sold? Under what conditions would this profit be obtained?

    b. Mr. Vestor sold the call option. What loss is incurred if the stock is trading at $62 at the expiration date?

    c. What is the minimum loss that will be incurred if after two months, with the stock trading at $63, Mr. Vestor decides to cut his losses by buying back the call?

8. A call option with strike 30 and time to expiration of two months trades at $6. Another call on the same stock has strike 30 and time to expiration of three months, and trades at $4. Construct a strategy that guarantees profit.

9. A put option with strike 30 and time to expiration of two months trades at $6. Another put on the same stock has strike 30, time to expiration 3 months, and trades at $4. Can one construct a strategy that guarantees profit? If so, what is this strategy?

10. A dont option is an option that you pay for only if you do not exercise the option by expiration. Do you think the premium of a dont call option would be higher or lower than the premium for a regular American call option? Justify your answer.

11. A trading range call option can be exercised only for the strike price, if the underlying stock price stays within a given range of prices. Would such an option be more or less valuable than an American call option? Explain your answer.

12. XYZ is selling at 40, and a one-month call option with strike 50 is selling for 1/2. Under what conditions would you sell the call option naked? What are the potential risks?

13. An investor with $5500 is bullish on XYZ. XYZ trades at $55. One possible investment is to buy 100 shares. An alternative is to buy one call option with a strike of 55 (assume the premium is $5) and invest the remaining $5000 in Treasury bonds for six months at 10 percent. Compare the two investments, assuming that the stock pays no dividends.

14. An XYZ April 50 call option is bought for $5. At expiration the stock is selling at $60. If the call is sold, the commission will be $25. If the call is exercised and

the stock is then sold, there will be a commission when the stock is bought and again when it is sold. Assuming a commission for each transaction of $65, compare the two strategies of selling versus exercising. Based on this analysis, how do commission costs affect option strategies?

15. A European option is identical to an American option except that it can be exercised only at the expiration date.
   a. Would you suspect a European call option to be worth more or less than its American counterpart? Explain.
   b. Would you expect a European put option to be worth more or less than its American counterpart? Explain.

16. Provide an intuitive explanation for the fact that put premiums drop when interest rates rise.

Appendix

Executing Option Orders and the Role of the Options Clearing Corporation

The option exchanges attempt to provide a continuous, competitive, and fair market environment for the purchase and sale of options. They determine the underlying securities on which options are traded, and they enforce rules applicable to the handling of accounts and execution of buy and sell orders. Specific information about exchange functions is readily available in rule books of the various exchanges and in publications put out by brokerage firms.

In this appendix the process of executing option orders through the option exchange is discussed. In addition, the central role of the Options Clearing Corporation is investigated, and the process of assigning exercise notices to investors with short positions is discussed.

PLACING OPTION ORDERS

To place an order with a broker, the investor must specify the name of the underlying security, the type of option (put or call), the number of contracts to buy or sell, the strike price, the expiration month, and the type of order. The type of order provides the broker with instructions on the price the customer is prepared to pay and the time for which the order is in effect. A *market order*, for example, is to be filled at the prevailing prices. A *limit order* is a buy (sell) order that is to be filled at a specific price or lower (higher). A *stop order* becomes a market order only if a specific price is penetrated. A *day order* is entered for one day only, and is cancelled if not filled by the end of the day. A *good till cancelled order* remains a valid order until filled or cancelled.

Example

The current price of XYZ is $50. A limit order to buy one April call option with strike 50 for $4 is placed with the broker. The order is a day order. If the option price is still above $4 by the end of the day, the order is cancelled.

EXECUTION OF ORDERS

After receiving an order from a customer, the broker will direct it to the appropriate exchange. A broker who represents the firm on the floor of the exchange will attempt to execute the order in a fashion consistent with the rules of the exchange. At the Chicago Board Options Exchange, for example, trading is done by a system of "open outcry." In this system, offers to buy and sell options on a particular stock are made to all traders present in a specified area. The broker may trade with three types of traders:

1. *Market makers* trade for their own accounts. Their activity on the floor of the exchange enhances liquidity and tightens the spread that may exist between bid and ask quotes.
2. *Order book officials* are exchange employees who can accept only public orders. They cannot trade for their own accounts. Their job is to see that public limit orders are executed as soon as their threshold prices have been attained.
3. *Other brokers* trade on behalf of their clients and their firm's accounts.

Once an oral agreement is reached between two floor traders, the transaction is reported to the Options Clearing Corporation and back to the original broker. Within a few minutes of placing an order, the customer will learn of the trade. Exhibit 2A.1 illustrates the transaction process.

THE OPTIONS CLEARING CORPORATION

Once a price is negotiated between two brokers on the floor of the exchange, the two cease to deal with each other. Instead, they deal with the Options Clearing Corporation (OCC). The OCC guarantees that all option obligations are met by breaking up every trade and becoming the seller for every buyer and buyer for every seller. Thus, all traders look to the OCC to maintain their side of the bargain, rather than to other traders.

Since the number of contracts purchased by the OCC equals the number sold, its net position is always zero. However, its position is not completely

EXHIBIT 2A.1
Option Order Execution Process

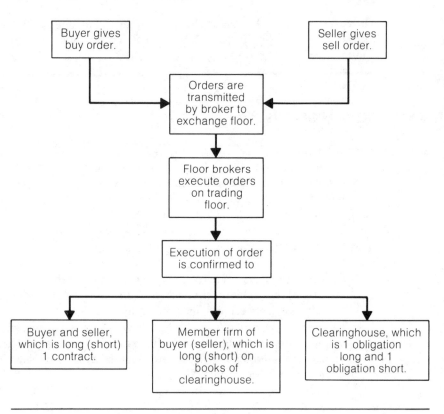

---

free of risk. To illustrate this, assume a particular investor exercises a call option. In this case the OCC is obliged to deliver 100 shares of the stock for the strike price. To accomplish this the OCC will, in effect, exercise one of its call options. If the investor to whom the exercise notice is assigned delivers the shares, the OCC covers its obligation. However, if the assigned writer fails to deliver the securities, the OCC must still fulfill its obligation.

To protect itself against the risk of default by sellers of options, the OCC requires that its member firms guarantee the obligations of all their particular customers. Toward this goal, the OCC requires that all member firms whose clients have short positions provide the OCC with collateral. These accounts are balanced daily. The clearing members, in turn, must ensure that their customers have sufficient funds to meet their potential obligations. They achieve this by requiring that their clients provide collateral for all their written positions. The exact amount of collateral required depends on the transaction and is discussed in the next chapter.

The breaking up of all trades by the OCC provides option traders with additional benefits. Since all members are, in essence, trading against the

OCC, they can easily cancel their positions. For example, a writer who sold a call option (to the OCC) can cancel his or her position by buying an option (at market-determined prices). In essence, this action results in a cancellation of the original transaction. Without the OCC, individual sellers would have to negotiate with individual buyers to establish a price at which both parties would settle.

EXERCISING OPTION CONTRACTS

Although most buyers and sellers of options close out their positions by an offsetting sale or purchase, there are occasions when a contract will be exercised. To exercise an option, the owner must instruct his or her broker to give exercise instructions to OCC. To ensure that an option is exercised on a particular day, this notice must be tendered before a particular time (which may vary across brokerage firms). The broker passes the exercise instructions to the OCC.

On the next business day, the OCC randomly assigns the exercise notice to a clearing member who has an account that contains a written option in the relevant security. The brokerage firm to which the notice is assigned then randomly allocates the assignment to a customer who has a written position. Once an exercise notice has been assigned to a writer, the writer can no longer effect an offsetting closing transaction, but must instead purchase (if the exercise notice is a put) or sell (if the notice is a call) the underlying securities for the strike price. Settlement between brokers on exercised options occurs on the fifth business day after exercise. Each broker involved in an exercise settles with his or her own customer.

3

Option Strategies

Chapter 2 was concerned with the basic terminology and properties of options. This chapter discusses categorizing and analyzing investment positions constructed by meshing puts and calls with their underlying securities. Options may be used to produce payouts that best reflect the expectations that an investor has for the future prospects of a security. As an example, consider an investor who believes that a news announcement will soon be released that will have major ramifications on the price of the stock of a particular company. Since it is not known whether the announcement will be good or bad, the investor is uncertain whether to buy or sell the security. We shall see that, by using options, one can construct a position on this security so that profits will be obtained, regardless of whether the news announcement is good or bad.

As a second example, consider an investor who attempts to "time" the market. Without options, such investors attempt to smooth out the fluctuations of their portfolio values by buying and selling their securities. Anticipating short-term declines in stock price, the investor may choose to sell the security, even if the long-term prospects appear good. Timing strategies can result in large transaction costs. With options, the anticipated short-term decline can be hedged without selling the stock. In fact, with options available, investors can choose precisely the degree of risk they want to bear. Unwanted risk associated with some aspects of stock ownership can be transferred to speculators who are willing to accept it.

In this chapter we shall consider a variety of option strategies that produce distinctive future payouts. We shall analyze these payouts by using profit diagrams.

For the most part, we shall ignore commissions, margin requirements, and dividends. We shall also assume that positions are maintained unchanged to the expiration date and that no premature exercising occurs.

The primary objectives of this chapter are the following:

1. To analyze almost any position containing several option contracts on a single underlying security;

2. To recognize the strategic role of options in investment management; and
3. To identify the most popular option strategies currently in use.

In this chapter we shall focus on option strategies for single securities; in Chapter 7 we shall consider hedge strategies for portfolios.

OPTION POSITIONS

There are four types of option positions:

1. *Naked positions* involve the purchase or sale of a single security, for example, the purchase or sale of a stock or a call or a put.
2. *Hedge positions* consist of the underlying stock together with options that provide partial or full protection from unfavorable outcomes.
3. *Spread options* consist of a long position in one option and a short position in another option on the same underlying security.
4. *Combinations* consist of portfolios containing either long or short positions in call and put options on the same security.

Exhibit 3.1 shows the price data that will be used to illustrate all the strategies discussed in this chapter.

EXHIBIT 3.1
Call and Put Option Prices
Stock Price = $40, Time to Expiration of Near Series = 12 Weeks

	Calls				Puts		
Strike	Near (April)	Middle (July)	Far (October)	Strike	Near (April)	Middle (July)	Far (October)
25	15.06	—	—	25	0.06	—	—
30	10.88	12.12	—	30	0.25	0.75	—
35	7.00	8.62	—	35	1.00	1.95	—
40	4.00	5.75	7.38	40	3.00	3.88	4.50
45	2.00	3.69	5.39	45	5.88	6.62	7.12
50	0.88	2.38	3.75	50	10.00	10.06	10.25

NAKED POSITIONS

Naked Positions in the Stock

Exhibit 3.2 illustrates the profit diagram for holding the stock for three months. Increases in stock price offer profits, whereas decreases in stock price offer losses.

EXHIBIT 3.2
Profit Table for Purchasing Stock

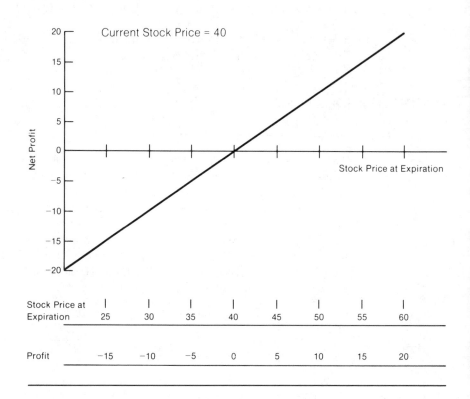

Stock Price at Expiration	25	30	35	40	45	50	55	60
Profit	−15	−10	−5	0	5	10	15	20

Exhibit 3.3 illustrates the profit diagram for selling the stock short. The short seller, anticipating stock declines, intends to return the securities by purchasing them in the market in the future at lower prices. Since the investor is liable for all dividends paid on the stock while it is outstanding, if the investor is to profit, the price declines must be significantly greater than the dividends. For the privilege of borrowing stock, the broker requires the investor to deposit collateral into a special margin account. Specifically, 50 percent of the short sale value must be deposited in cash or in interest-bearing securities with the broker. Furthermore, the proceeds of the sale of the borrowed stock are retained by the broker in a noninterest-bearing account until the stock is returned. If the stock moves favorably, some of the margin funds can be released to support other investments. No additional margin is required if the stock moves unfavorably until a lower maintenance margin requirement is violated. The details of margin requirements for short sales are discussed in the appendix to this chapter. Exhibit 3.3 shows the profit increasing as the stock price declines.

EXHIBIT 3.3
Profit Table for Selling Stock Short

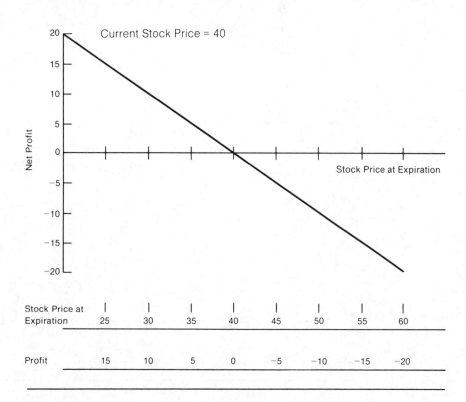

Current Stock Price = 40

Stock Price at Expiration	25	30	35	40	45	50	55	60
Profit	15	10	5	0	−5	−10	−15	−20

Naked Positions in Call Options

The solid line in Exhibit 3.4 illustrates the profit diagram associated with the strategy of buying a call. The diagram illustrates the payouts associated with buying the three-month at-the-money call contract.

One of the main attractions of buying call options is that they provide speculators with significant leverage. If the stock price in Exhibit 3.4 increases by $20, its return would be 50 percent, while the return on the option would be 400 percent. However, if the stock remained unchanged in price, its return would be 0 percent, compared to a 100 percent loss in the option. Even though the return on the option may be a very large percentage, the risk can never exceed the call premium, which is typically a fraction of the stock price.

The dashed line in Exhibit 3.4 indicates the profit diagram for the sale of the call. The naked call writer assumes the prospect of unlimited risk in return for a limited profit. Thus, this strategy is unsuitable for some investors. In Exhibit 3.4, the naked call writer will profit only if the stock price remains

EXHIBIT 3.4

Profit Table for Buying a Call Option

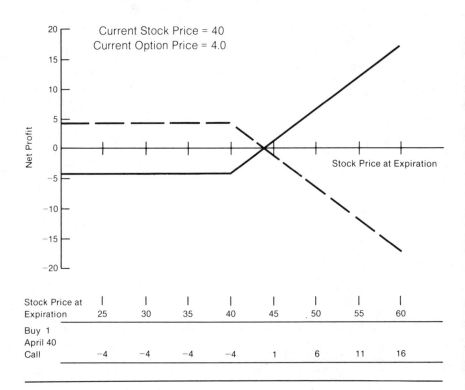

Stock Price at Expiration	25	30	35	40	45	50	55	60
Buy 1 April 40 Call	−4	−4	−4	−4	1	6	11	16

below $44. Recall that call writers have an obligation to deliver shares in the event that they are exercised. In order to ensure that the investor is able to deliver the underlying security, the broker will require the call writer to deposit collateral into a margin account. The exact margin requirements are discussed in the appendix to this chapter.

Naked Positions in Put Options

The solid line in Exhibit 3.5 illustrates the profit diagram associated with the strategy of buying a put option and holding it to expiration. The diagram illustrates the payouts associated with buying the three-month at-the-money put contract.

Like call options, put options are highly leveraged financial instruments. From Exhibit 3.5 it can be seen that if the stock drops to $25 (for a net loss of 37 percent), the return on the put would be 267 percent. As with call options, the maximum loss is limited to the put premium, which usually is a small fraction of the security price.

The dashed line in Exhibit 3.5 indicates the profit function for the sale of

EXHIBIT 3.5
Profit Table for Buying a Put Option

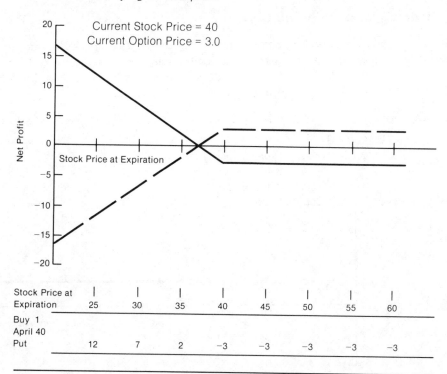

Current Stock Price = 40
Current Option Price = 3.0

Stock Price at Expiration	25	30	35	40	45	50	55	60
Buy 1 April 40 Put	12	7	2	-3	-3	-3	-3	-3

a put. Here the maximum profit equals the put premium, while the downside loss is only limited by the fact that the stock cannot go below zero.

Some investors who actually want to acquire stock will often write naked puts as well. The motivation for this is illustrated by the example below.

Example 3.1

An investor feels that XYZ would be a good buy at $36. With the stock priced at $40, the investor decides to place an open buy order with a limit price of $36. Three months later XYZ has drifted down to $37, but no lower. If the price rises rapidly, the investor will not participate in the rally, since the stock will not be owned.

Rather than place an open order at $36, the investor could have written a 40 put for $4. If XYZ is below $40 at expiration, the put will be exercised and the investor will be forced to pay $40 per share for the stock. Since $4 was received from the sale of the put, the net cost of the stock is $36.

The advantage of writing a put over placing an open buy order is that the strategy generates income when the stock price does not fall to the purchase level.

HEDGE POSITIONS

Hedging Stock with Call Options

A *covered hedge position* (often referred to as a *covered write position*) consists of a portfolio in which a call is written against every 100 shares held. Exhibit 3.6 shows the profit diagram of a portfolio in which a three-month at-the-money call option is written against the stock.

EXHIBIT 3.6
Profit Table for a Covered Call Option

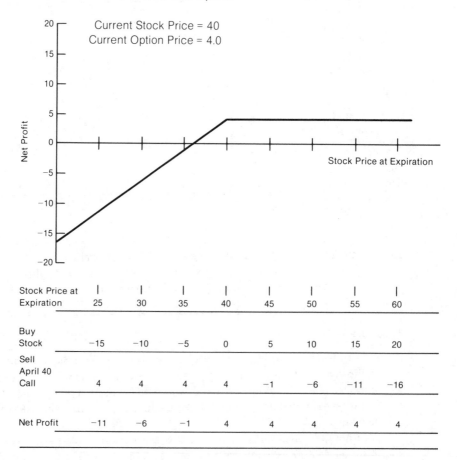

Stock Price at Expiration	25	30	35	40	45	50	55	60
Buy Stock	−15	−10	−5	0	5	10	15	20
Sell April 40 Call	4	4	4	4	−1	−6	−11	−16
Net Profit	−11	−6	−1	4	4	4	4	4

The solid line in Exhibit 3.7 illustrates the profit diagram for a covered hedge position in which the April 35 calls are sold against the stock. The profit diagram is compared to the previous position involving the sale of the April 40s.

EXHIBIT 3.7

Profit Table for a Covered Call Position

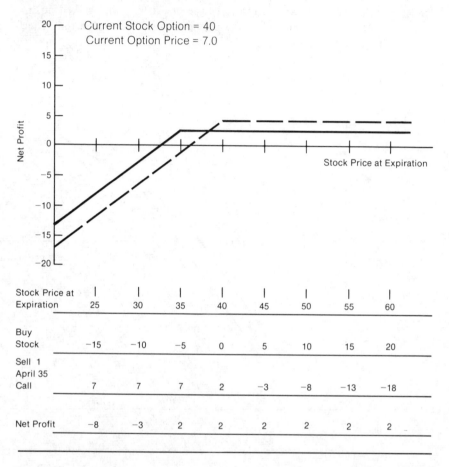

Current Stock Option = 40
Current Option Price = 7.0

Stock Price at Expiration	25	30	35	40	45	50	55	60
Buy Stock	−15	−10	−5	0	5	10	15	20
Sell 1 April 35 Call	7	7	7	2	−3	−8	−13	−18
Net Profit	−8	−3	2	2	2	2	2	2

Note that, by selling the 35s rather than the 40s, the investor sacrifices upside potential for downside protection. Specifically, the new position can make a maximum of only $2 (as opposed to $4). However, the position loses money only if the stock price falls below $33 (as opposed to $36). The choice between these two positions depends on the investor's beliefs about future prices as well as his or her attitudes toward risk and reward.

The fact that the option premium acts as partial compensation for potential declines in the underlying stock price has appeal to stockholders who believe that, over the short term, the stock price will be flat at best. Rather than sell the stock with the intention of buying it back in the future, such stockholders could sell calls against stock owned. Indeed, this strategy outperforms stock ownership if the stock price falls, remains the same, or even rises slightly.

A partially covered hedge position can be established by writing fewer calls than stock held. The ratio of calls written to stock held is called the *hedge ratio*. Exhibit 3.8 illustrates a 1:2 hedge where at-the-money call options are used. The dashed line indicates the profit line for a naked position in two stocks. Note that, unlike the previous position, this partial hedge does not place a ceiling on the upside potential.

EXHIBIT 3.8
Profit Table for a Partially Covered Hedge

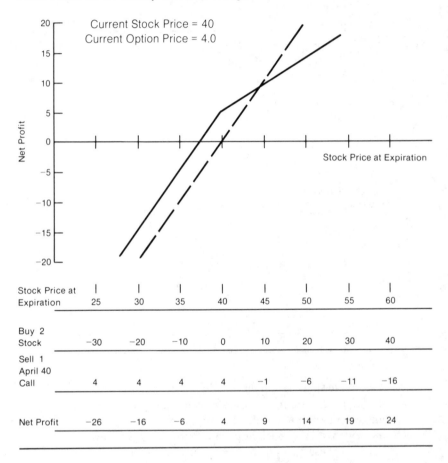

Stock Price at Expiration	25	30	35	40	45	50	55	60
Buy 2 Stock	−30	−20	−10	0	10	20	30	40
Sell 1 April 40 Call	4	4	4	4	−1	−6	−11	−16
Net Profit	−26	−16	−6	4	9	14	19	24

To be classified as a hedge, the ratio of calls sold to stock purchased should be close to one. If the number of call options exceeds the number of stocks held, the strategy is termed a *ratio write strategy*. Exhibit 3.9 illustrates the profit diagram for a 2:1 ratio write strategy.

The 2:1 ratio write strategy generally will provide larger profits than either the covered write strategy or naked writing if the underlying stock remains relatively unchanged over the life of the call options. However, should the stock price make a significant positive or negative move, losses could be substantial.

EXHIBIT 3.9
Profit Table for a 2:1 Ratio Write Strategy

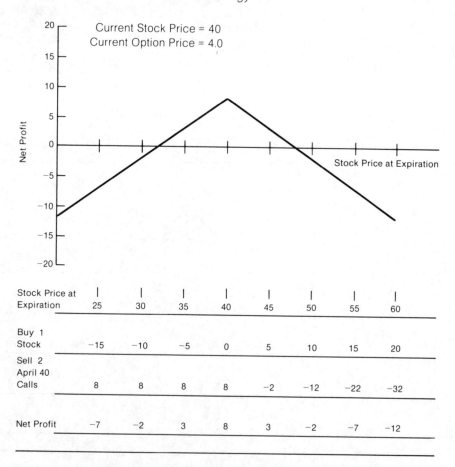

Current Stock Price = 40
Current Option Price = 4.0

Stock Price at Expiration	25	30	35	40	45	50	55	60
Buy 1 Stock	-15	-10	-5	0	5	10	15	20
Sell 2 April 40 Calls	8	8	8	8	-2	-12	-22	-32
Net Profit	-7	-2	3	8	3	-2	-7	-12

Generally, investors who establish a ratio write strategy are neutral in outlook regarding the underlying stock. This means that the at-the-money call is usually used in the strategy.

Note that the profit range in Exhibit 3.9 extends from $32 to $48. Although this interval appears large, the amount of dollars made in it can be small relative to the large losses that can be incurred if the stock price moves out of this range.

Hedging Stock with Put Options

Exhibit 3.10 shows the profit diagram of a long position in the stock and a put option. Note from the profit table that losses in the stock price below the strike are offset by increases in the put price. The put acts as an insurance policy providing price protection against stock declines below the strike. Note that this payout looks very similar to the payout of a call option. We shall have more to say about this in the next chapter.

EXHIBIT 3.10
Profit Table for Hedging a Stock with a Put

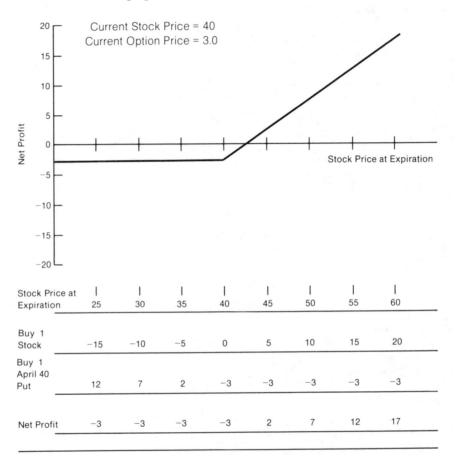

Stock Price at Expiration	25	30	35	40	45	50	55	60
Buy 1 Stock	−15	−10	−5	0	5	10	15	20
Buy 1 April 40 Put	12	7	2	−3	−3	−3	−3	−3
Net Profit	−3	−3	−3	−3	2	7	12	17

The solid line in Exhibit 3.11 illustrates the payouts achieved by hedging the stock by purchasing an April 35 put option. The previous profit diagram is also presented as a dashed line so that comparisons between the two alternatives can be made.

By paying $3, the investor buying the 40 put purchases protection against all price declines below $40. By paying $1, the investor buying the 35 put purchases protection against price declines below $35. By purchasing the cheaper put, the investor is bearing more downside risk. However, this risk is compensated by higher rewards should the stock price rise.

The put contract can be viewed as an insurance policy on the stock price. For a higher premium, an insurance policy that provides better protection against price declines can be obtained.

As with call options, the number of puts purchased against shares

EXHIBIT 3.11

Profit Table for Hedging a Stock with a Put

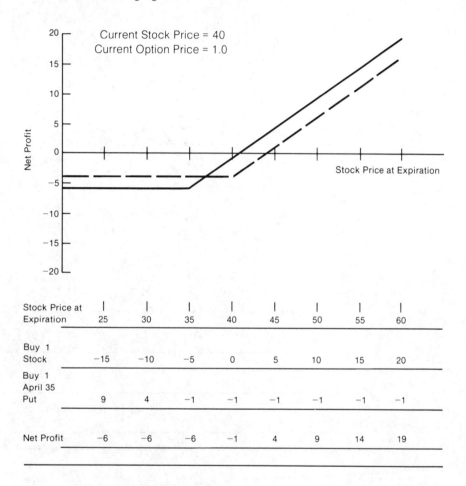

Stock Price at Expiration	25	30	35	40	45	50	55	60
Buy 1 Stock	−15	−10	−5	0	5	10	15	20
Buy 1 April 35 Put	9	4	−1	−1	−1	−1	−1	−1
Net Profit	−6	−6	−6	−1	4	9	14	19

owned need not be equal to one. The solid line in Exhibit 3.12 illustrates a profit diagram for a position with hedge ratios of 1:2. That is, one put is purchased for every two shares owned.

Exhibit 3.12 compares this strategy to the unhedged strategy of purchasing two shares and to the fully hedged strategy of purchasing two puts with the two shares. Note that the unhedged strategy produces the best results if the stock price appreciates significantly and the worst results if the stock price drops significantly. The fully insured position, on the other hand, performs the best, relatively, when the stock price drops significantly and the worst when the price appreciates. Although the partially hedged position does not truncate all the downside risk below the strike price, it offers more upside potential than the fully insured hedge.

EXHIBIT 3.12
Profit Table for Buying One Put for Two Stocks

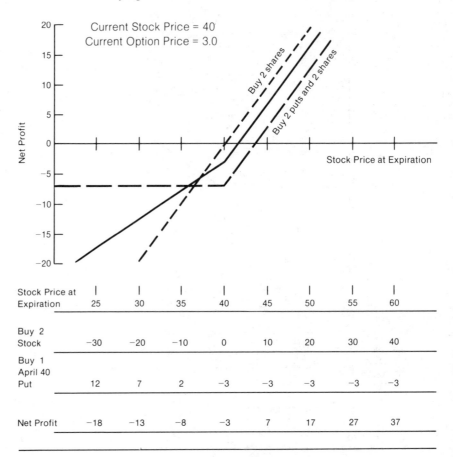

Stock Price at Expiration	25	30	35	40	45	50	55	60
Buy 2 Stock	−30	−20	−10	0	10	20	30	40
Buy 1 April 40 Put	12	7	2	−3	−3	−3	−3	−3
Net Profit	−18	−13	−8	−3	7	17	27	37

SPREADS

Simple spread positions are termed bullish (bearish) if the spread benefits from stock price increases (decreases). Spread positions can be categorized into three types: vertical, horizontal, and diagonal.

Vertical Spreads

A *vertical spread* involves the simultaneous purchase and sale of options, identical in all aspects except for the strike price. These spreads are often called *price spreads.*

Vertical bullish call spreads involve the sale of the option with the higher exercise price and the purchase of the option with the lower exercise price. The solid line in Exhibit 3.13 illustrates the profit diagram of a bullish call spread that is obtained by purchasing the April 35 call and simultaneously selling the April 45 call option.

Bull call spreads tend to be profitable if the underlying stock moves up in price. The spread has limited profit potential and limited risk. In general, since the in-the-money contract is purchased and an out-of-money contract sold, the initial investment for the position is positive. For example, the initial investment for the bullish call spread in Exhibit 3.13 is $5. The position always has a maximum profit if, at expiration, the stock price equals or exceeds the out-of-money strike price.

The maximum profit potential is obtained by computing the difference between the strike prices and subtracting the cost of the position (see Exercise 11). In the example, the difference in strike prices is $10, the cost of the position is $5, and the maximum profit is $5. To compute the breakeven point

EXHIBIT 3.13
Profit Table for a Bullish Call Spread

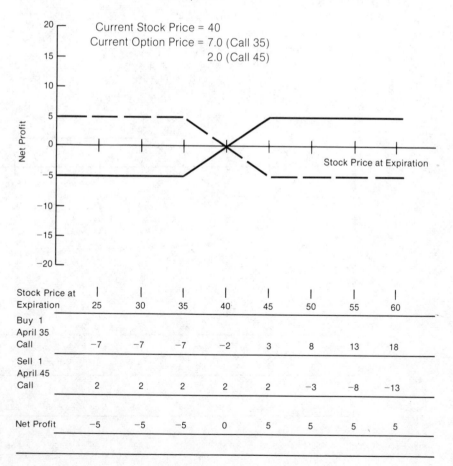

Stock Price at Expiration	25	30	35	40	45	50	55	60
Buy 1 April 35 Call	−7	−7	−7	−2	3	8	13	18
Sell 1 April 45 Call	2	2	2	2	2	−3	−8	−13
Net Profit	−5	−5	−5	0	5	5	5	5

for this spread, the investor simply adds the net cost of the spread to the lower strike price (see Exercise 12). In Exhibit 3.13, the breakeven point is $40.

The strike prices selected for a bullish call spread depend on the investor's beliefs concerning the stock price. A very bullish investor will select a very deep out-of-the-money option, while a more conservative (less bullish) strategy is to select adjacent contracts. Of course, an extremely bullish investor may not be interested in selling any deep out-of-the-money contract. That is, such an investor may prefer to hold a naked call.

A bearish call spread involves the purchase of the higher strike option and the simultaneous sale of the lower strike. For example, a bearish call spread could be established by buying the 45s and selling the 35s. Its payouts are indicated in Exhibit 3.13 by the dashed line.

Bullish vertical put spreads are constructed by selling puts with high strikes and buying puts with low strikes. Exhibit 3.14 illustrates the profit diagram of a bullish put spread that is obtained by purchasing the April 35 puts and selling the April 45 puts.

EXHIBIT 3.14
Profit Table for a Bullish Put Spread

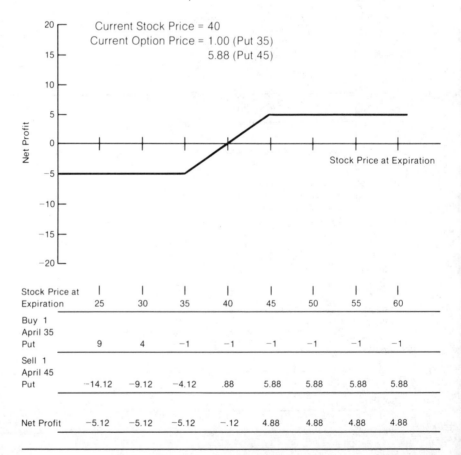

Stock Price at Expiration	25	30	35	40	45	50	55	60
Buy 1 April 35 Put	9	4	−1	−1	−1	−1	−1	−1
Sell 1 April 45 Put	−14.12	−9.12	−4.12	.88	5.88	5.88	5.88	5.88
Net Profit	−5.12	−5.12	−5.12	−.12	4.88	4.88	4.88	4.88

Current Stock Price = 40
Current Option Price = 1.00 (Put 35)
                       5.88 (Put 45)

Horizontal Spreads

A *horizontal* (or *time* or *calendar*) *spread* involves the simultaneous purchase and sale of options identical in all aspects except time to expiration. The principle behind a calendar spread is that, over time, the time premium of the near-term option will decay faster than the time premium of the long-term contract. While the initial price difference between two options with the same strike but different expiration dates may be modest, at expiration the price disparity should have grown, assuming little change in the price of the under-lying stock.

For example, consider the time spread set up by buying the July 40 call options for $12.12 and selling the April 40 for $10.88. The net cost of the position is $1.34. If the stock price remains unchanged, at the April expiration date the April call will be worth its intrinsic value of $10, while the July call will be worth more. If the July 40 call is worth more than $11.34, the net profit will be positive if it is sold. In order to obtain a profit function at the April expiration date, however, one would have to be able to value the July 30 contract in April. In later chapters we shall investigate how to plot the profit functions of options positions when some (or all) of the options still carry a time premium.

Diagonal Spreads

Exhibit 3.15 presents all the prices of all the call options available on the security. Vertical spreads get their name from the fact that options selected come from the same column. Horizontal spreads are so named because the options selected come from the same row. A *diagonal spread* involves the simultaneous purchase and sale of options that differ in both strike and time to maturity. For example, consider the purchase of a July 35 call option and the sale of an April 45 call contract. This position would constitute a diagonal spread.

EXHIBIT 3.15
Call Option Prices—Stock price = 40

Strike	April	July	October
25	15.06	—	—
30	10.88	12.12	—
35	7.00	8.62	—
40	4.00	5.75	7.38
45	2.0	3.69	5.39
50	0.88	2.38	3.75

Butterfly Strike Price Spreads

A *butterfly strike spread* is established when two middle strike options are purchased (written) and two options—one on either side—are sold (bought).

For example, consider a position consisting of buying two April 40 call options and selling the April 35 and April 45 contract. Exhibit 3.16 illustrates the profit diagram.

EXHIBIT 3.16
Profit Table for a Butterfly Strike Price Spread

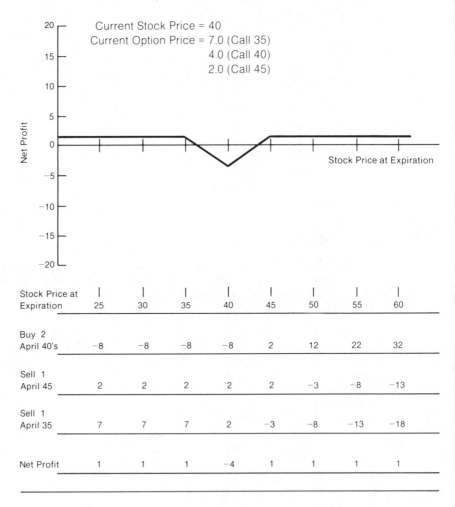

Stock Price at Expiration	25	30	35	40	45	50	55	60
Buy 2 April 40's	−8	−8	−8	−8	2	12	22	32
Sell 1 April 45	2	2	2	2	2	−3	−8	−13
Sell 1 April 35	7	7	7	2	−3	−8	−13	−18
Net Profit	1	1	1	−4	1	1	1	1

Note that the payouts take the shape of a butterfly, hence the name. The sale of the butterfly involves the sale of two April 40 together with the purchase of one April 45 and April 35 call option. The profit function is illustrated in Exhibit 3.17.

Like the 2:1 ratio write call strategy illustrated in Exhibit 3.9, the sale of the butterfly spread produces maximum profits if the stock price remains unchanged. Note, however, that the maximum profit of the butterfly is $4,

EXHIBIT 3.17
Profit Diagram for the Sale of a Butterfly Spread

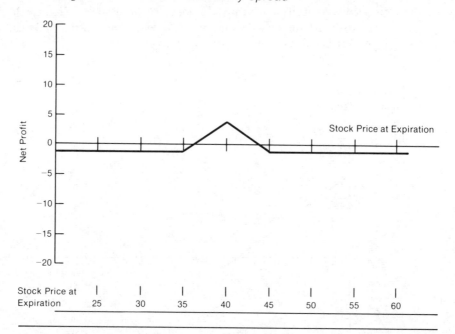

compared to $8 in the 2:1 ratio write strategy. Moreover, the profit interval of the butterfly sale extends from $36 to $44, compared to $32 to $48 for the ratio write. To compensate for the reduced upside potential, however, the sale of the butterfly creates a limit of only $1 on the downside. This is in contrast to the ratio write strategy, in which losses are unlimited.

Butterfly Time Spreads

Butterfly time spreads can be established by purchasing (selling) two options in the middle series and selling (buying) a near and far series option. All options have the same strike.

COMBINATIONS

Combinations consist of the simultaneous purchase (or sale) of put and call options.

Straddles

A *straddle* consists of the simultaneous purchase of a call option and a put option, with the same strike price and time to expiration. Exhibit 3.18 illustrates the profit diagram obtained from buying the April 40 call and the April 40 put. The breakeven points are 33 and 47.

Straddles are popular strategies to implement on securities that are highly volatile or are takeover candidates. Selling straddles involves more risk, since volatility can create large losses on both sides. To reduce the risk of large losses, a straddle seller may buy a put with a lower strike and a call with a higher strike. The resulting position looks similar to a butterfly spread.

EXHIBIT 3.18
Profit Table for a Straddle

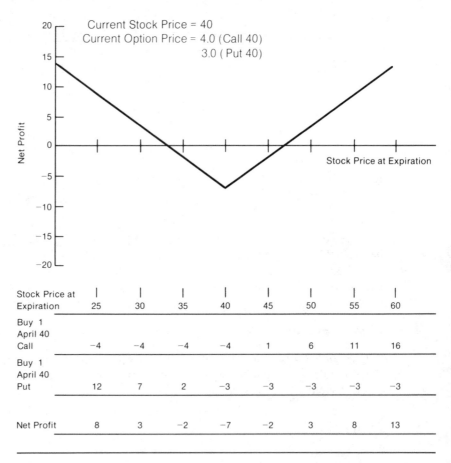

Stock Price at Expiration	25	30	35	40	45	50	55	60
Buy 1 April 40 Call	−4	−4	−4	−4	1	6	11	16
Buy 1 April 40 Put	12	7	2	−3	−3	−3	−3	−3
Net Profit	8	3	−2	−7	−2	3	8	13

Strips and Straps

A purchased *strip* consists of a long position in a call and put, together with an extra put. A *strap* consists of buying two calls and buying one put. Exhibit 3.19 illustrates the payouts of a strap consisting of buying two April 40 calls and one April 40 put.

EXHIBIT 3.19

Profit Table for a Strap

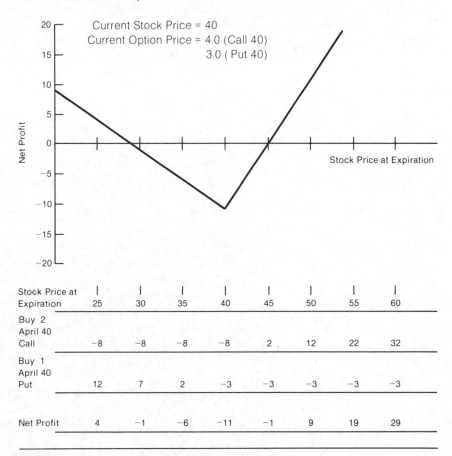

Current Stock Price = 40
Current Option Price = 4.0 (Call 40)
                       3.0 (Put 40)

Stock Price at Expiration	25	30	35	40	45	50	55	60
Buy 2 April 40 Call	−8	−8	−8	−8	2	12	22	32
Buy 1 April 40 Put	12	7	2	−3	−3	−3	−3	−3
Net Profit	4	−1	−6	−11	−1	9	19	29

Strangles

Consider the strategy of buying a call option with a strike price above the current stock price and a put option with a strike price below the current stock price: for example, buying the April 45 call options and the April 35 put options. Exhibit 3.20 illustrates the payouts. This position is referred to as a *strangle*. A strangle is similar to a straddle in that profits can be obtained only if the stock price moves significantly up or down. Note that the strangle profits if the stock price moves above $48 or falls below $32. In general, the stock price will have to move further than in a straddle for profits to be obtained. The strangle, however, has the advantage of having smaller maximum losses if the stock price does not move (compare Exhibit 3.20 with 3.18).

EXHIBIT 3.20
Profit Table for a Strangle

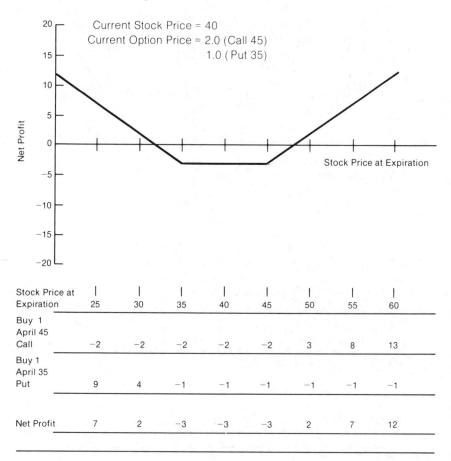

Stock Price at Expiration	25	30	35	40	45	50	55	60
Buy 1 April 45 Call	−2	−2	−2	−2	−2	3	8	13
Buy 1 April 35 Put	9	4	−1	−1	−1	−1	−1	−1
Net Profit	7	2	−3	−3	−3	2	7	12

OTHER COMBINATIONS

The number of ways options may be meshed around a particular stock is endless. To illustrate, consider call spread strategies in which the ratio of calls bought to calls sold is restricted to ratios of 1:1, 1:2, 1:3, 2:3, 3:4, and 4:5. With just these six ratios, and assuming six strike prices and all three series are available, the number of different call spread combinations is $2 \times 6 \times \binom{6}{2} \times \binom{3}{2} =$ 1080. If put options were also available, then 1080 put spreads could be constructed. The number of combinations would then be even larger (2276). This implies that there are over 4000 different spread positions that can be established using only one or two strike prices. If three strike prices (e.g., butterfly spreads) are considered, then the number of positions mushrooms further.

THE MOST POPULAR STOCK OPTION STRATEGIES

Buy Call Options/Buy T-Bills

Rather than purchasing the stock, a less risky strategy may be to place a small fraction of funds in call options and the remainder in T-bills. If the stock does appreciate, the investor will benefit by selling the option. If the stock does not appreciate, the premium on the call is lost but the holdings in T-bills cushion this loss.

Cash Secured Put Writing

Consider an investor who believes the current stock price is quite favorable. Rather than buying the stock, the investor sells an at- or out-of-the-money put option and deposits the exercise price in escrow. If the stock appreciates in value, the put is not exercised and the investor profits by the full premium. If the stock falls in value and the put is exercised, the investor accepts receipt of the stock at a price that was originally perceived to be favorable. Since there is significant risk associated with cash-secured put writing strategies, they should be attempted only when possession of the stock for the strike price is considered desirable.

Protective Put Purchasing

For every 100 shares held long, the investor purchases a put option. The put effectively provides insurance against price declines below the strike price. The selection of the most appropriate put contract depends on the price protection that is sought and the premium of the option. High strike prices imply that a great degree of price protection is required and may be appropriate for highly risk-averse investors.

Covered Call Writing

At- or out-of-the-money call options are written against stock owned. The objective is to earn additional income from securities that are not expected to significantly increase in value. However, if the stock does increase in value beyond the strike, losses from the sale of the call will be offset by the increased value of the underlying stock.

The Synthetic Short Sale

Rather than selling a stock short, an investor may consider buying a put and selling a call. The resultant position is referred to as a *synthetic short sale* because the profit function looks similar to the profit function associated with a short sale. The advantage of synthetic short sales over selling the stock short involves margin requirements and dividend payments. Specifically, margin requirements for the synthetic short sale are smaller, and the investor is not responsible for dividend payments to the stock lender.

CONCLUSION

The profit diagrams provide an extremely useful tool for comparing the risks and rewards among hedging alternatives. Although margin requirements, commissions, and dividends have not been included in the analysis, such adjustments are possible. It should be recognized, however, that the profit diagrams do not tell a complete story. First, they assume positions are maintained unchanged over time. Second, the profit diagram ignores the likelihood of early exercise. As an example, consider the sale of a straddle. If the underlying stock increases above the call strike and then decreases below the put strike, large losses can result. When the stock price increases, the in-the-money call may be exercised, in which case the straddle writer must deliver expensive stock for the strike. Then if the stock price decreases below the strike price of the put, the "cheap" stock may be put on the straddle writer for the higher strike price.

The purpose of this chapter has not been to provide a comprehensive treatment of the topic of selecting, monitoring, and revising hedge positions. Rather, we have attempted to provide an overview of the various strategies and to illustrate the immense patterns of distinct payouts that the meshing of options provides. The availability of stock options enables investors to design positions that reflect their preferences and outlooks for the underlying security.

References

The Options Clearing Corporation and the option exchanges publish many booklets that discuss the risks and rewards of specific option strategies and provide numerous examples. One limitation of our discussion in this chapter is that the analysis is static. In reality, option positions can be adjusted periodically as new information filters into the market. McMillan's textbook provides some insight into some dynamic strategies. (See References in Chapter 2 for this and other textbooks covering option strategies.) Indeed, his entire textbook is devoted to strategy.

Several stock and option market computer simulation/education games allow the investor to build and analyze stock option strategies and to adjust them periodically as price changes occur, as time to expiration nears, or as dividend dates approach. These games are especially useful for those investors who are genuinely interested in learning the real world constraints without having to invest real dollars. The computer games referenced below run on home computers.

Blue Chip Software. *Millionaire.* Chicago: Britannica Learning Corporation.

Commodities Exchange. *Comex.* New York: The Options Department of the Commodities Exchange.

Ritchken P., H. Salkin, and G. Getts. *Contemporary Portfolio Management.* Reading, Mass.: Addison-Wesley, 1987.

Torosian M. *The Margin Book.* Chicago: M.T.A. Financial Services, 1985.

Exercises

1. XYZ trades at $50. The call option prices are as follows:

	July	October	January
$45	7	9	11
$50	4	6	8
$55	1	3	5

 a. Mr. Vestor owns 100 shares of XYZ but wants to improve the yield on the stock by earning option premium income. Mr. Vestor, however, is anxious not to have XYZ called away from him. Of all options available, which is the most desirable to write?

 b. How far can the stock advance before the strategy loses money relative to not selling options?

 c. If Mr. Vestor sold the XYZ/October/50 option, over what price range (at the expiration date) will this strategy yield greater profits than merely holding onto the stock?

2. Ms. Vestor bought 100 shares of XYZ at $40 a share. It currently trades at $60. A July/60/call option trades at $6. Discuss the advantages of selling this option.

3. Mr. Vestor owns 200 shares of XYZ, purchased at $20 per share. Compare the strategy of writing one call at $15 and one call at $25 with that of writing two calls at $20. The current option prices are as follows:

Strike	Call Premium
15	8
20	5
25	3

4. XYZ stock is currently $53 a share. Ms. Vestor is unwilling to pay this price. Given that a put option with strike price of $50 trades at $2 a share, construct a strategy whereby the stock could effectively be purchased for less than $50. What is the disadvantage of this strategy?

5. Mr. Vestor owns 100 shares of XYZ, which were purchased when the stock was $52. The stock currently trades at $60. A 60 put option trades for $4, while a 65 put option trades for $7.

 a. Under what conditions (if any) should Mr. Vestor buy each option?

 b. Construct the payoff function if Mr. Vestor bought the 60 put option and sold the 65 put contract.

6. XYZ trades at $47 and the following options are available:

	Expiration Month		
Option	April	July	October
40	7 3/4	7 1/4	9
40p	1 1/2	1 3/4	2
45	2	3	4
45p	1 3/4	2 1/2	3
50	1 1/2	1 3/4	2
50p	7 3/4	8 1/4	9

    a. How many different straddle positions are available?

    b. Construct the payoff function for the XYZ $45 price April straddle.

    c. Under what conditions would you buy the straddle? When would you sell the straddle?

    d. Consider the $45 strike price July straddle. Plot the profit function at expiration. Compare the July straddle to the April straddle and state the conditions under which one straddle is preferable to the other.

7. Assume the $45 April straddle is bought. After two weeks, with the stock at $49, the call price has increased by $2. The investor believes the stock price will not increase further and so decides to sell the call. This strategy is referred to as "lifting a leg." Discuss the advantages and disadvantages of "lifting a leg." Under what conditions should the straddle be reestablished? If the stock increased to $51, for example, should the investor consider reestablishing the straddle?

8. With the price of XYZ at $40, Ms. Vestor buys an XYZ 40 straddle at a total cost of $6. With the stock price at $40, Ms. Vestor buys 100 shares. Plot the profit function at expiration and discuss the merits, if any, of such a strategy.

9. XYZ trades at $80. Under what conditions would it be desirable to sell the stock short? What alternative option strategy would yield a profit function similar to the "sell stock short" strategy?

10. XYZ trades at $65. A January 60 put sells for $2 and a January 70 call for $3. Ms. Vestor buys the 60 put and sells the 70 call. Plot the profit function and discuss the pros and cons of the strategy.

11. Show that the maximum profit potential for a bullish call spread is equal to the difference between the strike prices less the cost of the position.

12. Show that the breakeven point for a bullish call spread is obtained by adding the net cost of the spread to the lower strike price.

13. Obtain similar expressions to those listed above for vertical bear call spreads.

14. Obtain expressions for maximum profit and breakeven points for vertical bull (and bear) put spreads.

15. Obtain expressions for breakeven points for straddles and strangles.

16. Using the data in Exhibit 3.1, construct a synthetic short sale using the 40 call and 40 put. Provide a profit table and diagram.

17. a. With XYZ trading at $55, compute the margin requirement for a short position in the April 50 option, given that the call is worth $7.50.

    b. Compute the margin requirements for short positions in the April 50 XYZ option, assuming the stock price is $50, $45, and, finally, $40. The call prices in these three instances are $4, $1, and $.50, respectively.

18. If XYZ is at $55, compute the margin requirement for writing a put option with strike $50, given that its price is $1. What are the margin requirements if the stock price is $45 and the put premium is $7?

Appendix A
Commission Charges for Options

Since 1975, commissions for options have been negotiable. Exhibit 3A.1 below presents commission rates that may be somewhat representative of full service brokerage houses. The rates, of course, will vary among firms. Significant discounts can be obtained through discount brokers.

EXHIBIT 3A.1
Commission Charges

	Number of Contracts			
Option Price	**1**	**5**	**10**	**50**
1/8	$10	$10	$25	$125
1/2	$10	$25	$40	$200
1	$25	$45	$80	$300
2	$25	$50	$98	$325
5	$25	$80	$120	$450
10	$25	$100	$180	$700

The typical round-trip commission for one option contract that has value at expiration is $50. This can be a significant percentage of the price of the option and generally will be about 8 percent or more.

Although the commission charges are a high percentage of the option price, when a comparison is made with the commission charges incurred by buying and selling the stock itself, in absolute terms the option commissions are much less.

Appendix B
Margin Requirements for Stocks and Options

If stocks are sold short or if options are written naked, the broker will demand some form of collateral to guarantee performance in the event of unfavorable market movements. Such transactions are conducted in margin accounts. From a margin account, an investor can also buy securities that are financed by a loan from the broker. This appendix investigates margin accounts and the rules imposed on such accounts by the Federal Reserve Board, the New York Stock Exchange, and the option exchanges.

MARGIN ACCOUNTS

There are basically two types of brokerage accounts, cash and margin. In a cash account the investor pays for the security in full, while in a margin account the investor need only deposit a fraction of the transaction, the remainder being borrowed from the brokerage firm. The purchased security is kept by the firm as collateral against the loan. Interest charges on the loan continue until the investor sells the security.

INITIAL MARGIN REQUIREMENTS

The minimum allowable initial deposit that an investor must make to purchase a security in a margin account is established by the Board of Governors of the Federal Reserve Board and is binding on all brokers. Most brokerage firms set their initial margin requirements above the minimum requirements. At the present time, investors must deposit at least half the cost of the transaction. This fraction, referred to as the *margin percentage,* has remained the same since 1974. If the margin percentage were 100 percent, all purchases would have to be paid for in full. The lower the fraction, the greater the possible leverage investors can attain. Prior to the stock market crash of 1929, the percentage was about 10 percent. Many brokers in those years encouraged their customers to establish highly leveraged positions since commission charges were based on the size of the full transactions. The low margin percentage was one reason for the collapse of the stock market.

Margin accounts are used not only for purchasing securities. All short sales are conducted from such accounts. When an investor sells a security short, the stockbroker borrows the security from a third party so delivery can be made. To protect the brokerage firm, a margin deposit from the investor selling the security short is required. In addition, the broker retains the proceeds of the short sales in a noninterest-bearing account. At the present time the initial margin requirement for short sales is 50 percent of the transaction price.

Rather than deposit cash into the margin account, the investor can deposit marginable securities with a loan value equal to the required cash deposit. Regulation T of the Federal Reserve System specifies which securities can be used as marginable securities. Virtually all stocks traded on the major exchanges and many over-the-counter stocks qualify, as well as a large number of corporate and government bonds. The loan value of marginable securities is computed by multiplying the market value of the securities by the loan value percentage, 100 percent less the margin percentage. Currently the loan percentage for stocks is 50 percent.

In addition to the initial margin equity requirements specified by the Federal Reserve, the New York Stock Exchange requires a minimum initial equity in the margin account. Specifically, at the initiation of any new transaction, the investor must have equity of at least $2000 or its equivalent in marginable securities in the margin account.

Example 3B.1

An investor buys 100 shares of XYZ on margin. The current price of XYZ is $80. The initial margin requirement calls for a deposit of $4000 in the margin account or a deposit of marginable securities worth $8000.

If the investor sold 100 shares of XYZ short, a deposit of $4000 or a deposit of marginable securities worth $8000 into the account would be required. In addition, the $8000 generated by the sale would be held by the firm in a noninterest-bearing account.

RESTRICTED MARGIN ACCOUNTS

A margin account becomes restricted when the equity in the account falls below the Regulation T margin requirement. Such a situation occurs if the market moves against the investor's position or if interest charges, service fees, or dividend charges on short sales push the margin debit above its limit.

Example 3B.2

Consider the previous case, where an investor purchased 100 shares of XYZ on margin. The original margin debit is $4000. Suppose the stock price declines over time to $70. Assume the margin debit has increased to $4200, where the $200 represents the interest charge on the loan. The margin equity is currently $7000 – $4200 = $2800. Since the margin equity is below the original margin requirement of $4000, the account is restricted.

MAINTENANCE MARGIN REQUIREMENTS FOR PURCHASING SECURITIES LONG

When a margin account becomes restricted, the investor does not necessarily have to supply more funds or marginable securities to bring the account up to the initial margin requirements. However, if the market movements continue to be unfavorable, eventually the broker will require more collateral. The New York Stock Exchange requires that the equity in the margin account be at least 25 percent of the market value of the securities held in the account or $2000, whichever is greater. If the condition is violated, a margin maintenance call is issued requesting that additional cash or marginable securities be placed in the account.

Example 3B.3

An investor buys 100 shares of XYZ at $80 by depositing $4000 to comply with the Regulation T requirement and borrowing $4000 from the broker. The stock price immediately drops to $60. Twenty-five percent of $6000 is $1500. The margin equity is $6000 – $4000 = $2000. Since the account satisfies the NYSE requirement, no additional margin is required. If the stock drops to $52, however, 25 percent of the market value is $1300. The margin equity is $5200 – $4000 = $1200. In this case the broker will issue a margin maintenance call for $100.

An investor can meet a margin call by depositing cash equal to the maintenance call, or by depositing marginable securities with a market value equal to 4/3 of the call. In the previous example, rather than deposit $100, the investor could deposit marginable securities with a market value of $400/3 = $133.33. Note that in this case the new market value of the account is $5200 + $400/3 = $5333. Twenty-five percent of this value is $1333. The margin equity, on the other hand, is $5200 + $400/3 – $4000 = $1333. Hence, the margin maintenance condition is met.

An investor can establish the stock price at which a margin maintenance call will be issued by multiplying the initial margin debit by 4/3. In the previous example, no maintenance margin call is issued unless the stock price declines to $40 × 4/3 = $53.33.

If the investor does not respond to a maintenance call, the broker will sell sufficient securities in the account to meet the call.

MAINTENANCE MARGIN REQUIREMENTS FOR SELLING SECURITIES SHORT

The margin maintenance requirement for a short sale depends on the stock price and is summarized as follows:

Stock Price	Margin Maintenance
Below $2.50	$2.50 per share
$2.50–$5.00	100% of market value
$5.00–$16.75	$5 per share
Above $16.75	30% of market value

Example 3B.4

An investor sells 100 shares of XYZ short at $60 per share. The initial margin deposit of $3,000 together with the $6,000 received from the sale establishes the credit balance. The current equity in the account is $3,000, and margin maintenance is 30 percent of $6,000, which is $1,800. The market price increases to $75, so the market value of the security is now $7500. The credit balance remains at $9,000, but the margin equity drops to $9,000-$7,500 = $2,500. The margin maintenance is 30 percent of $7,500, which is $2,250. Hence, no margin maintenance call is issued. However, if the price increases to $80, the margin equity would be $1,000 and margin maintenance would be at 30 percent of $8,000, i.e., $2,400. In this case the account would be undermargined by $1,400.

As a second example, consider the short sale of 1,000 shares of a stock priced at $10. The initial margin deposit of $5,000 together with the $10,000 from the sale establishes the credit balance. The current equity is $5,000 and margin maintenance is $5 per share (i.e., $5,000). Thus, the margin maintenance requirement is just met. If the stock price increases by $1, the current equity is reduced by $1,000 to $4,000, while the margin maintenance remains at $5 per share. Hence, a margin maintenance call for $1,000 would be issued.

MARGIN REQUIREMENTS FOR OPTIONS

No option contracts can be purchased on margin. Therefore, the term *margin* in options transaction refers to the collateral brokers receive from option writers to ensure that they will fulfill their obligations in the event of exercise.

Investors who sell options typically deposit cash or securities in excess of the margin requirements so their investment strategies are not disturbed by frequent margin calls. In this section we shall summarize the margin requirements for several stock option positions.

MARGIN REQUIREMENTS FOR COVERED CALL WRITING AND CASH-SECURED PUT WRITING STRATEGIES

When an investor sells call options against an appropriate number of shares held long, no margin is required. Indeed, the covered option can be written from either the cash or margin account. Similarly, if an investor deposits cash equal to the aggregate strike price of the put option or equivalent collateral, the written put requires no additional margin.

MARGIN REQUIREMENTS FOR SELLING NAKED OPTIONS

The naked sale of options must be conducted in a margin account that has a minimum of $2000 equity at the time of the transaction. The investor must deposit and maintain a margin equal to 15 percent of the market value of the underlying security plus the option premium less the amount by which the option is out the money. The proceeds from the sale can be applied toward the margin. The minimum margin for each uncovered stock option, however, must exceed 100 percent of the premium plus 5 percent of the market value of the underlying security.

Example 3B.5

An investor sells one June 40 call option at $5. The market price of XYZ is $36. The margin requirement is determined as follows:

15% of $3600	$540
+ option premium	500
− amount out of the money	400
= margin required	$640
5% of market value	$180
+ call premium	500
= minimum margin	$680

Hence, $680 of margin is required. In order for the investor to sell the option, the margin account must have a minimum of $2000 equity.

MARGIN REQUIREMENTS FOR WRITING STRADDLES AND STRANGLES

If an investor owns the underlying security and deposits the aggregate exercise price of the put, there are no margin requirements. If the investor owns just the underlying security, the written call is covered but the put is not. The margin necessary in this instance would be the margin of a naked put. If both the call and put in the straddle have no coverage, the margin for a naked call and for a naked put is established and the maximum of the two margin requirements is taken as the margin requirement for the straddle. If the put and call sold have different strike prices, the margin requirement must be increased by adding the in-the-money amount of the option on the side of the transaction that was ignored.

Example 3B.6

An investor sells a June 40 call option with a premium of $4 and a June 30 put with a premium of $3. The price of the underlying stock is $35. The margins are calculated below:

Margin for a Naked Call		Margin for a Naked Put	
15% of $3500	$425	15% of $3500	$425
+ call premium	400	+ put premium	300
– amount out of the money	500	– amount out of the money	500
	$325		$225
5% of $3500	$175	5% of $3500	$175
+ call premium	400	+ put premium	350
	$575		$525

Hence, the margin requirement for the straddle if $575.

MARGIN REQUIREMENTS FOR SPREADS

For margin requirements, spreads can be classified as *qualified* or *unqualified*. In a qualified spread, the written option expires at the same time as, or before, the purchased option, whereas in an unqualified spread, the long option expires before the written option.

If a spread is unqualified, the investor pays for the long option and deposits the margin needed to cover the written side. If the spread is qualified, the investor may offset the cost of the long side by the premium received from the written option.

The margin requirements for qualified call (put) spreads are the lesser of the following two amounts:

1. The margin requirement for an uncovered call (put),
2. The difference between the aggregate exercise prices of the purchased call (written put) and the written call (purchased put).

Example 3B.7

An investor sells one three-month January 40 call at $3 and buys one six-month April 40 call on the same stock for $4. The stock is currently at $40. The margin calculation is as follows:

15% of $4500	$600
+ call premium	300
+ amount out of the money	0
= margin requirement	$900
5% of $4500	$200
+ call premium	300
= minimum margin	$500
= margin requirement	$900

The excess of aggregate exercise price of the long call over aggregate exercise price of short call is $4000 – $4000, or zero. Hence, the margin requirement is Min(0,900) = 0. There is no margin requirement for this spread.

MARGIN REQUIREMENTS FOR BUTTERFLY SPREADS

An investor must deposit a margin sufficient to cover any risks associated with the position.

Margin requirements for other hedge combinations can be computed by breaking the position into covered and spread positions together with naked positions. Actual margin requirements imposed by brokers may vary among firms. Also, margin requirements on other option contracts yet to be discussed will typically depend on the nature of the underlying instrument. Specific details of margin calculations and requirements can be obtained from brokerage firms. *The Margin Book,* by Torosian, provides an excellent discussion of the details of margin accounts.

Example 3B.8

An investor establishes the following spread:

Buy 1 XYZ	June 30 call	for $3
Sell 2 XYZ	June 25 calls	for $2 each
Buy 1 XYZ	June 20 call	for $5

In the event that both calls are exercised, the investor is committed to deliver 200 shares of stock for a total price of $5000. To offset this cost, the investor could exercise both calls. This would result in the receipt of 200 shares for $5000. Hence, there is no risk of default in this position. Since the net cost of the position is $300 + $500 – $400 = $400, the investor need deposit only $400.

4

Arbitrage Relationships for Call and Put Options

A risk-free arbitrage opportunity arises when an investment is identified that requires no initial outlays yet guarantees nonnegative payoffs in the future. Such an opportunity would not last long, as astute investors would soon alter the demand and supply factors, causing prices to adjust so that these opportunities would be closed off. In this chapter we shall use simple arbitrage arguments to obtain some basic boundary conditions for call and put options. The beauty of the pricing relationships obtained here derives from the fact that they require no assumptions on the statistical process driving security prices. Also, no severe assumptions are made concerning the risk behavior of investors. The simple requirement is that investors like more money than less.

This chapter also investigates conditions under which it is more appropriate to exercise options than to sell them. The final section explores some fundamental pricing relationships that exist between put and call options.

We shall adopt the following notation:

Current time = 0,
Time to expiration = T,
Time to first (second) ex-dividend date = $t_1(t_2)$,
Size of dividend declared at ex-dividend date $t_i = d_i$. $i = 1, 2$.

We are interested only in ex-dividend dates prior to expiration. In most cases, the number of dates in the interval is less than three.

EUROPEAN AND AMERICAN OPTIONS

A call option that can be exercised only at the expiration date (and not before) is called a *European option*. An *American* option must have a value at least as great as a European option, since the former has all the properties of the latter plus the additional early exercise feature. This property is used in several proofs in this chapter. The terms "American" and "European" have nothing to do with geographic location. In fact, most options trading in Europe are of the American variety.

DISCOUNT BONDS

Let $B(t_1,t_2)$ be the present value at time t_1 of \$1, to be received with certainty at time t_2. Equivalently, $B(t_1,t_2)$ can be thought of as the value at time t_1 of a riskless pure discount bond of face value \$1 that matures at time t_2. Then

$$B(t_1,t_2) = 1\exp[-r(t_2 - t_1)] \qquad (4.1)$$

where r is the continuously compounded riskless rate of return.

If K dollars are invested in the risk-free asset (bank) at time t_1, this amount of money will grow continuously at rate r, and at time t_2 the value will be $K/B(t_1,t_2)$.

Note from equation (4.1):

$$B(0,t) = \exp(-rt). \qquad (4.2)$$

Exhibit 4.1 shows how the discount rate, $B(0,t)$ behaves as t increases.

EXHIBIT 4.1
Present Value of \$1 Received at Time T

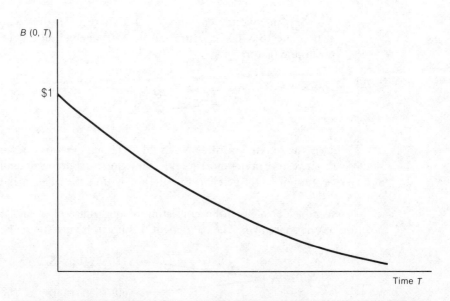

The present value of $1 to be received at a very distant date is not too valuable today. That is,

$$B(0,t_2) < B(0,t_1) < 1 \qquad \text{for } t_2 > t_1. \tag{4.3}$$

The purchase of K pure discount bonds at time t_1 that mature at time T guarantees a profit of $K[1 - B(t_1,T)]$ over the period.

One final relationship that follows directly from equations (4.1) and (4.2) is the following:

$$B(0,T) = B(0,t_1)B(t_1,T). \tag{4.4}$$

Throughout this chapter, we assume the risk-free rate r is a known constant.

AN ILLUSTRATION OF RISKLESS ARBITRAGE OPPORTUNITIES

Consider the following alternative investments:

1. For $70, an investor can buy (sell) a share of A that, at the end of the period will either appreciate to $120 or depreciate to $60, depending on whether the economy booms or not.

$$\$70 \begin{array}{c} \nearrow \$120 \\ \searrow \$60 \end{array}$$

2. For b, an investor can buy (sell) a share of B that will either appreciate to $100 or depreciate to $50, depending on the same economic factors.

What is the maximum price b can take? To answer this question, we shall assume investors prefer more wealth to less and can borrow or lend funds at a riskless rate of $r = 11$ percent. Finally, we assume the time period $T = 1$ year.

First, consider a portfolio consisting of one share of A and a short position of one share in B. The payouts of this portfolio are shown below:

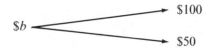

Clearly, all investors would prefer the final dollar payout of this portfolio to a certain payout of $10. To avoid a possible "free lunch," the present value of this portfolio must exceed the present value of $10. That is, $(70 - b) >$ $10\exp(-rT) = 9$, or $b < 61$.

If, for example, $b = \$64$, then a "free lunch" would exist. Specifically, an investor could establish a zero initial investment position by selling one share of B for $64, borrowing $6, and using the total proceeds to purchase one share of A. The $6 debt will grow to $6\exp(rT) = \$6.70$ in one year. The final payouts of this strategy are shown below:

$$\$0 \quad\begin{cases} \$120 - \$100 - \$6.70 = \$13.3 \\ \$60 - \$50 - \$6.70 = \$3.3 \end{cases}$$

To avoid this free lunch, the price of a share of B must satisfy $b < \$61$.

We shall use such arbitrage arguments frequently in this and later chapters.

The Law of One Price

Assume a third investment, C, provided the following payouts:

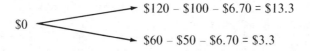

$$\$C \quad\begin{cases} \$120 \\ \$60 \end{cases}$$

To avoid riskless arbitrage, C must equal $70. To see this, note that this investment has identical payouts to A. If C exceeded $70, investors would buy A and sell C to lock into profits. Conversely, if C was lower than 70, investors would buy C and sell A to lock into profits.

The law of one price states that if two securities produce identical payouts regardless of the future, then to avoid riskless arbitrage, their current prices must be the same.

BOUNDING CALL OPTION PRICES

Bounding Call Values (With No Dividends)

Property 4.1

If there are no dividends prior to expiration, then to prevent arbitrage opportunities, the call price should never fall below
$$\text{Max}[0, S_0 - XB(0,T)] \tag{4.5}$$

Proof: Consider two portfolios, *A* and *B*. *A* contains one European call option and *X* pure discount bonds with a face value of $1 each and a maturity of *T*. *B* contains a long position in the stock.

Exhibit 4.2 illustrates the prices of the two portfolios at the expiration date of the option. Note that the future value of portfolio *A* is never lower than the future value of portfolio *B*.

EXHIBIT 4.2
Arbitrage Portfolio—Bounding Call Prices

Portfolio	Current Value	Value at Time T	
		$S_T < X$	$S_T \geq X$
A	$C_0 + XB(0,T)$	$0 + X$	$(S_T - X) + X$
B	S_0	S_T	S_T
		$V_a(T) > V_b(T)$	$V_a(T) = V_b(T)$

If an investor bought portfolio *A* and sold portfolio *B*, then at the expiration date the combined portfolio, *P*, would have value $V_p(T)$, given by $V_p(T) = V_a(T) - V_b(T)$ where $V_a(T)$ and $V_b(T)$ define the values of the portfolios *A* and *B* at time *T*.

If the call option expired in the money, then $V_a(T) = V_b(T)$ and, hence, $V_p(T) = 0$. However, if the call expired worthless, then, $V_p(T) = V_a(T) - V_b(T) \geq 0$.

The portfolio *P*, thus, can never lose money and has a chance of making money.

Let us now consider the initial cost of the portfolio, that is, $V_p(0)$. Since this portfolio has a nonnegative terminal value, it must be worth a nonnegative amount now.

Thus, $V_p(0) = V_a(0) - V_b(0) \geq 0$.
Equivalently, $V_a(0) \geq V_b(0)$.
That is, $C_0 + XB(0,T) \geq S_0$
and $C_0 \geq S_0 - XB(0,T)$.

Since a European call option must have value no less than $S_0 - XB(0,T)$, so must an American option. Of course, since call options offer the holder the right to purchase securities at a particular price, this right must have some value. Hence, $C_0 \geq 0$, from which we have the following result: $C_0 \geq \text{Max}[0, S_0 - XB(0,T)]$.

Example 4.1

Consider a stock currently priced at $55, with a three-month $50 strike price call available. Assume no dividends occur prior to expiration, and the riskless rate, *r*, is 12 percent. The lower bound on the price is given by the following:

$$C_0 \geq \text{Max}[0, S_0 - XB(0,T)]$$

(continued)

Example 4.1 (cont'd)

$$= \text{Max}(0.55 - 50\exp[-(0.12)(3/12)])$$

$$= \text{Max}(0.55 - 48.52) = 6.48.$$

Bounding Call Values (With Dividends)

Property 4.2

If a stock pays a single dividend of size d_1 prior to expiration, then to prevent arbitrage opportunities, the call price should never fall below Max(C_1, C_2, C_3),
where $C_1 = \text{Max}[0, S_0 - X]$,

$C_2 = \text{Max}[0, S_0 - XB(0, t_1)]$,

$C_3 = \text{Max}[0, S_0 - d_1 B(0, t_1) - XB(0, T)]$.

Proof: Each item (C_1, C_2, and C_3) is the value of a call option under a specific strategy.

Strategy 1: Exercise the Call Option Immediately   We know that the call price can never fall below its intrinsic value, C_1. If it did, an optimal strategy would be to exercise immediately.

Strategy 2: Exercise the Call Option Just Prior to Ex-Dividend Date
Assume the option is exercised just prior to the ex-dividend date. Then by using the same argument used to prove Property 4.1, it must be that the call price exceeds the stock price less the present value of the strike, or $S_0 - XB(0, t_1)$.

Strategy 3: Exercise the Call Option at Expiration   If the dividend is sacrificed and the option held to expiration, the call value must exceed C_3. We shall prove this result.

Consider two portfolios, A and B. A contains d_1 bonds that pay out $\$d_1$ at time t_1 and X bonds that pay out X dollars at time T. In addition, a call option is held. All dividends received at time t_1 are invested in the risk-free asset. Portfolio B contains a long position in the stock. Exhibit 4.3 illustrates the payoffs that occur if the strategy of exercising the call at the expiration date is followed.

Note that for portfolio A, the d_1 dollars received at time t_1 are reinvested in the riskless security and thus grow to $d_1/B(t_1, T)$ at expiration.

Since $V_a(T) \geq V_b(T)$, it must follow that to prevent arbitrage opportunities $V_a(0) \geq V_b(0)$. Hence, $C_0 \geq C_3$.

Since at the current time the optimal strategy is unknown, the actual call value should exceed the payoffs obtained under all three strategies. Hence, $C_0 \geq \text{Max}(C_1, C_2, C_3)$, and since $C_2 \geq C_1$, we have $C_0 \geq \text{Max}(C_2, C_3)$. This completes the proof.

EXHIBIT 4.3
Arbitrage Portfolio—Bounding Call Prices with Dividends

Portfolio	Current Value	Terminal Value $S_T < X$	$S_T \geq X$
A	$C_0 + XB(0,T)$ $+ d_1 B(0,t_1)$	$X + d_1/B(t_1,T)$	$S_T + d_1/B(t_1,T)$
B	S_0	$S_T + d_1/B(t_1,T)$ $V_a(T) \geq V_b(T)$	$S_T + d_1/B(t_1,T)$ $V_a(T) = V_b(T)$

Example 4.2

Consider the previous problem again, but now assume a dividend of $5 is paid after one month. The lower bound on the call price is given by $\text{Max}(C_1, C_2, C_3)$, where

$C_1 = \text{Max}(0, S_0 - X) = \text{Max}(0, 55 - 50) = \$5,$

$C_2 = \text{Max}[0, S_0 - X\exp(-rt_1)] = \text{Max}(0, 55 - 49.5) = \$5.50,$

$C_3 = \text{Max}[0, S_0 - d_1\exp(-rt_1) - X\exp(-rT)],$

$\quad = \text{Max}(0, 55 - 4.95 - 48.52) = 1.53.$

Hence, $C_0 \geq \$5.50.$

Note that the effect of dividends has been to lower the lower bound of the call option.

Two comments are worth noting here:

1. If the dividend was uncertain but bounds on its value could be established such that $d_{\min} \leq d_1 \leq d_{\max}$; then a lower bound on the call value could be obtained by using $d_{\max}$.
2. If there are two or more dividends prior to expiration, then lower bounds can be obtained by simple extensions to Property 4.2. For example, if two certain dividends d_1 and d_2 occur, then $C_0 \geq \text{Max}(C_1, C_2, C_3, C_4)$ where

$$C_1 = \text{Max}(0, S_0 - X)$$

$$C_2 = \text{Max}[0, S_0 - XB(0,t_1)]$$

$$C_3 = \text{Max}[0, S_0 - d_1 B(0, t_1) - XB(0, t_2)]$$
$$C_4 = \text{Max}[0, S_0 - d_1 B(0, t_1) - d_2 B(0, t_2) - XB(0, T)].$$

OPTIMAL TIMING FOR EXERCISING CALL OPTIONS

The previous result established bounds on the call prices by considering the effect of specific exercise strategies: namely, exercising immediately, just prior to an ex-dividend date, or at expiration. However, other exercising times are possible. In this section we show that, if exercising is ever appropriate for call options, it should be done at expiration or immediately prior to an ex-dividend date.

Property 4.3

Early exercising of a call option on a stock that pays no dividend prior to expiration is never optimal.

Proof: To prove this result we must show that, for a stock that pays no dividends over the lifetime of the option, the value of a call option unexercised is always equal to or greater than the value of the option exercised.

Let t_p be any time point prior to expiration. From Property 4.1, the lower bound on the call price at time t_p is the stock price, $S(t_p)$, less the present value of the strike, $XB(t_p, T)$. Hence, $C(t_p) \geq \text{Max}[0, S(t_p) - XB(t_p, T)]$. Note that the right-hand side of the equation exceeds the intrinsic value of the option, $S(t_p) - X$. Hence, early exercise is not optimal.

From Property 4.3 we see that early exercise of an American call option on a stock that pays no dividends over the lifetime of the option is never appropriate. Therefore, the value of the right to exercise the option prior to expiration must be zero. Thus, an American call option must have the same value as a European call.

Property 4.4

If a stock pays dividends over the lifetime of an option, then an American call option may be worth more than a European call option.

Proof: To prove this result, we shall show that just prior to an ex-dividend date there may be an incentive to exercise early.

To see this, consider an extreme case in which a firm pays all its assets as cash dividends. Clearly, any in-the-money call options should be exercised prior to the ex-dividend date, since after the date the call value will be zero. Note that if the option was European, its value before the ex-dividend date would be zero, whereas the American option would have positive value.

Property 4.5

Exercising of call options is optimal only at expiration, or possibly at the instant prior to an ex-dividend date.

Proof: Exercising of call options is appropriate only if the value of the call unexercised falls below the intrinsic value. Property 4.5 says that the only times the call value unexercised may equal or fall below its intrinsic value are immediately prior to an ex-dividend date and at expiration.

Let t_p be any possible exercising date. We have already seen that if t_p is set such that there are no more dividends prior to expiration, early exercise is not appropriate. If t_p is set before the ex-dividend date t_1, early exercise is again not appropriate. To see this, recall that the lower bound of a call price at time t_p is given by $C \geq \text{Max}(C_1, C_2, C_3)$, where $C_1 = \text{Max}[0, S(t_p) - X]$ is the intrinsic value, $C_2 = \text{Max}[0, S(t_p) - XB(t_p, t_1)]$ is the bound obtained by delaying exercise to immediately prior to the ex-dividend date, and $C_3 = \text{Max}[0, S(t_p) - XB(t_p, T)\ d_1 B(t_p, T)]$ is obtained by delaying exercise to expiration.

For $t_p < t_1$, the bound C_2 exceeds C_1. That is, the lower bound can never be equal to its intrinsic value. We have seen that with time remaining to an ex-dividend date or to the expiration date, exercising of options is not optimal. The only times it may be optimal must therefore be at an instant prior to the ex-dividend date or at expiration.

Dividend and Income Yield Analysis for Call Options

Property 4.5 states that if early exercise occurs, it should occur just prior to an ex-dividend date. The decision to exercise involves a trade-off between dividend income and interest income.

To illustrate this more precisely, consider a stock that pays a single dividend prior to expiration. The lower bound for the call value is: $\text{Max}(C_1, C_2, C_3)$. Moreover, since $C_2 > C_1$, the lower bound is $C_0 \geq \text{Max}(C_2, C_3)$. Early exercise just prior to the ex-dividend date is not appropriate if C_3 exceeds C_2.

Recall $C_2 = \text{Max}[0, S_0 - XB(0, t_1)]$,

$$C_3 = \text{Max}[0, S_0 - XB(0, T) - d_1 B(0, t_1)],$$

and $C_3 > C_2$ implies that

$$S_0 - XB(0, T) - d_1 B(0, t_1) > S_0 - XB(0, t_1),$$

from which

$$X[B(0, t_1) - B(0, T)] > d_1 B(0, t_1). \tag{4.7}$$

Now from equation (4.4) we have $B(0, T) = B(0, t_1) B(t_1, T)$.

Hence, equation (4.7) reduces to

$$XB(0,t_1)[1 - B(t_1,T)] > d_1 B(0,t_1)$$

and

$$X[1 - B(t_1,T)] > d_1. \qquad (4.8)$$

Equation (4.8) says that if the interest on the strike price from the ex-dividend date to expiration exceeds the dividend, early exercise is not appropriate. This leads to the following property.

Property 4.6

If the maximum dividend is less than the interest earned on the strike from the ex-dividend date to expiration, early exercise of an American call option is not optimal.

Example 4.3

In the previous example we had

$$C_0 \geq \text{Max}(C_1, C_2, C_3)$$

$$= \text{Max}(5.0, 5.50, 1.55)$$

$$= 5.50.$$

Since $C_2 > C_3$, early exercise may be appropriate. The size of the dividend $d_1 = \$5$. The size of foregone interest F is as follows:

$$F = X(1 - \exp[-r(T - t_1)])$$

$$= 50 \left[1 - \exp \left(\frac{-0.12 \times 2}{12} \right) \right]$$

$$= 0.99.$$

Since $d_1 > F$, premature exercise may be appropriate.

Note from equation (4.8), if d_1 is zero, then the right-hand side of the equation is zero and premature exercising is not optimal. Moreover, from equation (4.8), the option should not be exercised if the strike price exceeds the value X_{CRIT} where

$$X_{\text{CRIT}} = \frac{d_1}{[1 - B(t_1,T)]}. \qquad (4.9)$$

Thus, if it is optimal to exercise a particular strike-priced option, it is optimal to exercise all the call options with lower strikes.

BOUNDING PUT OPTION PRICES

In this section some arbitrage restrictions for American put options are derived. Unlike American call options, American put options can be exercised early, even if the underlying stock pays no dividends. This property will be proved in the next section. As with Property 4.3, we shall first obtain some put pricing bounds by considering specific exercise strategies for put options.

Property 4.7

Consider a stock that pays a certain dividend d_1 at time t_1. Then an American put option must satisfy the following:

$$P_0 \geq \text{Max}(P_1, P_2)$$

where

$$P_1 = \text{Max}(0, X - S_0)$$

$$P_2 = \text{Max}[0, (X + d_1)B(0, t_1) - S_0]. \qquad (4.10)$$

Proof: To obtain these bounds, we shall consider two strategies. The first strategy is to exercise immediately; the second strategy is to exercise immediately after the ex-dividend date. Other strategies, such as exercising immediately before the ex-dividend date or exercising at expiration, lead to weaker bounds.

Strategy 1: Exercise Immediately   Since a put option gives the holder the right (but not the obligation) to sell stock at the strike price, the put option must have nonnegative value. Furthermore, if exercised immediately, its intrinsic value is obtained with the loss of a possible time premium. Hence, $P_0 \geq P_1$.

Strategy 2: Exercise Immediately After the Ex-dividend Date t_1   Now consider the strategy of exercising the put option just after the ex-dividend date t_1. Then $P_0 \geq P_2$. To see this, consider two portfolios, A and B, where A consists of the put and B consists of a short position in the stock together with $(X + d_1)$ bonds that mature at time t_1. Exhibit 4.4 shows their values at time t_1, given that the put is exercised.

EXHIBIT 4.4
Arbitrage Portfolio—Bounding Put Prices

		Value at Time t_1	
Portfolio	Current Value ($t = 0$)	$S(t_1) \leq X$	$S(t_1) > X$
A	P_0	$X - S(t_1)$	0
B	$(d_1 + X)B(0, t_1) - S_0$	$X - S(t_1)$	$X - S(t_1)$
		$V_a(T) = V_b(T)$	$V_a(T) > V_b(T)$

To avoid risk-free arbitrage opportunities, it must follow that the current value of portfolio A exceeds that of B. That is, $P_0 \geq (d_1 + X) B(0,t_1) - S_0$. Hence, $P_0 \geq P_2$.

Strategy 3: Exercise the Put Option at Expiration   If the option is exercised only at expiration, then a weaker bound is obtained. To see this, consider two portfolios, A and B, where A consists of the put and B consists of a short position in the stock together with X bonds that mature at time T and d_1 bonds that mature at time t_1. Exhibit 4.5 shows their values at time T.

EXHIBIT 4.5
Arbitrage Portfolio—Bounding Put Prices

		Value at Expiration	
Portfolio	Current Value	$S_T \leq X$	$S_T > X$
A	P_0	$X - S_T$	0
B	$XB(0,T) + d_1 B(0,t_1) - S_0$	$X - S_T$	$X - S_T$
		$V_A(T) = V_B(T)$	$V_A(T) > V_B(T)$

Note that the dividend payment that is due (because of the short sale of the stock) can be met by the d_1 bonds that mature at the appropriate time. Since portfolio A dominates portfolio B, it must follow that its current price, $V_A(0)$, is no lower than $V_B0)$. That is,

$$P_0 > XB(0,T) + d_1 B(0,t_1) - S_0.$$

Note that this right-hand side value is less than P_2.

We leave it as an exercise to show that the strategy of exercising the put prior to the ex-dividend date also leads to weaker bounds. Intuitively, exercising the put prior to an ex-dividend date is not sensible, since immediately after the ex-dividend date the stock price will be lower.

Example 4.4

Consider a stock priced at $55, with a three-month put option with strike 60 available. Assume the riskless rate r is 12 percent and a dividend of size $2 is due in one month. Then, we have

$$P_0 \geq \text{Max}(P_1, P_2)$$

$$P_1 = \text{Max}(0, X - S_0) = \text{Max}(0, 60 - 55) = 5$$

$$P_2 = \text{Max}[0, (X + d_1)B(0,t_1) - S_0]$$

$$= \text{Max}\left[0, 62\exp\left(\frac{-0.12}{12}\right) - 55\right]$$

$$= 6.383.$$

OPTIMAL EXERCISING POLICY FOR PUT OPTIONS

Unlike call options, it may be optimal to exercise put options prior to expiration. To see this, consider a stock whose value falls to zero. In this case the put holder should exercise the options immediately. This follows, since if the investor delays action, the interest received from the strike price is lost.

European and American Put Option Prices

Immediately after an ex-dividend date, the holder of an in-the-money put option who also owns the stock may exercise the option. This is especially likely if the put is deep in the money and no more dividends are to be paid prior to expiration. By not exercising the option, the holder foregoes the interest that could be obtained from investing the strike price.

Since early exercise of American put options is a real possibility, these contracts will be more valuable than their European counterparts. And because American put options can be more valuable exercised than not exercised, it must follow that on occasion European put options could have values less than their intrinsic values. In other words, it is possible for European put options to command a negative time premium. This fact will be reconsidered later.

STRIKE PRICE RELATIONSHIPS FOR CALL AND PUT OPTIONS

Property 4.8

Let C_1, C_2, and C_3 (P_1, P_2, P_3) represent the cost of three call (put) options that are identical in all aspects except strike prices. Let $X_1 < X_2 < X_3$ be the three strike prices and, for simplicity, let $X_3 - X_2 = X_2 - X_1$. Then, to prevent riskless arbitrage strategies from being established, the option prices must satisfy the following conditions:

$$C_2 \le \frac{(C_1 + C_3)}{2}$$

and

$$P_2 \le \frac{(P_1 + P_3)}{2}. \tag{4.11}$$

Proof: Consider portfolio A, containing two X_2 call options, and portfolio B, containing one X_1 call option and one X_2 call option. Assuming the portfolios are held to expiration, Exhibit 4.6 illustrates the profits.

Since the future value of portfolio B is always at least as valuable as portfolio A, it must follow that the current value of B, $V_b(0)$, is no less than that of A, $V_a(0)$. That is,

$$V_b(0) \ge V_a(0)$$

EXHIBIT 4.6
Arbitrage Portfolio—Call Option Price Relationships

Portfolio	Current Value	$S_T \leq X_1$	$X_1 < S_T \leq X_2$	$X_2 < S_T \leq X_3$	$S_T > X_3$
A	$2C_2$	0	0	$2(S_T - X_2)$	$2(S_T - X_2)$
B	$C_1 + C_3$	0	$(S_T - X_1)$	$(S_T - X_1)$	$(S_T - X_1) +$ $(S_T - X_3)$
		$V_a(T) =$ $V_b(T)$	$V_b(T) \geq$ $V_a(T)$	$V_b(T) \geq$ $V_a(T)$	$V_a(T) =$ $V_b(T)$

and hence

$$C_1 + C_3 \geq 2C_2,$$

$$C_2 \leq \frac{(C_1 + C_3)}{2}.$$

If $C_2 > (C_1 + C_3)/2$, then an investor would sell portfolio A and buy portfolio B. The initial amount of money received would be $2C_2 - C_1 - C_3$. If held to expiration, additional arbitrage profits might become available. If, however, the X_2 options were exercised prior to expiration, when the stock was at S*, the amount owed could be obtained by exercising both the X_1 and X_3 calls. Hence, regardless of what price occurs in the future, riskless arbitrage strategies become available unless the middle strike call is valued less than the average of its neighboring strikes.

A similar result holds for put options.

Example 4.5

Consider the following option contracts:

Strike	Price
40	4.0
45	C_0
50	0.88

The upper bound for the 45 call option contract should be

$$C_0 \leq \frac{(4.0 + 0.88)}{2} = 2.44.$$

PUT-CALL PARITY RELATIONSHIPS

In this section we shall develop pricing relationships between put and call options.

European Put-Call Parity: No Dividends

Property 4.9

With no dividends prior to expiration, a European put should be priced as a European call price plus the present value of the strike price less the stock price. That is:

$$P_0^E = C_0^E + XB(0,T) - S_0 \qquad (4.12)$$

where the E superscript emphasizes the fact that the options are European.

Proof: Under the assumption of no dividends and no premature exercising, consider portfolios A and B, where A consists of the stock and European put and B consists of the European call with X pure discount bonds of face value $1 that mature at the expiration date. Exhibit 4.7 compares their future values.

EXHIBIT 4.7
Arbitrage Portfolio—Put-Call Parity

Portfolio	Current Value	Terminal Value	
		$S_T \leq X$	$S_T > X$
A	$P_0^E + S_0$	X	S_T
B	$C_0^E + XB(0,T)$	X	S_T
		$V_a(T) = V_b(T)$	$V_a(T) = V_b(T)$

To avoid riskless arbitrage opportunities, it must follow that the current value of the two portfolios are the same. That is,

$$P_0^E + S_0 = C_0^E + XB(0,T), \text{ or}$$

$$P_0^E = C_0^E + XB(0,T) - S_0.$$

This relationship is called the *European put-call parity equation*, since it precludes the possibility of premature exercise.

Note the equation 4.12 says that the price of a European put equals the price of a European call less the minimum price of a European call given by equation (4.5).

Example 4.6

Given the price of a stock is \$55, the price of a three-month 60 call is \$2, and the riskless rate is 12 percent, then the lower bound for a three-month 60 put option can be derived. Specifically, since

$$P_0{}^E = C_0{}^E + XB(0,T) - S_0,$$

we have

$$P_0{}^E = 2 + 60\exp\left[-0.12\left(\frac{3}{12}\right)\right] - 55$$

$$= 2 + 58.23 - 55$$

$$= 5.23$$

European Put-Call Parity Equations with Dividends

Property 4.10

Under the assumption of a single dividend of size d_1 at time t_1, the value of a European put option is given by

$$P_0{}^E = C_0{}^E + XB(0,T) + d_1 B(0,t_1) - S_0. \qquad (4.13)$$

Proof: Consider a stock that pays a dividend d_1 at time t_1. Consider the following two portfolios, A and B. Portfolio A contains the stock and put option. Portfolio B contains the call and X pure discount bonds of face value \$1 that mature at the expiration date, along with d_1 pure discount bonds that mature at time t_1. Exhibit 4.8 illustrates the terminal values under the assumption that all dividends or payouts are reinvested at the riskless rate.

EXHIBIT 4.8
Arbitrage Portfolio — Put-Call Parity with Dividends

Portfolio	Current Value	Terminal Value $S_T < X$	$S_T \geq X$
A	$P_0{}^E + S_0$	$X + d_1/B(t_1,T)$	$S_T + d_1/B(t_1,T)$
B	$C_0{}^E + XB(0,T) + d_1 B(0,t_1)$	$X + d_1/B(t_1,T)$	$S_T + d_1/B(t_1,T)$
		$V_a(T) = V_B(T)$	$V_a(T) = V_B(T)$

Since the terminal values of the two portfolios are the same regardless of the future stock price, it must follow that, to avoid riskless arbitrage opportunities, the current portfolio values must be the same. Hence,

$$P_0{}^E + S_0 = C_0{}^E + XB(0,T) + d_1 B(0,t_1),$$

and therefore,

$$P_0{}^E = C_0{}^E + XB(0,T) + d_1 B(0,t_1) - S_0.$$

The put-call parity equation not only values a European put option in terms of stocks, calls, and bonds, but also provides a mechanism for replicating a put option. That is, a portfolio containing one call option, X pure discount bonds maturing at time T, d_1 pure discount bonds maturing at time t_1, and a short position in the stock completely replicates the payouts of a put option.

Indirect Purchasing

The put-call parity relationship provides alternative methods of producing payouts equivalent to purchasing stock, calls, or puts. To illustrate this fact, we shall assume no dividends and shall consider European options.

Indirect Purchasing of Stock   Since

$$P_0{}^E = C_0{}^E + XB(0,T) - S_0,$$

we have

$$S_0 = XB(0,T) + C_0{}^E - P_0{}^E.$$

Hence, rather than buy the stock directly, one can buy it "indirectly" by purchasing X discount bonds maturing at time T, by buying a call option, and by selling a European put.

Indirect Purchasing of Calls   Since

$$P_0{}^E = C_0{}^E + XB(0,T) - S_0,$$

we have

$$C_0{}^E = S_0 + P_0{}^E - XB(0,T).$$

Thus, a call option can be replicated by buying the stock and put option and borrowing the present value of the strike.

Indirect Purchasing of a Long Position in the Call and a Short Position in the Put   From the put-call parity relationship, we have

$$C_0{}^E - P_0{}^E = S_0 - XB(0,T).$$

Hence, the portfolio of a call and written put is equivalent to a leveraged position in the stock, where the present value of the strike is borrowed to finance purchase of the stock.

AMERICAN PUT-CALL PARITY RELATIONSHIPS: NO DIVIDENDS

Property 4.11

With no dividends prior to expiration, the value of an American put option is related to the American call price by

$$P_0 \geq C_0 + XB(0,T) - S_0. \qquad (4.14)$$

Proof: Property 4.11 follows directly from Property 4.9 and the recognition that American puts are more valuable than European options (that is, $P_0 \geq P_0^E$).

Note from equation 4.12, since $C_0^E = C_0 \geq 0$, we have

$$P_0^E \geq XB(0,T) - S_0.$$

That is, a European put should always be priced to be no lower than the present value of the strike price less the stock price. Note that this lower bound is less than the intrinsic value, $X - S_0$. European put options could have negative time premiums.

Property 4.12

With no dividends prior to expiration, the value of an American put option is restricted by

$$P_0 \leq C_0 - S_0 + X. \qquad (4.15)$$

Proof: Consider portfolio A, which contains a call and $X/B(0,T)$ pure discount bonds that mature at time T, and portfolio B, which contains a put option together with the stock. Exhibit 4.9 shows the cash flows of the two portfolios. Since the value of portfolio B depends on whether the put was exercised prematurely, both cases must be considered.

EXHIBIT 4.9
Arbitrage Portfolio—Put-Call Parity

Portfolio	Current Value	Value at Time t (Put Exercised) $0 \leq t < T$	Value at Time T (Put Not Exercised) $S_T < X$	Value at Time T (Put Not Exercised) $S_T \geq X$
A	$C_0 + X$	$XB(t,T)/B(0,T) + C_t$	$X/B(0,T)$	$(S_T - X) + X/B(0,T)$
B	$P_0 + S_0$	X	X	S_T
		$V_A(t) > V_B(t)$	$V_A(T) > V_B(T)$	$V_A(T) > V_B(T)$

If the put is exercised early, the stock is delivered in receipt for X. Note that, in this case, the value of the bonds alone in portfolio A exceeds the value of portfolio B. If the put is held to expiration, then portfolio A will be more valuable than portfolio B, regardless of the future stock price. Clearly, to avoid risk-free arbitrage opportunities, the current value of portfolio A must be no smaller than the value of portfolio B. Hence,

$$C_0 + X \geq P_0 + S_0,$$

from which the result follows.

Example 4.7

Using the data for Example 4.6, we have

$$P_0 \leq C_0 + X - S_0 = 2 + 60 - 55 = 7, \text{ and}$$

$$P_0 \leq P_0^{E} = 5.23.$$

Hence, $5.23 \leq P_0 \leq 7$.

CONCLUSION

In this chapter arbitrage arguments have been used to derive bounds on option prices. In addition, the relationship between put and call options has been explored and optimal call and put exercise strategies have been investigated. Other bounds can be derived. For a comprehensive treatment of these bounds, refer to the references—especially the seminal paper by Merton.

Through arbitrage arguments alone, bounds on option prices can be constructed. The beauty of these arguments stems from the fact that they require only that investors prefer more wealth to less. If additional assumptions are placed on investor preferences, tighter bounds on option prices can be derived. This will be illustrated in the next chapter.

References

This chapter draws very heavily on Merton's article, published in 1973. Jarrow and Rudd provide a comprehensive treatment of this topic and include bounds for cases when dividends are uncertain and interest rates are random. Cox and Rubinstein also provide a rigorous treatment of these bounds. Empirical tests of these bounds are discussed by Gould and Galai; Klemkosky and Resnick; and surveyed by Galai.

Cox, J. C., and M. Rubinstein. *Option Markets.* Englewood Cliffs, N.J.: Prentice-Hall, 1985.
Galai, D. "Empirical Tests of Boundary Conditions for CBOE Options." *Journal of Financial Economics* 6(June–September 1978): 187–211.

Galai, D. "A Survey of Empirical Tests of Option Pricing Models." In *Option Pricing*, edited by M. Brenner. Lexington, Mass.: Lexington Books, 1983, 45–80.

Gould, J., and D. Galai. "Transaction Costs and the Relationship Between Put and Call Prices." *Journal of Financial Economics* 1(June 1974): 105–29.

Jarrow, R., and A. Rudd. *Option Pricing*. Homewood, Ill.: Richard Irwin Inc., 1983.

Klemkosky, R., and B. Resnick. "Put Call Parity and Market Efficiency." *Journal of Finance* 34 (December 1979): 1141–55.

Merton, R. "Theory of Rational Option Pricing." *Bell Journal of Economics and Management Science* 4(Spring 1973): 141–84.

Exercises

1. Consider the two investments below:

   a. Construct a riskless arbitrage portfolio.
   b. In an efficient market, what would happen to the prices of *A* and *B*?

2. XYZ trades at $50. One-dollar, face-value bonds currently trade at $0.90.

   a. Assuming the bonds mature at the expiration date of the option, compute the lower bound price of an at-the-money call option.
   b. If the call traded at $4, construct a profitable riskless arbitrage portfolio.

3. XYZ is currently trading at $50. It is about to declare a $0.50 dividend. An at-the-money, three-month call option is trading at $3. The riskless rate *r* is 10 percent.

   a. Compute the lower bound on the option price.
   b. How large must the dividend be before the investor will exercise?
   c. Construct a strategy that yields riskless arbitrage opportunities.

4. Explain why call options will be exercised (if at all) just prior to an ex-dividend date, while put options may be exercised at any point in time.

5. XYZ pays no dividends and trades at $50. The riskless rate *r* is 10 percent.

   a. What is the lowest price at which a six-month put with strike price 55 should be sold? If the put traded below this value, what could be done to lock into a guaranteed profit?
   b. How would the investment strategy above be affected if the stock paid dividends?

6. The six-month call prices on XYZ, which currently trades at $50, are shown below. XYZ pays no dividends. Construct a portfolio that will produce riskless profits.

Strike	Call Price
45	5.2
50	4.5
55	3.0
60	0.5

7. The call price on a six-month XYZ 50 call option is $6 and the riskless rate is 10 percent.

   a. Compute the lower bound on a six-month 50 put option. Assume the stock price is $52.

   b. If the underlying stock declares a dividend of $1 two months prior to expiration, would the lower bound increase, decrease, or remain the same? Explain.

8. XYZ trades at $60. The market price of an XYZ January 50 put is 1/16. The market price of the January 50 call is $11. Consider the strategy of buying the stock and put option and selling the call. Compute the initial investment and explain why a profit equal to the strike price less the initial investment is guaranteed.

9. Given XYZ trades at $30, the riskless rate of return is 12 percent, and an at-the-money call option with six months to expiration is trading at $4.

   a. Compute the price of a European put option.

   b. By plotting a profit function, show that the payouts of a stock can be replicated by a portfolio containing the six-month at-the-money call, a short position in the put, and borrowing funds at the riskless rate. How much needs to be borrowed?

10. Using arbitrage arguments alone, show that an American call option cannot be valued more than a stock.

11. Explain why a European put option could have a negative time premium, while an American put option could not.

5

The Economic Role of Options*

In Chapter 4, arbitrage arguments were used to obtain a lower bound for the price of a call option. A portfolio of stocks and bonds was constructed in such a way that, regardless of what occurred in the future, the value of the call could never fall below the value of the portfolio. This led to the observation that, in order to prevent riskless arbitrage opportunities, the current call price must not be lower than the current portfolio price.

If the payouts of an option could be perfectly replicated by a portfolio of traded securities, then by the law of one price, the option price would be unambiguously determined by the current value of the replicating portfolio. However, in this case the option would serve no economic role, since it would only duplicate payouts that could already be achieved by holding existing securities.

In this chapter we shall distinguish between economies in which options do and do not provide patterns of payouts that otherwise could not be constructed. To illustrate all the concepts, we shall simplify the analysis by considering a one-period problem in which no intermediate dividends occur.

In the first section we introduce the notion of market completeness. In such a market, investors can construct portfolios that provide patterns of payouts that exactly reflect their desired preferences. Indeed, in a complete market any type of future payout across the states of nature can be constructed from existing securities, and the introduction of new securities, including options, is not necessary. We shall see that, in a complete market, the price of an option contract is fully determined by the value of a unique replicating portfolio consisting of state contingent claims. We shall see that valuation of securities in complete markets can be simply accomplished by using a risk-neutral valuation argument. This argument is important in the theory of option pricing and will be applied in later chapters.

Complete markets are highly desirable since they allow investors to establish patterns of payouts in accordance with investors' desired prefer-

---

*This chapter, and all chapters and sections marked with an asterisk, can be skipped without loss of continuity.

ences. In an incomplete market, investors may be unable to achieve this goal. The introduction of new securities into this market may create new possibilities that can help. A less expensive alternative that is also considered is to introduce options on existing securities.

Since options may not be redundant in an incomplete market, they do serve an important economic role. Unfortunately, since no replicating portfolio exists, arbitrage arguments alone cannot be used to unambiguously value the option. By placing assumptions on the preferences of investors and on the behavior of the stock price, one can obtain tighter bounds than those derived in Chapter 4. Such bounds are discussed later in this chapter, on pages 105-107

COMPLETE MARKETS

Assume that all possible outcomes of nature and the economy can be classified into n mutually exclusive and exhaustive states. It is assumed that, at the end of a given period, all investors can easily identify which state has occurred. Thus, each state is well defined in terms of observable information.

We shall also assume the existence of a financial instrument that pays \$1 if a particular state, say state i, occurs and \$0 if any other state occurs. The current value of this instrument is e_i. Such a security is called a *state security*, a *contingent claim*, a *pure security*, or an *Arrow Debreu security*.

A market is said to be *complete* if a pure security exists for each state or if all n pure securities can be constructed from the portfolio of traded assets.

VALUATION OF SECURITIES IN COMPLETE MARKETS

Consider a particular security currently worth S_0. Let $\tilde{S}_T$ be a random variable representing its future value. Since there are n states of nature, the future value, $\tilde{S}_T$, is restricted to (at most) n distinct values. Let V_j be the value of the stock price, if state j occurs, $j = 1, 2, \ldots n$.

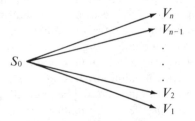

If two traded securities offer the same terminal values for all states, then clearly, to avoid riskless arbitrage opportunities, their current prices must be the same. This law of one price can be used to value any security in terms of the prices of pure securities. To see this, we shall devise a portfolio of pure securities that produces the same future outcomes as the traded security, regardless of which state occurs. The portfolio is constructed in the following manner:

Buy V_1 units of a pure security on state 1.
Buy V_2 units of a pure security on state 2.

.

.

.

Buy V_n units of a pure security on state n.

The cost of this portfolio, W_0, is

$$W_0 = \sum_{i=1}^{n} V_i e_i.$$

The future value of this portfolio, W_1, depends on which state occurs. Specifically, if state j occurs, the value of the portfolio is given by

$$W_1 = \sum_{\substack{i=1 \\ i \neq j}}^{n} V_i 0 + V_j 1 = V_j.$$

Thus, regardless of which state occurs, the terminal value of the portfolio will be identical to that of the traded security. Hence, to avoid riskless arbitrage, the current value of the security, S_0, must equal the current value of the portfolio, W_0. That is,

$$S_0 = \sum_{i=1}^{n} V_i e_i. \qquad (5.1)$$

Example 5.1

Consider a three-state economy. The future price of a security can be characterized by a vector consisting of three numbers, one for each state. Consider a security that is worth \$4 if state 1 occurs, \$6 if state 2 occurs, and \$10 if state 3 occurs. Let S_0 be the current price of the security. Then, we can represent the future prices as

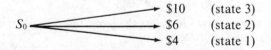

$$
\begin{array}{lll}
 & \$10 & (\text{state 3}) \\
S_0 & \$6 & (\text{state 2}) \\
 & \$4 & (\text{state 1})
\end{array}
$$

Assume the state securities are priced as follows:

$$e_1 = 0.5, \; e_2 = 0.25, \; e_3 = 0.2.$$

To avoid riskless arbitrage opportunities, the price of the security must satisfy the following equation:

$$S_0 = 4e_1 + 6e_2 + 10e_3$$

$$= 4(0.5) + 6(0.25) + 10(0.2) = 5.5.$$

The fact that, in a complete market, any security can be valued as a linear combination of the prices of pure securities has major ramifications. The result implies that once the prices of pure securities are determined, all other securities can be *unambiguously* valued. Preferences enter into the pricing only insofar as they determine the prices of pure securities. This will be discussed further on pages 95–96.

Before we establish how the prices of pure securities are set, it is important to recognize that they are fictitious securities and that their prices are not directly observable. However, in some cases the price of pure securities can be derived from the portfolio of traded securities. This is illustrated in the following example.

Example 5.2

Consider a three-state security market in which three assets are traded. The current prices and future values of the securities are illustrated below.

The future possible payouts of the securities can be represented by a matrix, A, where the columns represent the securities and the rows represent the states.

$$A = \begin{bmatrix} 0 & 1 & 1 \\ 3 & 2 & 0 \\ 1 & 1 & 2 \end{bmatrix}$$

In order to obtain a pure state 3 payout, we have to establish a portfolio of the currently traded assets. Let X_1, X_2, and X_3 be the amount of shares of type 1, 2, and 3 that are purchased. The payout of this portfolio is

$$0X_1 + 1X_2 + 1X_3$$

$$3X_1 + 2X_2 + 0X_3$$

$$1X_1 + 1X_2 + 2X_3$$

For this portfolio to replicate the pure state 3 payout, we must choose X_1, X_2 and X_3 such that

$$0X_1 + 1X_2 + 1X_3 = 1$$

$$3X_1 + 2X_2 + 0X_3 = 0$$

$$1X_1 + 1X_2 + 2X_3 = 0$$

The solution is given by

$$X_1 = -\frac{4}{5}, \ X_2 = -\frac{6}{5}, \ X_3 = -\frac{1}{5}.$$

(continued)

Example 5.2 (cont'd)

Hence, the payout of a state 3 pure security can be replicated by a portfolio consisting of 6/5 shares of security 2, together with a short position of 1/5 share of security 3, and 4/5 of a share of security 1.

$$-\frac{4S_1}{5} + \frac{6S_2}{5} - \frac{S_3}{5} \quad\Longrightarrow\quad \begin{matrix} 1 \\ 0 \\ 0 \end{matrix}$$

To avoid riskless arbitrage opportunities, the price of a pure state 3 security, e_3, must satisfy the following equation:

$$e_3 = -\frac{4S_1}{5} + \frac{6S_2}{5} - \frac{S_3}{5}.$$

The market is complete since portfolios of traded assets that replicate the payoffs of the other pure securities can be established. In particular, it can be shown that

$$e_2 = -\frac{S_1}{5} + \frac{S_2}{5} - \frac{S_3}{5}$$

$$e_1 = -\frac{2S_1}{5} - \frac{3S_2}{5} + \frac{3S_3}{5}.$$

VALUATION OF PURE SECURITIES

The previous example illustrated how the prices of pure securities could be generated from the prices of traded securities. In the example, three securities traded in an economy defined by three states. Moreover, each security was *distinct* in the sense that the payoffs of any one security could not be replicated by any portfolio containing the other two securities. In general, in order to obtain the prices of all pure securities, there must be at least as many distinct traded securities as states.

If there are fewer distinct securities than states, then unambiguous prices for some state securities cannot be obtained. In this case, there are some pure securities that cannot be constructed and the market is said to be *incomplete*.

In a complete market, any traded security can be valued once the state prices are known. The state security prices depend on several factors:

1. Clearly, the higher the likelihood of a particular state occurring, the higher the price of the state security. Hence, the consensus opinion of the likelihood of individual states affects the price of the pure state security.

2. The current value of a portfolio containing a pure security for each state is given by the following equation:

$$B_0 = \sum_{j=1}^{n} e_j. \tag{5.2}$$

Since this portfolio is riskless, its current price, B_0, represents the present value of $1. Since the sum of the state security prices is given by the riskless discount factor, individual state security prices will depend on the time value of money.

3. The price of state securities also depends on preferences of investors in the economy. To see this, let the states be ranked according to the aggregate level of wealth, where state 1 represents the lowest aggregate wealth state and state n represents the highest. (For example, state 1 could be the worst possible depression and state n the most prosperous state.) Since investors are risk averse, dollar payouts in lower states will be relatively more valuable than dollar payouts in higher states. As a result, investors will be prepared to pay more for pure securities in low wealth states than in high wealth states, even if the probabilities of the states' occurring were equal. As a result of this behavior, the low wealth states will provide investors with a lower expected return than higher wealth states. Equivalently, discount factors will be set such that they decrease as aggregate wealth increases. That is,

$$d_1 > d_2 > d_3 \ldots > d_n > 0 \tag{5.3}$$

where d_i is the discount factor for state i.

The actual size of discount factors will depend on the degree of risk aversion and the dispersion of aggregate wealth across the states. Note that if the *ex ante* probabilities of the states are given $(\pi_1, \pi_2, \ldots \pi_n)$, then the expected payout of a pure state j security at the end of the period is

$$1\pi_j + 0 \sum_{\substack{i=1 \\ i \neq j}}^{n} \pi_i = \pi_j.$$

The current value of a pure state j security is the expected future value discounted by the appropriate discount factor, d_j.

$$e_j = \pi_j d_j \tag{5.4}$$

VALUATION OF TRADED SECURITIES IN RISK-AVERSE COMPLETE MARKETS*

The current price of an asset will depend on the size of the future payouts the security provides, as well as on the states in which these payouts are obtained. All things being equal, securities that provide high payouts in states of low aggregate wealth should be priced so as to give a lower return than securities that provide high payouts in states of high aggregate wealth. This suggests that, all things being equal, securities positively correlated with aggregate wealth (the market) will provide higher expected returns than securities negatively correlated with the market. This phenomenon is captured by the capital asset pricing model (CAPM). Specifically, this model relates the expected return of a security to the beta value as follows:

$$E(\tilde{R}_S) = R_F + \beta[E(\tilde{R}_m) - R_F] \tag{5.5}$$

where $E(\tilde{R}_m)$ is the expected return of the market and β is the beta value of the security, given by

$$\beta = \frac{\text{Cov}(\tilde{R}_S, \tilde{R}_m)}{\text{Var}(\tilde{R}_m)}.$$

In the appendix, it is shown that the CAPM can be rewritten as

$$S_0 = \frac{[E(\tilde{S}_T) - \lambda\text{Cov}(\tilde{S}_T, \tilde{M}_T)]}{R_F} \tag{5.6}$$

where $\lambda = M_0[E(\tilde{R}_m) - R_F]/\text{Var}(\tilde{M}_T)$ is the market price of risk times the market value, M_0. Equation (5.6) says that the current price of a security can be obtained by computing the expected future price, subtracting a risk premium (which depends on the covariance term), and discounting this value at the riskless rate.

Now in a complete market, the stock price and market portfolio can be written as

$$S_0 = \sum_{i=1}^{n} V_i e_i$$

and

$$M_0 = \sum_{i=1}^{n} U_i e_i.$$

where V_i is the value of the security in state i and U_i is the aggregate wealth value in state i. Since the states of nature are ordered according to aggregate wealth, we have $U_1 \leq U_2 \leq U_3 \leq \ldots \leq U_n$, and

$$E(\tilde{S}_T) = \sum_{i=1}^{n} V_i \pi_i,$$

$$E(\tilde{M}_T) = \sum_{i=1}^{n} U_i \pi_i,$$

$$E(\tilde{S}_T \tilde{M}_T) = \sum_{i=1}^{n} U_i V_i \pi_i$$

where π_i is the probability of state i occurring. Substituting these expressions into equation (5.6) and simplifying yields

$$S_0 = \sum_{i=1}^{n} V_i d_i \pi_i \tag{5.7}$$

where

$$d_i = \frac{1 - \lambda[U_i - E(\tilde{M}_T)]}{R_F}.$$ (5.8)

Equation (5.8) indicates that as aggregate wealth (U_i) increases, the discount factor (d_i) decreases. For a given set of *ex ante* probabilities, the current value of a security will be high if the largest V_i values occur with the largest d_i values. Since high d_i values are provided in low aggregate wealth states, we conclude that securities that provide high payouts in low aggregate wealth states are relatively more valuable than securities that provide high payouts in high-aggregate-wealth states. Equivalently, securities that are negatively correlated with the market are relatively more valuable than securities positively correlated with the market.

INCOMPLETE MARKETS AND THE ROLE OF OPTIONS

In a complete market, investors can establish portfolios to suit their individual preferences based only on the n pure securities. In this market there is no need to create additional securities since all possible payout patterns can be created in the existing market.

In an incomplete market, however, combinations of existing securities are not sufficient to create all the state securities. As a result, some payout patterns cannot be achieved. The addition of new securities into this market may allow payouts to be created in a way that were not previously possible. Rather than introducing new securities, it may be cheaper, in terms of transaction costs, to increase the number of alternatives by creating options on existing securities. The following example illustrates the market-completing function of options.

Example 5.3

Assume there are three possible states and only one stock in the capital market. The stock has payoffs in all three states:

Suppose that call options C_2 and C_3 are created on this stock with strike prices 2 and 3, respectively. Then the payoffs are as shown:

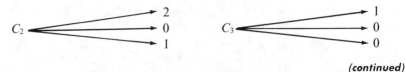

(continued)

Example 5.3 (cont'd)

For this situation, the three pure state securities can be constructed. Specifically, we have the following:

$$e_1 = C_2 - 2C_3$$

$$e_2 = \frac{S_0}{2} - \frac{3C_2}{2} + C_3$$

$$e_3 = C_3$$

Hence, the market is complete.

In general, the addition of call options alone on existing securities may not be sufficient to complete the market. For example, if the security in the previous problem had the payouts

then calls with strike 1, 2, and 3 would not complete the market.

The trading of put options together with call options may move the market closer to being complete. However, the introduction of both call and put options on securities may still not be sufficient to guarantee market completeness. Moreover, the introduction of so many contracts may be wasteful, in the sense that individual contracts may not add anything to completeness.

For economic reasons, it would be desirable to introduce the fewest contracts that would move the markets most rapidly toward being complete. In some situations market completeness can be achieved by trading options on a subset of all securities. In the next section, we provide a result that shows that, under certain conditions, market completeness can be achieved by trading option contracts on a *single* portfolio.

Ross's Theorem

If the payouts of all the securities taken together can distinguish among all the states, then market completeness can always be achieved by supplementing the traded securities with options written on a single portfolio. This portfolio need not be unique, but must have the property of producing different payouts in all states.

Example 5.4

To illustrate Ross's theorem, consider a four-state, two-security market. The payouts of the securities are

(continued)

Example 5.4 (cont'd)

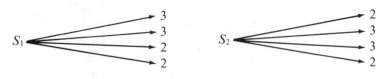

The introduction of call and put options with strike prices 2 and 3 on both stocks are not sufficient to complete the market. To see this, let $C_{ij}(P_{ij})$ denote a call (put) on stock i (i = 1, 2) with strike j (j = 2, 3). Then we have

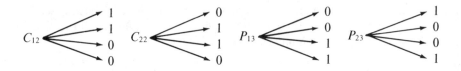

Note that

$$P_{23} = S_1 - S_2 + P_{13}$$

$$3C_{12} = S_1 - 2P_{13}$$

and $\qquad\qquad 3C_{22} = S_2 - 2P_{23}.$

Hence, the market contains only three distinct securities, S_1, S_2, and P_{13}, and is incomplete.

Note that the payouts of the two securities, taken together, do distinguish among all states. Specifically, let

$$A = \begin{bmatrix} 3 & 2 \\ 3 & 3 \\ 2 & 3 \\ 2 & 2 \end{bmatrix}$$

Since each row of the matrix A is unique, the conditions for Ross's theorem hold. That is, there exists a portfolio upon which, if options are traded, the market would be made complete.

For example, consider portfolio F, consisting of one unit of security 1 and two units of security 2.

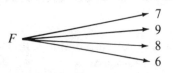

Note that this portfolio has distinct payouts in all states. By trading call and put options on this portfolio, by Ross's theorem, the market is completed. In fact, for this example, calls with strike prices 6 and 7 would complete the market.

Ross's theorem has important economic ramifications. It suggests that the move toward market completeness can be more readily accomplished by trading options on a single fund, rather than by trading options on individual securities. The theorem thus provides the justification for introducing options on portfolios. Options on portfolios are not equivalent to a portfolio of options and will be discussed in detail in Chapter 7.

THE GENERAL FORM OF AN OPTION PRICING MODEL

We shall now derive a general form for the price of an option in an economy characterized by n states in the future. We shall consider a single period in which the stock pays no dividends. As before, let the future value of the stock price in state j be V_j. Then, as seen earlier, by the law of one price the current stock price, S_0, can be written as follows:

$$S_0 = \sum_{j=1}^{n} V_j e_j$$

where e_j is the price of a pure security on state j and is fully determined if the market is complete. For convenience, we shall label the states such that $V_1 \leq V_2 \leq V_3 \leq \ldots \leq V_n$.

The value of a risk-free bond that pays $1 at the end of the period at time T is given by the following:

$$B_0 = \exp(-rT) = \sum_{j=1}^{n} e_j \tag{5.9}$$

Within this framework, the value of a call option with strike X and expiration date T, C_0, is given by the following:

$$C_0 = \sum_{j=1}^{n} e_j \text{Max}(V_j - X, 0)$$

$$= \sum_{j=k}^{n} e_j(V_j - X)$$

where k is the smallest integer such that $V_j \geq X$.

Hence,

$$C_0 = \sum_{j \geq k} e_j V_j - X \sum_{j \geq k} e_j \tag{5.10}$$

Example 5.5

Consider a two-state economy in which a stock and bond trade. The stock can appreciate or depreciate by 20 percent, while the riskless return is 5 percent.

Since the market is complete, the price of the pure two-state securities can be determined.

To replicate the payouts of a pure two-state security, consider a portfolio of H shares of stock, financed partially by borrowing $\$B$.

To replicate e_2, we require

$$120H - 1.05B = 1$$
$$80H - 1.05B = 0$$

from which

$$H = \frac{1}{40} = 0.025$$
$$B = \frac{2}{1.05} = 1.905$$

and, hence, $e_2 = 100H - B = 0.595$.

Thus, a pure two-state security can be constructed by borrowing $\$1.905$ and purchasing 0.025 shares of stock.

Similarly, we can show that the price of a one-state security e_1 is given by the following:

$$e_1 = 0.357.$$

Now consider a call option with strike 100 that expires at the end of the period. The payouts of the call are as follows:

(continued)

Example 5.5 (cont'd)

Hence, a call option is equivalent to ownership of 20 pure two-state securities, and $C_0 = 20e_2 = 11.9$.

Equivalently, a call option produces the same payouts as a portfolio containing $20(0.025) = 0.5$ shares of stock, partially financed by borrowing $20(1.905) = \$38.10$.

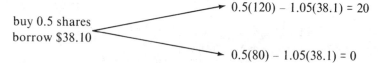

buy 0.5 shares
borrow $38.10

$0.5(120) - 1.05(38.1) = 20$

$0.5(80) - 1.05(38.1) = 0$

Hence, by the law of one price, $C_0 = H^* S_0 - B^*$, where $H^* = 0.5$ and $B^* = 38.1$.

Example 5.6

In Example 5.1 the prices of the three-state securities were $e_1 = 0.5$, $e_2 = 0.25$, and $e_3 = 0.2$. Hence,

$$B_0 = \sum_{j=1}^{3} e_j = 0.95.$$

Consider a stock that produces the following payouts:

$$S_0 \begin{array}{l} \longrightarrow 10 \\ \longrightarrow 6 \\ \longrightarrow 4 \end{array}$$

A call option with strike $X = 4$ produces the following payouts:

$$C \begin{array}{l} \longrightarrow 6 \\ \longrightarrow 2 \\ \longrightarrow 0 \end{array}$$

Now $S_0 = 4e_1 + 6e_2 + 10e_3 = 5.5$ and $C_0 = 2e_2 + 6e_3 = 1.7$. Unlike the previous example, the payouts of the call option cannot be replicated by a portfolio of stock and bonds alone. In a three-state security market, replicating the payouts of call options requires combining three traded securities. More generally, in an n state security market, replicating the payouts of a call option requires combining n distinct traded securities.

THE RISKLESS HEDGE AND THE RISK NEUTRALITY ARGUMENT

For the special case of a two-state economy, we have seen that a portfolio containing a particular number of shares of stock, partially financed by borrowing a certain amount of dollars, could be constructed to replicate the payouts of a call option. There are other situations in which the future payouts of call options can be replicated with the underlying stock and bonds alone. These conditions will be discussed in future chapters. Whenever this replication property holds, it is also possible to create a riskless portfolio using stock and call options alone.

Example 5.7

Reconsider Example 5.5, where $H^* = 0.5$, $B^* = 38.1$, and $C_0 = 11.9$. Since $C_0 = H^*S_0 - B^*$, we have the following:

$$B^* = H^*S_0 - C_0.$$

A portfolio containing $H^* = 0.5$ shares of stock and a written call option produces a guaranteed outcome.

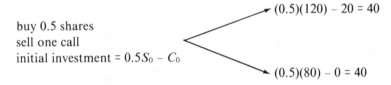

buy 0.5 shares
sell one call
initial investment = $0.5S_0 - C_0$

$(0.5)(120) - 20 = 40$

$(0.5)(80) - 0 = 40$

Since the portfolio is not risky, it should not command a risk premium. As a result, the portfolio should be priced in a risk-averse economy in the same way as in a risk-neutral economy. (Specifically, this portfolio should be priced to yield the riskless return of 5 percent.) That is, $(0.5S_0 - C_0)(1.05) = 40$, and for $S_0 = 100$, we can solve for C_0 to obtain $C_0 = 11.9$.

Note that, since the call option price derived in this fashion does not depend on preferences, its value in a risk-neutral economy is identical to its value in a risk-averse economy. For simplicity, then, a call option price could be generated by pretending the economy is risk neutral.

Example 5.8

Reconsider Example 5.7. We shall value the call by pretending that we are in a risk-neutral economy. Since the riskless rate is 5 percent, all securities should be priced so as to yield an expected return of 5 percent. Hence,

$$S_0 = \frac{E(\tilde{S}_T)}{1.05}$$

$$100 = \frac{[120p + 80(1 - p)]}{1.05}$$

where p is the assessed probability of an upward movement in this risk-neutral economy. Solving the above equation yields $p = 0.625$.

For the stock price to be an equilibrium price in a risk-neutral economy, the probability of an upward price movement must be $p = 0.625$.

(continued)

Example 5.8 (cont'd)

In this case, the expected call price is

$$E(\tilde{C}_T) = 20p + 0(1 - p) = 12.5$$

and, hence,

$$C_0 = \frac{E(\tilde{C}_T)}{1.05} = \frac{12.5}{1.05} = 11.9,$$

which is the result we obtained before.

THE RISK-NEUTRAL VALUATION RELATIONSHIP

Examples 5.7 and 5.8 suggest that if we somehow knew that a call option could be replicated by a portfolio containing the underlying stock and riskless assets (bonds) alone, then the value of the call option in a risk-averse economy could be obtained by pretending the economy was risk neutral and valuing the call as the future expected value (in this economy) discounted at the riskless rate.

Without restricting preferences of investors in the economy, this valuation methodology can be used only if such a replication exists. It is referred to as a *risk-neutral valuation relationship* (RNVR).

Example 5.9

Assume the following information,

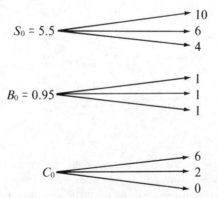

and

Since no portfolio of stock and bonds can be constructed to replicate the call option, the RNVR cannot be used to obtain an unambiguous call price.

OPTION PRICING IN INCOMPLETE MARKETS

Options can be unambiguously priced only by using arbitrage arguments and constructing a replicating portfolio. In this case, however, since the option can be replicated, it does not add to market completeness. Since it can be argued that the real economic role of options can be achieved only in incomplete markets, it is important to be able to value options in such markets.

Unfortunately, since in this case not all state securities can be valued and no replicating portfolio can be constructed, preference-free prices cannot be obtained. However, bounds on the option price can be established. In fact, in Chapter 4 we obtained bounds on option prices by assuming the law of one price, together with the fact that investors preferred more to less. In order to obtain tighter bounds on prices, one must make more assumptions. These include assumptions on prices and/or on preferences.

In an incomplete market, the value of the call, stock, and pure discount bond can be written as before, except now the values of the pure securities are not known. Hence, we have the following:

$$C_0 = \sum_{j=1}^{n} C_j e_j$$

$$S_0 = \sum_{j=1}^{n} V_j e_j$$

$$B_0 = \sum_{j=1}^{n} e_j.$$

If we assume the stock price, S_0, and the bond price, B_0, are observable, then the maximum and minimum prices for the call can be obtained by solving the following linear programming problems, where the pure security prices are the decision variables.

Maximize (or minimize) $C = \sum_{j=1}^{n} C_j e_j$
    $\{d_j\}$

subject to $\sum_{j=1}^{n} V_j e_j = S_0$ (5.11)

$$\sum_{j=1}^{n} e_j = B_0$$

$$e_j \geq 0.$$

These linear programming problems have a special property that allows the optimal solutions to be written down by inspection. Specifically, it can be shown that the optimal solution to the minimization problem is given by the following:

$$C_{min} = \text{Max}(0, S_0 - XB_0),$$ (5.12)

which is the same as equation (4.5).

The optimal solution to the maximization problem is

$$C_{max} = \frac{S_0 - XS_0}{V_n}.$$ (5.13)

Recall that V_n is the maximum stock price. In the worst case, equation (5.13) implies that the call price must be less than the stock price. However, if an upper bound can be placed on the stock price, the upper bound will be reduced.

By adding more restrictions to the linear programming problem, one can obtain tighter bounds. For example, in a risk-averse economy (where the state discount factors are set such that they decrease as aggregate wealth increases), tighter bounds on option prices can be obtained under suitable restrictions. Specifically, if it is assumed that the *ex ante* probabilities of the future states are provided ($\pi_1, \pi_2, \ldots \pi_n$), and if the payouts of the underlying security increase as aggregate wealth increases, then substituting $e_j = \pi_j d_j$ into the above linear program and adding the constraint that discount factors decrease as aggregate wealth increases, we obtain the following:

Maximize (or minimize)
$\{d_j\}$

$$C = \sum_{j=1}^{n} C_j \pi_j d_j$$

subject to

$$\sum_{i=1}^{n} V_j \pi_j d_j = S_0 \qquad (5.14)$$

$$\sum_{i=1}^{n} \pi_j d_j = B_0$$

$$d_1 \geq d_2 \geq d_3, \ldots \geq d_n \geq 0.$$

The solution to these optimization problems yields bounds tighter than those derived in Chapter 4. Details of these linear programming bounds and other methods for bounding option prices in incomplete markets are beyond the scope of this book. (The interested reader should refer to Perrakis and Ryan; Ritchken; and Levy, in the References at the end of this chapter.) The point to be gained here, however, is the fact that, by placing tighter assumptions on preferences or by making assumptions on the probability distribution of the underlying securities, tighter bounds on option prices can be derived.

CONCLUSION

In order to obtain an exact option price using arbitrage arguments alone, it is necessary to assume that a portfolio can be constructed that replicates the payouts of the option. In this case the option is redundant and, by the law of one price, it must be valued in exactly the same way as the replicating portfolio. An interesting observation is that if the payouts of a call can be replicated by a portfolio of stock and bonds, the option can be priced using a risk-neutral valuation argument. Risk-neutral valuation arguments can always be used if it can first be shown that the price of the security to be valued does not depend on preferences.

If options are priced by arbitrage arguments alone, they do not add to market completeness. In this case, the economic role of options is brought into question. If we assume that options offer new opportunities by creating patterns of payouts that were not previously attainable, then we are assuming that options move incomplete markets closer toward complete markets. In this case, no replicating portfolios can be constructed and no preference-free option price established. However, the bounds of Chapter 4 can be improved by placing tighter assumptions on the preferences of the investors in the economy.

In incomplete markets, options play an important economic role. However, Ross's theorem has illustrated that the creation of options on individual securities may not be an efficient method of moving markets toward completeness. In fact, rather than creating an abundance of such contracts, it may suffice to introduce options on a single fund. Ross's theorem provides firm theoretical foundations for the need to introduce option contracts on portfolios or on broadly based indexes. Such concepts are discussed in Chapter 7.

References

For a discussion on the role of options in moving incomplete markets toward complete markets, the papers by Ross, John, and Arditti and John are relevant. Both Banz and Miller and Breeden and Litzenberger provide applications of this theory. For discussions on valuation of options in discrete time, the papers by Brennan and Rubinstein are relevant. The risk-neutral valuation relationship is discussed by Cox and Ross and is discussed in discrete time by Brennan. Establishing bounds in discrete time by restricting investor preferences is also discussed by Perrakis and Ryan, by Ritchken, and by Levy. The Cox and Rubinstein textbook includes a chapter on innovations in option markets. The original specification of pure securities is provided by Debreu and by Arrow.

Arditti, F., and K. John. "Spanning the State Space with Options." *Journal of Financial and Quantitative Analysis* 15(March 1980): 1–9.

Arrow, K. "The Role of Securities in the Optimal Allocation of Risk Bearing." *Review of Economic Studies* (1964): 91–96.

Banz, R., and M. Miller. "Prices for State Contingent Claims: Some Estimates and Applications." *Journal of Business* 51(October 1978): 653–72.

Breeden, D., and R. Litzenberger. "Prices of State-Contingent Claims Implicit in Option Prices." *Journal of Business* 51(October 1978): 621–51.

Brennan, M. "The Pricing of Contingent Claims in Discrete Time Models." *Journal of Finance* 34(March 1979): 53–68.

Cox, J., and S. Ross. "The Valuation of Options for Alternative Stochastic Processes." *Journal of Financial Economics* 3(January–March 1976): 145–66.

Cox, J., and M. Rubinstein. *Option Markets*. Englewood Cliffs, N.J.: Prentice-Hall, 1985.

Debreu, G. *The Theory of Value*. New York: John Wiley, 1959.

John, K. "Efficient Funds in Financial Markets with Options: A New Irrelevance Proposition." *Journal of Finance* 37(June 1981): 685–95.

John, K. "Market Resolution and Valuation in Incomplete Markets." *Journal of Financial and Quantitative Analysis* 19(March 1984): 29–44.

Levy, H. "Upper and Lower Bounds of Put and Call Option Value: Stochastic Dominance Approach." *Journal of Finance* 40(4)(September 1985): 1197–1217.

Perrakis, S., and P. Ryan. "Option Pricing Bounds in Discrete Time." *Journal of Finance* 39(June 1984): 519–25.

Ritchken, P. "On Option Pricing Bounds." *Journal of Finance* 40(4)(September 1985): 1218–29.

Ross, S. "Options and Efficiency." *Quarterly Journal of Economics* 90(February 1976): 75–89.

Rubinstein, M. "The Valuation of Uncertain Income Streams and the Pricing of Options." *Bell Journal of Economics* 7(Autumn 1976): 407–24.

Exercises

1. Consider a single-period, three-state economy. The prices of the pure securities are as follows:

$$e_1 = 0.4, \; e_2 = 0.3, \; e_3 = 0.2.$$

   a. What is the single-period discount rate?
   b. Value a stock that is worth $5 in states 1 and 2 and $4 in state 3.

2. Consider a single-period, two-state economy in which a pure discount bond trades at $0.95 and a stock paying out $2 in state 1 and $5 in state 2 currently trades at $3.

   a. What is the value of the pure state securities?
   b. What is the value of a security that pays $6 in state 1 and $9 in state 2?
   c. Is the value of a security that pays out ten times as much in each state as the security in (b), worth ten times as much? Explain.
   d. What is the value of an option on the security in (b), given that the strike price is $7?
   e. What is the value of an option on the security in (c), given that the strike price is $70?

3. Construct an example of three securities that complete a three-state, single-period market. Your example should not include any pure state securities.

   a. Using your example, price the three-state securities. Make sure you identify the replicating portfolios.
   b. What is the risk-free rate in this economy?

4. Trading call options with different strike prices on a single security does not guarantee market completeness. Consider a security that yields the following payouts:

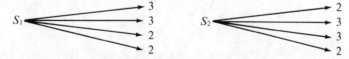

   Show that the addition of call options with strike prices 2 and 3 will not complete the market.

5. Consider the following four-state, two-security economy:

$$S_1 \begin{array}{l} \nearrow \; 3 \\ \rightarrow \; 3 \\ \rightarrow \; 2 \\ \searrow \; 2 \end{array} \qquad S_2 \begin{array}{l} \nearrow \; 2 \\ \rightarrow \; 3 \\ \rightarrow \; 3 \\ \searrow \; 2 \end{array}$$

   Consider introducing call options and put options with strikes 2 and 3 on both securities. Let $C_{ij}(P_{ij})$ represent a call option (put) option on stock $i(i = 1,2)$, with strike $j(j = 2,3)$. Then,

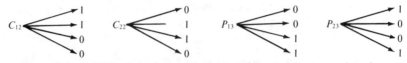

a. Show that the collection of securities and options does not complete the market.

b. Consider a portfolio of one share of security 1 and two shares of security 2. Show that call options with strike price 6 and 7 on this portfolio, together with the two securities, will complete the market.

c. Does Ross's theorem explain the results in (a) and (b)? Explain.

6. Using the data in Example 5.6, value a put option with strike 6.

7. a. Use the risk-neutral valuation relationship to value a call option with strike 70, given the data below.

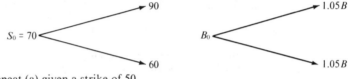

b. Repeat (a) given a strike of 50.

c. Repeat (a) for a put option.

8. a. Construct a replicating portfolio consisting of shares and bonds for the call option in 7(a).

b. Repeat for the put option.

9. Compute the price of the call option in 7(a) if interest rates were 7 percent, not 5 percent. What can you say about the behavior of option prices to interest rates? Try to justify your answer with an economic interpretation.

10. An option on a portfolio is not equivalent to a portfolio of options. Discuss the differences.

11. "In a complete market, options are redundant and, hence, worthless."
"In a complete market, options are redundant and their introduction does not create new possibilities."
"In a complete market, options are redundant, but nonetheless create payouts that were not easily constructed before. As such, options serve a beneficial role."
Discuss these three statements. Which, if any, is (are) true?

12. a. Using the data in Example 5.5, establish the value of a put option. What does the replicating portfolio consist of? Show that the put-call parity equation holds true.

b. If the call option traded at 10.9 and the put was "correctly" priced, what portfolio would you hold to obtain riskless arbitrage profits?

Appendix

Valuation of Securities in a Mean-Variance Complete Market

The capital asset pricing model provides the equilibrium relationship for securities in the market. Specifically, it is well known that the expected return of a security, $E(\tilde{R}_s)$, can be expressed as follows:

$$E(\tilde{R}_S) = R_F + \beta[E(\tilde{R}_m) - R_F]$$

where $\quad \beta = \text{Cov}(\tilde{R}_s, \tilde{R}_m)/\text{Var}(\tilde{R}_m)$

$\quad R_F = 1 + $ risk-free rate

$\quad \tilde{R}_s = $ return on security, s (in price relative form).

That is, $\tilde{R}_s = \tilde{S}_T/S_0$ where $\tilde{S}_T(S_0)$ is the end of period (current) price, and $\tilde{R}_m = \tilde{M}_T/M_0$ where $\tilde{M}_T(M_0)$ is the final (current) market price.

Equivalently, we have

$$E(\tilde{R}_s) = R_F + \text{Cov}(\tilde{R}_s, \tilde{R}_m)\lambda'$$

where $\lambda' = [E(\tilde{R}_m) - R_F]/\text{Var}(\tilde{R}_m)$ is the market price of risk.

Now

$$E(\tilde{R}_s) = E\left(\frac{\tilde{S}_T}{S_0}\right) = \frac{E(\tilde{S}_T)}{S_0}$$

$$E(\tilde{R}_m) = E\left(\frac{\tilde{M}_T}{M_0}\right) = \frac{E(\tilde{M}_T)}{M_0}$$

and

$$\text{Cov}(\tilde{R}_s, \tilde{R}_m) = \text{Cov}\left(\frac{\tilde{S}_T}{S_0}, \frac{\tilde{M}_T}{M_0}\right)$$

$$= \frac{\text{Cov}(\tilde{S}_T, \tilde{M}_T)}{M_0 S_0}.$$

Substituting these expressions into the capital asset pricing model and solving for S_0, we obtain

$$S_0 = \frac{[E(\tilde{S}_T) - \lambda \mathrm{Cov}(\tilde{S}_T, \tilde{M}_T)]}{R_F}$$

where $\lambda = \lambda'/M_0$.

6

Distribution of
Stock and Portfolio Returns

In this chapter we shall investigate the statistical process that drives the prices of securities. After characterizing this process, we can establish specific option pricing models. This will be accomplished in Chapters 8 and 9. This chapter also investigates the return distributions of portfolios. The returns on different securities tend to be positively correlated. Through diversification, total portfolio risk can be reduced without sacrifices being made in expected return. We shall review the single-index model and illustrate how total risk can be unbundled into market- and nonmarket-related components. Diversification and hedging strategies using options are important techniques in portfolio risk management. Hedging portfolios against general market downturns or specific industry-related risk, or against certain economic phenomena, will be discussed in the next chapter.

EFFICIENT MARKETS

The stock market provides an arena in which participants with similar investment goals and with access to the same information actively search for mispriced securities. The keen competition among the participants ensures that new information regarding securities is rapidly absorbed and reflected in prices. If security prices do fully reflect all available information, the market is said to be *efficient*. If the market were not efficient, then some information might not be rapidly used in the setting of prices. In this case, an astute investor might be able to use particular information to identify predictable cycles in stock prices. Based on these cycles, trading strategies yielding abnormal rates of return could be derived. Unfortunately, as soon as these strategies became apparent to investors, the information would soon be more efficiently used and abnormal profits would soon be eliminated.

In an efficient market, the process of determining prices is said to be a *fair game*. A fair game describes a process in which there is no way to use currently available information to earn a return above normal. This does not imply that returns are independent through time. For example, consider a company that increases its debt and risk over successive periods of time. Since the expected returns will tend to increase over time, to compensate for the increased risk the actual observed returns should also tend to increase. In this case, one might observe a correlation in the sequence of historical returns. However, in an efficient market this information could not be used to earn abnormal excess returns.

There are three forms of market efficiency. *Weak form efficiency* describes a market in which historical prices are efficiently impounded into the current price by market participants. *Semistrong efficiency* describes a market in which all publicly available information is efficiently digested by the participants. Finally, *strong form efficiency* describes a market in which not even those participants with privileged information can obtain above-fair-market returns.

Tests of weak form efficiency involve establishing whether or not the past price or past sequence of returns can be used to predict future returns in such a way as to generate abnormal returns. Most of the early tests were tests of the *random walk model*, a restrictive version of the fair game model. According to this model, successive returns are statistically independent and identically distributed. The independence assumption implies that historical returns cannot provide useful information on future returns. Since these returns are identically distributed, the expected return and variance of the returns are assumed to remain unchanged over time.

Researchers have conducted statistical autocorrelation and run tests to examine whether stock price returns are independent. Empirical tests for daily, weekly, and monthly stock price changes have provided support for this phenomenon.

THE DISTRIBUTION OF STOCK RETURNS

Let $\{S_t\}$ be a sequence of prices of a particular stock that are collected over periods of time (for example, daily). For simplicity, we shall assume the stock pays no dividends. Let z_t represent the price relative over the tth time period, and let R_t represent the total price relative over the t periods. Then,

$$z_t = \frac{S_t}{S_{t-1}} \tag{6.1}$$

and

$$R_t = \frac{S_t}{S_0}. \tag{6.2}$$

Moreover,

$$R_t = z_1 z_2 z_3 \ldots z_t = \prod_{i=1}^{t} z_i \tag{6.3}$$

The logarithmic return, r_t, is given by the following:

$$r_t = \sum_{i=1}^{t} ln\ z_i \qquad (6.4)$$

The logarithmic return is often referred to as the *continuously compounded return*. This return over t periods is just the sum of the continuously compounded returns in each period. If the successive logarithmic returns follow a random walk, then the logarithmic return over the t periods should, by the central limit theorem, be normally distributed.

Example 6.1

Assume each time increment corresponds to a day, and let R_t be the total price relative over a month (t days). If the daily logarithmic returns are independent and identically distributed random variables with mean μ and variance σ^2, then from equation 6.4 the logarithmic return r_t should, by the central limit theorem, be approximately normally distributed with mean μt and variance $\sigma^2 t$.

The shape of the statistical distribution of the price relative R_t, implied by the fact that its natural logarithm has a normal distribution, is shown in Exhibit 6.1.

EXHIBIT 6.1
The Lognormal Distribution

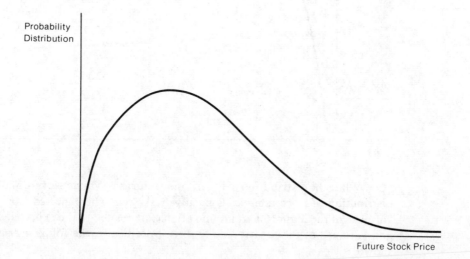

This statistical distribution is called the *lognormal distribution*. A random variable has a lognormal distribution whenever its logarithm has a normal distribution. Note that, unlike the normal random variable, which can take on any value, positive or negative, the lognormal random variable can take on only nonnegative values. To see this more clearly, recall the logarithmic transformation. From Exhibit 6.2 it can be seen that, associated with any value of r is a unique nonnegative value of R.

EXHIBIT 6.2
The Logarithmic Function

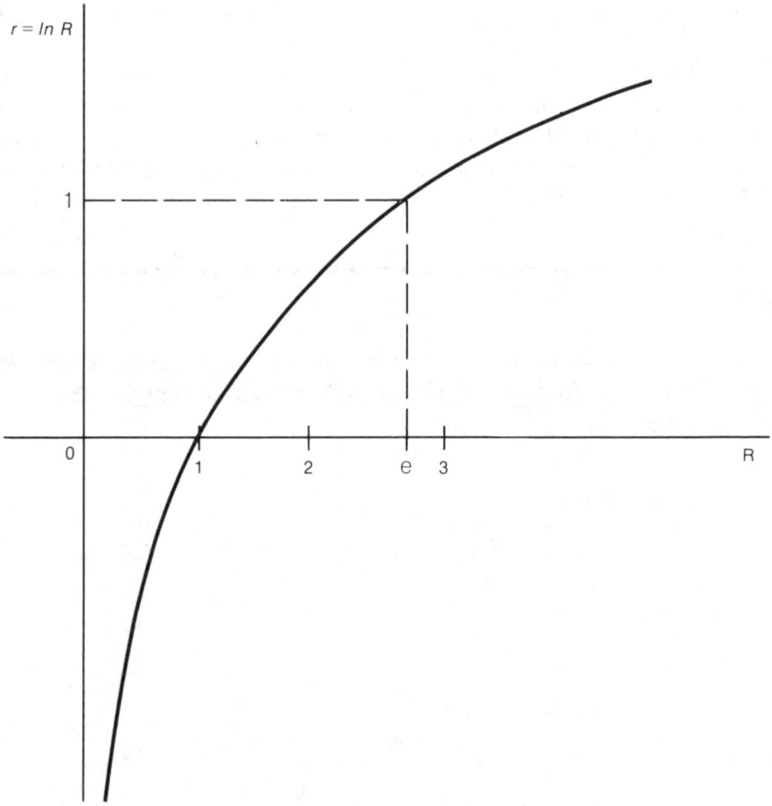

While the distribution of logarithmic returns is symmetric (normal), the distribution of price relatives is positively skewed. The expected value and variance of the lognormal random variable are related to the expected value and variance of the logarithmic returns. Specifically, the following can be shown:

$$E(R_t) = \exp\left(\mu t + \frac{\sigma^2 t}{2}\right)$$ (6.5)

and

$$\text{Var}(R_t) = E(R_t)^2[\exp(\sigma^2 t) - 1].$$ (6.6)

Example 6.2

Exhibit 6.3 shows daily closing prices of a nondividend-paying stock over a period of 10 consecutive days. The nine logarithmic returns are computed by $r_t = ln(S_t/S_{t-1})$. Assuming the daily logarithmic returns are independent and come from the same statistical distribution, then the daily logarithmic mean and variance can be estimated by the following:

$$\hat{\mu} = \sum_{i=1}^{9} \frac{r_i}{9} = 0.0112$$

$$\hat{\sigma}^2 = \sum_{i=1}^{9} \frac{(r_i - \hat{\mu})^2}{8} = 0.001987$$

and

$$\hat{\sigma} = 0.0445.$$

EXHIBIT 6.3
Computation of Logarithmic Price Relatives

Day	Price	Price Relative	Logarithmic Price Relative
1	$30.00	—	
2	31.00	1.033	0.0328
3	31.50	1.016	0.0159
4	30.00	0.952	-0.0492
5	32.00	1.066	0.0645
6	34.00	1.062	0.0606
7	32.00	0.941	-0.0606
8	32.50	1.015	0.0155
9	32.50	1.000	0.0000
10	31.25	0.9615	-0.0392

The estimate $\hat{\sigma}$ is referred to as the estimate of the daily logarithmic volatility.

From equations (6.5) and (6.6), estimates of the expected value and variance of the price relative over the next 30 days can be computed:

$$\hat{E}(R_t) = \exp\left(\hat{\mu}t + \frac{\hat{\sigma}t}{2}\right) = 1.44$$

$$\hat{\text{Var}}(R_t) = \hat{E}(R_t)^2[\exp(\hat{\sigma}^2 t) - 1] = 0.1276$$

and the standard deviation of the 30-day price relative is 0.357.

In Example 6.2 we assumed the price relatives were computed daily. Clearly, the time increments over which these price relatives are computed could be made smaller (e.g., every hour, minute, or even second). As long as the price relatives are independent and identically distributed random variables, the central limit theorem can be invoked to conclude that logarithmic returns over the period, such as a month, should be normal.

Mandelbrot argued that finite-period logarithmic returns would diverge from the normal distribution in two ways. First, because a higher percentage of stock price changes caused by the arrival of new information into the market would have little effect on prices, an excessive number of observations would cluster around the middle of the distribution. Second, because a small, but nonetheless significant, percentage of news announcements would result in significant changes in price, a larger number of observations would occur in the tail. Using daily data, Fama provided empirical support for Mandelbrot's hypothesis. However, for weekly data the normality assumption appeared to be reasonably well approximated.

In light of this evidence, the normal distribution for logarithmic returns, or the lognormal distribution for price relatives, has become the prototypical model used in analytical studies in the stock and options market.

THE WIENER PROCESS AND THE GEOMETRIC WIENER PROCESS

In many instances it may be necessary to specify how stock prices are generated through time, rather than merely to know their distribution after a given time interval. In the last section, for example, we did not need to know the distribution of daily price relatives. As long as these price relatives were independent and identically distributed, the central limit theorem suggested that the logarithmic return over the monthly interval would be normal.

If logarithmic returns over nonoverlapping intervals of any arbitrary but equal lengths constituted independent and identically distributed *normal* random variables having means and variances proportional to the length of the time increment, then the statistical process that generates the returns is referred to as a *Wiener process*.

Representation of a Wiener Process*

Specifically, if logarithmic returns follow a Wiener process over any arbitrary time interval, Δt, the logarithmic return $r_{\Delta t}$ has a normal distribution with mean $\mu\Delta t$ and variance $\sigma^2\Delta t$. μ and σ^2 are referred to as the *instantaneous mean* and the *variance of the logarithmic return*. The mean and variance of these logarithmic returns increase linearly with the time interval Δt.

Let $\tilde{z} = (\tilde{r}_{\Delta t} - \mu\Delta t)/\sigma\sqrt{\Delta t}$, or

$$\tilde{r}_{\Delta t} = \mu\Delta t + \sigma\sqrt{\Delta t}\,\tilde{z} \tag{6.7}$$

Since

$$\tilde{r}_{t+\Delta t} = \ln\left(\frac{\tilde{S}_{t+\Delta t}}{S_t}\right)$$

we have

$$\ln\left(\frac{\tilde{S}_{t+\Delta t}}{S_t}\right) = \mu\Delta t + \sigma\sqrt{\Delta t}\,\tilde{z}. \tag{6.8}$$

Taking exponentials of both sides, we obtain the following:

$$\tilde{S}_{t+\Delta t} = S_t \exp(\mu\Delta t + \sigma\sqrt{\Delta t}\,\tilde{z}). \tag{6.9}$$

That is, the stock price at time $(t + \Delta t)$ equals the stock price at time t multiplied by a lognormal random variable.

As the time interval Δt becomes small, equation (6.9) can be shown to reduce to the following*:

$$\frac{(S_{t+\Delta t} - S_t)}{S_t} = \left(\mu + \frac{\sigma^2}{2}\right)\Delta t + \sigma\sqrt{\Delta t}\,\tilde{z}. \tag{6.10}$$

If $\Delta S_t = S_{t+\Delta t} - S_t$, $m = \mu + \sigma^2/2$, and if Δw represents a normal random variable with mean zero and variance Δt, then equation (6.10) can be rewritten as follows:

$$\frac{\Delta S_t}{S_t} = m\Delta t + \sigma\Delta w. \tag{6.11}$$

In the limit as Δt tends to dt, Δw tends to dw and equation (6.11) can be written as

$$\frac{dS_t}{S_t} = m\,dt + \sigma\,dw \tag{6.12}$$

or

$$dS_t = mS_t\,dt + \sigma S_t\,dw. \tag{6.13}$$

Equation (6.12) says that the total returns for this process over the period dt is made up of a certain term, $m\,dt$, called the *drift component*, together with a stochastic (random) component $\sigma\,dw$.

If stock prices behave over time as above, the statistical process is said to follow a *geometric Wiener process*.

---

*Further details of this will be provided in Chapter 16.

Example 6.4

Stock XYZ is currently priced at $30. Its logarithmic returns follow a Wiener process with mean 0.02 and variance 0.03 per year.

The expected stock price after 0.25 years is given by

$$E(S_T) = S_0 \exp\left(\mu T + \frac{\sigma^2 T}{2}\right) = 30\exp(0.0214 + 0.0318) = 30.26.$$

The variance of the stock price at this time is

$$\text{Var}(S_T) = [E(S_T)]^2 [\exp(\sigma^2 T) - 1] = 6.893.$$

The probability that, at this point in time, the price exceeds some value, such as $35, can be computed. Specifically,

$$P(S_T > 35) = P\left(R_T > \frac{35}{30}\right) = P\left[r_T > \ln\left(\frac{35}{30}\right)\right]$$

$$= P(r_T > 0.154)$$

$$= P\left[\tilde{Z}_T > \frac{(0.154 - \mu T)}{\sigma\sqrt{T}}\right]$$

$$= P(\tilde{Z}_T > 1.72).$$

Upon using normal tables, we find this probability to be 0.043. Hence,

$$P(S_T > 35) = 0.043.$$

Ito Processes*

Geometric Wiener processes belong to a class of processes called *Ito processes*. An Ito process can be represented as follows:

$$dS_t = m(S_t, t)S_t dt + \sigma(S_t, t)dw. \tag{6.14}$$

For Ito processes, the change in stock price over small intervals of time, dt, depends at most on the current stock price and time. That is, the mean $m(S_t, t)$, and the volatility, $\sigma(S_t, t)$, need not be constant, but can depend on the stock price and time. Note that if the mean, $m(S_t, t)$, is a constant, m, and the volatility, $\sigma(S_t, t)$, is a constant, σ, then the Ito process reduces to the geometric Wiener process.

As an example of how a structure for $m(S_t, t)$ and $\sigma(S_t, t)$ can be established, we shall consider the Constant Elasticity of Variance model (CEV). This model was developed because of a limitation of the geometric Wiener process. Specifically, the latter process requires the variance of logarithmic price relatives in nonoverlapping time increments to be independent of the stock price. Empirical evidence, however, suggests that as the stock price increases, the variance of returns declines. The CEV model requires the standard deviation of returns to be related to the stock price as follows:

$$\sigma(S_t,t) = \sigma S_t^{a-1} \text{ with } 0 < a < 1. \tag{6.15}$$

Since $0 < a < 1$, the standard deviation of returns decreases as the stock price increases. The model gets its name because the elasticity of variance, with respect to the stock price, is constant. To see this, note that from (6.15), we have

$$\sigma^2(S_t) = \sigma^2 S_t^{2a-2}, \tag{6.16}$$

and the derivative, with respect to S_t, is

$$\frac{\partial \sigma^2(S_t)}{\partial S_t} = \sigma^2(2a - 2)S_t^{2a-3}. \tag{6.17}$$

The elasticity, e, is simply the percentage change in variance per percentage change in stock price. Hence,

$$e = \frac{\partial \sigma^2(S_t)}{\partial S_t} \cdot \frac{S_t}{\sigma^2(S_t)}. \tag{6.18}$$

Substituting (6.16) and (6.17) into (6.18) and simplifying, we obtain the following:

$$e = 2a - 2. \tag{6.19}$$

Note that if $a = 1$, there is no relationship between standard deviation and stock price. For $a = 1/2$ the model is referred to as the *square root model*, while for $a = 0$ the process is referred to as the *absolute process*.

The formal representation of the CEV model is

$$\frac{dS}{S} = m(S,t)dt + \sigma S^{a-1}dw \tag{6.20}$$

Equation (6.20) says the percentage change in stock price over a small interval, dt, is made up of a trend term that depends on the stock price and time and a normally distributed stochastic term. This component has variance $\sigma^2 s^{2a-2}dt$, which depends on the level of the stock.

Jump Processes*

In the continuous processes discussed so far, past stock prices, if continuously observed, can be graphed without lifting pencil from paper. Such continuous processes are said to generate continuous sample paths and are referred to as *diffusion processes*. The Wiener process, for example, generates continuous sample paths that are not differentiable. This implies that the stock price is in constant vibration, and no matter how small the time increment, it will not remain unchanged. An alternative approach to modeling continuous time processes is to assume that the process is characterized by a constant drift, except at random times, when it undergoes a sudden jump, the size of which could also be random. For example, we may hypothesize that stock prices remain unchanged until new information about a company reaches the marketplace. When this occurs, the price jumps to a new value.

The size of the jump, of course, depends on the content of the new information.

Ito processes, and in particular the geometric Wiener process, will be used in future chapters to characterize the behavior of stock prices over time.

DISTRIBUTION OF PORTFOLIO RETURNS

Observations of stock prices reveal that when the market goes up (as measured by a broad-based index), most stocks tend to appreciate. This suggests that stock prices are positively correlated with each other. In this section, we shall consider the behavior of finite period returns of portfolios. Toward this goal, let X_i be the fraction of funds invested in the ith asset, and let r_i be the return on the ith asset over a finite period. The return on the portfolio, r_p, is as follows:

$$r_p = \sum_{i=1}^{n} X_i r_i \tag{6.21}$$

where n is the number of different securities.

The actual distribution of the logarithmic return on the portfolio is dependent on the distribution of the individual security returns and on the degree of dependence among the returns of different securities. If the security returns are normal, then the portfolio returns will be normal, too. The expected return is the weighted average of individual expected returns,

$$E(r_p) = \sum_{i=1}^{n} X_i E(r_i) \tag{6.22}$$

and the variance is given by the following:

$$\text{Var}(r_p) = \sum_{i=1}^{n} X_i^2 \text{Var}(r_i) + \sum_{i=1}^{n} \sum_{\substack{j=1 \\ i \neq j}}^{n} X_i X_j \text{Cov}(r_i, r_j). \tag{6.23}$$

The effect of the covariance terms on the variance of portfolio returns is considerable. In fact, for large, well-diversified portfolios, the contribution of the covariances to the total variance is the dominant factor.

The Role of Diversification

In order to see the important contribution of the covariance terms, consider a portfolio with equal investments in all n assets. In this case $X_i = 1/n$ and equation (6.23) reduces to

$$\text{Var}(r_p) = \sum_{i} \frac{\text{Var}(r_i)}{n^2} + \sum_{i \neq j} \sum \frac{\text{Cov}(r_i, r_j)}{n^2}$$

$$= \frac{1}{n} \sum_{i} \frac{\text{Var}(r_i)}{n} + (n-1) \sum_{i \neq j} \sum \frac{\text{Cov}(r_i, r_j)}{(n-1)n} . \tag{6.24}$$

Let $\overline{V}$ be the average variance of return of all securities, and let $\overline{C}$ be the average covariance of return among all securities. Then

$$\overline{V} = \sum_{i=1}^{n} \frac{\text{Var}(r_i)}{n} \tag{6.25}$$

and

$$\overline{C} = \sum_{i \neq j} \sum \frac{\text{Cov}(r_i, r_j)}{n(n-1)}. \tag{6.26}$$

Hence,

$$\text{Var}(r_p) = \frac{\overline{V}}{n} + \frac{(n-1)\overline{C}}{n}. \tag{6.27}$$

Now in the limit as the number of securities tends to infinity, the first term tends to zero, while the second term tends to the average covariance, $\overline{C}$. Hence, $\text{Var}(r_p)$ tends to the average covariance, $\overline{C}$.

Since securities tend to react to economic factors by moving in a common direction, the average covariance is positive. This average covariance represents variance that cannot be eliminated through diversification. Exhibit 6.4 illustrates the size of total portfolio variance as the number of securities increase.

EXHIBIT 6.4
Risk Reduction Through Diversification

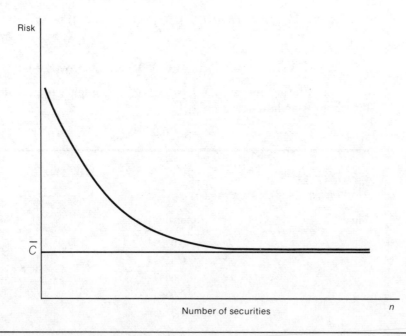

Example 6.5

The monthly rates of return for Company 1 and Company 2 are shown in Exhibit 6.5. Estimates of the expected return, variance, and covariance are as follows:

$$\bar{r}_i = \sum_{t=1}^{n} r_{it} \qquad\qquad i = 1,2 \qquad\qquad (6.28)$$

$$s_i^2 = \sum_{t=1}^{n} \frac{(r_{it} - \bar{r}_i)^2}{(n-1)} \qquad\qquad i = 1,2 \qquad\qquad (6.29)$$

and

$$s_{ij}^2 = \sum_{t=1}^{n} \frac{(r_{it} - \bar{r}_i)(r_{jt} - \bar{r}_j)}{(n-1)} \qquad\qquad (6.30)$$

where r_{it} is the return on security i in time period t.

Using equations (6.28), (6.29), and (6.30), we obtain the following:

$\bar{r}_1 = 0.0108$, $\bar{r}_2 = 0.098$, $s_1 = 0.0164$, $s_2 = 0.0342$, and $s_{12} = -0.00032$.

A portfolio with equal wealth allocated to each security has expected return and variance given by equations (6.22) and (6.23). Specifically, for this example we obtain

$$r_p = 0.5r_1 + 0.5r_2.$$

Hence,

$$\bar{r}_p = 0.5 \, (0.0108) + 0.5 \, 9(0.098) = 0.0544$$

and

$$\mathrm{Var}(r_p) = (0.5)^2 \mathrm{Var}(r_1) + (0.5)^2 \mathrm{Var}(r_2) + \mathrm{Cov}(r_1, r_2).$$

Substituting our estimates, we obtain the sample variance and, hence, the sample standard deviation, s_p:

$$s_p = 0.0064.$$

EXHIBIT 6.5
Monthly Rates

Time	Company 1	Company 2
1	0.03	0.05
2	0.025	0.09
3	0.005	0.12
4	0.004	0.14
5	−0.01	0.09

THE SINGLE-INDEX MODEL

The single-index model recognizes the simple fact that security returns tend to increase when the market increases and tend to decrease during market declines. The model, in fact, assumes that the only reason stock prices vary together is because of this common comovement with the market.

The return on a stock can be written as

$$\tilde{r}_i = \tilde{A}_i + \beta_i \tilde{r}_m$$

where $\tilde{A}_i$ is a random variable reflecting the component of security i's return that does not depend on the performance of the market, β_i is a constant reflecting the expected change in r_i per unit change in r_m, and $\tilde{r}_m$ is the return on a broad-based market index.

The variable $\tilde{A}_i$ reflects company-specific issues. The term can be represented by its expected value, α_i, together with a random deviation or error term, $\tilde{\epsilon}_i$, which has an expected value of zero, and variance σ_{ni}^2:

$$\tilde{A}_i = \alpha_i + \epsilon_i.$$

Hence, the index model can be rewritten

$$\tilde{r}_i = \alpha_i + \beta_i \tilde{r}_m + \epsilon_i. \tag{6.31}$$

Since the expected error term is zero, the future expected return on security i is linearly related to the expected return on the market index:

$$E(\tilde{r}_i) = \alpha_i + \beta_i \, E(\tilde{r}_m). \tag{6.32}$$

The slope β_i reflects the sensitivity of security i's expected return to the market index return.

MARKET RISK AND COMPANY-SPECIFIC RISK

The index model assumes that the error term is uncorrelated with market return. Together with (6.31), this assumption allows the variance of security i's returns to be expressed as follows:

$$\mathrm{Var}(\tilde{r}_i) = \beta_i^2 \, \mathrm{Var}(\tilde{r}_m) + \mathrm{Var}(\tilde{\epsilon}_i)$$

$$= \beta_i^2 \sigma_m^2 + \sigma_{ni}^2. \tag{6.33}$$

The equation says that the total variance of security i's return can be decomposed into two parts. The first term, $\beta_i^2 \sigma_m^2$, is market-related risk. The second term, σ_{ni}^2, is company-specific, or nonmarket, risk.

The final assumption for the index model concerns the error terms across different securities. It is assumed that these error terms are uncorrelated with each other and with the returns on the market. This assumption implies that the covariance of returns between securities i and j, σ_{ij} can be expressed by the following:

$$\sigma_{ij} = \text{Cov}(\alpha_i + \beta_i\tilde{r}_m + \tilde{\epsilon}_i, \alpha_j + \beta_j\tilde{r}_m + \tilde{\epsilon}_j)$$

$$= \text{Cov}(\beta_i\tilde{r}_m, \beta_j r_m)$$

$$\sigma_{ij} = \beta_i\beta_j\sigma_m^2. \tag{6.34}$$

Expected Returns and Variances of Portfolios

The single-index model can be used to simplify the expressions for the expected return and variance of a portfolio.

$$\tilde{r}_p = \sum_{i=1}^{n} X_i\tilde{r}_i = \sum_{i=1}^{n} X_i(\alpha_i + \beta_i\tilde{r}_m + \tilde{\epsilon}_i)$$

$$= \sum_{i=1}^{n} X_i\alpha_i + \sum_{i=1}^{n} X_i\beta_i\tilde{r}_m + \sum_{i=1}^{n} X_i\tilde{\epsilon}_i$$

$$= \alpha_p + \beta_p\tilde{r}_m + \tilde{\epsilon}_p$$

where

$$\alpha_p = \sum_{i=1}^{n} X_i\alpha_i, \quad \beta_p = \sum_{i=1}^{n} X_i\beta_i, \quad \tilde{\epsilon}_p = \sum_{i=1}^{n} X_i\tilde{\epsilon}_i.$$

Then the expectation can be obtained as follows:

$$E(\tilde{r}_p) = E(\alpha_p + \beta_p\tilde{r}_m + \tilde{\epsilon}_p) = \alpha_p + \beta_p E(\tilde{r}_m)$$

since

$$E(\tilde{\epsilon}_p) = \sum_{i=1}^{n} X_i E(\tilde{\epsilon}_i) = 0.$$

Also, the variance can be obtained as follows:

$$\text{Var}(\tilde{r}_p) = \text{Var}(\alpha_p + \beta_p\tilde{r}_m + \tilde{\epsilon}_p)$$

$$= \text{Var}(\beta_p\tilde{r}_m + \tilde{\epsilon}_p)$$

$$= \beta_p^2\text{Var}(r_m) + \text{Var}(\tilde{\epsilon}_p)$$

$$= \beta_p^2\sigma_m^2 + \sigma_{pn}^2. \tag{6.35}$$

where

$$\sigma_{pn}^2 = \text{Var}\left(\sum_{i=1}^{n} X_i\tilde{\epsilon}_i\right) = \sum_{i=1}^{n} X_i^2\sigma_{ni}^2$$

is the nonmarket-related risk of the portfolio and $\beta_p^2\sigma_m^2$ is the market-related risk.

As the number of different securities in the portfolio increases, the nonmarket term drops to zero. Thus, the primary risk of the well-diversified portfolio is comprised of market-related variance $\beta_p^2\sigma_m^2$.

The Beta Value

The beta value of a security measures the sensitivity of the returns on the security to market movements. Exhibit 6.6 illustrates the returns on a particular security plotted against the returns on a broad-based market index (for example, the Standard and Poor's index).

The slope of the regression line provides an estimate of the sensitivity of the returns on the security with respect to the returns on the market. The regression line is as follows:

$$\hat{r}_j = a_j + b_j r_m$$

where b_j, the slope, is an unbiased estimator of β_j, the true slope. The formula for the slope is the following:

$$\beta_j = \frac{\text{Cov}(\tilde{r}_j, \tilde{r}_m)}{\text{Var}(\tilde{r}_m)}. \tag{6.36}$$

This value is the beta value of the security.

For a particular security j, market-related risk $\beta_j^2 \sigma_m^2$ accounts for only 20–40 percent of total risk. However, for portfolios containing ten or more randomly selected securities, market-related risk $\beta_p^2 \sigma_m^2$ accounts for 80–95 percent of total risk.

EXHIBIT 6.6
Returns on Security and Index

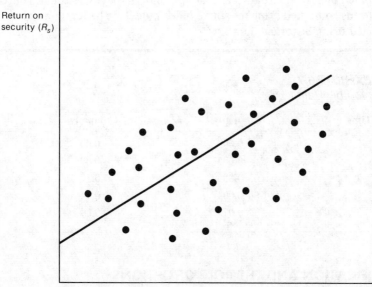

Example 6.6

The monthly rates of return for Company 1 and Company 2 are shown in Exhibit 6.7 together with the returns on a market index, m. The estimate of the beta value, b, is obtained by regressing the returns on each security with the returns on the market. The estimate of the beta value of stock i, given by equation (6.36), is as follows:

$$b_i = \frac{s_{im}}{s_m^2} \qquad (6.37)$$

where s_{im} is the covariance between the returns of stock and the returns of the market.

For the problem, we obtain $b_1 = -0.30$ and $b_2 = 0.786$.

The beta value of the portfolio, p, obtained by placing equal investments in securities 1 and 2, is given by using the following equation:

$$b_p = \sum_{i=1}^{n} X_i b_i \qquad (6.38)$$

where $n = 2$, $X_1 = X_2 = 0.5$. Hence, $b_p = 0.243$.

Note that, under the single index model, the estimate of the covariance between the returns of stocks 1 and 2 is given by equation (6.34). The estimate of this covariance is as follows:

$$s_{12} = b_1 b_2 s_m^2 = -0.000325. \qquad (6.39)$$

Note that this estimate differs from the monthly covariance estimate based on historical data (see Example 6.5). In general, estimates of covariance terms computed using the single-index model are better than estimates generated using historical data.

EXHIBIT 6.7
Monthly Rates

Time	Company 1	Company 2	m
1	0.04	0.05	0.06
2	0.025	0.09	0.06
3	0.005	0.12	0.10
4	0.004	0.14	0.15
5	−0.01	0.09	0.10

DIVERSIFICATION AND THE ROLE OF OPTIONS

Through diversification, portfolio risk can be reduced to levels proportional to the risk inherent in the market as a whole. If an investor is bullish, for example, then a high beta-valued portfolio is appropriate. Unfortunately, since fully diversified portfolios move in tune with the market, managers of such portfolios typically have to contend with this risk. By trading options on selected securities, the manager can obtain profits and losses that are not proportional to the profits and losses inherent in the market. However, while the relationship between an individual stock and its options are well understood, the impact of including several stock option strategies in a portfolio can be difficult to assess.

It thus appears that the simultaneous use of diversification and stock hedging as risk management devices can be extremely difficult. Within the portfolio context, managers may be more interested in hedging against a broad market decline or a specific industry-related risk than in hedging individual securities. For example, a portfolio manager who holds many shares of computer firms may want to hedge against the risk of a general downturn in the high technology area. Other managers may want to hedge against gold prices declining, or against the stock market as a whole depreciating significantly. Some investors may desire a hedge against changing economic phenomena, such as inflation, currency exchange rates, unemployment, or a movement in consumer price indices. In the next chapter we shall investigate how portfolio managers can use index options to hedge against such risks.

CONCLUSION

Characterizing the statistical evolution of stock prices over time is important, for it enables models to be developed for the pricing of options. Indeed, in Chapter 8 specific option-pricing models will be developed under the assumption that stock prices follow a geometric Wiener process.

The second part of the chapter focused on the return patterns of portfolios held over finite periods of time. The total risk of a portfolio can be unbundled into market and nonmarket factors. Through diversification, nonmarket-related risk can be eliminated. However, fully diversified portfolios are still susceptible to market-related risk. When several stock-option positions are put together into a portfolio, their net effects are very difficult to assess because of complex correlations that exist between positions on different securities. At the portfolio level, managers may be more interested in hedging against general market declines or specific industry-related risks than in hedging at the individual security level. In the next chapter we shall investigate how index option contracts can be used to achieve these portfolio goals.

References

The behavior of stock market returns is discussed by Fama (1976), Osborne, Mendelbrot, and others. The lognormal distribution and its properties are discussed by Aitchison and Brown. Discussions of Wiener, Jump, and Ito processes are usually found in probability theory textbooks and require some mathematics knowledge. Parzen and Karlin and Taylor have good discussions on Wiener processes. A more rigorous treatment is provided by Flemming and Rishel. Theory and applications of these processes in economics and finance are provided by Malliaris.

Several textbooks discuss the distribution of portfolio returns and modern portfolio management. In particular, the textbooks of Francis, Sharpe, Levy and Sarnat, and Elton and Gruber all provide a good introduction to the subject with a strong emphasis on the role of diversification.

Aitchison, J., and J. Brown. *The Lognormal Distribution.* Cambridge: Cambridge University Press, 1957.

Blattberg, R., and N. Gonedes. "A Comparison of the Stable and Student Distributions as Statistical Models for Stock Prices." *Journal of Business* (April 1974): 244–80.

Cheng, P., and M. Deets. "Portfolio Returns and the Random Walk Theory." *Journal of Finance* 26(1)(March 1971): 11–30.

Elton, E., and M. Gruber. *Modern Portfolio Theory and Investment Analysis.* 2d ed. New York: John Wiley, 1984.

Fama, E. *Foundations of Finance.* New York: Basic Books, 1976.

Fama, E. "Behavior of Stock Market Prices." *Journal of Business* (January 1965): 34–105.

Flemming, W., and R. Rishel. *Deterministic and Stochastic Optimal Control.* New York: Springer-Verlag, 1975.

Francis, J. C. *Investments: Analysis and Management.* New York: McGraw-Hill, 1976.

Karlin, S., and H. Taylor. *A First Course in Stochastic Processes.* New York: Academic Press, 1975.

Levy, H., and M. Sarnat. *Investments.* Englewood Cliffs, N.J.: Prentice-Hall, 1981.

Malliaris, A. G. *Stochastic Methods in Economics and Finance.* New York: North Holland Publishing Company, 1981.

Markowitz, H. *Portfolio Selection.* New York: John Wiley, 1959.

Mendelbrot, B. "The Variation of Certain Speculative Prices." *Journal of Business* (October 1963): 394–419.

Osborne, M. "Brownian Motion in the Stock Market." *Operations Research,* (March–April 1959): 145–73.

Parzen, E. *Stochastic Processes.* Oakland, Calif.: Holden Day, 1962.

Sharpe, W. *Investments.* Englewood Cliffs, N.J.: Prentice-Hall, 1981.

Tinic, S., and R. West. *Investing in Securities: An Efficient Markets Approach.* Reading, Mass.: Addison-Wesley, 1982.

Exercises

1. The following data are the closing prices on a nondividend-paying stock, XYZ:

Day	Price	Day	Price
1	$12.00	9	$14.50
2	12.50	10	15.00
3	13.00	11	14.50
4	13.25	12	14.25
5	13.25	13	14.00
6	13.25	14	13.00
7	14.50	15	12.00
8	14.25	16	10.00

   a. Compute the price relatives and daily logarithmic returns.

   b. Estimate the mean daily logarithmic return and standard deviation.

   c. Assuming that the logarithmic returns are normally distributed, estimate the expected price relative and standard deviation of price relatives over a period of 30 days.

   d. On day 16, the closing price is $10. If the process that generates returns remains unchanged, estimate the expected stock price in 30 days.

2. If a stock pays a dividend, the price relative over the period should be adjusted by including the dividend in the numerator. The following data give quarterly prices and dividend information for stock XYZ:

Price	Dividend
$30.00	—
42.00	0.5
37.00	—
41.00	0.7
42.00	—
45.00	0.8

   a. Compute the price relatives and logarithmic returns for each period.

   b. Compute the annual logarithmic mean and variance.

3. Below are actual price data for three nondividend-paying companies for each of six months.

Time	Security A	Security B	Security C
1	67 6/8	52	12
2	70 2/8	56 5/8	12 4/8
3	69 3/8	54 2/8	13
4	68 4/8	55 4/8	14 1/8
5	66 2/8	56 7/8	15
6	65	57	16 4/8

   a. Compute the rate of return for each company for each month.

   b. Compute the average rate of return and standard deviation for each company.

   c. Compute the covariance and correlation between all pairs of securities.

   d. Compute the average return and standard deviation for the following portfolios.

$$1/2A + 1/2B$$
$$1/2A + 1/2C$$
$$1/3A + 1/3B + 1/3C$$

4. The beta value of the XYZ is 1.2, while that for B is 0.6. A portfolio is established such that half the funds are allocated to each stock.

   a. Compute the beta value of the portfolio.

   b. Given that the variance of returns on the market index is 0.2, estimate the variance of the returns on this portfolio.

   c. Given that the expected market return is 10 percent, estimate the expected portfolio return.

   d. For this portfolio, comment on issues relating to nonmarket risk. That is, how does a portfolio with high nonmarket risk compare to a similar portfolio (same beta value) having low nonmarket risk?

5. Monthly return data are presented below for two stocks and the Standard and Poor's index.

| | | Security | |
Month	A	B	Index
1	12.0	-2.5	13.0
2	1.5	71.4	10.5
3	-8.6	13.4	0.6
4	-5.0	12.6	-5.5
5	6.0	14.2	2.5

a. Compute the mean return and variance of returns for both securities and the index.

b. Compute the covariance between each security and the index and between the two securities.

c. Estimate the beta value for security A and B.

d. Using the beta values, estimate the covariance between stocks A and B. Compare this estimate with that obtained in (b).

7

Index Options

In Chapter 6 the role diversification plays in reducing portfolio risk was discussed. The total risk of any security can be represented by the sum of market and nonmarket-related risks. Through diversification, portfolio risk can be reduced to levels proportional to the risk inherent in the market as a whole. Diversification, however, cannot reduce risk below market-related levels. Managers of well-diversified portfolios must either contend with this market risk or "time" the market. The latter strategy involves selecting times to enter and withdraw from the stock market and can result in large transaction costs.

In recent years, some investors have modified the buy-and-hold strategy as they have become more aware of the effects shorter-term market risks have on their longer-term investment goals. These risks can be hedged by purchasing put options on individual securities. However, this strategy can provide more protection than necessary. Specifically, investors may be willing to bear nonmarket-related risks, or they may have already reduced them to acceptable levels of diversification. In this case, investors require only a hedge against market-related risks.

This chapter investigates how index options can be used to hedge portfolios against market-related risks. Such contracts provide portfolio managers with a mechanism for smoothing out the volatilities of the stock market as a whole. They also provide a way to adjust the risk exposure of an entire portfolio without dramatically altering the portfolio's composition.

Index options began trading in March 1983, when the Chicago Board Options Exchange (CBOE) introduced options on the Standard and Poor's 100 Index (S & P 100). The American Stock Exchange followed with an option contract on the Major Market Index, and the New York Stock Exchange introduced options on the New York Stock Exchange Composite Index. Volume on the S & P 100 Index was so great that after 18 months the option pit in which it traded was the world's biggest trading arena after the New York Stock Exchange. After one year of trading, index options accounted for over 50 percent of the total volume of all options traded, and daily volume in the options amounted to over $4 billion in the underlying stock.

In this chapter we shall describe the index option market and emphasize the role these contracts play in portfolio management. The first section describes how indices are constructed. Then index options are described, and the differences between these contracts and stock option contracts are emphasized. Index options strategies, including hedged and spread positions, are also described.

INDICES

An *index* is a statistical measure designed to show changes in a variable or in a group of related variables over time. An index usually includes only a small portion of securities in the market it represents. For example, the Dow Jones Industrial Average contains only thirty securities from the industrial sector of the stock market. Each stock in an index is assigned a relative weight. There are three common weighting schemes: a market-value-weighted index, a price-weighted index, and an equally weighted index. To illustrate these weighting schemes, consider an index comprised of three stocks, A, B, and C, whose prices in the initial (or base) period and some future period, *t,* are shown in Exhibit 7.1. The exhibit also indicates the number of shares outstanding. Initially we shall assume that none of the shares split over the relevant time period.

EXHIBIT 7.1
Composition of a Three-Stock Index

Stock	Initial Price	Price at Time *t*	Shares Outstanding
A	$150	$150	50
B	$ 40	$ 80	100
C	$ 10	$ 30	500

Market-Value-Weighted Index

The market-value-weighted index at time *t* is obtained by computing the ratio of the market value of all outstanding shares that comprise the index at time *t* to the value at the initial period and multiplying by an initial index value.

Example 7.1

Let $MV(t)$ be the market value of all outstanding shares at time t, and let $I(t)$ be the index value at time t. Then we have

$$MV(0) = 150(50) + 40(100) + 10(500) = 16,500$$

$$MV(t) = 150(50) + 80(100) + 30(500) = 30,500.$$

Assuming $I(0) = 100$, we have

$$I(t) = \left[\frac{MV(t)}{MV(0)}\right] I(0) = \left(\frac{30,500}{16,500}\right) 100 = 184.85.$$

Note that stock splits have no effect on the index. However, adjustments to the formula are necessary to reflect capitalization changes over time.

Price-Weighted Index

A price-weighted index reflects the change in the *average* price of the stocks that comprise the index.

Example 7.2

The average stock price, $\overline{S}(0)$, at the initial period is

$$\overline{S}(0) = \frac{(150 + 40 + 10)}{3} = 66.667$$

and at time t

$$\overline{S}(t) = \frac{(150 + 80 + 30)}{3} = 86.67.$$

Assuming an initial index of 100, we have

$$I(t) = \left[\frac{\overline{S}(t)}{\overline{S}(0)}\right] I(0) = \left(\frac{86.67}{66.67}\right) 100$$

$$= 130.$$

Note that, in this example, the market-value-weighted index is considerably higher than the price-weighted index. The reason for this is that the price-weighted index gives the greatest weighting to the most expensive stock (Stock A), which in this example provides the lowest return.

The base value, $I(0)$, of the price-weighted index has to be adjusted from time to time to reflect specific events. As an example, consider what happens if a 2:1 split in Stock A occurs. Without the split, the index is $I(t) = 130$. In light of the split, we have

$$\overline{S}(t) = \frac{(75 + 80 + 30)}{3} = 61.67.$$

Without adjusting the index, we would obtain

$$I(t) = \left(\frac{61.67}{66.67}\right) 100 = 92.45.$$

To prevent stock splits from jolting the index value, the base value, $I(0)$, is adjusted (from 100) to a new value, which is set so that the new index value equals the old value. That is, $I(0)$ is chosen such that

$$130 = \left(\frac{61.67}{66.67}\right) I(0).$$

Hence,

$$I(0) = 140.6.$$

The base value is also adjusted when stocks in the index are changed. These changes may occur when companies go bankrupt, lose market share, or are taken over. If left unchanged, the dated index would not represent the group it was initially intended to represent.

Equally Weighted Index

In an equally weighted index, an equal dollar amount is invested in each stock comprised in the index.

Example 7.3

Assume $1,000 is invested in each stock in Exhibit 7.1. Then 6.667 shares of A, 5 shares of B, and 100 shares of C could be purchased. The investment in the base period would be $3,000. In time period t, the portfolio value would be $6,000. The new index in this case is

$$I(t) = \left[\frac{MV(t)}{MV(0)}\right] I(0) = 200.$$

In summary, value-weighted indices are appropriate benchmarks for index funds that attempt to invest "in the market"; price-weighted indices are appropriate benchmarks for investors who allocate wealth across stocks in ratios corresponding to their prices; finally, equally weighted indices are appropriate benchmarks for investors who allocate equal dollars among all stocks invested.

BROAD-BASED AND NARROW-BASED INDICES

A *broad-based market index* is designed to reflect the stock market as a whole. A *narrow-based index,* on the other hand, is designed to track the performance of a particular industry.

Exhibit 7.2 shows some broad-based market indices on which option contracts are traded. All but the Amex Major Market Index are market-value-weighted indices. The Amex Major Market Index is a price-weighted index.

EXHIBIT 7.2
Indices on Which Options Trade

Amex Major Market Index
Amex Market Value Index
New York Stock Exchange Composite Index
New York Stock Exchange Double Index
S & P 100 Index
S & P 500 Index

In addition, option contracts trade on narrow-based (market sector) indices such as computer technology, oil and gas, transportation, telephone, gaming/hotel, and gold/silver.

INDEX OPTIONS

Index options trade like stock options. Strike prices are expressed in dollars and are fixed at levels surrounding the current level of the underlying index. Additional contracts are introduced as index prices rise or decline. Like stock options, index options expire on the Saturday following the third Friday of the expiration month. When initially introduced, index options were assigned three-, six-, and nine-month expiration dates. From the beginning, however, investor interest concentrated in the nearby expiration months. As a result, option contracts with monthly expirations up to a maximum of four months trade at any time.

Call Index Options

A call index option provides the owner with the right to purchase, for a predetermined price, an amount of dollars equal to the index value multiplied by a given multiplier. The index value is determined by the closing price on the exercising date. This right exists up to a specific expiration date.

Example 7.4

Assume a call holder owns an April 120 index option with a multiplier of 100. If the holder exercises the option and the closing index price that day is 125, then ignoring transaction costs, the holder would receive $500.

Put Index Options

The put buyer obtains the right to sell, at a predetermined price, an amount of dollars equal to the index value, multiplied by a given multiplier. As with call options, the value of the index is determined by closing prices on the exercising date.

Example 7.5

Assume a put holder has an April 120 index option with a multiplier of 100. If the holder exercises the option and the closing price at the end of the day is 102, the put holder can deliver $10,200 in exchange for $12,000. The net transaction, ignoring transaction costs, will be receipt of $1,800.

Exhibit 7.3 shows the closing price of several index option contracts as they appear in the *Wall Street Journal.* Each point of premium represents $100. As with equity options, the minimum premium quotation is 1/16 of a point for premiums of less than 3 points and 1/8 of a point for premiums of 3 points or greater.

DIFFERENCES BETWEEN STOCK AND INDEX OPTIONS

There are several differences between index options and stock options. These differences are significant enough to cause strategies, arbitrage boundary relationships, and pricing mechanisms to differ between the two contracts. In this section the major differences are discussed.

The Underlying Asset

With index options, the underlying asset consists of a portfolio of the securities that comprise the index. From a practical point of view, it is virtually impossible to establish a portfolio that exactly reproduces the price of an index, such as the S & P 100. In order to do this, one would have to not only purchase the 100 stocks that comprise the index in the correct proportions, but also reinvest all the dividend flows in the appropriate fashion.

EXHIBIT 7.3
Index Option Prices

INDEX OPTIONS

Monday, July 14, 1986

Chicago Board

S&P 100 INDEX

Strike	Calls–Last			Puts–Last		
Price	Jul	Aug	Sep	Jul	Aug	Sep
205	....	....	24¾	....	⅛	⅝
210	17	17⅝	....	1/16	⅜	1⅜
215	....	12⅛	....	....	1	2 5/16
220	5½	7¾	10¼	5/16	2 5/16	3⅞
225	1⅞	4⅞	7½	1¾	4½	6
230	7/16	2 11/16	5⅛	5⅜	7½	8⅞
235	1/16	1 7/16	3¼	10⅛	11¼	11⅞
240	1/16	¾	2 3/16	15⅛	15⅛	16
245	1/16	⅜	1 5/16	20	20	20
250	1/16	⅛	¾	....	24	24
255	....	1/16	7/16	....	....	....

Total call volume 219,134 Total call open int. 687,861
Total put volume 269,660 Total put open int. 591,999
The index: High 229.21; Low 225.09; Close 225.16, −4.05

S&P 500 INDEX (NEW)

Strike	Calls–Last			Puts–Last		
Price	Jul	Aug	Sep	Jul	Aug	Sep
220	....	....	....	....	....	1 1/16
225	....	....	....	....	⅝	....
230	8¼	10⅝	....	⅛	1 11/16	....
235	4⅛	7¼	....	15/16	3⅝	5¼
240	13/16	4	7½	3½	5¼	7⅞
245	⅛	2⅜	5⅝	7⅜	8	....
250	1/16	1⅜	3½	11½	12	14¼
255	....	9/16	2¼	....	....	....
260	....	5/16	1⅜	....	....	22
265	....	1/16	....	....	....	....

Total call volume 5,163 Total call open int. 56,704
Total put volume 2,935 Total put open int. 59,051
The index: High 242.22; Low 238.04; Close 238.11, −4.11

American Exchange

MAJOR MARKET INDEX

Strike	Calls–Last			Puts–Last		
Price	Jul	Aug	Sep	Jul	Aug	Sep
320	....	26½	....	1/16	9/16	....
325	....	....	....	....	1⅛	....
330	....	....	....	1/16	2 3/16	4⅜
335	8¼	13	16⅞	⅜	3⅝	5⅝
340	4⅜	8⅞	13¾	1½	5½	8¾
345	1¾	6¼	9½	4⅛	8	10½
350	9/16	4⅛	7¾	8	11	13
355	3/16	2 11/16	6	12¾	15¼	16¼
360	1/16	1¾	4⅞	17¼	17½	18⅞
365	1/16	1 3/16	3⅝	21⅝	....	....
370	1/16	11/16	2¾	....	....	....
375	1/16	7/16	2	29¾	....	....
380	....	¼	1½	....	....	....
385	....	....	1⅛	....	....	....

Total call volume 46,097 Total call open int. 104,507
Total put volume 46,137 Total put open int. 74,672
The index: High 347.87; Low 342.34; Close 342.38, −5.49

COMPUTER TECHNOLOGY INDEX

Strike	Calls–Last			Puts–Last		
Price	Jul	Aug	Sep	Jul	Aug	Sep
105	....	....	....	1/16	....	....
110	1¼	....	....	1	....	....
115	1/16	1⅜	....	....	....	....
120	....	....	....	9	9	....

Total call volume 114 Total call open int. 1,378
Total put volume 145 Total put open int. 303
The index: High 112.67; Low 109.68; Close 109.72, −2.95

OIL INDEX

Strike	Calls–Last			Puts–Last		
Price	Jul	Aug	Sep	Jul	Aug	Sep
120	....	....	....	3/16	1½	2½
125	7/16	1⅜	2 9/16	2⅝	4⅛	....
130	1	....	....	7⅝	7⅝	....
135	....	....	7/16	11¾	....	....

Total call volume 113 Total call open int. 1,222
Total put volume 557 Total put open int. 1,083
The index: High 124.59; Low 122.54; Close 122.54, −2.02

AIRLINE INDEX

Strike	Calls–Last			Puts–Last		
Price	Jul	Aug	Sep	Jul	Aug	Sep
105	....	....	....	....	1¾	....
110	....	....	....	....	5	....
115	....	¾	....	....	....	....

Total call volume 5 Total call open int. 241
Total put volume 10 Total put open int. 93
The index: High 108.25; Low 106.19; Close 106.25, −1.28

NASD

NASDAQ 100 INDEX

Strike		Calls–Last			Puts–Last	
Price		Jul	Aug	Jul	Aug	
305	½	....	....	4	....	....
310	⅝	....	....	8	....	....

Total call volume 20. Total call open int. 133.
Total put volume 42. Total put open int. 79.
The index: High 305.95; Low 297.99; Close 298.57, −7.14

N.Y. Stock Exchange

NYSE OPTIONS INDEX

Strike	Calls–Last			Puts–Last		
Price	Jul	Aug	Sep	Jul	Aug	Sep
125	....	....	....	....	⅛	⅝
130	....	....	....	....	9/16	1½
135	2¼	4	6⅜	5/16	1⅞	3
140	3/16	1¾	3⅛	3⅝	4¾	5½
145	1/16	½	1½	8⅜	8⅛	....
150	....	⅛	....	....	....	....
155	....	1/16	5/16	....	....	....

Total call volume 6,203. Total call open int. 30,473.
Total put volume 3,681. Total put open int. 39,876.
The index: High 139.49; Low 137.23; Close 137.27, −2.24

NYSE DOUBLE INDEX

Strike	Calls–Last			Puts–Last		
Price	Jul	Aug	Sep	Jul	Aug	Sep
265	....	....	....	....	2	....
270	....	....	....	11/16	....	....
275	1½	5½	....	2¼	6	....
280	¼	4	....	5⅞	....	....
285	1/16	2⅜	....	9¾	....	....
290	1/16	1¼	....	....	....	....
295	....	11/16	....	....	....	....
300	....	¼	....	....	....	....
305	....	⅛	....	....	....	....

Total call volume 847. Total call open int. 6,989.
Total put volume 521. Total put open int. 12,100.
The index: High 278.98; Low 274.46; Close 274.54, −4.48

NYSE BETA INDEX

Strike	Calls–Last			Puts–Last		
Price	Jul	Aug	Sep	Jul	Aug	Sep
285	....	....	....	....	1 3/16	....
290	....	....	....	....	2⅞	....
295	4¾	....	....	¼	4½	6⅛
300	2¼	7⅛	....	⅞	6½	9¼
305	⅝	5¼	8⅛	2⅞	9⅜	11⅞
310	⅛	3⅛	....	6½	13⅞	....
315	1/16	1⅞	....	11⅛	....	....
320	1/16	1	3½	15¾	19 13/16	....
325	1/16	13/16	....	19	....	....
330	1/16	⅜	1 9/16	....	....	....
335	....	¼	....	....	....	....
340	....	3/16	....	....	....	....

Total call volume 1,944. Total call open int. 7,923.
Total put volume 3,214. Total put open int. 5,871.
The index: High 306.36; Low 299.14; Close 299.44, −6.96

Philadelphia Exchange

GOLD/SILVER INDEX

Strike	Calls–Last			Puts–Last		
Price	Jul	Aug	Sep	Jul	Aug	Sep
60	1⅛	2⅜	....	½	....	....
65	1/16	⅝	....	4⅛	....	....
70	....	¼	....	....	....	....

Total call volume 212 Total call open int. 2,238
Total put volume 20 Total put open int. 1,240
The index: High 61.92; Low 60.21; Close 60.87, −1.05

VALUE LINE INDEX OPTIONS

Strike	Calls–Last			Puts–Last		
Price	Jul	Aug	Sep	Jul	Aug	Sep
205	....	....	32¼	....	....	⅜
210	....	....	27¾	....	....	9/16
215	....	....	21¼	....	....	⅞
220	....	....	17½	....	....	1⅞
225	....	....	....	1/16	1⅜	3⅜
230	3½	5½	....	⅞	3½	5¼
235	9/16	2½	4½	4⅛	6½	8½
240	1/16	1¼	3¼	8⅝	10⅜	10¾
245	1/16	⅝	....	13¾	....	....
255	....	3/16	....	....	....	....
260	....	....	7/16	....	....	....

Total call volume 1,805 Total call open int. 17,103
Total put volume 1,532 Total put open int. 14,648
The index: High 236.79; Low 233.00; Close 233.09, −3.68

NATIONAL O-T-C INDEX

Strike	Calls–Last			Puts–Last		
Price	Jul	Aug	Sep	Jul	Aug	Sep
225	....	....	8⅞	....	....	....
230	2	5¼	....	....	....	....
240	....	....	....	12⅜	....	....

Total call volume 37 Total call open int. 311
Total put volume 1 Total put open int. 1,630
The index: High 232.83; Low 228.19; Close 228.60, −4.20

Pacific Exchange

TECHNOLOGY INDEX

Strike	Calls–Last			Puts–Last		
Price	Jul	Aug	Sep	Jul	Aug	Sep
110	2½	....	....	....	1⅜	....
115	....	....	....	....	3½	....
130	....	....	....	....	16¾	....

Total call volume 10 Total call open int. 1,073
Total put volume 41 Total put open int. 552
The index: High 114.99; Low 112.34; Close 112.38, −2.58

In practice, proxy portfolios are constructed that closely follow the underlying index. These portfolios typically contain only the most highly liquid stocks that comprise the index. The weights of the stocks in the portfolio are chosen so that the proxy portfolio tracks the index quite closely. Nonetheless, since exact duplication of the index prices is not possible, the arbitrage arguments used in Chapter 4 to obtain bounds on stock option prices may not hold for index options.

The risk involved with particular strategies can be greater with index options than with stock options. Covered call writing strategies, for example, are not possible with index options. Call writers who hold a proxy portfolio must bear the risk of the index value's expanding more rapidly than their portfolio values. Similarly, put holders who purchase protection for their proxy portfolios run the risk of their portfolios' depreciating faster than the index.

Cash Settlement

When index options are exercised, no underlying securities are delivered. Instead, settlements are made in cash. The size of the payment is the difference between the exercise price of the option and the closing value of the index on the day of exercise, multiplied by the multiplier. This settlement process introduces two types of risk that are not present with stock options.

Exercise Risk   Unlike the stock options, when an option holder exercises an index option, the exact amount received remains uncertain until the closing price of the index becomes available. If the final closing price is lower (higher) at the close of the day than the strike price of the exercised option, the call (put) holder is obliged to pay the writer. To reduce the likelihood of this occurring, if an index option is to be exercised, the order should be delayed as long as possible. The latest time of day at which exercise notice for index options can be made, the *cutoff time*, is usually set by the brokerage firm and may be earlier than the cutoff time for stock options.

Timing Risk   The amount of cash received when an option holder exercises his or her contract is determined at the close of the market on the exercising day. The writer will not learn that assignment has been made until the next business day at the earliest. The time between exercise and notice of assignment poses no risk for covered call writers if the underlying asset is to be delivered. However, in the case of an index option, the writer is obliged to pay a fixed amount. If the investor held a perfectly matched portfolio and the security prices remained unchanged over the lag time, then it would theoretically be possible to liquidate the portfolio and use the proceeds to cover the debt. In practice, stock prices will have changed and liquidation of the portfolio may not cover the debt. The risk caused by this delay is termed *timing risk*. Timing risk limits the ability to reduce risk exposure by holding the underlying stock positions.

Margin Requirements

Margin requirements for index options are similar to those for stock options. All option purchases must be paid in full. Margin requirements for naked written positions on indices are similar to those for stock options. Specifically, the initial margin is the current option premium plus 5 percent of the aggregate index value reduced by any out-of-the-money amount. The minimum margin consists of the current premium plus 2 percent of the market value of the index.

Narrow market-based index options require more margin. Specifically, naked written positions require the margin to be the current option premium plus 15 percent of the aggregate index value reduced by any out-of-the-money amount. The minimum margin amount is the current premium plus 5 percent of the aggregate index value.

Since covered call writing is not possible with index options, some margin is always required. Although certain index option spreads may qualify for a reduced margin, the requirements are generally higher than for stock option spreads.

Index Price Reporting Problems

Although the index value is reported throughout the trading day, the reported level may not provide the most recent information. For example, if trading is interrupted in some stocks used in the index, the index information will be based on the most recently reported levels of all trading securities and the last reported price for those stocks not trading. A halt in the trading of index options may occur if trading is interrupted in a large portion of the index value. In this case holders of options may be prohibited from exercising their right, and special arrangements may be introduced if the interruptions persist through the expiration date.

Dividend Streams on the Index

In Chapter 4 we saw that dividend payments have an impact on the pricing of options. For call options, early exercise is optimal only if the dividend captured exceeds the foregone interest on the strike. This is most likely to occur if the dividend yield is high relative to interest rates and if the option is deep in the money. If the dividend stream is continuous and the spread between the dividend yield and interest rate widens, the probability of early exercise of call options diminishes. The dividend stream for index options is more complex than for stock options. However, for well-diversified, broad-based indices, the dividend stream is more continuous than that for stocks. With the spread between interest rates and dividend yield being quite high, early exercise of all but the most deep-in-the-money options is quite unlikely. This suggests that, for the most part, American call index options may behave and be priced as European call index options.

STRATEGIES WITH INDEX OPTIONS

Like stock option strategies, index option strategies can be classified according to whether the positions are naked, hedged, or spread.

Naked Strategies

An investor who anticipates an increase in the price level of the stock market as a whole could purchase shares in a diversified mutual fund. A more speculative strategy would be to buy broad-based market index options. Such a purchase allows the investor to participate in profits if market prices increase, while limiting downside risk to the size of the option premium. Purchasing call options may also be appropriate for investors who anticipate that future funds will become available for investments in the market yet are keen to participate in an early bullish market.

Call index options are sold naked by speculators who anticipate stable or decreasing market prices. In a bearish market, an alternative strategy would be to purchase put index options.

Hedging Diversified Portfolios with Put Index Options

Consider the owner of a well-diversified portfolio who anticipates that the market will experience a short-term decline. Liquidation of the portfolio for the short term is not realistic because of high transaction costs, dividend income, and tax consequences. Without financial hedging devices, the owner may have to bear the risk of a short-term declining market. With index options available, the investor may hedge against market-related risk by purchasing put index options. The effectiveness of this strategy depends on the degree of correlation between the index and the portfolio. In a worst case situation, the portfolio value could depreciate while the market index appreciates. However, this event is unlikely if the stock index on which the option trades is highly correlated with the portfolio. The maximum risk associated with this strategy (relative to an unhedged position) is limited to the full premium of the option.

To establish how many put options should be purchased to insulate the portfolio from market risk, assume the current portfolio value is $160,000. Moreover, assume the index level is 80 and at-the-money put options are to be purchased. The exercise price of each option is $80 \times 100 = $8,000. The purchase of 20 put options would represent an aggregate exercise price of $160,000, which equals the value of the portfolio.

If the beta value of the portfolio, computed with respect to the market index on which the option trades, is 1, the portfolio value is expected to appreciate or depreciate at the same rate as the market index. In this case, the purchase of 20 put options will provide an appropriate insurance against market declines. However, the hedge is not perfect, since the portfolio may decline more or less than the overall market. Indeed, the actual portfolio may depreciate rapidly while the index remains stable. In this case the protective puts would not produce offsetting profits. On the other hand, if the investor had picked superior stocks, profits could be realized in a declining market from the protective puts, even though no losses were incurred on the portfolio.

If the beta value is greater than 1, then the rate of decline of the portfolio is expected to be greater than the rate of decline in the market index. In this case, to obtain insulation against market declines, one must purchase more put options. For example, if the beta value is 1.5, then 30 (rather than 20) options would be appropriate.

Example 7.6

Assume the S & P 100 is selected as the index that correlates best with the portfolio being hedged. With the index at 150, each put option with strike 150 hedges $15,000 of equity. If the current portfolio value were $100,000 and its beta value with respect to the S & P 100 index were 1.0, the number of protective puts to purchase would be 100,000/15,000 = 6.67. Hence, 6 or 7 puts would provide adequate protection against market declines. If the beta value were 1.3, the number of protective puts to purchase would be (6.67)(1.3) = 8.6 (i.e., 8 or 9 puts).

Hedging Diversified Portfolios with Call Index Options

If the owner of a fully diversified portfolio anticipated a flat or slightly bearish market, additional income could be earned by writing call index options. This strategy is similar to selling call options on stock owned in that the premium income earned provides a cushion to reduce losses in declining markets. However, upside potential is limited, since increases in the portfolio value if the market booms will be offset by losses in the call index contracts. Theoretically the risk of writing index calls is unlimited, since individual stock portfolios may not always follow general market trends.

Example 7.7

An investor manages a well-diversified portfolio that has a beta value of 1.5. This beta value is computed with respect to the S & P 100 Index. The dividend yield on the portfolio is 5 percent. Current money market yields are 9 percent. The portfolio value has recently declined, but the investor believes the market is about to stabilize and over the long term there will be significant growth. To improve the short-term return, the investor decides to sell S & P 100 index options against the portfolio. The price of at-the-money, two-month call options with strike 150 is $3. Given that the current value of the portfolio is $150,000, the maximum reasonable number of call options to sell is given by 10(1.5) = 15. The sale of any additional calls could result in losses in a bullish market. However, the market might surge ahead, creating losses in the calls without the portfolio's producing offsetting gains.

In hedging diversified portfolios, the actual number of calls sold or puts purchased is often set at values lower than those dictated by the beta value. For put options this implies that only partial insurance against market declines is obtained, while for call options it implies that not all upside potential is limited.

The Role of Index Options in Small Portfolios

Market index options need not be used only as hedging instruments for large, diversified portfolios. Suppose an investor feels comfortable with picking stocks but is unsure of market timing and direction. The risk components of the small portfolio can be unbundled into market and nonmarket components, thus allowing hedging against market risk. The investor can lay off market risk associated with market declines by buying protective put options.

Examples 7.8

As an extreme example, consider a portfolio containing only one security. Assume that, of the total risk of the stock, only 20 percent can be accounted for by market forces. Assume the beta value of security is 1.2. Using the single-index model, we have

$$\sigma^2 = \beta^2 \sigma_m^2 + \sigma_n^2$$

where σ^2 is the total risk of a single security, σ_m^2 is the market risk, and σ_n^2 is the nonmarket risk.

The significant amount of nonmarket risk is not of concern to the investor because she believes the company is positioned to perform well. However, the investor is concerned about the direction of the market and, hence, may buy protective puts on the market index.

The Role of Narrow-Based Index Options in Small Portfolios

Some investors are comfortable ranking companies within a given industry but are unwilling to predict the future direction of the industry as a whole. With industry options available, insurance against poor industry performance can be obtained, and the investor may be able to profit from his or her ability in picking stocks.

Example 7.9

Consider an investor who believes that company XYZ should outperform other companies in the transportation sector but is unsure how the transportation sector as a whole will perform. By buying the stock together with put options on the S & P Transportation Index, the investor can partially hedge

(continued)

Example 7.9 (cont'd)

industry-related risks. The number of puts to purchase can be determined by establishing the sensitivity of rates of return on XYZ relative to rates of return on the index. This sensitivity can be obtained by regressing the returns on XYZ against the returns on the index and estimating the slope.

Spreads

Spread positions can be established with index options. However, because of timing risk, these strategies are more risky than the equivalent strategies using stock options.

Example 7.10

Consider an investor who buys a June XYZ 80 put and sells a March 80 put on the same index. On Monday the option is exercised. The closing price is $72, which means the investor must pay $800. The investor learns about the exercise notice on Tuesday and decides to offset the loss by exercising the June XYZ 80 put. However, since the closing price on Tuesday was $76, the investor will receive only $400 and sustain a net loss of $400. Rather than exercise the put and lose the time premium, a superior strategy would have been to sell the put early on Tuesday.

INTERMARKET SPREADING

The broad-based market indices are highly correlated with each other. However, if the returns on one index are regressed against the returns on another, the resulting slope could be significantly different from 1. For example, if the S & P 500 is used as the base index and the New York Stock Exchange Index is regressed against it, a beta estimate of, say, 1.23 could be obtained. This implies that the New York Stock Exchange could rise approximately 23 percent more than the S & P 500 Index in a bull market. An investor who perceives a bullish market could buy the "high beta" option contract and sell the "low beta" option in anticipation of the spread widening in favor of the high beta index. Conversely, in a declining market, the low beta option could be bought and the high beta option sold in anticipation of the spread narrowing.

EMPIRICAL TESTS FOR INDEX OPTION BOUNDARY CONDITIONS

There is overwhelming empirical support for the stock option boundary conditions established in Chapter 4. Our discussion of differences between stock and index options makes clear that index options may not satisfy the same bounds. For example, the American call option price need not exceed the intrinsic value of the option. To see this, note that if the index option were less than its intrinsic value, then purchasing the call and immediately exercising it would not be riskless since the relevant index value is the value of the index at the close. In order to come close to obtaining risk-free arbitrage profits, the investor who purchased the call would have to sell the index. As discussed, this would require selling short several stocks in a proxy portfolio, which could be difficult.

Evnine and Rudd have conducted empirical tests to establish whether index options would satisfy the stock option boundary conditions. Using data collected over a two-month period starting in June 1984, they showed that in over 2 percent of occasions the call asking price was less than the intrinsic value. Moreover, on a significant number of occasions both the European and American put-call parity relationships (with dividend adjustments) were violated. Although they acknowledge some concern about the prices they used in their analysis, they concluded that the violations of the boundary conditions were significant.

CONCLUSION

Index option trading accounts for over half the volume of all option contracts traded. To a certain degree, investors have used index options as an alternative to stock options. As a result, the liquidity of the stock option market has suffered. The theoretical justification for this phenomenon is partially provided by Ross's theorem (see Chapter 5).

Index options provide a mechanism for hedging portfolios against market- or industry-related risk. Rather than time the market by buying and selling securities, investors can smooth out the volatilities over the short term by trading one-, two-, or three-month contracts. Index options differ from stock options in that they have cash settlements. Since the underlying index cannot be owned, hedging strategies are not perfect and exact profit functions of positions at the expiration date of the contract cannot be constructed. Nevertheless, index options do allow unwanted market- or industry-specific risk to be traded away.

Pricing of index options may differ somewhat from pricing of stock options. Indeed, since the underlying portfolio cannot be held and index options are settled in cash, index options may not satisfy the boundary conditions for stock options that were established in Chapter 4.

References

The Options Clearing Corporation and the option exchanges publish booklets describing specific index option contracts and illustrating alternative investment strategies. Two chapters in the text *Stock Index Futures* discuss options on stock indices, their pricing, and their role in portfolio management.

Evnine, J., and A. Rudd. "Index Options: The Early Evidence." *Journal of Finance* 40(3)(July 1985): 743–56.

Faboozi, F., G. Gastineau, and S. Wunsch. "Introduction to Options on Stock Indexes and Stock Index Futures Contracts." In *Stock Index Futures,* edited by F. Faboozi and G. Kipnis. Homewood, Ill.: Dow Jones-Irwin, 1984.

Faboozi, F., G. Gastineau, and A. Madansky. "Options on Stock Indexes and Stock Index Futures: Pricing Determinants, Role in Risk Management, and Option Evaluation." In *Stock Index Futures,* edited by F. Faboozi and G. Kipnis. Homewood, Ill.: Dow Jones-Irwin, 1984.

Khoury, S. *Speculative Markets.* New York: Macmillan, 1984.

Exercises

1. An investor managers a portfolio comprised of twenty major oil and gas companies. The dividend yield on the portfolio is 5 percent. Current money market yields are 9 percent. The portfolio value has recently declined as oil and gas prices have dropped. The investor believes that this industry has stabilized and that long term there will be significant growth. Establish a strategy that will achieve a higher return without trading stocks. Which index option would be used, and how many contracts should be purchased or sold?

2. An investor has significant investments in a money fund. The investor believes that the market will bottom out in about two months. Then some excellent buying opportunities will occur. Assuming the investor will buy stocks selected from the S & P 100 Index, construct a strategy that is consistent with these beliefs.

3. An investor has been aggressively buying shares of computer companies that produce certain printing devices. Recently, however, there have been rumors that the industry could face reduced profits because of new products introduced by foreign competition. How can index options be useful in offsetting this industry-specific risk?

4. Index options have affected the liquidity of the stock option market. Investors that previously traded stock options have replaced their strategies with index option strategies. Provide several reasons for this occurrence.

5. The greatest activity in index options is always focused on the near series. Index options with time to maturity exceeding four months were never actively traded. Offer several reasons why strategies using index options are short term.

6. Can arbitrage arguments like those developed in Chapter 4 be used to obtain bounds on index option prices? In particular, what problems, if any, are caused by the fact that the underlying stocks in the index pay out dividends?

7. Why is it important for an arbitrager to know how the index of a particular indicator is developed? How will an arbitrager attempt to profit from "mispriced" index options?

8. An option to buy 100 shares of a specific fully diversified mutual fund is not the same as an index option. Explain the differences. If options on particular mutual funds were available, could the arbitrage arguments of Chapter 4 be applied, or would special restrictions prevent their applications?

9. A portfolio of call options is different from an option on a portfolio. Explain the differences.

10. If you could introduce two new index option contracts, which two would you introduce? Explain why these contracts would be useful in the current economy. Specifiy the underlying index.

11. If a call option on the S & P 100 Index was overpriced according to the American put-call parity equation, what strategy could be adopted to obtain riskless arbitrage profits. What risks (if any) would be involved in this strategy?

8

The Black-Scholes
Option Pricing Model

In order to obtain an exact theoretical stock option price, we must make more assumptions than those made in Chapter 4. In this chapter we shall assume that the statistical process driving security prices is the geometric Wiener process. We shall also assume that stock/option positions can be revised infinitely, frequently with no transaction costs, and that interest rates are constant. With these assumptions, Black and Scholes were able to derive an exact price for a European call and put option. In this chapter we provide an intuitive approach to the development of their model and establish the properties of theoretical option prices. With this pricing model, we can establish profit diagrams of hedge strategies prior to expiration. This is important, since it illustrates how profits may evolve over time.

The Black-Scholes model is applicable to American call options on nondividend-paying stock. The final sections of this chapter illustrate how these prices can be used to approximate prices for American call and put options on dividend-paying securities. Discussion of the theoretical foundations behind the results of this chapter and a formal derivation of the Black-Scholes equation are deferred to Chapters 9 and 15.

THE OPTION PRICING LINE—AN INTUITIVE APPROACH

In Chapter 4 we obtained the lower boundary price for an option on a stock that paid no dividends prior to expiration. This lower value was given by the stock price less the present value of the strike. Exhibit 8.1 illustrates the actual price line of a call option at some time prior to expiration.

If the current stock price is S_0, then the call price is given by C_0. The slope of the price line at point P indicates the sensitivity of the call price to small instantaneous changes in the stock price. For calls deep out the money, call price changes are insensitive to stock price movements, whereas for calls deep in the money, the call price changes dollar for dollar with the stock price.

EXHIBIT 8.1
The Call Pricing Line

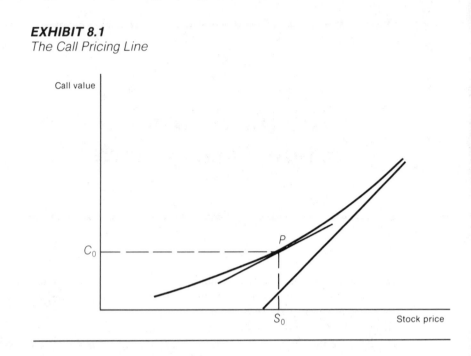

A PERFECT INSTANTANEOUS HEDGE

For an infinitesimal stock price change, ΔS, the call price will change by ΔC. Clearly the size of ΔC depends on the slope of the call line. Let H be the current slope of the line when the stock price is S_0. Then

$$\Delta C = H\Delta S. \tag{8.1}$$

Now consider a portfolio containing H shares of stock and a written call. For the infinitesimal stock price change ΔS, the H shares appreciate by $H\Delta S$ and the written call depreciates by ΔC. The net change in portfolio value, however, will be zero. Hence, at this instant in time the portfolio is free of risk. This portfolio is called the *perfect instantaneous hedge.*

It should be emphasized that this portfolio is free of risk only if the change in stock price is small. Furthermore, after an arbitrary time interval, Δt, the hedge will not be free of risk even if the stock price remains the same. To emphasize this point, consider a perfect hedge established at time t_0 when the stock price is S_0 and the call price is C_0 (point P in Exhibit 8.2). At time $t_0 + \Delta t$, the call price corresponds to a point on the new option line. If the stock value changes by ΔS, the call price is given by point Q. The change in option price is represented by the distance QR. The line RT represents the change in the value of H shares of stock. The distance QT thus represents the net change in value of the instantaneous hedge held over a small time period, Δt. Note that the size of this value depends on the value of ΔS and Δt. As Δt tends to zero, the hedge becomes free of risk. However, over finite periods, the hedge is not free of risk.

EXHIBIT 8.2
Change in Option Pricing Line Over a Time Increment

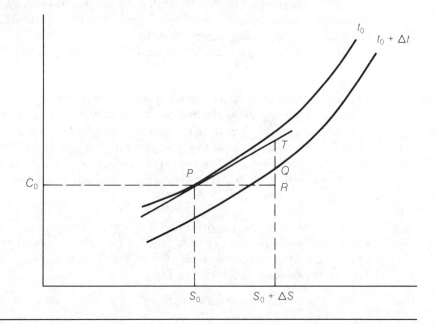

THE CONTINUOUS TRADING ASSUMPTION

The slope of the option pricing line, *H,* changes as the stock price changes or as time passes. Thus, like the call value, the slope can be expressed as

$$H = H(S_t, t). \tag{8.2}$$

To maintain a risk-free position over time, the revision process of buying *H* shares and selling one call must be continuous. The ability to achieve this without incurring transaction costs is called the *continuous trading assumption.*

Under a continuous trading assumption, it is possible to maintain a portfolio of stock and calls over finite time periods in such a way that the portfolio is free of risk. This is discussed more fully below.

AN INTUITIVE LOOK AT THE BLACK-SCHOLES MODEL

We shall assume that the stock, bond, and option markets are frictionless. That is, there are no transaction costs, no margin requirements, and no taxes, all shares are infinitely divisible, and continuous trading can be accomplished. We shall also assume that all investors can borrow or lend at a constant, known risk-free rate, *r,* and that the stock price follows a geometric Wiener process. This implies that the distribution of stock prices at any future point in time is lognormal. The stock pays no dividends prior to the expiration date, T.

If we could establish a portfolio of stock and bonds in such a way that the payoffs and properties of a call option were completely replicated, then to prevent riskless arbitrage opportunities from occurring, their current values would have to be identical. In order to replicate an option, the following two requirements are necessary.

The Equivalence-of-Value Requirement   The value of the replicating portfolio consisting of stocks and bonds must equal the value of the call option at all points in time until the option is exercised or expires. Since the stock pays no dividends prior to expiration, early exercise of the option is not optimal. Hence, the equivalence of value should be maintained until expiration, at which time the portfolio value, V_T, should satisfy the condition

$$V_T = \text{Max}(0, S_T - X).$$

Assume the replicating portfolio initially contains H_0 shares held long and B_0 dollars borrowed. The borrowed funds can be viewed as a short position in N_0 pure discount bonds of face value \$1, which mature at time T. The current value of each bond, F_0, is

$$F_0 = \exp(-rT) \tag{8.3}$$

and

$$B_0 = N_0 F_0.$$

The current portfolio value is

$$V_0 = H_0 S_0 - B_0$$

$$= H_0 S_0 - N_0 F_0. \tag{8.4}$$

Since the value of this portfolio replicates the cash flows of the call option at all points prior to expiration, to avoid riskless arbitrage opportunities, its current value, V_0, must be equal to the current call value, C_0.

The Self-Financing Requirement   Once an option is purchased, no additional funds are needed to maintain the position. The only cash flows that occur will be the terminal flows when the option is sold. The replicating portfolio must also have this property. Thus, if additional shares need to be purchased to maintain the replication, these funds must be obtained by additional borrowing. If shares are sold, the income must be used to reduce the size of the loan. This requirement of not allowing any external funds to be added to or removed from the portfolio is called the *self-financing requirement*.

To understand this point, consider the initial replicating portfolio of H_0 shares held long and N_0 bonds held short. If this portfolio is maintained unchanged over period Δt, then the new value, V_1, is

$$V_1 = H_0(S_0 + \Delta S) - N_0(F_0 + \Delta F). \tag{8.5}$$

where ΔS is the change in the stock price and ΔF is the change in the bond price over period Δt. Furthermore, the change in bond price in a small time interval, Δt, is just the continuously compounded return, r, multiplied by the time interval. That is, $\Delta F = r\Delta t$.

Assume at this time the "target" replicating portfolio consists of H_1^* shares, and N_1^* bonds held short, where

$$H_1^* = H_0 + \Delta H \tag{8.6}$$

and

$$N_1^* = N_0 + \Delta N. \tag{8.7}$$

The value of this portfolio, V_1^*, is equal to the call value and is

$$V_1^* = H_1^*(S_0 + \Delta S) - N_1^*(F_0 + \Delta F) \tag{8.8}$$

$$= (H_0 + \Delta H)(S_0 + \Delta S) - (N_0 + \Delta N)(F_0 + \Delta F) \tag{8.9}$$

$$\begin{aligned} &= H_0(S + \Delta S) - N_0(F_0 + \Delta F) \\ &\quad + \Delta H(S_0 + \Delta S) - \Delta N(F_0 + \Delta F) \end{aligned} \tag{8.10}$$

$$= V_1 + \Delta H(S_0 + \Delta S) - \Delta N(F_0 + \Delta F). \tag{8.11}$$

The self-financing requirement implies that the dollar adjustments required by buying ΔH shares must be made by adjusting the size of the loan by ΔN bonds. That is,

$$\Delta H(S_0 + \Delta S) - \Delta N(F_0 + \Delta F) = 0. \tag{8.12}$$

In the limit as Δt tends toward zero, this requirement (equation) becomes a differential equation that must hold for all instants in time prior to expiration. Of course, as Δt becomes smaller, the frequency of revisions become greater and, in the limit, a continual revision process is attained.

Example 8.1

To understand the self-financing requirement, assume that at time zero a call option could be replicated by buying 0.742 shares of a stock partially financed by borrowing $29.48. The replication holds well for time increment Δt. At this time the call price equals the portfolio value but the new replicating portfolio consists of 0.738 shares. That means 0.004 shares must be sold. The self-financing requirement implies that the income generated from the sale of these shares is used to offset the size of the loan (which has accrued interest over the time increment). The resulting portfolio will then replicate the payout of the call for another small time increment. As Δt tends toward zero, the frequency of revisions increases and the replication becomes more precise.

The Black-Scholes Equation

Equation (8.12) describes how the rate of change of the slope of the option pricing line (ΔH) relates to the rate of change in the number of bonds purchased, ΔN, given changes in the stock price. Under the continuous trading assumption in a lognormal securities market, the limiting form of equation (8.12) can be shown to be:

$$\frac{1}{2}\sigma^2 S^2 C_{SS} - rSC_S + rC - C_t = 0, \tag{8.13}$$

where

$$C_{SS} = \frac{\partial^2 C}{\partial S^2}, \; C_S = \frac{\partial C}{\partial S}, \; C_t = \frac{\partial C}{\partial t}.$$

The derivation of this equation is left for Chapter 16. What is important to note is that this equation, obtained under the self-financing requirement, together with the boundary conditions

$$C(S_T, T) = \text{Max}(0, S_T - X) \tag{8.14}$$

$$S_t \geq 0, 0 \leq t \leq T,$$

can be solved to obtain a unique call price. This call price is given by

$$C_0 = H_0 S_0 - B_0 \tag{8.15}$$

where

$$H_0 = N(d_1)$$

and

$$B_0 = X\exp(-rT)N(d_2)$$

where

$$d_1 = \frac{\ln(S_0/X) + (r + \sigma^2/2)T}{\sigma\sqrt{T}}$$

$$d_2 = d_1 - \sigma\sqrt{T}$$

and $N(\;)$ is the cumulative standard normal distribution function. That is,

$$N(d_j) = (2\pi)^{-1/2} \int_{-\infty}^{d_j} \exp\left(\frac{-t^2}{2}\right) dt.$$

This equation is the Black-Scholes price of a call option. If an option is priced above this value, then under the continuous trading assumption, it is possible to form a riskless arbitrage portfolio that initially consists of the replicating portfolio of H_0 shares, partially funded by borrowing B_0 dollars, together with a short position in the call. By continually adjusting the replicating portfolio, one can offset any losses (gains) on the call by gains (losses) on the portfolio. At expiration, the replicating portfolio gains (losses) will be exactly offset by losses (gains) on the option and the arbitrager will obtain a profit equal to the initial difference between the call price and the replicating portfolio value (together with interest).

Example 8.2

Given the following information:

$$S_0 = 50, \ X = 45, \ T = 3 \text{ months}, \ \sigma^2 = 0.20, \ r = 6\%,$$

Then,

$$d_1 = \frac{ln(S_0/X) + (r + \sigma^2/2)T}{\sigma\sqrt{T}}$$

$$= \frac{ln(50/45) + (0.06 + 0.20/2)0.25}{[(0.20)(0.25)]^{1/2}}$$

$$= 0.65$$

$$d_2 = d_1 - \sigma\sqrt{T} = 0.426.$$

Then

$$N(d_1) = 0.742, \ N(d_2) = 0.665$$

and

$$H_0 = N(d_1) = 0.742$$

$$B_0 = X\exp(-rT)N(d_2) = (45)\exp[(-0.06)(0.25)](0.665)$$

$$= 29.48$$

and

$$C_0 = H_0S_0 - B_0 = 50(0.742) - 29.48$$

$$= \$7.62.$$

Suppose the market price of the call option was \$8.62. Since the call is overvalued, an arbitrager would sell it and buy the replicating portfolio, which initially consists of 0.742 shares of stock partially financed by borrowing \$29.48. By continually adjusting the replicating portfolio until the option price aligns itself, the arbitrager could earn a riskless profit of \$1.00, together with interest. This alignment might occur prior to expiration. In the worst case, however, continual readjustments might have to be made to the expiration day, at which time

$$C_T = \text{Max}(0, S_T - X).$$

Share Equivalents

According to the Black-Scholes equation, at any point in time a call option is equivalent to a portfolio containing H_0 shares of stock, some of which are financed by borrowing B_0 dollars. Under the conditions of the model, call options are redundant in the sense that their payoff patterns can always be replicated by continually changing the amount of leverage in a particular portfolio. The current number of shares (H_0) in this unique replicating portfolio is referred to as the *share equivalents*. Under the Black-Scholes assumptions, the analysis of risk and reward opportunities for call options at this point in time is equivalent to the analysis of the risk and reward of the replicating leveraged portfolio.

Example 8.3

The analysis of the instantaneous risk and reward of the call option in Example 8.2 can be analyzed by investigating the risks and rewards of a leveraged position consisting of 0.742 shares partially financed by borrowing $29.48.

Role of Leverage in Risk Management

In order to analyze the risk and reward of option positions, we first must investigate how risks and rewards of leveraged stock positions can be analyzed.

Consider an investor with current wealth W_0 fully invested in shares of fund p. Assume the expected return (in price relative form), variance, and beta value of the fund are $E(R_p)$, $\sigma^2(R_p)$, and β_p, respectively.

If the investor borrows Q_0 dollars at risk-free rate R_F and invests in additional shares of the fund, the new portfolio, q, is leveraged and exposed to greater risks and rewards. To see this, consider the leveraged portfolio, q. The return on this portfolio is

$$\tilde{R}_q = \frac{[(Q_0 + W_0)\tilde{R}_p - Q_0 R_F]}{W_0}$$

$$= a\tilde{R}_p + (1 - a)R_F \qquad (8.16)$$

where a = (Total funds invested)/(Total funds-borrowing)
That is,

$$a = \frac{(Q_0 + W_0)}{W_0}$$

and is called the *leverage ratio*. The expected return and variance of the leveraged portfolio, q, are given by

$$E(\tilde{R}_q) = aE(\tilde{R}_p) + (1 - a)R_F \qquad (8.17)$$

$$\text{Var}(\tilde{R}_q) = \text{Var}[a\tilde{R}_p + (1 - a)R_F]$$

$$= a^2 \text{Var}(\tilde{R}_p) \qquad (8.18)$$

The beta value is given by

$$\beta_q = \frac{\text{Cov}(\tilde{R}_q, \tilde{R}_m)}{\text{Var}(\tilde{R}_m)}$$

$$= \frac{\text{Cov}[a\tilde{R}_p + (1 - a)R_F, \tilde{R}_m]}{\text{Var}(\tilde{R}_m)}$$

$$= \frac{a\text{Cov}(\tilde{R}_p, \tilde{R}_m)}{\text{Var}(\tilde{R}_m)} = a\beta_p \qquad (8.19)$$

Note that if funds are borrowed, the leverage ratio a exceeds 1 and hence the beta value and expected return exceed the values of the unleveraged portfolio. On the other hand, if funds are lent (Q_0 is negative), then risk (as measured by variance or beta value) and reward (as measured by expectation) of portfolio q fall below the values of the unleveraged portfolio, p.

Example 8.4

Consider a stock priced at $100. Its beta value is 1.2, its expected return is 12 percent, and its standard deviation is 3 percent.

An investor buys the stock by putting down $75 and borrowing $25 at 8 percent ($Q_0 = 25$, $W_0 = 75$). Hence $a = 100/75 = 1.33$.

From equations (8.17), (8.18), and (8.19) we have

$$E(\tilde{R}_p) = 1.33(0.12) - (0.33)(0.08) = 0.133$$

$$\text{Var}(R_p) = 1.33^2(0.03)^2 = 0.0016$$

and

$$\beta_p = (1.33)(1.2) = 1.596.$$

Note that if $50 were borrowed, then the leverage ratio would be 2 and the beta value would be 2.4. On the other hand, if the investor has $125 and lent $25 at the risk-free rate, then $W_0 = 125$, $Q_0 = -25$, and $a = 100/125 = 0.75$. In this case the leverage ratio is less than 1 and the beta value is

$$\beta_p = a\beta_s = 0.75(1.2) = 0.9.$$

Leverage Ratios for Call Options and Elasticity

Since a call option is equivalent to a portfolio of H_0 shares partially financed by borrowing B_0 dollars, we have

     Total funds invested $= H_0 S_0$
     Borrowed Funds $= B_0$

and hence the leverage ratio, a, is given by

$$a = \frac{H_0 S_0}{H_0 S_0 - B_0} = \frac{H_0 S_0}{C_0} \qquad (8.20)$$

The elasticity of a call option, e, measures the percentage change in the call value for a percentage change in the stock value:

$$e = \frac{\Delta C / C_0}{\Delta S / S_0} = \frac{\Delta C}{\Delta S} \cdot \frac{S_0}{C_0} \qquad (8.21)$$

Now $\Delta C / \Delta S$ is the change in the call price per unit change in the stock price. As the time interval, Δt, tends toward zero, this ratio tends toward the slope of the call price line at the current stock price. Hence, equation (8.21) reduces to

$$e = \frac{H_0 S_0}{C_0} \qquad (8.22)$$

The elasticity of a call option is just the leverage ratio of the replicating portfolio. The higher the elasticity (leverage), the greater the risk of the option.

Example 8.5

In Example 8.2 we had $S_0 = 50$, $H_0 = 0.742$, $B_0 = 29.48$, $C_0 = 7.62$.
The elasticity of the call option is

$$e = \frac{H_0 S_0}{C_0} = \frac{(0.742)(50.0)}{7.62}$$

$$= 4.87$$

Thus, for each percentage change in stock price, the percentage change in the call value is 4.87 percent.

The elasticity, or leverage value, for call options increases as the strike price increases. Thus, calls deep out of the money are more risky (higher leveraged) than calls at or in the money. Calls deep in the money are the least leveraged options, and tend to behave most similarly to stock.

Instantaneous Measures of Risk and Reward for Options

Since a call option can be replicated by a unique leveraged portfolio, it follows that the instantaneous return on a call, $\hat{r}_c$, must equal the instantaneous return on the replicating portfolio. Hence,

$$\hat{r}_c = a\hat{r}_s + (1 - a)r \qquad (8.23)$$

where $\hat{r}_s$ is the instantaneous return on the stock and r is the instantaneous risk-free rate.

The instantaneous expected return on the call, μ_c, variance, σ_c^2, and call beta, β_c, can be computed using equations (8.17), (8.18), and (8.19) to obtain

$$\mu_c = a\mu_s + (1 - a)r \qquad (8.24)$$

$$\sigma_c^2 = a^2\sigma_s^2 \tag{8.25}$$

$$\beta_c = a\beta_s \tag{8.26}$$

where μ_s, σ_s^2, and β_s are the instantaneous expected return, variance, and beta value for the stock.

Example 8.6

Consider the security of Example 8.2 with the following additional parameters:

$$\beta_s = 1.2,\ \mu_s = 0.15,\ \sigma_s^2 = 0.20,\ r = 0.05.$$

Then the beta value, expected return, and standard deviation of the call option can be established by analyzing the beta value, expected return, and standard deviation of the replicating portfolio. For the call option in the previous example, we had $H_0 = 0.742$, $B_0 = 29.48$.

The leverage ratio, a, is given by

$$a = \frac{H_0 S_0}{H_0 S_0 - B_0} = \frac{(0.742)(50)}{7.62} = 4.87$$

Hence,

$$\beta_c = a\beta_s = 4.87(1.2) = 5.84$$

$$\mu_c = a\mu_s + (1 - a)r = (4.87)(0.15) - (3.87)0.05 = 0.5370$$

$$\sigma_c = a\sigma_s = (4.87)(0.20)^{1/2} = 2.18$$

Note that since the replicating portfolio value changes as time passes and the stock price changes, the instantaneous beta value, expected return, and standard deviation of the call price change. Thus, the values computed above hold true only over small time intervals and only if the stock price changes are small.

Risks and Rewards of Portfolios Containing Options

The risks and rewards of a portfolio containing options can be computed by translating all call options into their equivalent leveraged stock positions. For example, to illustrate the risks and rewards of a covered call writing strategy, we duplicate the sale of a call option by the sale of the leveraged stock position. The buy stock/sell call position is thus equivalent to a portfolio of $1 - H_0$ shares of the stock and the purchase of B_0 bonds. In this case, since the leverage ratio, a, is less than 1, the risk of the position is less than the risk of buying 1 share of stock.

Example 8.7

Reconsider Example 8.1, in which we had

$$S_0 = 50, \ C_0 = 7.62, \ H_0 = 0.742, \ B_0 = 29.48, \text{ and } \beta_s = 1.2$$

$$\mu_s = 0.15, \ \sigma_s = 0.2, \text{ and } r = 0.05.$$

Now consider a portfolio containing a long position in the stock and a written call. This call is equivalent to selling 0.742 shares and lending $29.48. Using share equivalents, at this point in time the portfolio is equivalent to a long position in $(1 - H_0)$ shares and lending B_0 dollars at the risk-free rate.

The equivalent portfolio consists of $(1 - 0.742) = 0.258$ shares held long and an investment of $29.48 in the bank.

The current value of the portfolio is

$$W_0 = 0.258(50) + 29.48 = \$42.38$$

and the amount of dollars borrowed at the riskless rate is

$$Q_0 = -29.48.$$

Hence the leverage ratio is

$$a = \frac{(Q_0 + W_0)}{W_0}$$

$$= \frac{(42.38 - 29.48)}{42.38}$$

$$= 0.304.$$

The instantaneous beta value for this position is β_p, where

$$\beta_p = a\beta_s = 0.304(1.2) = 0.365.$$

Moreover, from equations (8.24) and (8.25), the instantaneous expected return, μ_p, and variance of return, σ_p^2, can be computed. Specifically,

$$\mu_p = a\mu_s + (1 - a)r = 0.304(0.15) + 0.696(0.05) = 0.0804$$

$$\sigma_p^2 = a^2\sigma_s^2 = (0.304)^2(0.20) = 0.018$$

To compensate for the risk involved in this position, its expected return exceeds the risk-free rate of 5 percent.

By translating portfolios containing options into equivalent leveraged stock positions, we may compute the relationship between a portfolio's expected return and its beta value. Exhibit 8.3 illustrates the relationship for a few call option strategies.

Put Pricing

Black and Scholes use arbitrage arguments to establish the following differential equation for the put option, P:

EXHIBIT 8.3

Risk-Reward Relationships for Options

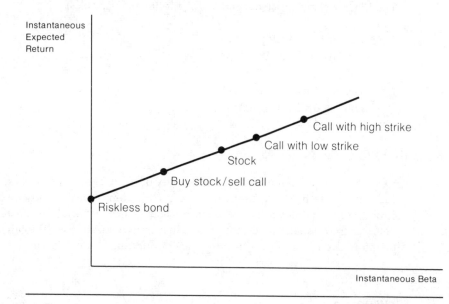

$$\frac{1}{2}\,\sigma^2 S^2 P_{SS} + rSP_S - rP + P_t = 0 \qquad (8.27)$$

where the subscripts denote partial differentiation. (Compare this equation to equation 8.13.) In addition, the put price must satisfy certain further conditions, including

$$P(S,T) = \text{Max}(X - S_T, 0)$$

$$P(S,T) \geq \text{Max}(X - S_T, 0) \qquad (8.28)$$

$$P(S,T) \leq X$$

$$P(S,T) \geq 0.$$

Although the deviation of this equation is beyond the scope of this chapter, it is of interest that no simple closed-form solution exists for the American put option.

If the option is European, then assuming no dividends, the following put-call parity relationship can be used to establish the Black-Scholes put price:

$$P_0^E = C_0^E - S_0 + X\exp(-rT). \qquad (8.29)$$

Given the Black-Scholes value for C_0^E, the put price can be determined. Substituting the Black-Scholes price into the above equation and simplifying terms, we obtain

$$P_0 = X\exp(-rT)N(-d_2) - S_0N(-d_1). \qquad (8.30)$$

PROPERTIES OF THE BLACK-SCHOLES PRICE

The Black-Scholes price depends on the following variables:

The current stock price, S_0,
The strike price, X,
The time to expiration, T,
The variance rate, σ^2, and
The risk-free rate of return, r.

Sensitivity to Stock Prices

Exhibits 8.4 and 8.5 illustrate the sensitivity of the near, middle, and far call and put option prices to the stock price. The exhibits clearly show that as option contracts move into the money, their values increase. Moreover, as time to expiration increases, the price also increases. In all cases, the call time premium is positive. Deep in-the-money put options trade at parity.

EXHIBIT 8.4
Sensitivity of the Call Price to the Stock Price

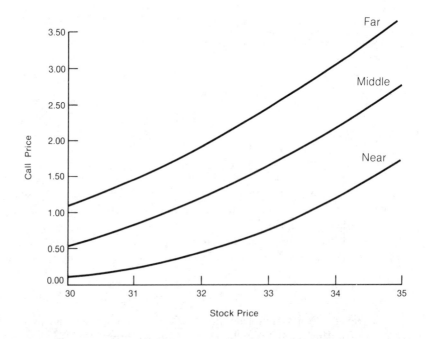

EXHIBIT 8.5
Sensitivity of the Put Price to the Stock Price

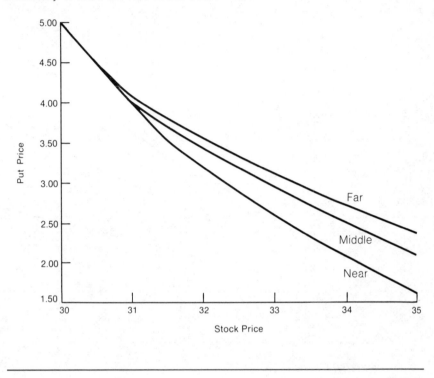

The sensitivity of the option price to stock price, $\partial C/\partial S$, can be shown to be equal to H_0. That is,

$$\frac{\partial C}{\partial S} = H_0 = N(d_1).$$

This value is often referred to as the *delta value*. A position in the stock can be "immunized" by ensuring the ratio of calls sold to stock purchased is equal to delta. The process of maintaining this immunized portfolio over time is often referred to as *delta hedging* and is discussed in Chapter 10.

Sensitivity to Interest Rates

Exhibits 8.6 and 8.7 illustrate the sensitivity of option prices to interest rates. As interest rates increase, call prices increase and put prices decrease. The reasons behind these results were discussed in Chapter 2.

EXHIBIT 8.6
Sensitivity of the Call Price to the Risk-Free Rate

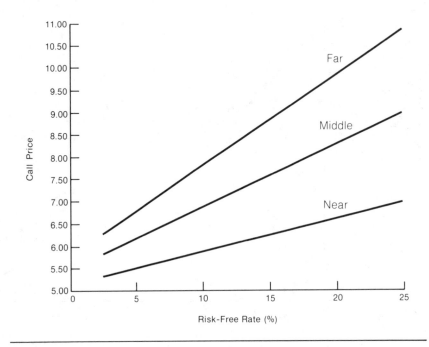

EXHIBIT 8.7
Sensitivity of the Put Price to the Risk-Free Rate

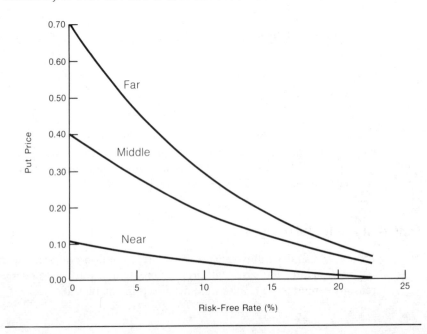

Sensitivity to Volatility

Option prices increase as volatility increases, as illustrated in Exhibits 8.8 and 8.9. The exhibits also illustrate that the time premiums of call options decrease as time to expiration decreases. In Exhibit 8.9 the time premiums of put options dropped off toward zero for options deep in the money. As discussed in Chapter 4, European put options could carry a negative time premium.

THE BLACK-SCHOLES PRICE AND THE RISK-NEUTRALITY ARGUMENT*

Under the Black-Scholes assumption, call and put prices depend on the stock price, S_0, the strike price, X, the time to expiration, T, the volatility, σ, and the riskless rate, r. Surprisingly, the prices do not depend on the total expected return from the stock, μ, or on investors' preferences. This being the case, the value of an option in a risk-neutral economy must be the same as the value of an option in a risk-averse economy. Thus, for mathematical simplicity, we may assume the option is to be valued in a risk-neutral economy. If we can derive the fair value of a call option in this risk-neutral economy, this price must be the fair price in other economies.

EXHIBIT 8.8
Sensitivity of the Call Price to Volatility

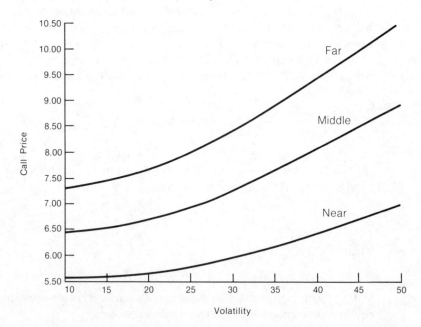

EXHIBIT 8.9
Sensitivity of the Put Price to Volatility

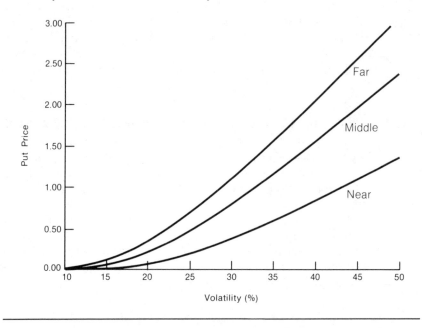

Recall that in a risk-neutral economy, investors are indifferent between a gamble, G, which has an expected return, $E(G)$, and a certain riskless return of $E(G)$. In such an economy, investors pay no attention to variances and higher moments. In equilibrium, all assets are priced to have the same expected return as the risk-free rate.

Let $R_F = \exp(rT)$. Then an investment of B_0 dollars in the riskless asset will grow to $R_F B_0$. In this economy, at the expiration date, T, we should have

$$B_1 = R_F B_0 \tag{8.31}$$

$$E(\tilde{S}_T) = R_F S_0 \tag{8.32}$$

$$E(\tilde{C}_T) = R_F C_0 \tag{8.33}$$

Hence, the current call price, C_0, would be the expected call price at expiration $E(\tilde{C}_T)$ discounted to the present:

$$C_0 = \frac{E(\tilde{C}_T)}{R_F} \tag{8.34}$$

where

$$\tilde{C}_T = \text{Max}(\tilde{S}_T - X, 0) \tag{8.35}$$

and $\tilde{S}_T$ has a lognormal distribution, with parameters set according to the equilibrium conditions in the risk-neutral economy.

Recall that the price, $\tilde{S}_T$, can be represented as follows:

$$\tilde{S}_T = S_0\exp(\mu T + \sqrt{T}\,\tilde{Z})$$

and

$$E(\tilde{S}_T) = S_0\exp\left(\mu T + \frac{\sigma^2 T}{2}\right) \tag{8.36}$$

where μ and σ^2 are the instantaneous mean and variance, respectively. Hence, in a risk-neutral economy, from equations 8.32 and 8.36 we have

$$R_F S_0 = \exp\left(\mu T + \frac{\sigma^2 T}{2}\right) S_0$$

and hence

$$R_F = \exp\left(\mu T + \frac{\sigma^2 T}{2}\right) \tag{8.37}$$

Substituting $R_F = \exp(rT)$ into the left-hand side of equation 8.37 and solving for μ, we obtain

$$\mu = r - \frac{\sigma^2}{2} \tag{8.38}$$

That is, in a risk-neutral economy, securities having lognormal distributions must have their instantaneous expected value, μ, satisfying equation (8.38). The call price, C_0, is given by

$$C_0 = \frac{E(\tilde{C}_T)}{R_F}$$

where

$$E(\tilde{C}_T) = \text{Max}(\tilde{S}_T - X, 0) \tag{8.39}$$

In the appendix, it is shown that this expectation is given by

$$E(\tilde{C}_T) = E(\tilde{S}_T)N(d_1{}^*) - XN(d_2{}^*) \tag{8.40}$$

where

$$d_1{}^* = \frac{\ln(S_0/X) + \mu T + \sigma^2 T}{\sigma\sqrt{T}}$$

$$d_2{}^* = d_1{}^* - \sigma\sqrt{T} \tag{8.41}$$

Now since in a risk-neutral economy $\mu = r - \sigma^2/2$, we have

$$E(\tilde{C}_T) = E(\tilde{S}_T)N(d_1) - XN(d_2) \tag{8.42}$$

where

$$d_1 = \frac{\ln(S_0/X) + (r + \sigma^2/2)T}{\sigma\sqrt{T}}$$

$$d_2 = d_1 - \sigma\sqrt{T}$$

Finally, since $C_0 = E(\tilde{C}_T)/R_F$, with $R_F = \exp(rT)$, we have

$$C_0 = S_0 N(d_1) - X\exp(-rT)N(d_2), \qquad (8.43)$$

which is the Black-Scholes equation.

In Chapter 5 we showed that, in a complete market, options could be valued using a risk-neutral valuation relationship. Under the assumptions of Black and Scholes, the risk-neutral valuation relationship is also applicable. The reason for this stems from the continuous trading assumption. With this assumption, a portfolio can be constructed that replicates the payouts of the call. This results in the option being a redundant security, which by the law of one price can be unambiguously valued. Since preferences do not enter the pricing relationship, the risk-neutrality argument is applicable.

APPROXIMATE OPTION PRICING MODELS FOR DIVIDEND-PAYING STOCKS

The Black-Scholes model values a European call option and, hence, an American call option on a stock that pays no dividends. If the stock declares dividends prior to the expiration date, then an American call may be more valuable exercised than not exercised. In this case the Black-Scholes price may understate the value of an American option. In some instances simple adjustments to the model may result in very reasonable approximations. We shall discuss one such method. References are then provided for more accurate approximations. For simplicity, we shall assume that a known dividend of size d_1 occurs at time t_1 prior to expiration, T. In this case, if the dividend is forfeited and the option not exercised prematurely, the call value is given by

$$C' = C(S_A, X, T) \qquad (8.44)$$

where $C(S_A, X, T)$ is the Black-Scholes call price based on a stock price of S_A, strike of X, and time to expiration, T, and S_A is the current stock price adjusted by deducting the present value of the dividend.

Clearly, since the call may be exercised early, we have

$$C \geq C(S_A, X, T). \qquad (8.45)$$

In Chapter 4 it was shown that if the option was to be exercised early, it should be exercised at time t_1, just prior to the ex dividend date. If exercised at this time, the holder pays X dollars to receive the stock. However, a part of this payment is offset by the dividend received at that time. Hence, the effective strike is $X - d_1$. The value of a call exercised at time t_1 with this strike is

$$C'' = C(S_A, X - d_1, t_1). \qquad (8.46)$$

Hence, the value of the call should be no lower than C^*, where

$$C^* = \text{Max}(C', C''). \qquad (8.47)$$

   If there are two dividends prior to expiration, then it can be shown that the call price should be no lower than C^*, where

$$C^* = \text{Max}(C', C'', C''') \tag{8.48}$$

and

$$C' = C(S_A, X, T) \tag{8.49}$$
$$C'' = C(S_A, X - d_1 - d_2\exp[-r(t_2 - t_1), t_1] \tag{8.50}$$
$$C''' = C(S_A, X - d_2, t_2) \tag{8.51}$$

and

$$S_A = S_0 - d_1\exp(-rt_1) - d_2\exp(-rt_2). \tag{8.52}$$

   These formulae are approximations of the American call option price when early exercise is possible. Since an American call can be exercised at any time, its value should not fall below C^*.

   More accurate pricing of American call options on dividend-paying stocks is discussed in the references by Geske, Roll, and Whaley.

APPROXIMATE PUT OPTION PRICING MODELS

Let $P(X)$ be the price on an American put option on a nondividend-paying stock. Margrabe has shown that the price of this option is bounded above by the price of a European put option with identical terms except for the strike price, which is increased from X to $X\exp(rT)$, where r is the riskless rate and T is the time to expiration. Hence,

$$P^E(X) \leq P(X) \leq P^E(Xe^{rT})$$

where the E superscript denotes the European option. Johnson has postulated that the actual price can be written as a linear combination of these bounds. That is,

$$P(X) = \alpha P^E(X) + (1 - \alpha)P^E(Xe^{rT}).$$

The value of α is not a constant, but a complicated function of the stock price, strike time to expiration, volatility, and interest rate. Johnson established the following formula for α:

$$\alpha = \left[\frac{rT}{3.9649rT + 0.032325}\right]^\lambda$$

$$\lambda = \frac{\ln(S_0/S_c)}{\ln(X/S_c)}$$

and S_c is the calculated by

$$S_c = X\left(\frac{\gamma}{1 + \gamma}\right)^m$$

where

$$\gamma = \frac{2r}{\sigma^2}$$

and

$$m = \frac{\sigma^2 T}{(1.0408\sigma^2 T + 0.00963)}.$$

These approximations can be extended to account for stocks that pay dividends.

The problem with such approximations is that there is no way to ensure the results are arbitrarily accurate. Geske and Johnson have established an analytic formula for American put options. Although this formula consists of an infinite series of terms, it is an exact pricing equation. Although quite complex, it is possible to establish polynomial expressions that can be used for approximations. The advantage of this model is that by adding terms, the approximation can be improved. Geske and Johnson provide equations that ensure the result is within pennies of the analytical result.

CONCLUSION

This chapter has provided an intuitive explanation of the Black-Scholes option pricing equation. The sensitivity of the Black-Scholes price to its parameters was illustrated. The Black-Scholes price depends on the stock price, strike price, time to expiration, volatility, and interest rates. Surprisingly, the value does not depend on expectations and preferences. The reason for this stems from the continuous trading assumption that allows a portfolio of stocks and bonds to replicate the payouts of the option.

Under the Black-Scholes assumption, a call option can be viewed as a continually adjusted, leveraged position in the stock. As such, at any point in time the analysis of the risk and reward of any position can be addressed by translating all options into their equivalent leveraged positions.

When dividends occur, American call options cannot be valued exactly by the Black-Scholes equation. For American put options, no simple closed-form valuation equation exists. As a result, approximate models are available. In the final section of this chapter, approximations based on adjustments to the Black-Scholes model were described. Other approximations are possible and are discussed in the next chapter.

References

The original Black-Scholes pricing model was developed by Black and Scholes in 1973. Their article requires advanced mathematics. An introduction to this mathematics and a rigorous deviation of the Black-Scholes equation are provided in Chapter 16. Jarrow and Rudd provide an excellent coverage of this topic that requires only modest strength in mathematics. The characterization of self-financing portfolio strategies is discussed by Bergman.

The review paper by Smith provides a history of the early attempts that were made to price options before the Black-Scholes model. A number of call option pricing models have been proposed in which the underlying stock pays dividends (see Geske, Roll, and Whaley). American put option pricing models are also referenced (see Geske and Shastri, Geske and Johnson, and Johnson).

Applications of the Black-Scholes model are deferred to Chapter 10. Alternative derivation and generalizations of the model are presented in Chapters 9 and 10.

Bergman, Y. "A Characterization of Self-Financing Portfolio Strategies." Working paper, School of Business Administration, University of California at Berkeley, 1981.

Black, F. "Fact and Fantasy in the Use of Options." *Financial Analysts Journal* (July/August 1985): 36–72.

Black, F., and M. Scholes. "The Pricing of Options and Corporate Liabilities." *Journal of Economics* (May 1973): 637–59.

Geske, R. "A Note on an Analytical Valuation Formula for Unprotected American Call Options on Stocks with Known Dividends." *Journal of Financial Economics* 7(December 1979): 375–80.

Geske, R., and K. Shastri. "The Early Exercise of American Puts." *Journal of Banking and Finance* (1985): 207–19.

Geske, R., and H. Johnson. "The American Put Option Valued Analytically." *Journal of Finance,* 39(5)(December 1984): 1511–24.

Jarrow, R., and A. Rudd. *Option Pricing.* Homewood, Ill.: Richard Irwin, 1983.

Johnson, H. "An Analytic Approximation for the American Put Price." *Journal of Financial and Quantitative Analysis* 18(March 1983): 141–48.

Margrabe, W. "The Value of an Option to Exchange One Asset for Another." *Journal of Finance* 33(March 1978): 177–86.

Merton, R. "Theory of Rational Option Pricing." *Bell Journal of Economics and Management Science* 4(Spring 1973): 141–83.

Roll, R. "An Analytic Valuation Formula for Unprotected Call Option on Stocks with Known Dividends." *Journal of Financial Economics* (November 1977): 251–58.

Smith, C. "Option Pricing: A Review." *Journal of Financial Economics* (January 1976): 3–51.

Sterk, W. "Test of Two Models for Valuing Call Options on Stocks with Dividends." *Journal of Finance* (December 1982): 1229–37.

Whaley, R. "On the Valuation of American Call Options on Stocks with Known Dividends." *Journal of Financial Economics* 9(June 1981): 207–12.

Exercises

1. A nondividend-paying stock is currently priced at $50. An American call with strike 45 and time to expiration 0.25 years is to be valued. The riskless interest rate is 10 percent and the stock volatility is 0.5.
   a. Using the Black-Scholes equation, price the call option.
   b. If the annual volatility were 0.25, not 0.5, what would the price of the option be?

2. Using the above data, value a European put option. If dividends were paid out on the stock, would the put price be higher or lower? Discuss.

3. From the data in question 1 together with the fact that the stock's beta value is 1.3, compute the following:
   a. The elasticity of the option,
   b. The instantaneous beta value of the option.

4. For the stock in question 1, compute the value of an at-the-money option contract.
   a. Using this value, compute the elasticity and beta value of the option.
   b. By comparing your answers in questions 3 and 4, what can you conclude about the risk of option contracts?

5. Stock XYZ is at $50. A three-month at-the-money call option is written against the stock. The volatility of the stock is 0.5, and interest rates are 10 percent.
   a. Compute the leverage ratio, a, for this position.
   b. Compute the beta value of this position assuming the beta value of the stock is 1.2.

6. Repeat question 5 for a position where two calls are written against the stock (i.e., a 2:1 ratio write). Is the instantaneous risk of this position greater or less than the risk of the covered write strategy in question 5?

7. Consider a bullish call spread where the 50s are sold and the 45s are purchased.
   a. Using the Black-Scholes prices derived in question 1 and 5, compute the number of share equivalents and the beta value of this position.
   b. Would you expect this beta value to be very sensitive to price fluctuations in the stock and to time to maturity? Explain.

8. Compute the number of share equivalents for the put option in problem 2. Interpret the initial replicating portfolio for the put option. Finally, calculate the beta value for the purchase of a put option, given a stock beta of 1.3.

9. Using the 50 call and 50 put prices computed in problems 1 and 2, compute the number of share equivalents in a straddle position. Interpret the answer. Finally, compute the beta value for the position.

10. Discuss the implications of the continuous trading assumption. How do transaction costs inhibit this assumption?

11. Under the Black-Scholes assumption, the stock price follows a geometric Wiener process. The Black-Scholes hedge ratio, $H[H = N(d_1)]$, must be continually updated. Could a Black-Scholes riskless hedge be maintained if the stock price remained unchanged over a finite time period? Discuss.

Appendix A
Calculation of the Expected Call Price at Expiration

The call price at expiration is

$$\tilde{C}_T = \text{Max}(0, \tilde{S}_T - X). \qquad\qquad \text{A(8.1)}$$

Hence,

$$E(\tilde{C}_T) = \int\limits_{S_T > X} (S_T - X) f(S_T) dS_T \qquad\qquad \text{A(8.2)}$$

where $f(S_T)$ is the probability density function of the stock price at expiration. For a lognormal distribution, we have

$$\tilde{S}_T = S_0 \exp(\mu T + \sigma \sqrt{T} \, \tilde{Z}) \qquad\qquad \text{A(8.3)}$$

where $\tilde{Z}$ is the standard normal density.

From A(8.2) we have

$$E(\tilde{C}_T) = \int\limits_{S_T > X} S_T f(S_T) dS_T - X P(\tilde{S}_T > X). \qquad\qquad \text{A(8.4)}$$

We shall now compute the two terms in equation A(8.5).

$$P(\tilde{S}_T > X) = P[S_0 \exp(\mu T + \sigma \sqrt{T} \, \tilde{Z}) > X]$$

$$= P\left[Z \geq -\frac{\ln(S_0/X) + \mu T}{\sigma \sqrt{T}}\right]$$

$$= N(d_2^*) \qquad\qquad \text{A(8.5)}$$

where

$$d_2^* = -\frac{\ln(S_0/X) + \mu T}{\sigma \sqrt{T}}$$

and $N(\ )$ is the cumulative normal distribution.

The first term in A(8.4) is computed similarly. Specifically,

$$\int_{S_T > X} S_T f(S_T) dS_T = S_0 \exp(\mu T)(2\pi)^{-1/2} \int_{d_2^*}^{\infty} \exp\left(\sigma\sqrt{T}\, Z - \frac{Z^2}{2}\right) dZ.$$

$$\text{A(8.6)}$$

Completing the square and simplifying reduces the expression to

$$\int_{S_T > X} S_T f(S_T) dS_T = S_0 \exp\left(\mu T + \frac{\sigma^2 T}{2}\right) N(d_1^*) \qquad \text{A(8.7)}$$

where

$$d_1^* = \frac{\ln(S_0/X) + \mu T + \sigma^2 T}{\sigma\sqrt{T}}$$

Substituting A(8.5) and A(8.7) into A(8.4), we obtain, after simplification,

$$E(\tilde{C}_T) = E(\tilde{S}_T) N(d_1^*) - X N(d_2^*). \qquad \text{A(8.8)}$$

Appendix B

Computer Program for Black-Scholes Prices

The following computer program calculates the Black-Scholes prices of European put and call options.

```
10   REM  *********************************************************************
20   REM     A PROGRAM USED TO CALCULATE OPTION PRICES USING THE BLACK-
30   REM     SCHOLES OPTION PRICING FORMULA
40   REM
50   REM        written by GREGORY B. GETTS
60   REM
70   REM     List of variables used in the program
80   REM
90   REM        CO     - CALL PRICE
100  REM        PO     - PUT PRICE
110  REM        STRIKE - STRIKE PRICE
120  REM        SIG    - THE STAND. DEV. OF THE STOCK
130  REM        RATE   - SHORT TERM INTEREST RATE
140  REM        PRICE  - PRICE OF THE COMMON STOCK
150  REM        TIME   - DAYS UNTIL THE OPTION EXPIRES
160  REM        ATIME  - ANNUAL TIME UNTIL EXPIRATION
170  REM
180  REM  *********************************************************************
190       DOALL=1
200       GOSUB 600
210       ATIME=TIME/365
220       GOSUB 370
230       CO=PCO
240  REM
250       PO=CO-PRICE+STRIKE*EXP(-RATE*ATIME)
260       X=STRIKE-PRICE
270       IF X>PO THEN PO=X
280  REM
290  REM    PRINT OUT RESULTS
300  REM
310       CLS:LOCATE 22,8:PRINT "The call price is: ";CO
320       LOCATE 23,8:PRINT "The put price is:  ";PO
330       GOTO 200
```

```
340 REM ******************************************************************
350 REM This section calculates the B/S option price
360 REM ******************************************************************
370     D1=(LOG(PRICE/STRIKE)+(RATE+SIG/2)*ATIME)/(SIG*SQR(ATIME))
380     D2=D1-SIG*SQR(ATIME)
390     ZVAL=D1
400     GOSUB 490
410     XND1=XN
420     ZVAL=D2
430     GOSUB 490
440     PCO=PRICE*XND1-STRIKE*EXP(-RATE*ATIME)*XN
450     RETURN
460 REM ******************************************************************
470 REM This section calcualtes the area under the curve
480 REM ******************************************************************
490     Z1=ABS(ZVAL)
500     IF Z1>=5 THEN XN=1:GOTO 550
510     Z2!=1/(1+.2316419*Z1)
520     Z3!=.3989423*EXP(-ZVAL*ZVAL/2)
530     XN=(((1.330274*Z2!-1.821256)*Z2!+1.781478)*Z2!-.3565638)*Z2!+.3193815
540     XN=1-Z3!*Z2!*XN
550     IF ZVAL<0 THEN XN=1-XN
560     RETURN
570 REM ******************************************************************
580 REM   INPUT THE INFORMATION FOR THE OPTION
590 REM ******************************************************************
600   IF DOALL=1 THEN GOTO 750
610   LOCATE 3,8:PRINT "THE FOLLOWING OPTIONS EXIST:"
620   LOCATE 5,8:PRINT "0) Calculate the option prices"
630   LOCATE 6,8:PRINT "1) Change the current stock price      ";PRICE
640   LOCATE 7,8:PRINT "2) Change the standard deviation       ";SIG
650   LOCATE 8,8:PRINT "3) Change the strike price             ";STRIKE
660   LOCATE 9,8:PRINT "4) Change the days until expiration    ";TIME
670   LOCATE 10,8:PRINT "5) Change the risk free interest rate";RATE
680   LOCATE 13,8:PRINT "6) Enter a completely new option"
690   LOCATE 14,8:PRINT "7) Exit the system"
700   O$="ENTER A NUMBER BETWEEN 0 AND 7:":GOSUB 870
710   INPUT I%
720   IF I%<0 OR I%>7 THEN BEEP:LOCATE 18,12:PRINT SPACE$(40):GOTO 700
730   IF I%=0 THEN RETURN
740   ON I% GOTO 750,770,790,810,830,850,860
750   O$="ENTER THE CURRENT STOCK PRICE:":GOSUB 870
760   INPUT PRICE:IF DOALL=0 THEN GOTO 610
770   O$="ENTER THE CURRENT STANDARD DEVIATION:":GOSUB 870
780   INPUT SIG:IF DOALL=0 THEN GOTO 610
790   O$="ENTER THE STRIKE PRICE:":GOSUB 870
800   INPUT STRIKE:IF DOALL=0 THEN GOTO 610
810   O$="ENTER THE NUMBER OF DAYS UNTIL EXPIRATION:":GOSUB 870
820   INPUT TIME:IF DOALL=0 THEN GOTO 610
830   O$="ENTER THE CURRENT RISK FREE RATE OF RETURN:":GOSUB 870
840   INPUT RATE:DOALL=0:GOTO 610
850   DOALL=1:GOTO 750
860   CLS:SYSTEM
870   LOCATE 18,8:PRINT SPACE$(70):LOCATE 18,8:PRINT O$;:RETURN
```

9

Binomial Option Pricing Models

In Chapter 8 a closed-form solution for the price of an American call option on a stock that pays no dividends prior to expiration was derived. Unfortunately, no closed-form solution can be obtained for an American put option. In this case, numerical procedures are often used to approximate the fundamental partial differential equation governing the option price. Rather than approximate the differential equation, option prices can often be derived in a simple fashion by first approximating the stochastic process of the stock price.

The approximation of stock price processes is often accomplished by means of a binomial model. In the first section of this chapter, the binomial approximation is investigated. The second section investigates how options can be priced, assuming stock prices follow the binomial model. This approach was first discussed by Sharpe, and formally analyzed by Cox, Ross, and Rubinstein and by Rendleman and Bartter. The results in this chapter draw heavily on their analyses. The model they established, referred to as the *binomial option pricing model* (BOPM), is extremely useful. We shall see, for example, that as the binomial approximation to the geometric Wiener process becomes more precise, the BOPM converges onto the Black-Scholes model. Unlike the Black-Scholes model, however, the BOPM can be used to value American put options and to price option contracts when the underlying stock pays dividends. A computer program that provides these theoretical prices is included.

In addition to providing numerical procedures for valuing options under a variety of assumptions, this chapter also provides further explanation of the Black-Scholes model and the risk-neutrality argument. Indeed, the binomial option pricing model should provide the reader with a deep understanding of arbitrage relationships and the law of one price.

DISCRETE RANDOM WALK MODELS

Processes whose outcomes are influenced by random effects throughout time are referred to as *stochastic processes*. In characterizing any process, it is first necessary to specify a time set, T^*. If this set consists of an interval with observations recorded continuously, the process is called a *continuous process*. An example of a continuous process would be the geometric Wiener process, discussed in Chapter 6. If observations are made periodically, then T^* consists of a sequence of times and the process is referred to as a *discrete process*. We shall first consider a discrete process where the time interval, say $(0, T)$, is partitioned into n time increments of width Δt and stock prices are observed at the end of each increment. We shall reference the observations by consecutive integers. Then T^* is defined as $T^* = \{0, 1, 2, 3, 4, \ldots, n\}$, and the collection of stock prices observed at these points in time constitute the stochastic process. Let $\{\tilde{S}_t\}$ represent this collection. Note that as the partition of the interval $(0, T)$ increases, the number of observations increases and the discrete process converges onto a continuous process. In this section we shall consider a discrete binomial random walk process. This process is extremely useful, since it serves as an approximation to a variety of continuous stochastic processes, including the geometric Wiener process.

We shall assume stock price changes over the time increments of width Δt are independently and identically distributed random variables. In this case, we have

$$\tilde{S}_1 = S_0 + \Delta \tilde{S}_1$$

$$\tilde{S}_2 = \tilde{S}_1 + \Delta \tilde{S}_2 = S_0 + \Delta \tilde{S}_1 + \Delta \tilde{S}_2$$

and finally

$$\tilde{S}_n = S_0 + \sum_{i=1}^{n} \Delta \tilde{S}_i. \tag{9.1}$$

The stock price at the end of the time period $(0, T)$ can be represented by the original stock price together with the sum of n random variables. From equation (9.1), we have

$$E(\tilde{S}_n) = S_0 + nE(\Delta \tilde{S}) \tag{9.2}$$

$$\text{Var}(\tilde{S}_n) = n\text{Var}(\Delta \tilde{S}). \tag{9.3}$$

This model is referred to as a *simple random walk process*. The independence assumption implies that historical trend analysis will not help predict the direction of future movements. Moreover, the actual change in the stock price does not depend on the level of the stock price.

To illustrate the random walk model for stock prices, we could hypothesize that in each time increment, Δt, the stock price could either increase by a fixed amount, u, with probability p, or decrease by amount d with probability q. In the ith time increment, we have

$$\Delta \tilde{S}_t = \Delta \tilde{S} = u \text{ with probability } p$$

$$= d \text{ with probability } q.$$

The expected stock price change and variance are

$$E(\Delta \tilde{S}) = up + dq \tag{9.4}$$

$$\text{Var}(\Delta\tilde{S}) = E(\Delta\tilde{S}^2) - [E(\Delta S)]^2$$
$$= u^2p + d^2q - (up + dq)^2,$$

which simplifies to

$$\text{Var}(\Delta\tilde{S}) = (u - d)^2pq. \tag{9.5}$$

Given $E(\Delta\tilde{S})$ and $\text{Var}(\Delta\tilde{S})$, the expected stock price and variance after n time increments, computed using equations (9.2) and (9.3), are

$$E(\tilde{S}_n) = S_0 + n(up + dq) \tag{9.6}$$

$$\text{Var}(\tilde{S}_n) = (u - d)^2npq. \tag{9.7}$$

Example 9.1

Consider a stock currently priced at \$50. Assume $u = 4$, $d = -3$, and $p = 0.6$. Exhibit 9.1 illustrates the possible realizations over three periods. From equations (9.6) and (9.7), the expected stock price and variance after three periods are given by

$$E(\tilde{S}_3) = 50 + 3[4(0.6) + (-3)(0.4)] = 53.6$$

$$\text{Var}(\tilde{S}_3) = (4 + 3)^2 3(0.6)(0.4) = 35.28.$$

EXHIBIT 9.1
Possible Stock Price Realizations

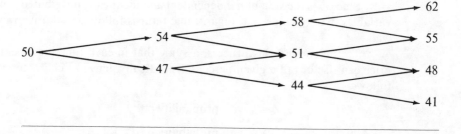

THE GEOMETRIC RANDOM WALK

The hypothesized structure imposed on the stock prices in the additive model has several undesirable features. First, the stock price could become negative. Second, the stock price changes do not depend on the current stock price. A \$10 price change in a stock currently valued at \$10 is as likely as the same price change if the stock were priced at \$100.

To remedy these problems, rather than place restrictions on the *absolute* price change, we shall place restrictions on the *relative* pricing behavior. Toward this goal, consider the process generated by the price relatives. Let $\tilde{Z}_t = \tilde{S}_t / \tilde{S}_{t-1}$ represent the price relative over the tth time increment. Then, given the original stock price is S_0, future stock prices can be represented by a multiplicative process, as follows:

$$\tilde{S}_1 = S_0 \tilde{Z}_1$$

$$\tilde{S}_2 = \tilde{S}_1 \tilde{Z}_2 = S_0 \tilde{Z}_1 \tilde{Z}_2$$

and finally

$$\tilde{S}_n = S_0 \tilde{Z}_1 \tilde{Z}_2 \ldots \tilde{Z}_n = S_0 \prod_{i=1}^{n} \tilde{Z}_i.$$

Let $\tilde{R}_t$ represent the total return (from time 0 to time t) in price relative form. Then,

$$\tilde{R}_t = \frac{\tilde{S}_t}{S_0} = \prod_{i=1}^{t} \tilde{Z}_i \quad \text{for } t = 1, 2, \ldots n. \tag{9.8}$$

If the sequence of price relatives, $\{Z_i\}$, are independent and identically distributed random variables, then the process is referred to as a *geometric random walk process*. The total return over the period $(0, T)$ is

$$\tilde{R}_n = \frac{\tilde{S}_n}{S_0} = \prod_{i=1}^{n} \tilde{Z}_i.$$

Let $\tilde{r}_n = ln(\tilde{R}_n)$ represent the logarithmic return. Then,

$$\tilde{r}_n = \sum_{i=1}^{n} ln \, \tilde{Z}_i. \tag{9.9}$$

Since $\tilde{r}_n$ is the sum of n independent and identically distributed random variables, we conclude that logarithmic returns follow an additive random walk.

To understand this process, assume that in each time increment, the price can rise or fall a given percent. Specifically, let $\tilde{Z}_i$ be characterized as follows:

$$\tilde{Z}_i = u \text{ with probability } p$$

$$= d \text{ with probability } q \ (q = 1 - p).$$

From equation (9.9),

$$\tilde{r}_n = ln(\tilde{R}_n) = \sum_{i=1}^{n} \tilde{V}_i \tag{9.10}$$

where $\tilde{V}_i = ln(\tilde{Z}_i)$ and its distribution is given by

$$\tilde{V}_i = a = ln(u) \text{ with probability } p$$

$$= b = ln(d) \text{ with probability } q.$$

Using equations (9.6) and (9.7), we have

$$E(\tilde{r}_n) = n(ap + bq) \qquad (9.11)$$

$$\text{Var}(\tilde{r}_n) = (a - b)^2 npq. \qquad (9.12)$$

Example 9.2

Exhibit 9.2 illustrates the evolution of prices for $S_0 = 50$ when it is assumed that in each increment the stock can either appreciate by 10 percent ($u = 1.1$) with probability 0.6, or depreciate by 10 percent ($d = 0.9$) with probability 0.4.

The expected logarithmic return and variance over three periods is computed using equations (9.11) and (9.12). Specifically,

$$a = ln(1.1) = 0.09531, b = ln(0.9) = -0.10536,$$

and hence

$$E(r_3) = 3[(0.09531)0.6 + (-0.10536)0.4] = 0.045$$

$$\text{Var}(r_3) = (0.09531 + 0.10536)^2 3(0.6)(0.4) = 0.290.$$

EXHIBIT 9.2
Possible Stock Price Realizations

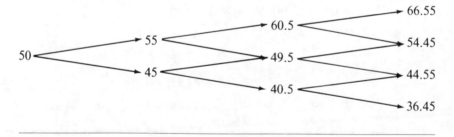

The actual probability distribution of stock prices after n time increments can be derived. Toward this end, let S_{nj} represent the stock price after n periods, given that j upward movements and $n - j$ downward movements have occurred. Exhibit 9.3 illustrates the stock price behavior.

After n periods, the stock price is given by

$$S_{nj} = u^j d^{n-j} S_0 \qquad j = 0, 1, 2, 3, \ldots n. \qquad (9.13)$$

The probability that the stock price in the nth period, $\tilde{S}_n$, takes on the value S_{nj} is merely the probability that in n periods (trials) there are j upward movements (successes) and $(n - j)$ downward movements (failures). This probability is given by the binomial probability law. Hence, we have

$$P(\tilde{S}_n = S_{nj}) = \binom{n}{j} p^j q^{n-j} \qquad j = 0, 1, 2, 3, \ldots n. \qquad (9.14)$$

EXHIBIT 9.3
A Geometric Binomial Random Walk Process

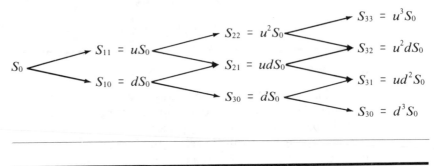

Example 9.3

In the previous example we had $n = 3$, $p = 0.6$, $u = 1.1$, and $d = 0.9$. Moreover, from Exhibit 9.2, we had

$$S_{33} = (1.1)^3 50 = 66.55$$

$$S_{32} = (1.1)^2(0.9)50 = 54.45$$

$$S_{31} = (1.1)(0.9)^2 50 = 44.55$$

and $S_{30} = (0.9)^3 50 = 36.45.$

Using equation (9.14), we have

$$P(\tilde{S}_3 = 66.55) = 0.216$$

$$P(\tilde{S}_3 = 54.45) = 0.432$$

$$P(\tilde{S}_3 = 44.55) = 0.288$$

$$P(\tilde{S}_4 = 36.45) = 0.064.$$

BINOMIAL APPROXIMATIONS OF CONTINUOUS STOCHASTIC PROCESSES

The discrete geometric binomial random walk model is important because it can be used to approximate a variety of well-known continuous stochastic processes. This is accomplished by partitioning the time interval $(0, T)$ into smaller and smaller segments. As the width of each segment, Δt, decreases, the size of the jump values (a and b) and their probabilities (p and q) must be adjusted. Depending on how these jumps and probabilities are linked to the width of the time increment, different limiting models result.

To see this more clearly, consider the case when the time period $(0, T)$ is partitioned into n segments, with $n = T/\Delta t$. Then from equations (6.11), (6.12), and (6.14), we have

$$E(\tilde{r}_n) = \frac{T(ap + bq)}{\Delta t} \qquad (9.15)$$

$$\text{Var}(\tilde{r}_n) = (a - b)^2 \frac{pqT}{\Delta t} \qquad (9.16)$$

and

$$P(\tilde{S}_n = S_{nj}) = \binom{n}{j} p^j q^{n-j} \qquad j = 0, 1, 2, 3, \ldots n. \quad (9.17)$$

As the partition of the interval of interest $(0, T)$ becomes finer and finer, the discrete stochastic process converges onto a continuous stochastic process. The logarithmic return over the period, r_n, converges onto the continuously compounded return. Let r_T represent this return. Its expected value and variance are given by

$$E(\tilde{r}_T) = \lim_{n \to \infty} E(\tilde{r}_n) \qquad (9.18)$$

$$\text{Var}(\tilde{r}_T) = \lim_{n \to \infty} \text{Var}(r_n). \qquad (9.19)$$

The expectation, variance and, indeed, the limiting distribution of the logarithmic return at time T are well characterized once values for a, b, and p are developed in terms of time increment Δt.

By suitably defining the values for a, b, and p, one can make the binomial process for logarithmic returns converge onto a variety of diffusion and jump processes.

As an example, if we let

$$a = \sigma \sqrt{\Delta t} \qquad (9.20)$$

$$b = -\sigma \sqrt{\Delta t} \qquad (9.21)$$

$$p = \frac{1}{2} + \frac{\mu}{2\sigma} \sqrt{\Delta t} \qquad (9.22)$$

then equation (9.15) is given by

$$E(\tilde{r}_n) = \mu T \qquad (9.23)$$

and equation (9.16) reduces to

$$\text{Var}(\tilde{r}_n) = (\sigma^2 - \mu \Delta t) T. \qquad (9.24)$$

In the limit, we have

$$E(\tilde{r}_T) = \mu T \qquad (9.25)$$

$$\text{Var}(\tilde{r}_T) = \sigma^2 T, \qquad (9.26)$$

and by a special version of the central limit theorem, it can be shown that $\tilde{r}_T$ has a normal distribution.

Exhibit 9.4 shows how, by suitable definitions of a, b, and p, the binomial model can be used to approximate other diffusion and jump processes.

EXHIBIT 9.4
Binomial Approximations to Three Statistical Processes

Up Parameter	Down Parameter	Probability P	Limiting Distribution of Stock Price
$\sigma\sqrt{\Delta t}$	$-\sigma\sqrt{\Delta t}$	$\dfrac{1}{2} + \dfrac{\mu}{2\sigma}\sqrt{\Delta t}$	Geometric Wiener
$\sigma(S,t)\sqrt{\Delta t}$	$-\sigma(S,t)\sqrt{\Delta t}$	$\dfrac{1}{2} + \dfrac{\mu(S,t)}{2\sigma(S,t)}\sqrt{\Delta t}$	Constant elasticity of variance if $\sigma(S,t) = \sigma S_t^{a-1}$ $0 < a < 1$
$a = k_1$	$b = k_2\Delta t$	$p = \lambda\Delta t$	Pure jump process (k_1 and k_2 are constants)

BACKGROUND TO BINOMIAL OPTION PRICING

In the next few sections we shall investigate how options can be priced under the assumption that stock prices follow a geometric binomial random walk process over the time period to expiration. To understand the key concepts of what follows, consider a stock currently priced at $100 and assume that there is one period to go to expiration. Assume that in this period the stock can either rise to $120 or fall to $80. Assume further that a call option with strike 100 is available. Finally, assume that money can be borrowed or lent at a 10 percent rate and that the stock and call can be bought or sold at the given prices. Exhibit 9.5 illustrates the information, where C is the call price.

EXHIBIT 9.5
Evaluation of a Call Option

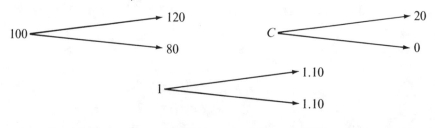

With this information, what is the value of the call? At first glance this question appears impossible to answer, for we are not given the probability, p, of the stock price moving up. As a result, the final distribution of stock and option prices is not known, and expectations, for example, cannot be computed.

Say we were given $p = 0.75$. Then the expected terminal stock and option price could be computed. Specifically,

$$E(\tilde{S}_T) = 120(0.75) + 80(0.25) = 110,$$

$$E(\tilde{C}_T) = 20(0.75) + 0(0.25) = 15.$$

Furthermore, a risk-neutral investor would be indifferent between buying the stock and investing in the riskless asset, since they provide the same expected return. Moreover, the risk-neutral investor would buy the call only if it gave a net expected return in excess of 10 percent. With this logic, the maximum price the investor would pay for the call would be $15/1.10 = 13.64$. That is, for $p = 0.75$, a *risk-neutral* investor would buy the call, provided its value was less than 13.64. Since a *risk-averse* investor will demand a higher expected return than 10 percent before buying the call, to entice the investor away from investments in the riskless asset, the current call price would have to be less than 13.64.

At first glance it appears that, to obtain a fair value for the call option, we need to know the value, p, and we also need to know more about the preferences of the investor.

We now present a somewhat surprising result. The value of the call in Exhibit 9.5 does not depend on p, nor does it depend on preferences! Indeed, for this problem the price of the call must be $13.64. If the market sets the price of the call option at any other value, a riskless arbitrage opportunity (free lunch) exists.

To see why the call option has to be priced at $13.64, consider a portfolio containing 1 stock and a short position in 2 calls. The initial value of this position, V_0, is

$$V_0 = 100 - 2C_0.$$

If the stock price rises, the portfolio value, V_1, will be given by

$$V_1 = 120 - 2(20) = 80$$

and if the stock price falls, the portfolio value will be given by

$$V_1 = 80 - 2(0) = 80.$$

Hence, regardless of what occurs in the future, the terminal value of this portfolio is $80.

Now consider placing $72.73 into the riskless asset (bank). At the end of the period, this wealth would have grown to $72.73(1.10) = $80.

We thus have two riskless alternatives. Either we can buy 1 stock and sell

2 calls, or we can put $72.73 in the bank. To avoid riskless arbitrage opportunities it must follow that the current values of these portfolios must be equal. Hence, $100 - 2C_0 = 72.73$ or, $C_0 = \$13.64$.

If, for example, the cost of the call was $12.64, then by selling the portfolio, the investor would receive $100 - 2(12.64) = \$74.73$. By investing $72.73 of this in the riskless asset, the investor would have $2 left over. At the expiration date the value of the riskless asset would be $72.73(1.10) = \$80$, and the value of the portfolio would also be $80. Thus, regardless of what occurred in the future, the $80 received from the riskless asset would always be sufficiently large to cover the value of the portfolio. Hence, regardless of what occurred, the investor would make $2 without requiring any initial investment.

Since many arbitragers would attempt this strategy, the price of the option would soon rise to $13.64. With the option at this value, no free lunch would exist.

In the next few sections we shall show how these replicating portfolios can be constructed. (For example, how did we know that a portfolio of 1 stock purchased long and 2 calls sold short would produce a riskless return?) In addition, we shall extend this simple 1-period 2-outcome problem to more realistic situations.

THE SINGLE-PERIOD BINOMIAL MODEL

Consider a stock currently priced at S_0. We assume that at the end of the period, which coincides with the expiration date, the stock price, $\tilde{S}_1$, can either increase to S_{11} or decrease to S_{10}. The price movements can be represented as follows:

$$S_0 \begin{array}{c} \nearrow S_{11} = uS_0 \\ \searrow S_{10} = dS_0 \end{array}$$

where $u > d$.

The current value of a call option with strike X is C_0. At expiration the call value, $\tilde{C}_1$, will be C_{11} or C_{10} where

$$C_{11} = \text{Max}(S_{11} - X, 0) \tag{9.27}$$

$$C_{10} = \text{Max}(S_{10} - X, 0) \tag{9.28}$$

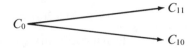

$$C_0 \begin{array}{c} \nearrow C_{11} \\ \searrow C_{10} \end{array}$$

In addition, we assume the riskless one-period interest rate for borrowing and lending is $r - 1$.

To avoid arbitrage opportunities, we shall assume that $d < r < u$.

Clearly, if r exceeded u, an investment in the riskless asset would dominate an investment in the risky security. Conversely, if r was lower than d, no investor would purchase the riskless asset.

Replicating the Payoffs of a Call Option

Consider a portfolio containing H shares of stock and a short position of B_0 dollars in the riskless asset (i.e., B_0 dollars are borrowed). The current value of the portfolio, V_0, is

$$V_0 = HS_0 - B_0.$$

At the expiration date the portfolio value, V_1, can be either

$$V_{11} = HS_{11} - rB_0$$

or

$$V_{10} = HS_{10} - rB_0.$$

We shall select the number of shares H, and dollars borrowed, B_0, such that the terminal values V_{11} and V_{10} are exactly equal to the call values C_{11} and C_{10}. That is, we require

$$HS_{11} - rB_0 = C_{11}$$

and

$$HS_{10} - rB_0 = C_{10}.$$

Since there are two equations in two unknowns, a unique solution for H and B_0 can be obtained. The solution is

$$H^* = \frac{(C_{11} - C_{10})}{(S_{11} - S_{10})} \tag{9.29}$$

and

$$B_0^* = \frac{(C_{11}S_{10} - C_{10}S_{11})}{(S_{11} - S_{10})r}. \tag{9.30}$$

A portfolio containing H^* shares partially financed by borrowing B_0^* dollars produces identical payoffs to the call option at expiration. Hence, to avoid riskless arbitrage opportunities, the initial portfolio value must be equal to the price of the call. That is,

$$C^* = H^*S_0 - B_0^*. \tag{9.31}$$

Example 9.4

Assume a stock is currently valued at $50. A one-period call option with strike price 50 is to be valued. The stock can either increase 10 percent to $55 or decrease 10 percent to $45. The riskless rate is 5 percent.

The stock prices can be represented by

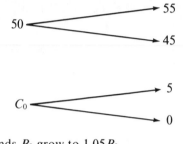

The call prices are

and the borrowed funds B_0 grow to $1.05 B_0$

From the information we have $u = 1.1$, $d = 0.9$, $r = 1.05$, and $S_{11} = 55$, $S_{10} = 45$, $C_{11} = 5$, and $C_{10} = 0$. Hence,

$$H^* = \frac{(5 - 0)}{(55 - 45)} = 0.5$$

and

$$B^* = \frac{5(45) - 0(55)}{1.05(55 - 45)} = \$21.40.$$

A portfolio containing 0.5 shares held long partially financed by borrowing $21.40 is the replicating portfolio. Its current value V_0 is

$$V_0 = H^* S_0 - B_0^* = \$3.60.$$

After one period this portfolio will either increase to V_{11} or decrease to V_{10}:

$$V_{11} = H^* S_{11} - r B_0^* = \$5,$$
$$V_{10} = H^* S_{10} - r B_0^* = \$0.$$

To avoid riskless arbitrage opportunities between the call and replicating portfolio, it must follow that

$$C_0^* = H^* S_0 - B_0^* = \$3.60.$$

(continued)

Example 9.4 (cont'd)

Assume the actual market price of the call option was $2.60. Then an astute investor will buy the call and sell the replicating portfolio. The net income from this transaction is $1.00. Since at expiration gains (or losses) in the replicating portfolio will be exactly offset by losses (gains) in the call, the investor will have earned $1.00 with no risk and no initial investment.

One-Period Model for Put Options

The same procedure can be used for put options. Let P_0 be the price of the put option with strike X, and let P_{11} and P_{10} represent the terminal prices.

$$P_0 \nearrow \begin{array}{l} P_{11} = \text{Max}(X - S_{11}, 0) \\ \\ P_{10} = \text{Max}(X - S_{10}, 0) \end{array}$$

Consider a portfolio of H_p shares and B_p dollars borrowed. Let V_0 be the current value, i.e., $V_0 = H_p S_0 - B_p$, and let V_{11} and V_{10} be the two possible terminal values of the portfolio. In order for the portfolio to replicate the payoffs of the put, we must have

$$H_p{}^* = \frac{(P_{11} - P_{10})}{(S_{11} - S_{10})} \tag{9.32}$$

$$B_p{}^* = \frac{(P_{11}S_{10} - P_{10}S_{11})}{(S_{11} - S_{10})r} \tag{9.33}$$

and to avoid riskless arbitrage opportunities, it must follow that

$$P_0 = H_p{}^* S_0 - B_p{}^*. \tag{9.34}$$

Example 9.5

Return to our earlier example, $S_0 = 50$, $u = 1.1$, $d = 0.9$, $r = 1.05$. Assume a put option is traded with strike $X = 50$. Then we can price the put as follows

$$P_0 \nearrow \begin{array}{l} P_{11} = 0 \\ \\ P_{10} = 5 \end{array}$$

and

$$H_p{}^* = \frac{(0 - 5)}{(55 - 45)} = -0.5,$$

(continued)

Example 9.5 (cont'd)

$$B_p^* = \frac{0(45) - 5(55)}{(55 - 45)1.05} = -26.2.$$

That is, the put option can be replicated by selling 0.5 shares and lending $26.20. Hence,

$$P_0 = H_p^* S_0 - B_p^* = -0.5(50) + 26.2 = 1.2.$$

The put price could have been derived using the put-call parity relationship instead. That is,

$$P_0 = X\exp(-rT) + C_0 - S_0$$

where $X\exp(-rT)$ is the present value of the strike. In our example the discount factor is $1/1.05$. Hence, we have

$$P_0 = \frac{50}{1.05} + 3.6 - 50 = 1.2.$$

But this value is precisely what we had before.

PROPERTIES OF BINOMIAL OPTION PRICES

1. The fair price of the call option does not depend on investor preferences. The price was obtained by simply recognizing that if it were not priced at this value, riskless arbitrage profits could be obtained. These profits would soon disappear because astute investors would continue to exploit these opportunities until the set of prices adjusted. Since this price is the correct price in all types of economies, it must also hold true in particular economies. For example, the same price must exist in economies consisting solely of risk-averse, risk-seeking, or risk-neutral investors.

2. The fair price does not depend on the probability of an upward or downward movement. In the example the fair value of the call is $3.60, regardless of whether the probability of an upward movement is 0.95 or 0.05.

3. In view of the fact that probabilities appear unimportant, it must follow that expectations do not enter the analysis. In the example the fair value of a call is $3.60, regardless of whether the expectation is high or low. However, variances cannot be ignored. The variance is a measure of spread, and this was clearly an important consideration. As u and d change, the call price changes.

4. The call pricing equation, $C_0 = H^* S_0 - B_0^*$, can be simplified further. By substituting the value of H^* and B^* into the equation, we obtain

$$C_0 = \left[\frac{(C_{11} - C_{10})}{(S_{11} - S_{10})}\right] S_0 - \left[\frac{(C_{11}S_{10} - C_{10}S_{11})}{r(S_{11} - S_{10})}\right]. \qquad (9.35)$$

By rearranging the terms, we can express C_0 in terms of its future values C_{11} and C_{10}. That is,

$$C_0 = \left[\frac{(rS_0 - S_{10})}{r(S_{11} - S_{10})}\right] C_{11} + \left[\frac{(S_{11} - rS_0)}{r(S_{11} - S_{10})}\right] C_{10} \qquad (9.36)$$

Finally, we substitute $S_{10} = dS_0$ and $S_{11} = uS_0$ into the expression to obtain

$$C_0 = \left(\left[\frac{(r - d)}{(u - d)}\right] C_{11} + \left[\frac{(u - r)}{(u - d)}\right] C_{10}\right) \Big/ r \qquad (9.37)$$

$$= \frac{[\theta C_{11} + (1 - \theta)C_{10}]}{r} \qquad (9.38)$$

where

$$\theta = \frac{(r - d)}{(u - d)}. \qquad (9.39)$$

Thus, the call price can be viewed as the discounted expected value of the terminal call price, where the probability of an upward movement is given by θ. An interpretation of θ is provided in the next section.

5. The value of a call depends solely on u, d, r, X, and S_0. It does not make any assumptions about the stock price relative to other security prices, nor does it impose any security equilibrium conditions. Thus, market factors and covariance terms are not relevant.

CALL PRICES IN A RISK-NEUTRAL ECONOMY

Recall from Chapter 8 that in a risk-neutral economy, investors are indifferent between a gamble, G, that has an expected return $E(G)$ and a certain riskless return of $E(G)$. That is, variances and higher moments play no role. Since investors are not compensated according to the size of second and higher moments, prices are set such that the call option has the same expected return as other securities. In such an economy, the future price of riskless bonds, stocks, and options will satisfy

$$B_1 = rB_0$$

$$E(\tilde{S}_1) = rS_0 \qquad (9.40)$$

$$E(\tilde{C}_1) = rC_0. \qquad (9.41)$$

Now the expected stock and call prices in this economy are

$$E(\tilde{S}_1) = pS_{11} + (1 - p)S_{10} \qquad (9.42)$$

$$E(\tilde{C}_1) = pC_{11} + (1 - p)C_{10} \tag{9.43}$$

where p is the probability of the stock price moving up. Hence, from equation (9.40) and (9.42)

$$rS_0 = pS_{11} + (1 - p)S_{10}$$

or, equivalently,

$$rS_0 = puS_0 + (1 - p)dS_0. \tag{9.44}$$

Solving the expression for p, we obtain

$$p = \frac{(r - d)}{(u - d)} = \theta.$$

Furthermore, from equation (9.41) and (9.43),

$$rC_0 = pC_{11} + (1 - p)C_{10}$$

and hence

$$C_0 = \frac{[\theta C_{11} + (1 - \theta)C_{10}]}{r}. \tag{9.45}$$

But this equation is exactly the general call pricing equation we obtained in equation (9.38). This result implies that the fair price of a call can be obtained by valuing the call as if it were trading in a risk-neutral economy. The result motivates a general risk-neutral proof technique argument for establishing call prices. This argument was briefly discussed in Chapters 5 and 8 and is repeated here.

If we have to value an option, and *if somehow we know that the fair value does not depend on preferences,* then for simplicity assume a risk-neutral economy. Derive the equilibrium call price in this economy (the present value of the expected terminal call price). The call price obtained in this economy is also the fair value for all economies.

THE RISK-FREE HEDGE

Since a call option can be replicated by a portfolio containing H^* shares partially financed by borrowing B_0^* dollars, it is a redundant asset. In the theory of finance, we say the option does not add to the completeness of the market. It was only because the option was redundant that we could price it uniquely. This is a general result. That is, if redundant assets are introduced into an economy, arbitrage arguments can be used to obtain their unique fair values.

Furthermore, since $C_0 = H^*S_0 - B_0^*$, it follows that the amount borrowed, B_0^*, is $H^*S_0 - C_0$. Equivalently, a long position of H^* shares of stock and a short position in the call option must produce a return equivalent to that of an investment in the riskless asset.

To emphasize this point, consider our illustrative problem again. We shall construct a portfolio containing a long position of 0.5 shares (H^* shares) and a short position of 1 call option. The current value of this portfolio is $V_0 = 0.5S_0 - C_0 = \$21.40$.

The terminal value of this portfolio is either V_{11} or V_{10}, i.e.,

$$V_{11} = 0.5S_{11} - C_{11} = 0.5(55) - 5 = 22.5$$

or

$$V_{10} = 0.5S_{10} - C_{10} = 0.5(45) - 10 = 22.5.$$

Hence, regardless of what stock price occurs in the future, the portfolio value is known (\$22.50). If the initial investment (\$21.40) were placed in the riskless asset, the terminal value would be

$$B_1 = rB = (1.05)(21.4) = 22.5.$$

Thus, a bond may be replicated by buying H^* shares and selling 1 call. The ratio of shares bought per call sold, H^*, is called the *hedge ratio*. The hedge ratio in the example is 0.5 (or 1:2).

THE TWO-PERIOD BINOMIAL MODEL

We now extend the one-period model to a two-period model where an opportunity exists to revise the position at the beginning of each period. The stock price movements are represented as follows:

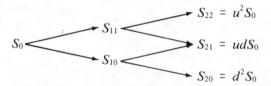

$$
\begin{array}{c}
S_{22} = u^2 S_0 \\
S_{11} \\
S_0 \qquad\qquad S_{21} = udS_0 \\
S_{10} \\
S_{20} = d^2 S_0
\end{array}
$$

As before, we assume that in each period the stock price rises by factor u or decreases by factor d. We now consider the pricing of a call contract with two periods to go prior to expiration. The call price movements can be represented as follows:

$$
\begin{array}{c}
C_{22} = \text{Max}(u^2 S_0 - X, 0) \\
C_{11} \\
C_0 \qquad\qquad C_{21} = \text{Max}(udS_0 - X, 0) \\
C_{10} \\
C_{20} = \text{Max}(d^2 S_0 - X)
\end{array}
$$

With one period to go to expiration, the stock price is either at S_{11} or S_{10}. If the stock price is at S_{11}, then faced with a one-period problem, the theoretical fair call value C_{11} can be obtained. Similarly, if the stock price is at S_{10}, the theoretical call value C_{10} can be obtained.

Example 9.6

Consider a stock currently priced at $45.45. Assume in each period the stock can appreciate or depreciate by 10 percent. As before, assume a riskless rate of 5 percent per period and consider a call option with strike $X = \$40$. Then $u = 0.9$, and the stock prices can be represented as follows:

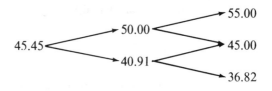

Case 1. Assume the stock price goes to $50. Then in the last period we have

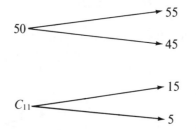

In this case, $H^* = (15 - 5)/(55 - 45) = 1$, $B_0^* = 15(45) - 5(55)/[10(1.05)] = 38.10$ and $C_{11}^* = H^* S_{11} - B_0^* = 1(50) - 38.10 = 11.90$.

Thus, at the beginning of period 1, if the stock price is $50 and if the call price is not $11.90, riskless arbitrage opportunities exist.

Case 2. Assume the stock price in period 1 is $40.91:

40.91
45
36.82

(continued)

$$5 = \text{Max}(45 - 40.00)$$

C_{10}

$$0 = \text{Max}(36.82 - 40.00)$$

Now $H^* = (5 - 0)/(45 - 36.82) = 0.61$
and $B_0^* = (36.81)(5)/(8.18)(1.05) = 21.43$.
Thus, $C_{10}^* = (0.61)(40.91) - 21.43 = 3.57$.

If we knew with certainty that at the end of the first period the call price would either be C_{11}^* or C_{10}^*, then to obtain the current fair value we could reapply the 1-period model. Specifically, we would have

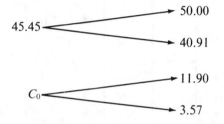

45.45

50.00

40.91

C_0

11.90

3.57

Hence, the replicating portfolio consists of $H^* = (11.90 - 3.57)/(50 - 40.91) = 0.92$
and $B^* = [11.90(40.91) - 50(3.57)]/[9.09 (1.05)] = 32.30$
and hence $C_0^* = H^* S_0 - B_0^* = = (0.92)(45.45) - 32.30 = \$9.35$.

Exhibit 9.6 summarizes all the calculations.

Assume that the market price of the call option is $10.35. According to our analysis, the option is overpriced by $1.00. The arbitrager will sell the call and purchase the replicating portfolio. Specifically, the arbitrager will sell 1 call option and borrow $32.30 to raise a total of $42.65. Then the arbitrager will purchase 0.92 shares of the stock for $41.65. The remaining $1.00 could be put in the bank. Regardless of what occurs in the future, this position will not lose money and could make additional profits. To see this, assume the stock price rises to $50.00. In this case the replicating portfolio increases in value to $11.90. If the call price equals its theoretical value of $11.90, the portfolio can be sold and the call purchased. If the call value is less than $11.90, then additional profits can be made by liquidating the entire position. However, by the same logic, if the call price exceeds the value of the replicating portfolio, liquidation could result in net losses. In this case, however, since the call value is above $11.90, the optimal strategy for the second period is to sell the call and buy the replicating portfolio, which consists of 1 share financed by borrowing $38. The value of the required replicating portfolio is $11.90, which is the exact value of the current replicating portfolio. Hence, all that is

EXHIBIT 9.6
Summary Calculations for the Two-Period Binomial Option Model

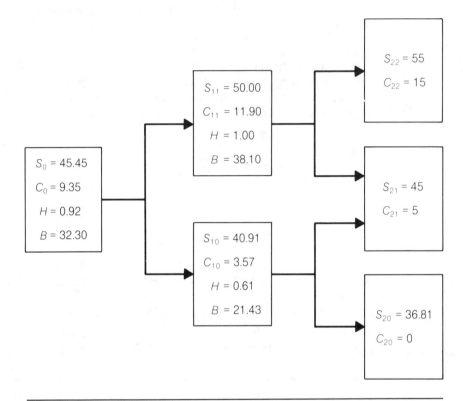

required is an adjustment in the portfolio composition. Specifically, the amount of stock in the replicating portfolio is increased from 0.92 to 1.0 by increasing the borrowing from $32.30 (plus one period interest) to $38.10 (plus one period interest).

Once this is accomplished, the arbitrager is guaranteed that at expiration no losses (or profits) will be obtained. Thus, the original $1.00 is obtained without any risk or initial investment.

We have seen that if the option is overpriced at the end of the first period, the arbitrager must extend the strategy to the expiration date, when the option prices will come into line. However, this strategy could be thwarted if the option is exercised. For example, if the option price in period 1 is $12.90, then the arbitrager cannot close out the position without loss. However, if the option is exercised, the investor must purchase the stock for $50 and deliver it at the strike price of $40. In this case the net cost is $10, which is less than the $11.90 value of the replicating portfolio.

Thus, if for one reason or another the option is exercised early, the arbitrager will benefit and obtain additional riskless arbitrage profits. Of course, with the option trading at a value above the strike price of $10, early exercise is not optimal and the investor who tendered the exercise notice would have been better off selling the option.

The example illustrates the fact that, even if call prices do not adjust to their theoretical fair values until expiration, a self-financing strategy can still be devised to protect the original arbitrage profits. If other investors behave irrationally or the market option prices overadjust, this can never hurt the strategy; on the contrary, it will result in additional profits.

REWRITING THE TWO-PERIOD OPTION PRICING MODEL

We have seen that the call price C_0 can be written as

$$C_0 = \frac{[\theta C_{11} + (1 - \theta)C_{10}]}{r}$$

where $\theta = (r - d)/(u - d)$
and

$$C_{11} = \frac{[\theta C_{22} + (1 - \theta)C_{21}]}{r}$$

$$C_{10} = \frac{[\theta C_{21} + (1 - \theta)C_{20}]}{r}.$$

Substituting C_{11} and C_{10} into the expression for C_0, we obtain

$$C_0 = \frac{[\theta^2 C_{22} + 2\theta(1 - \theta)C_{21} + (1 - \theta)^2 C_{20}]}{r^2},$$

which can be rewritten as

$$C_0 = \left[\sum_{j=0}^{2} \binom{2}{j} C_{2j} p_{2j} \right] \Big/ r^2 \qquad (9.46)$$

where

$$p_{2j} = P(\tilde{S}_2 = S_{2j}) = \binom{2}{j} \theta^j (1 - \theta)^{2-j} \quad j = 0, 1, 2$$

and

$$C_{2j} = \text{Max}(S_0 u^j d^{2-j} - X, 0) \qquad j = 0, 1, 2.$$

The equation states the call price can be derived as the present value of the expected terminal value of the option in a risk-neutral economy.

THE n PERIOD BINOMIAL OPTION PRICING MODEL

The two-period model generalizes to n periods. Assume that the time to expiration is broken down into n periods.

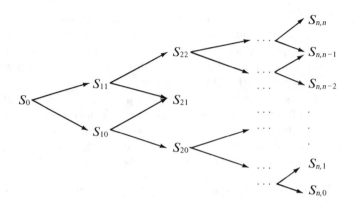

After n periods the stock price $\tilde{S}_n$ takes on one of the values $S_{n,j}$ for $j = 0$, $1, 2, \ldots n$. The index j refers to the number of upward price movements that have occurred over the previous n periods (see Chapter 6). Since in each period the stock price increases by factor u or decreases by factor d, we have

$$S_{n,j} = u^j d^{n-j} S_0$$

and

$$P(\tilde{S}_n = S_{n,j}) = \binom{n}{j}\theta^j(1 - \theta)^{n-j} \quad \text{for } j = 0, 1, 2, \ldots n \qquad (9.47)$$

where $\theta = (r - d)/(u - d)$.

The value of the call for each state is known at expiration. That is,

$$C_{n,j} = \text{Max}(S_{n,j} - X, 0)$$

$$= \text{Max}(u^j d^{n-j} S_0 - X, 0). \qquad (9.48)$$

Let k be the minimum number of upward stock price movements that is necessary for the option to terminate in the money. Then the probability that the call expires in the money is

$$P(\tilde{S}_n > X) = \sum_{n=k}^{n} \binom{n}{j}\theta^j(1 - \theta)^{n-j} \qquad (9.49)$$

and

$$C_{n,j} = 0 \quad \text{for } j = 0, 1, 2, \ldots k - 1.$$

Given the terminal option values, the fair values in period $(n - 1)$ can be computed. Specifically, since early exercise is not a factor, we have

$$C_{n-1,j} = \theta C_{n,j+1} + (1 - \theta)C_{n,j} \quad \text{for } j = 0, 1, 2, \ldots n - 1. \qquad (9.50)$$

This process can be repeated recursively throughout the network until the fair value C_0 is obtained.

The call value, C_0, is obtained as the present value of the terminal payout assuming a risk-neutral economy. This is valid since the stock pays no dividend, early exercise is not optimal and therefore the value of an American call is equivalent to its European counterpart.

Thus
$$C_0 = \frac{E(\tilde{C}_n)}{r^n}.$$
(9.51)

Now the expected terminal call price is easily evaluated:

$$E(\tilde{C}_n) = \sum_{j=0}^{n} C_{n,j} p_{n,j}$$

$$= \sum_{j=k}^{n} C_{n,j} p_{n,j}$$

$$= \sum_{j=k}^{n} (u^j d^{n-j} S_0 - X)(\tbinom{n}{j}) \theta^j (1-\theta)^{n-j}$$

$$= \sum_{i=k}^{n} (\tbinom{n}{j})(u\theta)^j [d(1-\theta)]^{n-j} S_0 - X \left[\sum_{j=k}^{n} (\tbinom{n}{j}) \theta^j (1-\theta)^{n-j} \right].$$

Hence

$$C_0 = \left(\sum_{j=k}^{n} (\tbinom{n}{j}) \left(\frac{u\theta}{r} \right)^j \left[\frac{(d - d\theta)}{r} \right]^{n-j} \right) S_0$$

$$- X \left[\sum_{j=k}^{n} (\tbinom{n}{j}) \theta^j (1-\theta)^{n-j} \right] \Big/ r^n.$$
(9.52)

Now let $\alpha = u\theta/r$. Then $0 < \alpha < 1$ and $1 - \alpha = (d - d\theta)/r$.

With these results equation (9.52) reduces to the n period binomial option pricing equation:

$$C_0 = HS_0 - B_0$$
(9.53)

where

$$H = \sum_{j=k}^{n} (\tbinom{n}{j}) \alpha^j (1-\alpha)^{n-j}$$
(9.54)

$$B_0 = X \left[\sum_{j=k}^{n} (\tbinom{n}{j}) \theta^j (1-\theta)^{n-j} \right] \Big/ r^n$$
(9.55)

$$\alpha = \frac{u\theta}{r}$$

$$\theta = \frac{(r-d)}{(u-d)}.$$

THE BLACK-SCHOLES MODEL AND OTHER OPTION PRICING MODELS

The way in which u and d are chosen clearly depends on the width of the intervals over which u and d are defined and the time to expiration, T. If we choose the parameters of the binomial model, u, and d, and the probability of an upward movement, p, as

$$u = \exp(\sigma\sqrt{\Delta t})$$

$$d = \exp(-\sigma\sqrt{\Delta t}), \text{ and} \qquad (9.56)$$

$$p = \frac{1}{2} + \frac{\mu}{2\sigma}\sqrt{\Delta t}$$

where

$$\Delta t = \frac{T}{n},$$

then, as discussed on page 182, the stock price distribution will converge onto the lognormal distribution. In this case the binomial option pricing model can be shown to converge onto the Black-Scholes model.

That is,

$$C_0 = H^*S_0 - B^* \qquad (9.57)$$

where

$$H^* = N(d_1)$$

$$B^* = X\exp(-rT)N(d_2)$$

where

$$d_1 = \frac{\ln(S_0/X) + (r + \sigma^2/2)T}{\sigma\sqrt{T}}$$

$$d_2 = d_1 - \sigma\sqrt{T}$$

By defining a, b, and p in different ways, one can approximate alternative stochastic processes for the underlying stock. In many limiting cases, the binomial option pricing model can be shown to reduce to special formulas.

OPTION PRICING WITH DIVIDENDS*

When a stock pays dividends, early exercise of the call option may be optimal. In this case the preceding analysis is not correct and the option cannot be valued as the present value of the expected terminal price in a risk-neutral economy. However, the binomial model can still be applied to obtain a solution for the call value.

To see this, consider a stock that pays a constant yield, f, on each ex-dividend date. Then at the ex-dividend date, t, the stock price will drop by the dividend amount, fS_t.

Let δ_t be a variable given by

$$\delta_t = 1 \qquad \text{if there is no dividend in period } t,$$

$$\delta_t = 1 - f \qquad \text{if there is a dividend in period } t.$$

Then the stock price can be represented as follows:

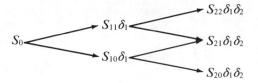

After t periods the stock prices $\tilde{S}_t$ can take on any of the $(t+1)$ values:

$$S_{tj} = u^j d^{t-j} \left(\prod_{i=1}^{t} \delta_i \right) \qquad \text{for } j = 0, 1, 2, \ldots t.$$

Let $k(t)$ be the number of ex-dividend dates in the first t periods. Then

$$\prod_{i=1}^{t} \delta_i = (1-f)^{k(t)}$$

and the stock price value can be represented by

$$S_{tj} = u^j d^{t-j} (1-f)^{k(t)} S_0 \qquad \text{for } j = 0, 1, 2, \ldots t. \tag{9.58}$$

Furthermore, the probability that the stock price is in state j at time t is p_{tj} where

$$p_{tj} = P(\tilde{S}_t = S_{tj}) = \binom{t}{j} \theta^j (1-\theta)^{t-j} \qquad \text{for } j = 0, 1, 2, \ldots t. \tag{9.59}$$

If the option were a European option, the risk-neutrality argument could be invoked and the call value could be established. Specifically,

$$C_0 = \frac{E(\tilde{C}_n)}{r^n}$$

$$= \sum_{j=0}^{n} \frac{\text{Max}[S_0 u^j d^{n-j} (1-f)^{k(n)} - X, 0] p_{tj}}{r^n}. \tag{9.60}$$

This equation is identical to the earlier expression except that the stock prices have been adjusted for dividends.

For the American call option, however, early exercise is a possibility. To see this, assume a dividend occurs in the last period. In time period $n-1$, consider a state, j, chosen so that regardless of the last stock price movement, the call expires in the money.

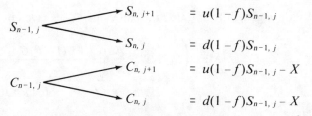

In this case the value of the call unexercised is

$$C_{n-1, j} = \frac{[\theta C_{n, j+1} + (1-\theta) C_{n, j}]}{r}. \tag{9.61}$$

Substituting the values of $C_{n, j+1}$ and $C_{n, j}$, we obtain

$$= \frac{(\theta[u(1 - f)S_{n-1, j} - X] + (1 - \theta)[d(1 - f)S_{n-1, j} - X])}{r}$$

$$= \frac{[S_{n-1, j}(1 - f)(u\theta - d\theta + d) - X]}{r}.$$

Now since $\theta = (r - d)/(u - d)$, $\theta(u - d) = r - d$, and the above equation for the value of the call unexercised is

$$C_{n-1, j} = S_{n-1, j}(1 - f) - \frac{X}{r}. \tag{9.62}$$

The value of the call exercised is its intrinsic value $S_{n-1, j} - X$.

Early exercise is appropriate if the value of the call exercised exceeds the value of the call unexercised. Hence, the early exercise is appropriate if

$$S_{n-1, j} - X > S_{n-1, j}(1 - f) - \frac{X}{r}$$

or equivalently if

$$S_{n-1, j}f > X - \frac{X}{r}. \tag{9.63}$$

size, $fS_{n-1,j}$, exceeds the foregone interest on the strike $(X - X/r)$. Note that for $f = 0$, early exercise is not appropriate (see Chapter 4). The lowest stock price for which early exercise should be considered is the value $S*$ for which

$$S*f = X - \frac{X}{r} \quad \text{or} \quad S* = \frac{(X - X/r)}{f}.$$

When dividends are a factor, the recursive call pricing equation has to be modified to take into account the possibility of early exercise. Specifically, for the n period problem we have

$$C_{n-1, j} = \text{Max(Value of the call exercised, Value of the call unexercised)}$$

$$C_{n-1, j} = \text{Max}\left(S_{n-1, j} - X, \frac{[\theta C_{n, j+1} + (1 - \theta)C_{n, j}]}{r}\right) \tag{9.64}$$

and $\theta = (r - d)/(u - d)$.

More generally at time t the call value $C_{t, j}$ is given by

$$C_{t, j} = \text{Max}\left(S_{t, j} - X, \frac{[\theta C_{t+1, j+1} + (1 - \theta)C_{t+1, j}]}{r}\right) \tag{9.65}$$

$$\text{for } j = 0, 1, 2, \ldots t$$

where

$$S_{t, j} = u^j d^{t-j}(1 - f)^{k(t)} S_0 \quad \text{for } j = 0, 1, 2, \ldots t \tag{9.66}$$

and $C_{t+1, j+1}$ and $C_{t+1, j}$ are obtained from earlier recursions.

Finally, the current fair call price is obtained

$$C_0 = \text{Max}(S_0 - X, [\theta C_1 + (1 - \theta)C_{10}]/r).$$

Again the hedge ratio would be

$$H = \frac{(C_{11} - C_{10})}{(S_{11} - S_{10})}$$

and

$$B = \frac{(C_{11}S_{10} - C_{10}S_{10})}{r(S_{11} - S_{10})}.$$

OTHER DIVIDEND POLICIES*

The binomial model provides a numerical procedure to value call options for a variety of different dividend policies. The constant dividend yield policy, however, is possibly the easiest to analyze. This results from the fact that the policy does not increase the number of distinct terminal stock prices. This does not occur with other dividend policies. For example, if we assume a constant dividend size of v, the number of possible stock prices mushrooms as illustrated below.

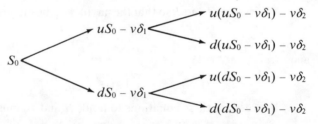

where $\delta_i = 1$ of a dividend is declared in period i and 0 otherwise.

In this case each additional period may double the number of possible causing the tree to explode quite rapidly. Contrast this situation with the constant yield policy, where the addition of each period causes the states to by 1. Although this is cumbersome, the same principles can be used to value the call option. That is, we start off at the end of the tree and work backwards to obtain the current fair value.

PUT OPTION PRICING MODELS

Using the put-call parity relationship, one can value European put options. However, even in the case of no dividends, early exercise of American put options may be optimal. In this case, the binomial model provides an effective mechanism for approximating the true price.

Let $P_{n,j}$ represent the terminal put price of a stock that may declare dividends. Then, assuming a constant dividend yield policy, the terminal put price is given by

$$P_{n,j} = \text{Max}(X - S_{n,j}, 0) \qquad j = 0, 1, 2, \ldots n$$

where

$$S_{n,j} = u^j d^{n-j}(1 - f)^{k(n)} S_0 \qquad j = 0, 1, 2, \ldots n.$$

Let $P_{n-1,j}$ represent the price of a put option with 1 period to go. Then

Consider a portfolio of H shares partially financed by borrowing B dollars. The value of such a portfolio, $V_{n-1,j}$ is

$$V_{n-1,j} = HS_{n-1,j} - B. \qquad (9.67)$$

At expiration the terminal value of the portfolio is either $V_{n,j+1}$ or $V_{n,j}$ where

$$V_{n,j+1} = HS_{n,j+1} - rB \qquad (9.68)$$

$$V_{n,j} = HS_{n,j} - rB. \qquad (9.69)$$

We choose H and B so that the payoffs of the put are replicated. That is,

$$V_{n,j+1} = P_{n,j+1}$$

and

$$V_{n,j} = P_{n,j}.$$

In order for these equations to hold, H and B_0 must be given as

$$H = \frac{(P_{n,j+1} - P_{n,j})}{(S_{n,j+1} - S_{n,j})} \qquad (9.70)$$

$$B_0 = \frac{(P_{n,j+1}S_{n,j} - P_{n,j}S_{n,j+1})}{(S_{n,j+1} - S_{n,j})r}. \qquad (9.71)$$

Given that the option will not be exercised in period $n - 1$, to avoid riskless arbitrage opportunities, the value of the put should equal the value of the replicating portfolio. Hence,

$$P_{n-1,j} = HS_{n-1,j} - rB_0.$$

Substituting in equations (9.47) and (9.48) and rewriting, we obtain

$$P_{n-1,j} = \frac{[\theta P_{n,j+1} + (1 - \theta)P_{n,j+1}]}{r} \qquad j = 0, 1, 2, \ldots n - 1. \qquad (9.72)$$

This value can be lower than the intrinsic value of $X - S_{n-1,j}$. If this is the case, the optimal strategy is to exercise the put. Thus, the value of the put is

$$P_{n-1,j} = \text{Max}\left(X - S_{n-1,j}, \frac{[\theta P_{n,j+1} + (1 - \theta)P_{n,j}]}{r}\right) \quad j = 0, 1, 2, \ldots n. \quad (9.73)$$

This equation defines a recursive relationship that enables the put price in each period to be computed.

THE BINOMIAL OPTION PRICING COMPUTER PROGRAM

The binomial option pricing model can be used to approximate put and call values under a variety of dividend and stochastic process assumptions. A BASIC computer program that provides option prices for calls and puts when underlying stock has a constant yield policy and the stochastic process is geometric Brownian motion is provided in the appendix.

To use the binomial model, we require knowledge on the stock price, S_0, the strike price, X, the time to expiration, T, the dividend yield, f, the time to first ex-dividend date, t_1, the time to the second ex-dividend date, t_2, and the time to the third ex-dividend date, t_3. In addition, we require the annual volatility, σ, and the annual interest rate, r. All these values are observable except the annual interest rate and the stock volatility. In addition, the number of periods to use needs to be specified. Clearly, the finer the partition, the better the approximation.

In Chapter 10 we shall discuss alternative methods for estimating the volatility and specifying the interest rate. For the moment, we assume these values are given. The empirical issue of determining the number of periods to use in the binomial model is addressed here.

For a given n, $\Delta t = T/n$, and $a = \sigma\sqrt{\Delta t}$, $b = -\sigma\sqrt{\Delta t}$. The annual interest rate r must then be converted into an interest rate per period, r_n, say. To do this, let m denote the number of compound periods per year. Then $m = n/t$. If r_F is the annual rate of interest, then we require r_n to satisfy

$$\left(1 + \frac{r_n}{m}\right)^m = 1 + r_F. \quad (9.74)$$

and hence $r_n = m[(1 + r_F)^{1/m} - 1]$.

As an example, if the effective annual interest rate is 6 percent, the time to expiration 0.5 years, and the number of periods is 4, then the period-by-period rate, r_n, is

$$r_n = \left(\frac{4}{0.5}\right)[(1.06)^{0.125} - 1] = 0.05848,$$

and the appropriate value to use in the binomial model is 1.05848.

For stocks paying no dividends, using 30 to 100 periods in the binomial option model produces prices that are within cents of the Black-Scholes price.

CONCLUSION

Approximating stock price movements over time by a discrete binomial model allows call and put option models to be developed that can easily take into account dividend policies. Moreover, by carefully defining the up and down values and their probabilities of occurrence, one can make the binomial model converge onto almost any diffusion or jump process. If the binomial process converges onto the geometric Wiener process, the binomial option pricing model converges onto the Black-Scholes model. This chapter has illustrated the value of the binomial option pricing model. Other models for approximating option prices are available. For example, rather than approximate the stochastic process of stock prices, an alternative is to approximate the differential equation that option prices satisfy and use numerical methods to obtain answers. Such procedures are briefly considered in Chapter 16.

References

The binomial option pricing model was first fully developed by Cox, Ross, and Rubinstein and by Rendleman and Bartter. Variants of the binomial option pricing model and development of other limiting forms have been investigated (Cox and Rubinstein, 1985 and 1983). Applications of the binomial option pricing model to value other types of options and securities will be considered in later chapters.

Cox, J., S. Ross, and M. Rubinstein. "Option Pricing: A Simplified Approach." *Journal of Financial Economics* 7(September 1979): 229–63.
Cox, J., and M. Rubinstein. *Option Markets.* Prentice-Hall, 1985.
Cox, J., and M. Rubinstein. "A Survey of Alternative Option Pricing Models." In *Option Pricing,* edited by M. Brenner. Lexington, Mass.: D. C. Heath, 1983, pp. 3–33.
Rendleman, R., and B. Bartter. "Two-State Option Pricing." *Journal of Finance* 34(December 1979): 1093–110.

Exercises

1. a. Price a call option using the one-period binomial model assuming the following data:

$$S_0 = 129, X = 80, u = 1.5, d = 0.5, \text{ and } r = 1.1.$$

   b. What does the replicating portfolio consist of?

2. Using data from problem 1, compute the put price and validate the put-call parity relationship.

3. a. Price a call option using the two-period binomial model assuming the following data:

$$S_0 = 129, X = 80, u = 1.5, d = 0.5, \text{ and } r = 1.1.$$

   b. What is the hedge ratio for this call option?

    c. If the call option were priced at $55, what would an arbitrager do? Discuss the exact strategy.

4. In the first period the stock can appreciate or depreciate by 50 percent and the interest rate 10 percent ($r = 1.1$). In the second period the stock can only appreciate or depreciate by 25 percent and r is 15 percent.

    a. Plot the tree of possible stock prices.

    b. Price a call option with strike price 80 and maturity in two periods.

5. Consider a stock that in any period can appreciate, remain unchanged, or depreciate. Assume a riskless asset was traded and an option was to be valued. Can an unambiguous option price be established? Explain why the arbitrage argument works or fails in this case.

6. A *down-and-out* call option differs from other call options in that if the stock falls below a specified value before maturity, the option contract becomes void. Modify the binomial model to handle the down-and-out option.

7. A *trading-range* option is a call option that can be exercised only if the stock price is in a given range. Modify the binomial model to handle valuation of such an option.

8. A *lookback* option is a call option that allows the holder to buy the stock at the minimum stock price that occurred over the period to expiration. Can the binomial model be used to find the price of such a contract?

9. A *don't* option is a call option that one pays for at the expiration date if one did not exercise the call. Can the binomial model be modified to value such a contract?

10. Using the binomial model, establish the conditions under which early exercise of the put is optimal.

11. Assume that calls and puts with the same strike price are traded on a stock. Without using the stock, can a portfolio of puts and bonds be used to value the call? Using the one-period binomial, explain whether put-call parity conditions can be established. If possible, extend the analysis to two periods. Comment on any problems with this approach.

Appendix

The Binomial Option Pricing Computer Program

The computer program below calculates call and put prices on a dividend-paying stock using the binomial model.

```
10  REM  ****************************************************************
20  REM     A PROGRAM USED TO CALCULATE OPTION PRICES USING THE
30  REM     BINOMIAL OPTION PRICING FORMULA
40  REM
50  REM        written by GREGORY B. GETTS
60  REM
70  REM     List of variables used in the program
80  REM
90  REM     CO      - CALL PRICE
100 REM     PO      - PUT PRICE
110 REM     STRIKE  - STRIKE PRICE
120 REM     SIG     - THE STAND. DEV. OF THE STOCK
130 REM     RATE    - SHORT TERM INTEREST RATE
140 REM     PRICE   - PRICE OF THE COMMON STOCK
150 REM     TIME    - DAYS UNTIL THE OPTION EXPIRES
160 REM     DAYDIV  - WEEKS UNTIL FIRST DIVIDEND
170 REM     N       - THE NUMBER OF ITERATIONS
180 REM
190 REM  ****************************************************************
200      DEFINT I-J
210      DIM IDAY(4),IEX(20),EX(20)
220 REM
230      DOALL=1
240      GOSUB 800
250      XDIV=DIV/4
260      IDAY(1)=DAYDIV
270      FOR I=2 TO 4:IDAY(I)=IDAY(I-1)+91:NEXT
280      ITYPE=2:GOSUB 410
290      CO=OPTPRC
300      ITYPE=3:GOSUB 410
310      PO=OPTPRC
320 REM
330 REM   PRINT OUT RESULTS
340 REM
350      CLS:LOCATE 22,8:PRINT "The call price is: ";CO
```

```
360      LOCATE 23,8:PRINT "The put price is:   ";PO
370      GOTO 240
380 REM ******************************************************************
390 REM      CALCULATE THE OPTION PRICE
400 REM ******************************************************************
410      PD=1-XDIV/PRICE
420      IF ITYPE=2 THEN DEL=1 ELSE DEL=-1
430      IF DEL*(PRICE-3)<DEL*STRIKE THEN N=10 ELSE N=6
440      NN=N+1
450      X=TIME/N:IT=1
460 REM
470      FOR II=1 TO NN
480         IF II>INT(IDAY(IT)/X) THEN IT=IT+1
490         IEX(II)=IT-1
500      NEXT
510 REM
520      U=EXP(SIG*SQR(X/365))
530      D=1/U
540      RR=(1!+RATE)^(X/365)
550      P=(RR-D)/(U-D):Q=1-P
560 REM
570      FOR JJ=1 TO NN
580         J=JJ-1
590         EX(JJ)=DEL*(U^J*D^(N-J)*PD^IEX(NN)*PRICE-STRIKE)
600         IF EX(JJ)<0 THEN EX(JJ)=0
610      NEXT JJ
620 REM
630      FOR LL =1 TO N
640         K=N-LL
650         KK=K+1
660         IF   KK=1 THEN 760
670 REM
680         FOR JJ=1 TO KK
690            J=JJ-1
700            X=DEL*(U^J*D^(K-J)*PD^IEX(KK)*PRICE-STRIKE)
710            Y=(P*EX(JJ+1)+Q*EX(JJ))/RR
720            IF X>Y THEN EX(JJ)=X ELSE EX(JJ)=Y
730         NEXT JJ
740      NEXT
750 REM
760      X=DEL*(PRICE-STRIKE)
770      Y=(P*EX(2)+Q*EX(1))/RR
780      IF X>Y THEN OPTPRC=X ELSE OPTPRC=Y
790      RETURN
800 REM ******************************************************************
810 REM  INPUT THE INFORMATION FOR THE OPTION
820 REM ******************************************************************
830    IF DOALL=1 THEN GOTO 1000
840    LOCATE 1,8:PRINT "THE FOLLOWING OPTIONS EXIST:"
850    LOCATE 3,8:PRINT "0) Calculate the option prices"
860    LOCATE 4,8:PRINT "1) Change the current stock price      ";PRICE
870    LOCATE 5,8:PRINT "2) Change the standard deviation       ";SIG
880    LOCATE 6,8:PRINT "3) Change the strike price             ";STRIKE
890    LOCATE 7,8:PRINT "4) Change the days until expiration    ";TIME
900    LOCATE 8,8:PRINT "5) Change the risk free interest rate ";RATE
910    LOCATE 9,8:PRINT "6) Change the annual dividend          ";DIV
920    LOCATE 10,8:PRINT "7) Change weeks until first dividend  ";DAYDIV
```

```
930    LOCATE 13,8:PRINT "8) Enter a completely new option"
940    LOCATE 14,8:PRINT "9) Exit the system"
950    O$="ENTER A NUMBER BETWEEN Ø AND 9:":GOSUB 1170
960    INPUT I%
970    IF I%<Ø OR I%>9 THEN BEEP:LOCATE 18,12:PRINT SPACE$(4Ø):GOTO 950
980    IF I%=Ø THEN RETURN
990    ON I% GOTO 1ØØØ,1Ø2Ø,1Ø4Ø,1Ø6Ø,1Ø8Ø,11ØØ,113Ø,115Ø,116Ø
1ØØØ   O$="ENTER THE CURRENT STOCK PRICE:":GOSUB 1170
1Ø1Ø   INPUT PRICE:IF DOALL=Ø THEN GOTO 84Ø
1Ø2Ø   O$="ENTER THE CURRENT STANDARD DEVIATION:":GOSUB 1170
1Ø3Ø   INPUT SIG:IF DOALL=Ø THEN GOTO 84Ø
1Ø4Ø   O$="ENTER THE STRIKE PRICE:":GOSUB 1170
1Ø5Ø   INPUT STRIKE:IF DOALL=Ø THEN GOTO 84Ø
1Ø6Ø   O$="ENTER THE NUMBER OF DAYS UNTIL EXPIRATION:":GOSUB 1170
1Ø7Ø   INPUT TIME:IF DOALL=Ø THEN GOTO 84Ø
1Ø8Ø   O$="ENTER THE CURRENT RISK FREE RATE OF RETURN:":GOSUB 1170
1Ø9Ø   INPUT RATE:IF DOALL=Ø THEN GOTO 84Ø
11ØØ   O$="ENTER THE CURRENT ANNUAL DIVIDEND:":GOSUB 1170
111Ø   INPUT DIV:IF DOALL=Ø THEN GOTO 84Ø
112Ø   IF DIV=Ø THEN DAYDIV=Ø:DOALL=Ø:GOTO 84Ø
113Ø   O$="ENTER THE NUMBER OF DAYS UNTIL FIRST DIVIDEND IS PAID:":GOSUB 1
114Ø   INPUT DAYDIV:DOALL=Ø:GOTO 84Ø
115Ø   DOALL=1:GOTO 1ØØØ
116Ø   CLS:SYSTEM
117Ø   LOCATE 18,8:PRINT SPACE$(7Ø):LOCATE 18,8:PRINT O$;:RETURN
```

10

Applications and Support for the Black-Scholes Model

Since the development of the Black-Scholes model, there has been a rapid growth in the literature in option pricing. Where possible, adjustments to the formula have been made to reflect real world behavior. The rapid growth of this literature, however, reflects more than a desire by economists to seek explanations for observed market prices. The option pricing model can also be used to guide trading strategies, to construct "synthetic" or theoretical prices when no market prices are available, and to study market behavior, especially market efficiency.

After briefly describing a few practical applications of option pricing models, this chapter investigates methods for estimating the required parameters. Then the limitations caused by the assumptions of the Black-Scholes model are discussed. The final test of option pricing models is determined by their ability to explain current market prices, and is an empirical issue. The final section reviews the empirical tests that have been conducted.

REQUIREMENTS OF THE BLACK-SCHOLES MODEL

To price options using the Black-Scholes model requires knowledge of the stock price, strike price, time to expiration, interest rates, and volatility. The first two variables are directly observable. The time to expiration is obtained by counting the number of days to expiration and dividing by 365. Methods for estimating the last two variables are discussed below.

Interest Rates

The interest rate, r, can be determined using the price of a Treasury bill maturing at the same time as the option. The current price of a Treasury bill with face value $10,000 can be determined using information from the *Wall*

Street Journal. Specifically, let B be the bid discount and A the asked discount for the T-bill with maturity n days. Then the price of the T-bill, B_0, is

$$B_0 = 10,000 \left[1 - 0.01 \left(\frac{A+B}{2} \right) \left(\frac{n}{360} \right) \right].$$

An investment of B_0 today results in a certain return of $10,000 in n days. Let $T = n/365$ be the time to expiration in years. Then we have

$$B_0 = 10,000 \exp(-rT)$$

from which

$$r = \frac{\ln \left(\dfrac{10,000}{B_0} \right)}{T}.$$

For a further discussion of Treasury bills, see Chapter 13.

Volatility

The Black-Scholes model requires that the volatility of logarithmic returns, σ, remains constant over time. Specifically, the model requires that the underlying statistical process driving stock prices has the following representation:

$$\frac{dS}{S} = \mu(s,t)dt + \sigma dw.$$

Let $\{\tilde{S}_t\}$ represent a sequence of stock prices collected over n periods, and let represent the logarthmic return.

$$\tilde{r}_t = \ln(\tilde{R}_t) = \ln \left(\frac{\tilde{S}_t}{\tilde{S}_{t-1}} \right) \qquad t = 1, 2, \ldots n$$

If we assume that the expected return, $\mu(s,t)$, remains the same (i.e., $\mu(s,t) = \mu$), the logarithmic returns can be considered a simple random sample from a normal distribution, with mean μ, and variance, σ^2. In this case let $\bar{r}$ and s^2 be estimators of the mean and variance per period. Then

$$\bar{r} = \sum_{t=1}^{n} \frac{r_t}{n}$$

$$s^2 = \frac{1}{n-1} \sum_{t=1}^{n} (r_t - \bar{r})^2$$

The estimate of the variance, s^2, is then annualized to obtain an estimate for σ^2. For example, if stock prices are observed weekly, then we have $\hat{\sigma}^2 = 52s^2$ where $\hat{\sigma}^2$ is the annualized estimator for σ^2. The estimator for the volatility, σ, is then given by $\hat{\sigma} = \sqrt{\hat{\sigma}^2}$.

Example 10.1

Consider a stock XYZ whose closing prices at the beginning of each of the past 20 weeks are shown in Exhibit 10.1.

$$\bar{r} = 0.0144195$$

$$s = 0.0406$$

and the annualized volatility $\hat{\sigma} = 52s = 0.29$.

EXHIBIT 10.1
Computation of Logarithmic Returns

Week	Price	Weekly Price Relative	Logarithmic Return
1	$20.50	—	—
2	21.00	1.042	0.02409
3	22.00	0.9545	0.0465
4	22.125	1.0056	0.00566
5	23.25	1.0508	0.04959
6	23.50	1.010	0.01069
7	21.25	0.9042	−0.10064
8	20.50	0.9647	−0.035932
9	20.75	1.0122	0.01212
10	20.825	1.0036	0.003607
11	21.75	1.0444	0.04345
12	24.25	1.1149	0.1088
13	26.375	1.0876	0.08399
14	26.375	1.00	0.0
15	27.25	1.033	0.0326
16	28.00	1.027	0.02715
17	27.00	0.9642	−0.03636
18	26.25	0.972	−0.02817
19	26.50	1.00952	0.009478
20	27.00	1.0188	0.0186

It can be shown that $\hat{\sigma}^2$ is an unbiased estimator of σ^2. That is, $E(\hat{\sigma}^2) = \sigma^2$. Unfortunately, $\hat{\sigma}$ is a biased estimator of a σ [i.e., $E(\hat{\sigma}) \neq \sigma$]. To correct for this bias, $\hat{\sigma}$ should be adjusted by a factor $K(n)$, which depends only on the sample size. Exhibit 10.2 gives values of $K(n)$ for small sample sizes. Note that as

EXHIBIT 10.2
Factors for Adjusting the Bias in Standard Deviation Calculations

n	K(n)
4	1.0854
5	1.0638
6	1.0509
7	1.0423
8	1.0363
9	1.0314
10	1.0281

sample size increases, bias decreases. For sample sizes exceeding 20, the bias can be ignored.

Other Estimators of Volatility

The disadvantage of the above estimation procedure is that it requires the simultaneous estimation of σ and μ. The historical estimate of μ may not be a good estimate of the future expectation. Indeed, the Black-Scholes model is still valid if μ changes over time. Hence, it seems advantageous to obtain an estimator of σ that does not require estimation of μ.

Let $\{r_t\}$ be a sequence of logarithmic returns drawn from independent normal distributions with the same variances but different means. Recall that we had as our estimator of σ^2 the equation

$$s^2 = \frac{1}{(n-1)} \sum_{i=1}^{n} (r_i - \bar{r})^2$$

$$= \frac{\sum_{i=1}^{n} r_i^2 - n\bar{r}^2}{(n-1)}.$$

Fortunately, with weekly logarithmic returns, the $n\bar{r}^2/(n-1)$ term does not contribute significantly to s^2. One reason for this is that both expectation and variance are proportional to the time period. For small time intervals the contribution of the mean squared term is negotiable. Hence,

$$s^2 \approx \frac{\sum_{i=1}^{n} r_i^2}{(n-1)}.$$

Although this estimator is not an unbiased estimator of σ^2, it avoids the requirement of estimating μ.

Example 10.2

In Example 10.1 the value $n\bar{r}^2/(n-1)$ is 0.000219. This value is about 13 percent of the sample variance. If it is ignored, the estimate of the annual volatility is 0.273.

In practice the volatility of a stock may not remain the same over time. Hence, establishing the periodicity of data (daily or weekly, for example), and the number of historic values to use is important. The most common method is to use daily intervals over a period of about 20 weeks. Since option prices are sensitive to volatility, significant efforts have been made to devise better estimating procedures. These methods include the use of daily high, low, open, and close prices. Other methods use time series models that revise the estimate based on historical values by taking into account economic variables, such as inflation and market/industrial sector factors. Indeed, volatilities of different stocks tend to be highly correlated with each other. This suggests that a common market volatility factor may explain a large percentage of the variability of individual stocks. In addition, extreme volatilities of stocks in a particular industry tend to regress toward the mean values for their industry. As a result, extremely volatile stocks should have their forecasts dampened slightly, while low-volatility stocks should have their forecasts enhanced a bit. Volatilities that shift in response to stock prices, market forces, and other variables are inconsistent with the basic assumptions of volatility in the Black-Scholes model. Nonetheless, very practical results can be obtained by using the model in conjunction with volatilities that are frequently revised by more sophisticated methods than analysis of historical variability.

Implicit Volatility

If the assumptions of the Black-Scholes model held true and all the parameters were known, the market price of a call option on a nondividend-paying stock would equal the Black-Scholes price. With the volatility unknown, however, different investors would estimate it differently and would disagree over the theoretical price. Since call prices are observable, however, rather than use the Black-Scholes equation to compute a fair price, an investor could take the price as given and use the equation to obtain the volatility that equates the theoretical price to the observed price.

Unfortunately, no explicit equation for σ^2 can be obtained from the Black-Scholes model, and numerical search procedures must be used. The method is quite simple. Conceptually, one guesses a value for σ, puts it into the Black-Scholes equation, and computes the fair value. If this value equals the actual market price, the guess is correct. If the computed call price is too large (small), then a smaller (larger) value for σ is tried. The value of σ that equates the market and theoretical price is called the *implicit volatility*. It can be viewed as the current best consensus estimate by the market's participants regarding future volatility over the time period to expiration.

In practice, different options on the same stock may result in different implicit volatilities. If the volatility changes over time, options with the same strike but different maturities should have different implicit volatilities. Options with the same maturity but different strikes may also have different implicit volatilities. This may be especially true for stocks that pay dividends and for some deep-in-the-money contracts where early exercise may be appropriate and the market's opinion on the volatility reflects only the time to the next ex-dividend date. A more important reason why implicit volatilities differ is measurement errors in the stock and option prices. Specifically, the closing prices of options may not represent the actual prices that could be obtained. This measurement error is discussed in more detail on page 227.

Let σ_i^* represent the implicit volatility of an option belonging to a given strike and maturity class. The simplest method of deriving a single forecast of implicit volatility is to compute the average implicit volatility, $\bar{\sigma}^*$, across all contracts

$$\bar{\sigma}^* = \sum_{i=1}^{m} \frac{\sigma_i^*}{m}$$

where m is the number of different contracts.

The simple averaging process gives equal weight to all options. However, since option prices are not equally sensitive to volatility, it appears reasonable to give extra weight to those contracts that are most sensitive to the volatility parameter. These contracts are the at-the-money contracts. Let W_i be the weight assigned to the ith contract. Then

$$\bar{\sigma}^* = \sum_{i=1}^{m} W_i \sigma_i^*$$

where

$$\sum_{i=1}^{m} W_i = 1.$$

Different weighting schemes have been proposed. One measure of the sensitivity of the call to volatility is given by the slope of the call pricing line with respect to volatility, $\partial C/\partial \sigma$. In this case the weights W_i are proportional to $\partial C_i/\partial \sigma$. Chiras and Manaster recommend that a weighting scheme based on the elasticity of variance be adopted. Beckers, however, has shown that using only the implicit volatility of the option nearest the money produces predictions as good as any other method.

Empirical evidence confirms that forecasts of future volatility based on implicit volatility are generally better than predictions based on historically computed volatilities using weekly data.

EXTENSIONS OF THE BLACK-SCHOLES MODEL

The original Black-Scholes model has been extended to take into account several real world factors. In this section we shall briefly review some of the areas in which extensions have been made.

The Stock Price Process

The original Black-Scholes model assumes stock prices follow a geometric Wiener process with a constant and known volatility. Option pricing models for alternative diffusion processes have been derived. In addition, option pricing models for jump processes and diffusion jump processes have been established. Nonetheless, while there are closed-form solutions to option prices for other statistical distributions, the Black-Scholes model remains the most popular.

The Black-Scholes and other continuous trading option models assume the volatility is constant and known with certainty. If the volatility were not known, riskless hedges could not be maintained. Extensions of the Black-Scholes model to handle changing volatilities have not been accomplished.

Taxes, Margin Requirements, and Borrowing Rates

The original Black-Scholes model ignores taxes, margin requirements, and differential borrowing and lending rates. If the option is priced according to one given marginal tax rate, then investors in other tax brackets will perceive riskless arbitrage opportunities. Somehow the correct option price has to be established for an "average" tax bracket. Modifications to the Black-Scholes model that adjust for this have been proposed. The effect of margin requirements and the differential borrowing and lending rates can also be taken into account.

Interest Rates

The Black-Scholes model requires that interest rates be known. That is, the yield curve must be well specified. A constant interest rate is not necessary. For example, with the binomial model, the value of the interest rate can differ in each period. However, if the interest rates not only change over time, but do so in a way that is unpredictable, the usual arbitrage theory breaks down.

Dividends

In Chapter 8 we discussed how the Black-Scholes model could be adjusted to approximate option prices on dividend-paying securities. More precise option pricing models that explicitly take dividends into account have been established and are referenced in that chapter.

Discrete Trading Opportunities

The Black-Scholes model requires a perfect capital market where continuous trading can be conducted. This assumption allows a risk-free position to be created with stocks and options alone. A continual revision of the portfolio is necessary for the riskless position to be maintained. If adjustments can be made only at discrete points in time or if they involve transaction costs, riskless positions could not be maintained and options prices would diverge from the Black-Scholes value.

One big advantage of the continuous trading approach is that the option price can be derived *relative* to the stock price, regardless of whether the stock price is in equilibrium or not. The option price so derived is termed a *fair price* since all investors, regardless of their preferences, would conclude that, if the option price were set at any other value, riskless arbitrage opportunities would arise.

If continuous trading could not be accomplished, the option could not usually be priced free of preferences because the option could no longer be replicated by a leveraged position in the stock. In this situation, option prices could be established only if assumptions were made about the stock price process and the preferences of investors in the economy. Implicit in discrete time models, therefore, is a capital asset pricing model.

In a single-period model, it may at first glance be quite tempting to compute the call price by using the "usual" capital asset pricing model. Specifically, for the stock we have

$$E(\tilde{R}_s) = R_F + \beta_s[E(\tilde{R}_m) - R_F]$$

and for the option we require

$$E(\tilde{R}_c) = R_F + \beta_c[E(\tilde{R}_m) - R_F].$$

Finally, the stock and call are related by the no-arbitrage opportunity at expiration. That is,

$$\tilde{C}_T = \text{Max}(\tilde{S}_T - X, 0).$$

With these three equations, it is possible to solve for the current call price C_0. This call price will depend on market expectation terms, as well as on volatility terms that are not directly observable. Unfortunately, this approach is not very useful. The "usual" discrete time capital asset pricing model assumes securities all have normal distributions. Under this premise, basing decisions on means and variances can be shown to be optimal. However, with options in the investment opportunity set, the return payouts can have truncated distributions. Indeed, the return distributions can be molded into almost any shape. With non-normal distributions, a mean variance framework may no longer be appropriate.

If all investors had logarithmic utility (or more generally, constant proportional risk aversion), then the resulting discrete time model for option prices would be given by the Black-Scholes model again. Although the model in discrete time is preference dependent, it does not require that all investors have identical forecasts of volatility. This result was first derived by Rubinstein. His result thus provides further credibility for the Black-Scholes equation and for using a continuous trading assumption to derive option prices.

APPLICATION OF OPTION PRICING MODELS

There are four primary areas in which option pricing models are useful.

To Guide Transactions

The most obvious application is to provide a decision aid to investors who are establishing stock-option/hedge positions. Such investors attempt to buy underpriced options and/or sell overpriced contracts. Theoretical pricing models can be used to establish which contracts are not fairly priced. In addition, the Black-Scholes model can be used to obtain the hedge ratio, H_0, which measures the sensitivity of the call price to a small change in the stock price.

The Black-Scholes model is so popular that it is often included as a hardware function in financial handheld calculators. The role of option pricing models to guide transactions is discussed in more detail in the next section.

To Construct Synthetic Prices

If no option prices are available for a particular option at a particular point in time, a model can be used to estimate the price that would have been established by the market had trading occurred. Such prices are established by dealers, for example, who issue options privately. The models are also useful for valuing financial arrangements that have optionlike terms in them. Such applications of option pricing will be discussed in Chapters 13 and 14.

To Study Market Behavior

A frequent studied aspect of market behavior is efficiency. An unavoidable step in such studies is specifying a model of price determination. With option pricing at hand, market efficiency tests can be conducted. The resulting tests are actually joint tests of the market itself and of the pricing model used to study the market. In order to study the functioning of the option markets, a model such as the Black-Scholes model is necessary. If observed option prices diverge systematically from their theoretical prices, then the market is either inefficient or not well specified. Empirical tests of the Black-Scholes model and efficiency are discussed later in this chapter.

To Obtain Implicit Parameters

Option prices can contain useful information. Call premiums tend to expand in some periods and shrink in others. The size of these premiums depends primarily on interest rates and volatility expectations over the period. By analyzing option premiums, one can obtain useful information about how investors in the aggregate perceive the future of the market. For example, if call option premiums expand, the reason may be the fact that there is a consensus among investors that future volatility in the stock market will exceed historical volatility.

OPTION STRATEGIES AND OPTION PRICING

In Chapter 3 we introduced several option strategies and analyzed them by investigating their profit functions at expiration. With an option pricing model available, further analyses on positions can be accomplished.

Buy and Sell Decisions

An investor purchasing (selling) an option would like to buy (sell) an underpriced (overvalued) contract. By using an option pricing model, he or she can establish a benchmark on prices. When observed prices deviate significantly from their theoretical price, this signals some event. On the one hand, it could be an investment opportunity; on the other hand, it could reflect a change in the market's consensus opinion on the future volatility of the stock.

Profit Functions and Strategy Evaluation

With an option pricing formula in hand, profit functions can be plotted out prior to the expiration date. This is especially important for positions involving options with different maturities. For example, consider a horizontal call spread. When the near option expires, the far option still has a time premium. Using an option pricing model, one can compute these time premiums for different stock prices. Exhibit 10.3 illustrates the payout of a horizontal call spread evaluated at the expiration date of the near series. The options traded have a strike of $40.

Option pricing models also allow investors to investigate how the profit function of any position evolves over time. Exhibit 10.4, for example, illustrates how the profit function of a vertical call spread evolves over time. This is accomplished by plotting the profit function at three points in time. The strike prices of the options in the spread are $35 and $45. As time to expiration nears, the profit function converges onto the piecewise linear graph ($T = 0$). Note that the convergence rate increases as time to expiration decreases.

Option Deltas, Gammas, Thetas, and Lambdas

Option pricing models provide more than the fair price of a call option. They provide the initial replicating portfolio. Using share equivalents provided by

EXHIBIT 10.3

A Horizontal Call Spread at the Maturity Date of the Near Option

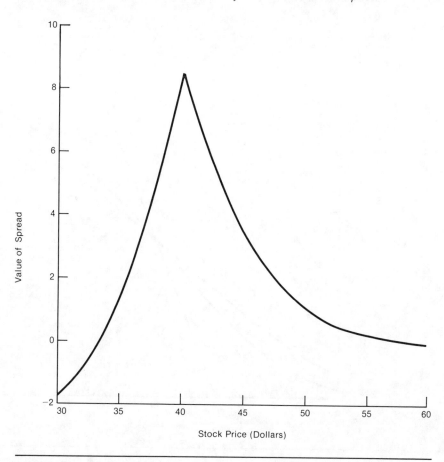

such models, one can analyze risk and reward for any stock-option position. This analysis was illustrated in Chapter 8.

Recall that the share equivalent, H_0, is the slope of the option pricing line. In the trade it is often referred to as the *delta value,* since it measures the change in option price for a dollar change in stock price. If delta equals 0.3, this implies that the option premium should move up 30 cents for every dollar advance in the underlying stock. The delta value for call options ranges from 0 to 1; out-of-the-money call options have low slopes (delta near 0), at-the-money options have deltas near 0.5, and deep-in-the-money options have deltas near 1. Put deltas will range in value from 0 to –1. Unfortunately, since the delta value depends on the stock price and time to expiration, it does not remain constant.

The *neutral ratio* is the reciprocal of delta. If delta equals 0.30, then the neutral ratio is 3.33 options. The neutral ratio establishes the number of

EXHIBIT 10.4
A Vertical Call Spread with T *Months to Maturity*

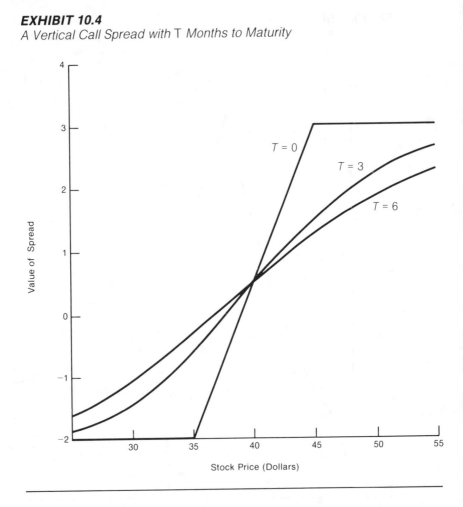

options that must be used to hedge the underlying stock. A neutral ratio of 3.33 implies that 10 option contracts are currently needed to hedge every 300 shares of the underlying stock.

Unfortunately, delta hedges have to be monitored continuously.

Example 10.3

Assume the current stock price is $30 and an investor wants to hedge his or her position in 400 shares with call options. The current delta value of the in-the-money option that is used is 0.8. The neutral ratio is 1/0.8 = 1.25 options. Hence, 5 options are required in the hedge. If the stock price moves down to 27 and the delta value adjusts to 0.6, the new neutral ratio is 1/0.6 = 1.667 and 6.67 (i.e., 1.667 × 4) options are now required in the hedge.

Delta measures the change in option premiums relative to a given price change in the underlying security. Since delta varies with the price and with time, its stability plays an important role in the successful design of a neutral hedge. If the delta value is extremely sensitive to the underlying price or time, frequent portfolio revisions may be necessary to maintain an effective hedge. Note that delta values become more unstable as expiration approaches. In this case, call deltas move rapidly toward 0 or 1.

Gamma is a measure of the rate of change in delta. As such, gamma is nothing more than a measure of the rate of change of the slope of the option price line. The gamma value is maximum for calls at the money and near expiration. Both puts and calls have positive gamma values.

The *theta value* measures the sensitivity of the option value with respect to the passage of time, assuming the stock price remains unchanged. Stock options with high theta values can lose their time premium rapidly, even if the stock price remains unchanged. Theta values change the most as maturity approaches. They represent the income stream to an option writer provided the stock price remains unchanged. Since a European call option decreases in value as time to expiration nears (assuming the stock price remains unchanged), it has a negative theta. European puts usually also have negative thetas. Stocks, of course, have zero theta values.

The Black-Scholes assumption of an unchanging and known volatility parameter is quite restrictive. Most option market practitioners believe volatilities are stochastic. In the absence of an option model that allows stochastic volatility, practitioners use the existing model by periodically updating estimates. One measure that captures the risk attributable to a changing volatility is provided by the option *lambda,* which is just the partial derivative of the option value with respect to volatility. If the lambda value is large, then the risk attributable to changing volatility is substantial.

Exhibit 10.5 summarizes the formula for deltas, thetas, lambdas, and gammas for call options. These formulas are based on the Black-Scholes equation.

Position Deltas, Gammas, and Thetas

The position delta measures the current sensitivity of the position to small changes in the stock price. If the position delta is zero, then the position is immunized from small stock price changes. However, if it is a large positive (or negative) number, then the position is extremely sensitive to stock price changes.

Example 10.4

Consider an investor who buys n_1 calls with strike price X_1 at price C_1 each, and n_2 calls with strike price X_2 at price C_2 each. The value of the position is

$$V_0 = n_1 C_1 + n_2 C_2.$$

(continued)

Example 10.4 (cont'd)

The position delta value, Δ, is given by

$$\Delta = \frac{\partial V_0}{\partial S_0} = n_1 \frac{\partial C_1}{\partial S_0} + n_2 \frac{\partial C_2}{\partial S_0}$$

$$= n_1 H_1 + n_2 H_2.$$

For the position delta value to be zero we must require

$$n_1 H_1 = -n_2 H_2$$

or

$$n_1 = -\frac{H_2}{H_1} n_2.$$

Thus, for every call option with strike X_2 that is bought, (H_2/H_1) calls with strike X_1 should be sold for the hedge to be immunized over a small instant in time. Note that the hedge will only be immunized over a small time interval if stock price changes are small. If the stock price should suddenly jump, the slopes of the call prices at their new levels could be significantly different and the position would no longer be immunized.

EXHIBIT 10.5
Formulas for the Delta, Theta, Lambda, and Gamma of a Call Option

$$\text{Call option delta } \Delta = \frac{\partial C}{\partial S} = N(d_1)$$

$$\text{Call option theta } \theta = -\frac{\partial C}{\partial t} = -\left[Xe^{-rT}N(d_2) + S\sigma\sqrt{T}\frac{n(d_1)}{2}\right]$$

$$\text{Call option lambda } \lambda = \frac{\partial C}{\partial \sigma} = S\sqrt{T}n(d_1)$$

$$\text{Call option gamma } \Gamma = \frac{\partial \Delta}{\partial S} = \frac{n(d_1)}{S\sigma\sqrt{T}}$$

where

$$d_1 = \frac{\ln(S/X) + (r + \sigma^2/2)T}{\sigma\sqrt{T}}$$

$$d_2 = d_1 - \sigma\sqrt{T}$$

$$n(d_1) = \frac{\exp(d_1^2/2)}{\sqrt{2\pi}}$$

$N(d_1)$ = the cumulative normal distribution function

As the underlying stock price changes, the position delta changes and the investor may have to readjust the portfolio to bring the position delta back into line. Ideally, a position should be established such that the desired delta value is quite robust to stock price changes. The measure of the robustness of a position is provided by the position gamma. If the position gamma is close to zero, then the delta value of the position will be robust.

In Example 10.4 the position delta is $n_1 H_1 + n_2 H_2$ and the position gamma is

$$\Gamma = \frac{\partial \Delta}{\partial S} = n_1 \frac{\partial H_1}{\partial S} + n_2 \frac{\partial H_2}{\partial S}.$$

A position with a zero delta value and a low absolute position gamma will be better immunized than if the position gamma was larger in absolute value. Equivalently, a position with a low absolute gamma value should require less frequent portfolio revisions to keep the position delta constant than a position with a higher absolute gamma value.

Similarly to the position delta, it is possible to establish the theta value of a position. This measure indicates the income stream on the position provided the stock price remains unchanged. As an example, the position theta of the call spread, θ, in example 10.4 is given by

$$\theta = -\frac{\partial V_0}{\partial t} = -n_1 \frac{\partial C_1}{\partial t} - n_2 \frac{\partial C_2}{\partial t}$$

$$= n_1 \theta_1 + n_2 \theta_2$$

where θ_1 and θ_2 are the theta values of the two call options.

Example 10.4 illustrates how positions can be constructed with definite investment goals in sight. If an investor is bullish, a high delta portfolio may be appropriate. If an investor is neutral about a stock and constructs a position by selling calls against stock held, then a portfolio with a high theta value and low absolute gamma value may be appropriate.

Regardless of the goals of an investor, the very fact that option positions can be translated into a portfolio of share equivalents whose sensitivity to price changes and to time can be analyzed is very useful.

EMPIRICAL TESTS OF THE BLACK-SCHOLES MODEL

The first test of prices of listed stock options was conducted by Galai in 1977. Using data from the first seven months of trading on the CBOE, Galai set up a trading rule and tested it to determine whether abnormal profits could be generated. If abnormal profits could be obtained, he would have concluded that the market was inefficient and use of the Black-Scholes model could lead to abnormal profits. If the model did not yield abnormal profits, then either the Black-Scholes model was correct and the market efficient or the model was misspecified. The trading rule used by Galai was a feasible strategy in that decisions based on information available at the end of any day were implemented at the closing prices at the end of the next day. If an option was overpriced (according to the Black-Scholes model), the call was sold and the hedge ratio of shares was purchased. Conversely, if the call was underpriced, the option was bought and the hedge ratio of shares sold short. With positions revised daily, the net abnormal returns generated by the trading strategy (after transaction costs were included) disappeared.

The Galai study, like several that followed, suffered from a severe drawback, namely, the policy of using closing prices. In contrast to stock prices, use of closing option prices is plagued with problems, which will be discussed later in this section.

An alternative experimental design based on comparing actual option prices with theoretical option prices, computed using weighted average implied volatilities as estimates in the Black-Scholes equation, has also been considered. Trippi, using weekly closing prices and a trading rule that purchased (sold) options if the market price deviated by 15 percent less (more) than its theoretical value, showed that abnormal average returns could be generated. Chiras and Manaster obtained similar results. When transaction costs were included, however, the abnormal profits were significantly reduced. MacBeth and Merville were able to identify common characteristics of option contracts that were overpriced. They concluded that the Black-Scholes formula overvalues out-of-the-money options and undervalues in-the-money contracts. Similar studies by other investigators lead to the following general conclusions:

1. The Black-Scholes model is extremely good for pricing at-the-money options, especially when time to expiration exceeds two months and no dividends occur.
2. For deep-in-the-money and out-of-the-money contracts, significant deviations between market prices and model prices can occur.
3. Short-term (less than a month) contracts are often mispriced.
4. Options on extremely low and extremely high volatility stocks are often mispriced.

The biases reported in the empirical studies are not consistent over time. For example, the strike price bias from Black-Scholes values is significant, and tends to be in the same direction at any point in time. However, the direction of bias may change from period to period.

Most empirical tests conducted prior to 1980 used closing prices of options. These closing prices can be very misleading and on occasion indicate that arbitrage opportunities based on the pricing relationship in Chapter 4 are available. The errors in using closing prices are caused by liquidity problems, non-simultaneity of stock and option closing prices, and the bid-ask spread. These issues are discussed next.

Non-simultaneity of Stock and Option Prices   Most option trading takes place in near-the-money short-term contracts. Low liquidity in far-from-the-money contracts increases the likelihood that the last option trade occurred some time before trading ceased in the stock. This means that the reported option price need not reflect the actual price an option could be bought or sold for when the stock stopped trading at the end of the day.

The Bid-Ask Spread   Investors who purchase (sell) options will probably get the ask (bid) price quoted in the trading pit. By looking at the closing price, the investor does not know if the trade took place at the bid, at the ask, or in between. If, for example, the spread is ½ and the closing price is 3, then if the last transaction took place at the bid (ask), the bid-ask spread is 3–3½ (2½–3). Hence, given a closing price of 3, the bid-ask spread creates uncertainty in prices between 2½ and 3½. This spread is 33 percent of the closing price.

To overcome these difficulties, Rubinstein used the CBOE's own record of all reported trades and quotes over a two-year period. This data base provided a time-stamped record to the nearest second of option trade prices and quotes together with the stock prices at the same time. Rubinstein found the quality of these data to be extremely high, primarily because of the CBOE's computerized error-checking procedures. Using nonparametric statistical tests, Rubinstein compared several option pricing model results to observed prices and concluded that (1) out-of-the-money options with short expirations were relatively overpriced, (2) a strike bias existed but its direction changed according to the time period, and (3) no model provided results consistently superior to the Black-Scholes model. Rubinstein suggested that a combination of these model prices could produce better results and that biases observed in any period could be correlated with macroeconomic variables such as the level of stock market prices, volatilities, and interest rates.

The strike-price and time-to-expiration biases displayed by the Black-Scholes model can be explained to a certain degree by the nontreatment of dividends. In fact, Whaley and Sterk found that, for options on stocks paying exactly one dividend during the term of the option, strike-price and time-to-expiration biases could be removed by applying option models that took dividends into account. Geske and Roll argue that some of the volatility biases recorded for the Black-Scholes model are not attributable to model misspecifications, but rather to the errors induced by estimation methods for the volatility.

The overall conclusions, however, are that the Black-Scholes model provides an extremely good fit to actual data and that the pricing model does serve as a useful valuation tool.

CONCLUSION

In this chapter the requirements for using the Black-Scholes model were discussed and the use of the Black-Scholes model in option strategies was investigated. Although profit diagrams for hedge positions can be generated over time, it is often useful to obtain measures of the sensitivity of the current position to small stock price changes or to the passage of time. The delta, gamma, and theta measures provide the sensitivity measures.

Testing of any option pricing model is made difficult by several problems, including transaction costs, nonsimultaneity of prices, and lack of knowledge about volatility. Nonetheless, empirical evidence supports the Black-Scholes model, especially for at-the-money call options.

References

The most important estimate required for practical use of the Black-Scholes model is volatility. Rather than using closing prices, Parkinson used daily high and low values. Garman and Klass improved this procedure by including more information, including the opening and closing prices. Unfortunately, their estimators are developed under the assumption that stock prices follow a geometric Wiener process, and may not be robust. Implicit volatilities may provide the best estimators. Latane and Rendleman, and Beckers, provide convincing evidence that these methods provide good estimates.

Applications of delta, gamma, and theta values for constructing and screening positions in such a way that the resulting positions reflect the preferences of the investor are well discussed by Cox and Rubinstein. Black provides a summary of the "facts and fantasies" associated with options and option strategies.

For a comprehensive review of the empirical tests of parity relationships and of option pricing models, see Galai and Rubinstein. For discussions of strike price biases caused primarily by dividends, see Geske and Roll; Whaley; and Sterk. Although the Black-Scholes formula for nondividend paying stock is often contained as a built-in function in some handheld calculators, if it is not available, a direct graphical procedure for computing the theoretical price is. Specifically, graphs that show contours of option prices as a function of the important variables have been developed by Dimson.

Numerical methods other than the binomial option pricing model have been used to approximate option prices for American options. Specifically, discrete difference equations are used to approximate the differential equations set up using the Black-Scholes no-arbitrage methodology. For a discussion of such methods, see Brennan and Schwartz and Courtadon. These methods are briefly discussed in Chapter 16.

Beckers, S. "The Constant Elasticity of Variance Model and Its Implications for Option Pricing." *Journal of Finance* 35(June 1980): 661–73.

Beckers, S. "Standard Deviations Implied in Option Prices as Predictors of Future Stock Price Variability." *Journal of Banking and Finance* 5(September 1981): 363–82.

Bhattacharya, M. "Empirical Properties of the Black-Scholes Formula Under Ideal Conditions." *Journal of Financial and Quantitative Analysis* 15(December 1980): 1081–95.

Black, F., and M. Scholes. "The Valuation of Option Contracts and a Test of Market Efficiency." *Journal of Finance* 27(May 1972): 399–418.

Black, F. "Fact and Fantasy in the Use of Options." *Financial Analysis Journal* 31(July–August 1975): 36–41, 61–72.

Blomeyer, E., and R. Klemkosky. "Tests of Market Efficiency for American Call Options." In *Option Pricing,* edited by M. Brenner. Lexington, Mass.: D. C. Heath, 1983, pp: 101–21.

Bookstaber, R. "Observed Option Mispricing and the Nonsimultaneity of Stock and Option Quotations. *Journal of Business* 54(January 1981): 141–55.

Boyle, P., and A. L. Ananthanarayanan. "The Impact of Variance Estimation in Option Valuation Models." *Journal of Financial Economics* 5(December 1977): 375–88.

Boyle, P., and D. Emanuel. "Discretely Adjusted Option Hedges." *Journal of Financial Economics* 8(September 1980): 259–82.

Brennan, M., and E. Schwartz. "The Valuation of American Put Options." *Journal of Finance* 32(May 1977): 449–62.

Brennan, M., and E. Schwartz. "Finite Difference Methods and Jump Process Arising in the Pricing of Contingent Claims: A Synthesis." *Journal of Financial and Quantitative Analysis* 13(September 1978): 461–74.

Chiras, D., and S. Manaster. "The Information Content of Option Prices and a Test of Market Efficiency." *Journal of Financial Economics* 6(June–September 1978): 213–34.

Courtadon, G. "A More Accurate Finite Difference Approximation for the Valuation of Options." *Journal of Financial and Quantitative Analysis* 17(December 1982): 697–703.

Cox, J., and S. Ross. "The Valuation of Options for Alternative Stochastic Processes." *Journal of Financial Economics* 3(January–March 1976): 145–66.

Cox, J., and M. Rubinstein. *Option Markets.* Englewood Cliffs, N.J.: Prentice-Hall, 1985.

Dimson, E. "Option Valuation Nomograms." *Financial Analysis Journal* (November–December 1977): 71–74.

Finnerty, J. "The CBOE and Market Efficiency." *Journal of Financial and Quantitative Analysis* 13(March 1978): 29–38.

Galai, D. "Tests of Market Efficiency of the Chicago Board Option Exchange." *Journal of Business* 50(April 1977): 167–97.

Galai, D. "Empirical Tests of Boundary Conditions for CBOE Options." *Journal of Financial Economics* 6(June–September 1978): 187–211.

Galai, D. "A Convexity Test for Traded Options." *Quarterly Review of Economics and Business* 19(Summer 1979): 83–90.

Galai, D. "A Survey of Empirical Tests of Option Pricing Models." In *Option Pricing,* edited by M. Brenner. Lexington, Mass.: D. C. Heath, 1983, pp. 45–80.

Garman, M., and M. Klass. "On the Estimation of Security Price Volatilities from Historical Data." *Journal of Business* 53(January 1980): 67–78.

Geske, R. "Pricing of Options with Stochastic Dividend Yield." *Journal of Finance* 33(May 1978): 618–25.

Geske, R., and R. Roll. "On Valuing American Call Options with the Black-Scholes Formula." *Journal of Finance* 39(June 1984): 443–55.

Geske, R., and K. Shastri. "Valuation by Approximation: A Composition of Alternative Option Valuation Techniques." *Journal of Financial Quantitative Analysis* 20(March 1985): 45–71.

Gould, J., and D. Galai. "Transactions Costs and the Relationship Between Put and Call Prices." *Journal of Financial Economics* 1(June 1974): 105–29.

Hayes, S., and M. Tennenbaum. "The Impact of Listed Options on the Underlying Shares." *Financial Management* 8(Winter 1979): 72–77.

Ho, T., and R. Macris. "Dealer Bid-Ask Quotes and Transaction Prices: An Empirical Study of Some AMEX Options." *Journal of Finance* 39(March 1984): 23–45.

Klemkosky, R., and B. Resnick. "Put-Call Parity and Market Efficiency." *Journal of Finance* 34(December 1979): 1141–55.

Latane, H., and R. Rendleman, Jr. "Standard Deviations of Stock Price Ratios Implied in Option Prices." *Journal of Finance* 31(May 1976): 369–82.

Leland, H. "Option Pricing and Replication with Transaction Costs." *Journal of Finance* 40(December 1985): 1283–1301.

MacBeth, J., and L. Merville. "An Empirical Examination of the Black-Scholes Call Option Pricing Model." *Journal of Finance* 34(December 1979): 1173–86.

Manaster, S., and R. Rendleman, Jr. "Option Prices as Predictors of Equilibrium Stock Prices." *Journal of Finance* 37(September 1982): 1043–58.

McDonald, R., and D. Siegel. "Option Pricing When the Underlying Asset Earns a Below-Equilibrium Rate of Return: A Note." *Journal of Finance* 39(March 1984): 261–65.

Parkinson, M. "The Extreme Value Method for Estimating the Variances of the Rate of Return." *Journal of Business* 53(January 1980): 61–65.

Phillips, S., and C. Smith, Jr. "Trading Costs for Listed Options: The Implications for Market Efficiency." *Journal of Financial Economics* 8(June 1980): 179–201.

Rogalski, R. "Variances of Option Prices in Theory and Evidence." *Journal of Portfolio Management* 4(Winter 1978): 43–51.

Rubinstein, M. "Nonparametric Tests of Alternative Option Pricing Models." Working Paper No. 117. University of California, Berkeley, Research Program in Finance, 1981.

Rubinstein, M. "The Valuation of Uncertain Income Streams and the Pricing of Options." *Bell Journal of Economics* 7(Autumn 1976): 407–425.

Schmalensee, R., and R. Trippi. "Common Stock Volatility Expectations Implied by Option Premia." *Journal of Finance* 33(March 1978): 129–47.

Scholes, M. "Taxis and the Pricing of Options." *Journal of Finance* 31(May 1976): 319–32.

Smith, C., Jr. "Option Pricing: A Review." *Journal of Financial Economics* 3(January–March 1976): 3–51.

Sterk, W. "Tests of Two Models for Valuing Call Options on Stocks with Dividends." *Journal of Finance* 37(December 1982): 1229–38.

Sterk, W. "Comparative Performance of the Black-Scholes and Roll-Geske-Whaley Option Pricing Models." *Journal of Financial and Quantitative Analysis* 18(September 1983): 345–54.

Trennepohl, G. "A Comparison of Listed Option Premiums and Black and Scholes Model Prices: 1973-1979." *Journal of Financial Research* 4(Spring 1981): 11–20.

Whaley, R. "Valuation of American Call Options on Dividend Paying Stocks: Empirical Tests." *Journal of Financial Economics* 10(March 1982): 29–58.

Exercises

1. How does the delta value change as the call option moves from being out of the money to being in the money? How does the delta value of the put option change?

2. a. "The price of an option depends on the total volatility of the stock."
   b. "The price of a security depends on the total amount of nondiversifiable risk inherent in the stock."
   Are these two statements inconsistent? Should option prices depend only on the level of nondiversifiable risk? If not, explain.

3. Explain the implied volatility of a stock. Why would you obtain different implied volatilities when using options with different expiration dates and with different strikes.

4. If options traded in the market with time to expiration of 2 or 3 years, would the Black-Scholes model provide good fits to data? Provide possible reasons for poor fits.

5. Describe the empirical tests that have been conducted to establish the validity of the Black-Scholes model.

6. Using the data in Exhibit 10.1 together with the fact that the annual short-term interest rate is 8 percent, compute the up and down values u and d for the binomial model. Assume the option has 6 months to expiration and 10 periods are used in the analysis.

7. "Under a discrete trading assumption, option prices are preference dependent." Is this statement always true? If not, provide an example.

8. Let H_1 and H_2 be the hedge ratios for two call options with strikes 60 and 70. Compute the delta values for a bullish call spread. For what stock price would you suspect the position delta to be most sensitive? That is, for what stock price is the position gamma value the largest? Explain your answer.

9. A land option allows the holder to purchase a specific property for a particular price. This right lasts for a particular time period. Land options are not traded in secondary markets. Could the Black-Scholes model be used to construct a synthetic price for the contract? Explain the difficulties in using such a model.

10. An investor is extremely bullish on a stock. Unfortunately, according to the Black-Scholes model, the option is overpriced. Does that mean the option should not be purchased? Provide reasons for your answer.

11. If a call option is underpriced but the put-call parity condition holds, is the put overpriced? If both are mispriced, can a position be constructed that takes advantage of both mispricings?

12. "Delta-neutral trading is usually done by market makers on the floor of the exchange." Explain why this is true.

13. "Traders who engage in delta hedging by selling calls against stock held ideally would like to construct positions with a negative gamma, positive theta, and small lambda." Is this true? Justify your answer.

11

Forward and Futures Contracts and Their Options

This chapter provides an introduction to forward and futures markets. Contracts traded in these markets often serve similar functions to options. Futures contracts, for example, can be used in hedging strategies to reduce risks associated with stock ownership. The primary purpose of this chapter is to introduce these contracts and contrast them with options. The second purpose is to discuss option contracts that trade on futures. Such contracts accomplish very similar risk management objectives to option contracts on the cash commodities. For example, options on stock index futures may serve as an alternative to options on stock indices. Differences between options on cash and options on futures contracts are discussed, and illustrations of hedging strategies involving futures and options on futures are provided. Then pricing of European and American options on futures and forward contracts is discussed, and put-call parity relationships are investigated. The final section explores similarities and differences between options on spot and options on futures.

FORWARD CONTRACTS

An investor who holds a long (short) position in a forward contract agrees to buy (sell) a specific quantity of a specific asset at a specified date for a specified price.

The contract can be viewed as a side bet on the future delivery price. The payoff of this bet is equal to the difference between the agreed price, called the *forward price,* and the final delivery price. The contract is simply a sales agreement established in an over-the-counter market in which delivery and payments are deferred. If an investor considered the agreed price (forward price) to be very low, he or she would be prepared to pay a premium to obtain such a contract. Conversely, if the fixed price was considered too high, the contract would have inherent value to the seller. Clearly, there is some intermediate forward price at which the contract will carry a zero value. This fixed price corresponds to the forward price. Thus, when a contract is initiated, the forward price is set so that there are no initial cash flows between the parties of the transaction. Let $FO(T)$ be the forward price that exists at time zero, with T periods to go to settlement.

ESTABLISHING FORWARD PRICES—THE COST-OF-CARRY MODEL

The difference between the forward price and spot price is called the *basis:*

$$\text{Basis = Spot Price – Forward Price.} \qquad (11.1)$$

The basis reflects the net carrying charges (and convenience yield) between the present time and the delivery date. The carrying costs include interest costs, insurance, and storage charges, while the convenience yield represents the benefits accruing from holding stock of a commodity today, instead of the cash for purchasing that commodity in the future. As the delivery date nears, this net charge diminishes. At the delivery date, the basis is zero and the forward price (for immediate delivery) must equal the spot price. If this were not the case, arbitrage opportunities would exist. If, for example, forward prices were lower than spot prices at the delivery date, investors would find it cheaper to purchase the commodity by buying the forward contract and taking immediate delivery, rather than buying on the spot market. Exhibit 11.1 illustrates how the basis shrinks as the delivery date draws near. In "normal" markets, the basis is just sufficient to cover storage, insurance, inspection and other carrying costs incurred by holding the commodity for future delivery. The basis thus compensates speculators for the expense of buying the commodity and storing it for future sale.

Example 11.1

Consider a storable asset such as gold or silver. The price of the item is $100. The net cost of carrying the asset over a period of three months, including net capital costs, insurance, storage, commissions and so forth, comes to $8. To break even, the price of the asset must appreciate by $8. An investor could earn riskless arbitrage profits if a sales price exceeding $108 could be guaranteed. If forward prices, for example, were $110, then by borrowing $100, buying the asset, and selling a forward contract, the investor could lock into a $2 profit. This arbitrage opportunity would not last long. In equilibrium, the forward price would adjust until it equalled the spot price plus the net cost of carrying.

If h represents the continuous rate of cost of carrying the item and if we assume that the carrying charge depends on the cost of the item, then the forward price, $FO(T)$, is given by $FO(T) = S_0\exp(hT)$. This gives rise to Property 11.1.

EXHIBIT 11.1
Shrinkage of the Basis

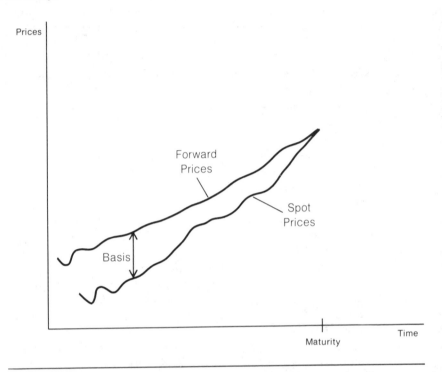

Property 11.1

The forward price for a storable commodity whose net cost of carrying is h percent is given by

$$FO(T) = S_0 \exp(hT). \qquad (11.2)$$

In some cases the cost of carrying may not depend solely on the spot price, and the pricing relationship in equation (11.2) will not hold.

Occasionally the market in some commodity becomes "inverted." In this case, the forward price is less than the spot price, and the basis is positive. Such situations can occur when the current supply of a commodity is short (and prices high) while the future supply is expected to be high (and prices low). The forward price could also be lower than the current price if the commodity itself provided a yield, that is, if the commodity provides payouts to its owners over the period.

Example 11.2

A commodity currently priced at \$100 provides a continuous yield of 12 percent. Since its carrying charge is 9 percent, the net rate of return on holding the commodity is 3 percent. In this case, the net cost of carry is 3 percent ($h = -3$ percent), and the breakeven point, K_T, is

$$K_T = S_0\exp(hT) = 100 \exp(-0.03) = 97.04.$$

FORWARD PRICES AND EXPECTED PRICES

Consider a storable security that provides no payouts (dividends). The expected future price is related to the current price by the equation

$$S_0 = \exp(-\rho_s T)E(\tilde{S}_T), \tag{11.3}$$

where $\rho_s > r$ reflects the riskiness of the security.

The forward price on this security is $FO(T) = S_0\exp(hT)$, where h is the cost of carrying. By substituting equation (11.3) into the above equation, we obtain

$$FO(T) = \exp(-\rho_s T)E(S_T)\exp(hT)$$

$$= \exp(hT - \rho_s T)E(S_T). \tag{11.4}$$

If $\rho_s > h$, then the forward price is set lower than the expected value.

Example 11.3

Assume the spot price is \$100 and the total carrying charge to maturity of the forward contract is \$2. Then according to the cost-of-carry model, the forward price should be \$102. If the expected future price were \$102.50, an expected profit of \$.50 could be made by buying now and carrying forward. However, there is risk involved. If the investor were risk averse, the additional expected compensation of \$.50 might not be high enough to compensate for the risk borne. The extent to which the market expectation is above the forward price depends on the aggregate degree of risk aversion in the market.

The cost-of-carry model for forward prices is based on the assumption that the underlying commodity is storable. Not all commodities, however, are storable. For example, produce may not store well. Financial instruments may also not be storable. In addition, the cost-of-carry model assumes that the commodity is always the deliverable item. However, in some instances settlement may be conducted by cash. This can create difficulties for the cost-of-carry model.

SPREADS

The size of the basis can be accounted for by interest rates, carrying charges, and yields. In addition to relationships between forward prices and spot prices, there are relationships among forward contracts of the same security with different maturities. The difference between two forward prices is known as the *spread*. Let T_1 and T_2 be the maturities of two forward contracts. Then the spread, S_p, is given by

$$S_p = FO(T_2) - FO(T_1). \tag{11.5}$$

VALUATION OF FORWARD CONTRACTS

Consider an investor who at time 0 enters into a long position in a forward contract with settlement date T days away. Let the forward price be $FO(T)$. Recall that this price is established so that the value of the contract is zero. Let $V[FO(T),T]$ represent the value of the contract, with T days to expiration. Then we have

$$V[FO(T),T] = 0. \tag{11.6}$$

Although the initial price paid for the forward contract is zero, over time its value will change.

At the settlement date, the value of the contract will be the difference between the forward price and settlement price. That is,

$$V[FO(T),0] = S_T - FO(T). \tag{11.7}$$

To see this, note that the buyer is obligated to take delivery at price $FO(T)$. Since the spot price at this time is S_T, the value of the contract must be the difference.

In this section we shall value the forward contract at an arbitrary point in time between the original date (time 0) and the settlement date (time T). To do this, consider the investor with the long position at time t_1. The current value of this position is $V[FO(T),T - t_1]$. The new contracts that are being established at this time have forward price $FO(T - t_1)$ and zero value. That is, $V[FO(T - t_1),T - t_1] = 0$.

To establish a formula for $V[FO(T),T - t_1]$ we shall assume that at time t_1 the investor offsets the long commitment by selling a forward contract with price $FO(T - t_1)$. The value of the portfolio at this point in time, $V_p(t_1)$ say, is given by

$$V_p(t_1) = V[FO(T),T - t_1] - V[FO(T - t_1),T - t_1]$$

$$= V[FO(T),T - t_1]. \tag{11.8}$$

At time T the value of the portfolio, $V_p(T)$, is given by

$$V_p(T) = V[FO(T),0] - V[FO(T - t_1),0]$$

$$= [S_T - FO(T)] - [S_T - FO(T - t_1)]$$

$$= FO(T - t_1) - FO(T). \tag{11.9}$$

Now this value will be known with certainty at time t_1. Hence, over the period t_1 to T, the investor is carrying a riskfree portfolio. To avoid riskless arbitrage opportunities, this portfolio should earn the riskless rate. Hence,

$$V_p(t_1) = V_p(T)B(t_1, T),$$

where $B(t_1, T)$ is the riskless discount factor. Specifically,

$$B(t_1, T) = \exp[-r(T - t_1)].$$

Substituting for $V_p(t_1)$ and $V_p(T)$ we obtain

$$V[FO(T), T - t_1] = [FO(T - t_1) - FO(T)]B(t_1, T).$$

This leads to the following property.

Property 11.2

At time t_1, the value of a forward contract entered into at time 0 is just the present value of the change in forward price:

$$V[FO(T), T - t_1] = [FO(T - t_1) - FO(T)]B(t_1, T). \tag{11.10}$$

Example 11.4

Assume a forward contract calling for delivery in six months was entered into at a forward price of $100. Assume two months later the forward price is $110. By selling this forward contract, the investor is obliged to buy at $100 and sell at $110. Thus, the investor is guaranteed $10. The current value of the net position is just the present value of $10. Given $T = 6$, $t_1 = 2$, $B(t_1, T) = 0.9$, then from equation (11.12), we have

$$V[FO(T), T - t_1] = [FO(T - t_1) - FO(T)]B(t_1, T)$$

$$= [110 - 100]0.9$$

$$= \$9.00.$$

FINANCIAL FORWARD CONTRACTS

A *financial forward contract* is an obligation to buy (sell) a specified amount of a specific financial instrument at some future date at a specific price. The net effect of such a contract is to lock in the price and interest rate for the period beginning at the expiration date of the contract and extending over the life of the underlying instrument.

As an example, consider a forward contract on an M-day maturity riskless discount bond of face value \$1. The delivery date is time T, and the current forward price $FO(T)$. The buyer of such a contract is assured of receiving an M-day maturity riskless discount bond for $FO(T)$ dollars at time T. Essentially, the investor has locked into an interest rate over the period T to $T + M$. Assuming the total carrying costs for the discount bond is the riskless rate, we have from equation (11.2):

$$FO(T) = S_0\exp(rT) = \frac{S_0}{B(0,T)}.$$

Since the deliverable is an M-day maturity discount bond and since the delivery date is T days away, the underlying commodity consists of a $T + M$-day maturity discount bond. The current value of such a bond, S_0, is

$$S_0 = B(0, T + M)1.$$

Hence,

$$FO(T) = \frac{B(0, T + M)}{B(0, T)}. \tag{11.11}$$

Example 11.5

A pure discount bond maturing in three months is currently valued at \$0.95, while one maturing in six months is valued at \$.90. A forward contract calling for delivery of a three-month pure discount bond in three months has a forward price given by equation (11.11).

$$FO(T) = \frac{B(0, T + M)}{B(0, T)}$$

$$= \frac{0.9}{0.95}$$

$$= 0.947.$$

The value of the forward contract initially is zero:

$$V[FO(T), T] = 0. \tag{11.12}$$

After t days, the value of this contract is the present value of the change in forward prices. That is, from Property 11.2,

$$V[FO(T), T - t] = [FO(T - t) - FO(T)]B(t, T).$$

If forward prices are set in accordance with equation (11.11), then

$$FO(T) = \frac{B(0, T + M)}{B(0, T)}$$

$$FO(T - t) = \frac{B(t, T + M)}{B(t, T)}$$

and hence,

$$V[FO(T), T - t] = \left[\frac{B(t, T + M)}{B(t, T)} - \frac{B(0, T + M)}{B(0, T)} \right] B(t, T). \quad (11.13)$$

Equation 11.13 describes the value of the forward contract with $T - t$ days to go to settlement. Using this equation at expiration date T, we have

$$V[FO(T), 0] = B(T, T + M) - \frac{B(0, T + M)}{B(0, T)}. \quad (11.14)$$

Note that the last term in equation (11.14) is just the forward price. Hence, at settlement we have

$$V[FO(T), 0] = B(T, T + M) - FO(T). \quad (11.15)$$

Note that (11.15) is consistent with equation (11.7) since $B(T, T + M)$ is just the spot price of an M-day maturity pure discount bond at the settlement date.

REPLICATING FORWARD CONTRACTS IN THE SPOT MARKET

Consider a forward contract on an M-day maturity pure discount bond. (That is a bond with face value of one dollar.) The delivery date is time T and the forward price, $FO(T)$. To replicate the forward contract, the value of the portfolio must equal the value of the forward contract, given by equation (11.13) at all points in time.

Consider a portfolio containing one pure discount bond maturing at time $T + M$ and a short position in N discount bonds maturing at time T where

$$N = \frac{B(0, T + M)}{B(0, T)} = FO(T).$$

The current value of the portfolio, $V_p(0)$, is given by

$$V_p(0) = B(0, T + M) - \left[\frac{B(0, T + M)}{B(0, T)} \right] B(0, T) = 0. \quad (11.16)$$

The value of the portfolio at time t, with $T - t$ days to delivery, is $V_p(t)$, where

$$V_p(t) = B(t, T + M) - \left[\frac{B(0, T + M)}{B(0, T)} \right] B(t, T). \quad (11.17)$$

At delivery date, T, the portfolio value is $V_p(T)$, where

$$V_p(T) = B(T, T + M) - \frac{B(0, T + M)}{B(0, T)}. \quad (11.18)$$

Now equations (11.16), (11.17), and (11.18) are exactly equal to the value of the forward contracts (see equations 11.12, 11.13, and 11.14).

Thus, a portfolio containing a long position in the $(T + M)$ maturity bond, together with a specific short position in the T maturity bond, produces identical payouts to a forward contract.

Example 11.6

A forward contract on a three-month maturity discount bond with a settlement date of six months has a fairly set forward price of 0.9. To replicate the payoffs of this contract requires buying a pure discount bond that matures in nine months and selling 0.9 pure discount bonds that mature in six months.

RELATIONSHIPS BETWEEN FORWARD CONTRACTS AND EUROPEAN OPTIONS

Property 11.3

A forward contract can be replicated by a portfolio containing a long position in a European call option and a short position in a European put option where the options have strikes equal to the forward price.

To see this, consider the strategy of selling a forward contract, buying a call contract, and selling a put contract.

All contracts have the same expiration (delivery) date, T, and the same strike (forward) price, FO. Exhibit 11.2 illustrates the future payouts.

EXHIBIT 11.2
Replication of Forward Contracts

	Initial Cost	Final Value $S_T < FO$	Final Value $S_T \geq FO$
Sell Forward Contract	0	$FO - S_T$	$FO - S_T$
Buy Call	C_0^E	0	$S_T - FO$
Sell Put	$-P_0^E$	$S_T - FO$	0
Net Value	$C_0^E - P_0^E$	0	0

To avoid riskless arbitrage opportunities, the forward price, *FO*, must be established so that the call price equals the put price. That is, the strike price of the option must be set such that $C_0^E - P_0^E = 0$.

Now using the put-call parity relationship (see equation 4.13), we know that for a non-dividend paying security;

$$C_0^E - P_0^E = S_0 - XB(0,T).$$

Hence, the forward price must be set such that

$$S_0 - FO\exp(-rT) = 0.$$

Hence,

$$FO = S_0\exp(rT).$$

Thus the price of a forward contract is determined by the interest rate that can be obtained over the period to maturity.

Note that if the asset provided a dividend payment, d_1, at time t_1, the European put-call parity relationship is given by

$$C_0^E - P_0^E = S_0 - d_1B(0,t_1) - XB(0,T).$$

Hence, the forward price must be set such that

$$S_0 - d_1B(0,t_1) = FOB(0,T).$$

Hence,

$$FO = \frac{[S_0 - d_1B(0,t_1)]}{B(0,T)}.$$

If the asset provided a continuous yield of *d*, then the forward price would be lower than if no dividend were provided, reflecting a lower net cost of carry. That is,

$$FO = S_0\exp(hT)$$

where $h = r - d$.

HEDGING WITH FORWARD CONTRACTS

Investors wishing to avoid the risk of future prices moving in a direction that would cause them to lose money could hedge against this risk by using forward contracts.

The Long Hedge

A *long hedge* is a purchase of a forward contract to protect against price rises. Commodity users, for example, may buy forward contracts to eliminate the risk of prices rising further in the future. As an example, consider a manufacturer who has committed the firm to delivery of produced items at a given price. To protect the firm from rising prices, forward contracts on particular raw materials should be bought.

By buying a forward contract, the investor is locking into a future price. Regardless of the future market price, the investor will buy the raw materials for $FO(T)$. Thus, the strategy eliminates price risk completely, at the expense of the future commodity price being lower than the forward price.

The Short Hedge

A *short hedge* involves selling forward contracts to avoid losses from possible price declines on a security currently owned. Farmers, for example, may sell forward contracts on their produce to lock into firm sales prices. If commodity prices do decline, the strategy will reduce losses. However, if a shortage develops and prices soar, the farmer will not participate in the unforeseen profits.

FUTURES CONTRACTS

A *futures contract* is an arrangement in which the seller agrees to deliver a well-defined asset of a certain quality and amount to the buyer at a specific date for a specific price.

Like forward contracts, futures contracts are bets on the future delivery price. However, unlike forward contracts, futures contracts are traded on federally designated exchanges. More important, futures contracts have *daily resettlements*.

To see this, let $F(T)$ be the future price for settlement in T days. Then, like forward contracts, the value $F(T)$ is chosen so that the current worth of the futures contract is zero. That is,

$$V[F(T),T] = 0. \tag{11.19}$$

Suppose that the futures price of a newly created futures at the end of the day is $F(T-1)$. Then, like forward contracts, newly issued contracts satisfy the condition that

$$V[F(T-1),T-1] = 0. \tag{11.20}$$

Unlike forward contracts, cash flows into and out of the futures account during the life of the contract. As the futures price changes, the party in whose favor the price change occurred is paid the full amount of the futures price change by the losing party.

Thus,

$$V[F(T),T-1] - V[F(T),T] = F(T-1) - F(T). \tag{11.21}$$

At the end of the day, the original futures contract is rewritten by the clearing house at the closing futures price, $F(T-1)$. If the futures contract is sold during the day at time S, say, with $0 \leq S \leq 1$, the value is

$$V[F(T),T-S] - V[F(T),T] = F(T-S) - F(T). \tag{11.22}$$

Property 11.4

Futures contracts give the buyer the change in value of the futures price computed over each day up to the time in which the position is closed.

Example 11.7

Assume an investor buys a futures contract at $150. If at the end of the day the futures price is $156, the investor makes a $6 profit. However, if at the end of the day the futures price is $143, the investor loses $7. To ensure that the investor can pay up against losses, the broker will require an initial margin deposit. Further margin may be required if the futures prices continue to move against the investor. The process of daily resettlements is termed *marking to the market*.

With futures, the difference between the final spot price, S_T, and the initial futures price, $F(T)$, will have been received or paid in daily installments throughout the life of the contract, whereas with forward contracts, no cash flows occur until settlement.

THE RELATIONSHIP BETWEEN FORWARD PRICES AND FUTURES PRICES

Forward contracts are different from futures. As a result, forward prices need not be the same as futures prices. In this section we shall investigate conditions under which the two prices are the same.

Property 11.5

If interest rates are certain, then futures prices and forward prices are equal.

$$FO(t) = F(t) \qquad 0 \le t \le T.$$

If interest rates are not certain, then futures prices may differ from forward prices.

To see this, consider a case in which risk-free rates are certain. With one day to go to delivery, consider a portfolio consisting of a long position in the forward contract and a short position in the futures contract. The initial investment is zero. At the end of the day, the value of the forward contract is

$S_T - FO(1)$ and the value of the short position in the futures is $F(1) - S_T$. The net portfolio value of $F(1) - FO(1)$ is certain. With an initial zero dollar investment, it is thus possible to earn a certain return of $F(1) - FO(1)$. To avoid riskless arbitrage opportunities, it must follow that the forward price equals the futures price.

Now consider the case with two days to go. As before, let $B(t, T)$ be the value of a default-free discount bond at time t, which pays \$1 at time T. Consider the strategy of buying $1/B(T-1, T)$ forward contracts and selling one futures contract. Again the initial investment is zero. At the end of the day, the value of each forward contract is given by

$$[FO(1) - FO(2)]B(T-1, T)$$

and the value of the futures contract is $F(2) - F(1)$.

At the end of the day, the value of the portfolio is

$$[FO(1) - FO(2)] \frac{B(T-1, T)}{B(T-1, T)} + F(2) - F(1)$$

$$= FO(1) - FO(2) + F(2) - F(1)$$

$$= F(2) - FO(2).$$

Thus, to avoid riskless arbitrage opportunities, it must follow that $F(2) = FO(2)$.

If the interest rates are deterministic, this argument can be repeated successively to demonstrate that $F(T) = FO(T)$ for all T. This result can only be obtained because the proper hedge ratio between forward and futures contracts can be established. However, if the risk-free rates are not deterministic, the hedge factor is uncertain and the arbitrage portfolio cannot be constructed. In this case, forward prices and futures prices may differ. With uncertain interest rates, futures prices will depend on factors such as correlation effects between the commodity and interest rates. For a discussion on this topic, see Cox, Ingersoll, and Ross.

FUTURES MARKETS AND PRICES

In 1848 the first centralized market in futures contracts in the United States was established by the Chicago Board of Trade. Today there are twelve exchanges (Exhibit 11.3), with the Chicago Board of Trade the largest.

Exhibit 11.4 illustrates the prices of several futures contracts as they appear in the *Wall Street Journal*. For each commodity traded, the exchange where it is traded is shown, together with some terms of the contract. This includes the amount of the commodity per contract and the units of price. From Exhibit 11.4 it can be seen that gold futures trade on the Commodity

EXHIBIT 11.3
Futures Exchanges

Chicago Board of Trade
Chicago Mercantile Exchange
Coffee, Sugar, and Cocoa Exchange (New York)
Commodity Exchange, Inc. (New York)
Kansas City Board of Trade
Mid-America Commodity Exchange (Chicago)
Minneapolis Grain Exchange
New York Cotton Exchange, Inc.
Citrus Associates of the New York Cotton Exchange, Inc.
Petroleum Associates of the New York Cotton Exchange, Inc.
New York Futures Exchange
New York Mercantile Exchange

Exchange, New York (CMX). The unit is 100 troy ounces, and the price is quoted as $ per troy ounce. Details of these contracts will be provided later.

The deliveries (expiration months) of all contracts currently trading are listed in the first column. The next three columns give the daily opening, high, and low prices for each contract. The fifth column indicates the settlement price, which usually is the last trading price for the day. In some cases, if no trading has occurred toward the end of the day, a settlement price (fair value) is determined by a committee. The sixth column indicates the change in settlement prices since the previous day. The next two columns indicate the lifetime high and low prices for the contract. The last column indicates the number of contracts outstanding.

EXAMPLES OF FUTURES CONTRACTS

In this section gold futures and stock index futures are described. Futures on financial instruments are discussed in Chapter 13.

Gold Futures Contracts on the Commodity Exchange, New York (CMX)

A gold futures contract calls for delivery of a specific grade of gold in a specific quantity during a specified delivery month. Trading of CMX gold futures is conducted for delivery in the current month, the next two months, and any February, April, June, August, and December within a 23-month period. Exhibit 11.5 shows price quotations of gold futures contracts as reported in the *Wall Street Journal.*

EXHIBIT 11.4

Futures Prices from the Wall Street Journal

FUTURES PRICES

Monday, July 14, 1986

Open Interest Reflects Previous Trading Day.

–GRAINS AND OILSEEDS–

CORN (CBT) 5,000 bu.; cents per bu.

	Open	High	Low	Settle	Change	Lifetime High	Lifetime Low	Open Interest
July	207½	209½	204	208	+ 5½	286	191	4,111
Sept	173¼	175	172	173½	....	270	170½	26,122
Dec	172½	175	171½	173	– ¾	235½	172¼	65,660
Mar87	184	185	182	183	– ¾	242½	182	11,417
May	188	189½	187¼	188¾	....	242	186¾	4,716
July	189¾	192	189¼	190½	+ ½	227	190	1,985
Sept	184½	186½	184½	185	....	201½	183	322

Est vol 16,000; vol Fri 18,223; open int 114,333, +440.

OATS (CBT) 5,000 bu.; cents per bu.

	Open	High	Low	Settle	Change	Lifetime High	Lifetime Low	Open Interest
July	101½	102½	100	101½	+ 2¾	139¾	97	83
Sept	99½	105½	99½	101½	+ 1½	136¾	98½	1,264
Dec	107¼	111¾	107¼	109¾	+ 1½	142	105½	1,426
Mar87	....	....	....	111½	+ 1¼	119	108	162

Est vol 350; vol Fri 297; open int 2,982, +64.

SOYBEANS (CBT) 5,000 bu.; cents per bu.

	Open	High	Low	Settle	Change	Lifetime High	Lifetime Low	Open Interest
July	524½	532¼	524½	531½	+ 4	658	497	4,459
Aug	506½	510¾	506	510	+ 1¼	609	498½	12,015
Sept	488	493	486	491	– ¾	555½	484	6,789
Nov	484½	490	482½	489	+ 1	556½	479½	29,625
Jan87	492	498¼	492	497½	+ 1	565	488	4,632
Mar	501	506½	501	506½	+ 1	576	497½	1,908
May	507	513	507	512½	+ 1½	574	504½	528
July	512	516¾	512	515½	+ ¾	577½	506½	548

Est vol 22,000; vol Fri 20,737; open int 60,516, –438.

SOYBEAN MEAL (CBT) 100 tons; $ per ton.

	Open	High	Low	Settle	Change	Lifetime High	Lifetime Low	Open Interest
July	151.40	154.50	151.40	154.50	+ 1.30	167.00	134.00	4,373
Aug	144.30	141.80	140.50	141.30	– .20	163.50	135.50	12,893
Sept	140.50	141.80	140.50	141.30	– .20	160.50	137.50	6,107
Oct	138.00	140.00	138.00	139.30	....	162.10	136.00	6,755
Dec	139.00	141.50	139.00	141.10	+ .20	162.10	136.00	18,037
Jan87	140.50	143.20	140.50	142.50	+ .30	163.10	136.10	2,543
Mar	143.50	145.00	143.50	144.20	+ .20	163.10	143.00	1,183
May	....	....	....	146.70	+ .30	169.70	143.00	656
July	....	....	....	149.50	+ 1.50	157.00	146.10	229

Est vol 11,000; vol Fri 12,328; open int 52,780, –1,326.

SOYBEAN OIL (CBT) 60,000 lbs.; cents per lb.

	Open	High	Low	Settle	Change	Lifetime High	Lifetime Low	Open Interest
July	16.20	16.20	15.98	16.03	– .26	25.25	15.98	1,485
Aug	16.17	16.20	16.02	16.06	– .23	25.15	16.02	16,858
Sept	16.33	16.35	16.17	16.22	– .26	24.05	16.17	10,210
Oct	16.42	16.45	16.27	16.30	– .24	22.80	16.27	7,028
Dec	16.82	16.90	16.75	16.81	– .15	22.50	16.65	22,029
Jan87	17.00	17.02	16.85	16.87	– .13	22.35	16.85	3,913
Mar	17.26	17.35	17.20	17.21	– .21	20.25	17.20	1,345
May	17.60	17.60	17.51	17.51	– .09	20.90	17.51	807
July	17.76	17.80	17.76	17.80	– .20	18.70	17.76	497

Est vol 10,000; vol Fri 8,462; open int 64,218, –558.

WHEAT (CBT) 5,000 bu.; cents per bu.

	Open	High	Low	Settle	Change	Lifetime High	Lifetime Low	Open Interest
July	263½	271	262½	269¾	+ 6¼	310	241	3,046
Sept	258½	261½	257¼	259½	+ 1¾	299	239	12,765
Dec	258	261½	257¾	259	+ ¾	309	244	12,054
Mar87	253	256½	252¾	253½	+ ¾	308	243½	3,444
May	242½	244½	240	240	– 1	300	233¼	1,961
July	231	233½	230	230	+ ¼	250	223¼	1,000

Est vol 14,000; vol Fri 22,177; open int 34,270, –2,517.

WHEAT (KC) 5,000 bu.; cents per bu.

	Open	High	Low	Settle	Change	Lifetime High	Lifetime Low	Open Interest
July	246½	249½	246	246¾	+ 1¼	298½	232½	397
Sept	241¼	245	241¼	244½	+ 2¼	291	233½	9,780
Dec	246¾	251½	246¾	250¼	+ 2¾	298	240½	8,155
Mar87	245½	249	245½	248½	+ 2	302½	239¾	937

Est vol 3,613; vol Fri 4,902; open int 19,397, –96.

WHEAT (MPLS) 5,000 bu.; cents per bu.

	Open	High	Low	Settle	Change	Lifetime High	Lifetime Low	Open Interest
July	260	264¼	260	263	+ 2	328	247½	576
Sept	264	268¼	263¾	266	+ 1¼	350	258½	4,610
Dec	270	273¾	269½	271½	+ 1	321½	262	1,577
Mar87	271	271	271	271	....	283	268	133

Est vol 1,189; vol Fri 1,696; open int 6,816, –19.

BARLEY (WPG) 20 metric tons; Can. $ per ton

	Open	High	Low	Settle	Change	Lifetime High	Lifetime Low	Open Interest
July	....	....	....	108.30	– .10	119.17	86.70	867
Oct	84.00	84.20	83.90	83.90	– 1.00	106.00	83.40	3,814
Dec	84.00	84.20	83.90	83.90	– .70	99.50	83.60	3,162
Mar87	85.20	85.20	84.80	84.80	– .90	91.40	81.50	792

Est vol 400; vol Fri 898; open int 8,635, +259.

FLAXSEED (WPG) 20 metric tons; Can. $ per ton

	Open	High	Low	Settle	Change	Lifetime High	Lifetime Low	Open Interest
July	250.50	250.50	250.00	250.00	+ .30	325.20	248.90	63
Oct	258.00	258.10	257.90	258.00	– .50	333.80	257.90	2,978
Dec	263.00	263.50	262.60	262.70	– .80	325.00	262.30	1,892
Mar87	271.50	271.50	271.40	271.50	– .50	287.60	271.40	406

Est vol 720; vol Fri 486; open int 5,339, –16.

RAPESEED (WPG) 20 metric tons; Can. $ per ton

	Open	High	Low	Settle	Change	Lifetime High	Lifetime Low	Open Interest
Sept	259.60	260.50	259.00	259.20	– 1.20	351.00	259.00	7,784
Nov	265.30	266.50	265.10	265.20	– 1.50	352.00	266.00	5,954
Jan87	271.80	272.60	271.10	271.40	– 1.90	354.90	271.10	2,594
Mar	278.00	278.30	277.10	277.10	– 1.70	318.50	277.10	789
Jun	287.00	287.00	286.90	286.90	– 1.10	291.50	284.00	110

Est vol 3,060; vol Fri 3,134; open int 17,231, +138.

RYE (WPG) 20 metric tons; Can. $ per ton

	Open	High	Low	Settle	Change	Lifetime High	Lifetime Low	Open Interest
July	103.00	103.00	101.20	101.20	+ 2.60	130.00	95.50	76
Oct	103.50	103.50	101.50	101.50	+ 1.40	127.50	97.70	1,670
Dec	....	....	....	103.00	– 1.20	127.40	99.00	731
Mar87	....	....	....	106.00	– .20	111.50	105.70	245

Est vol 120; vol Fri 842; open int 2,722, +206.

–FOOD & FIBER–

COCOA (CSCE)–10 metric tons; $ per ton.

	Open	High	Low	Settle	Change	Lifetime High	Lifetime Low	Open Interest
July	1,802	1,825	1,780	1,842	+ 24	2,429	1,658	5
Sept	1,840	1,885	1,835	1,879	+ 24	2,430	1,730	8,087
Dec	1,890	1,934	1,887	1,931	+ 27	2,425	1,790	5,788
Mar87	1,931	1,975	1,925	1,972	+ 28	2,385	1,840	3,005
May	1,951	1,991	1,951	1,991	+ 18	2,184	1,875	1,546
July	1,990	2,005	1,990	2,020	+ 32	2,200	1,908	1,364
Sept	2,000	2,050	2,000	2,045	+ 32	2,055	1,925	2,053
Dec	....	....	....	2,080	+ 27	....	....	738

Est vol 3,736; vol Fri 1,671; open int 22,586, –102.

COFFEE (CSCE)–37,500 lbs.; cents per lb.

	Open	High	Low	Settle	Change	Lifetime High	Lifetime Low	Open Interest
July	174.75	178.75	174.25	179.38	+ 8.38	278.38	135.50	241
Sept	176.10	182.40	175.25	181.88	+ 9.28	282.78	137.50	9,163
Dec	178.24	178.24	178.24	178.24	+ 4.00	287.10	138.00	4,048
Mar87	....	....	....	181.45	+ 4.00	290.33	156.75	1,796
May	183.73	183.73	183.73	183.73	+ 4.00	291.83	169.95	563
July	185.75	185.75	185.75	185.75	+ 4.00	266.25	178.50	179

Est vol 3,769; vol Fri 4,225; open int 16,042, +408.

COTTON (CTN)–50,000 lbs.; cents per lb.

	Open	High	Low	Settle	Change	Lifetime High	Lifetime Low	Open Interest
Aug	....	....	....	30.07	– .23	38.00	38.00	1
Oct	30.15	30.45	30.02	30.07	– .23	65.50	30.02	3,201
Dec	30.80	30.98	30.48	30.50	– .40	59.25	30.48	13,925
Mar87	31.60	31.73	31.30	31.34	– .28	49.50	31.30	1,983
May	32.30	32.60	32.08	32.12	– .38	52.75	32.08	735
July	33.15	33.25	32.90	32.90	– .40	46.80	32.90	670
Oct	34.60	34.60	34.24	34.18	– .47	65.50	34.10	335
Dec	35.64	35.55	35.00	35.02	– .42	37.40	35.00	202

Est vol 2,000; vol Fri 3,801; open int 21,111, +214.

ORANGE JUICE (CTN)–15,000 lbs.; cents per lb.

	Open	High	Low	Settle	Change	Lifetime High	Lifetime Low	Open Interest
July	102.00	102.00	99.00	99.65	– 2.75	157.50	83.50	217
Sept	101.00	101.00	97.30	99.50	– 2.55	127.25	82.00	2,858
Nov	102.20	102.20	99.00	100.50	– 2.50	125.00	82.50	985
Jan87	101.50	101.75	99.00	101.30	– 2.45	113.00	83.75	777
Mar	103.00	103.00	100.30	102.15	– 2.90	122.00	83.90	1,612
May	103.00	103.00	101.10	103.15	– 2.95	109.90	84.50	666
July	....	....	....	104.25	– 2.95	109.60	84.75	346

Est vol 1,300; vol Fri 729; open int 7,555, –40.

SUGAR–WORLD (CSCE)–112,000 lbs.; cents per lb.

	Open	High	Low	Settle	Change	Lifetime High	Lifetime Low	Open Interest
Sept	5.20	5.20	5.15	5.35	+ .16	9.42	4.05	533
Oct	5.55	5.65	5.41	5.63	+ .02	9.40	4.02	47,952
Jan87	5.62	5.70	5.53	5.69	+ .02	9.50	5.53	225
Mar	6.28	6.40	6.17	6.36	....	9.64	6.03	21,800
May	6.43	6.54	6.35	6.53	– .02	9.82	6.35	6,637
July	6.58	6.70	6.53	6.69	– .01	9.92	6.53	4,880
Oct	6.75	6.90	6.66	6.90	– .03	9.60	6.66	2,326

Est vol 12,909; vol Fri 11,966; open int 84,354, +744.

SUGAR–DOMESTIC (CSCE)–112,000 lbs.; cents per lb.

	Open	High	Low	Settle	Change	Lifetime High	Lifetime Low	Open Interest
Sept	20.97	21.03	20.97	21.02	+ .06	21.95	19.70	2,531
Nov	20.71	20.75	20.71	20.72	....	21.70	20.40	2,047
Jan87	....	....	....	20.71	....	21.31	20.42	251
Mar	20.73	20.73	20.73	20.79	+ .03	21.40	20.50	1,089
May	....	....	....	20.83	– .02	21.15	20.60	104
July	20.97	20.98	20.97	21.00	+ .01	21.00	20.65	556

Est vol 247; vol Fri 347; open int 6,603, –55.

–METALS & PETROLEUM–

COPPER (CMX)–25,000 lbs.; cents per lb.

	Open	High	Low	Settle	Change	Lifetime High	Lifetime Low	Open Interest
July	58.40	58.40	58.40	58.40	– .75	72.55	58.15	212
Sept	59.05	59.10	58.65	58.80	– .80	70.90	58.65	37,682
Dec	59.70	59.75	59.30	59.40	– .80	70.30	59.30	18,886
Mar87	60.20	60.20	59.75	59.90	– .80	70.00	59.75	3,152
May	60.00	60.40	60.00	60.25	– .80	70.00	60.00	675
July	60.50	60.70	60.50	60.55	– .80	69.95	60.50	1,898
Sep	60.85	60.85	60.85	60.85	– .80	70.35	60.85	217
Dec	61.80	61.80	61.20	61.30	– .80	69.50	61.20	264

Est vol 4,700; vol Fri 6,156; open int 63,067, –1575.

GOLD (CMX)–100 troy oz.; $ per troy oz.

	Open	High	Low	Settle	Change	Lifetime High	Lifetime Low	Open Interest
July	344.80	345.90	344.80	345.30	– 1.40	349.50	342.50	3
Aug	346.80	347.40	346.00	346.40	– 1.40	427.50	328.00	41,667
Oct	350.10	350.50	349.10	349.40	– 1.50	395.70	331.50	8,264
Dec	353.60	353.80	352.30	352.60	– 1.50	392.00	336.50	19,697
Feb87	356.40	356.40	356.30	355.90	– 1.50	397.50	337.30	7,907
Apr	359.20	359.20	359.20	359.10	– 1.50	405.00	346.30	8,237
June	363.20	363.20	363.20	362.40	– 1.60	409.00	350.50	9,118
Aug	....	....	....	365.90	– 1.60	408.50	356.00	7,144
Oct	....	....	....	369.40	– 1.60	420.00	361.00	5,675
Dec	....	....	....	373.20	– 1.60	399.40	365.00	4,496
Feb88	378.00	378.00	378.00	377.20	– 1.60	389.00	371.50	6,650
Apr	....	....	....	381.30	– 1.60	392.50	378.00	2,947

Est vol 14,000; vol Fri 13,573; open int 121,805, –3,335.

PLATINUM (NYM)–50 troy oz.; $ per troy oz.

	Open	High	Low	Settle	Change	Lifetime High	Lifetime Low	Open Interest
July	438.00	438.00	435.00	435.30	– 1.50	455.50	273.00	464
Oct	438.00	438.50	436.00	436.50	– 2.30	459.50	303.50	13,194
Jan87	441.00	441.00	439.20	439.20	– 2.30	462.00	347.00	2,373
Apr	443.00	443.50	442.00	442.00	– 2.30	463.00	361.00	1,112

Est vol 1,704; vol Fri 1,775; open int 17,217, –187.

PALLADIUM (NYM) 100 troy oz.; $ per troy oz.

	Open	High	Low	Settle	Change	Lifetime High	Lifetime Low	Open Interest
July	111.25	111.25	111.25	110.50	– .60	111.25	107.00	3
Sept	111.80	112.00	111.20	111.25	– .60	119.00	91.70	3,762
Dec	112.10	112.25	112.00	111.50	– .60	120.00	94.25	1,284
Mar87	112.20	112.20	112.20	111.75	– .60	127.50	90.00	268

Est vol 175; vol Fri 117; open int 5,330, –11.

SILVER (CMX)–5,000 troy oz.; cents per troy oz.

	Open	High	Low	Settle	Change	Lifetime High	Lifetime Low	Open Interest
July	503.0	504.0	501.0	502.1	– 4.5	945.0	487.0	520
Sept	506.0	509.0	505.0	506.7	– 4.5	940.0	493.0	22,695
Dec	515.0	517.5	513.0	515.2	– 4.6	799.0	503.0	16,235
Jan87	518.0	519.0	518.0	518.1	– 4.6	789.0	510.5	113
Mar	523.5	524.5	523.0	523.7	– 4.5	770.0	511.0	7,017
May	531.0	532.5	529.0	529.5	– 4.8	752.0	520.0	10,672
July	536.0	536.0	536.0	535.2	– 4.8	746.0	524.0	4,308
Sept	544.0	544.0	544.0	541.4	– 5.0	729.2	532.0	1,409
Dec	555.0	555.0	551.0	550.8	– 5.0	694.0	543.5	1,832
Mar88	563.0	563.0	563.0	560.9	– 5.1	610.0	560.0	545

Est vol 5,300; vol Fri 2,488; open int 65,370, +41.

	Open	High	Low	Settle	Change	Lifetime High	Lifetime Low	Open Interest
Mar	.3300	.3300	.3225	.3325	– .0050	.4385	.3225	772
Apr	....	....	....	.3190	– .0045	.4180	.3280	649
May	.3100	.3140	.3090	.3095	– .0040	.4175	.3200	603

Est vol 13,841; vol Fri 13,654; open int 61,486, +182.

GAS OIL (IPEL) 100 metric tons; $ per ton

	Open	High	Low	Settle	Change	Lifetime High	Lifetime Low	Open Interest
Aug	90.50	90.50	86.50	87.00	– 5.75	230.00	90.00	3,270
Sept	95.00	95.00	90.50	90.75	– 6.50	208.00	90.50	2,765
Oct	98.50	99.25	94.25	94.50	– 7.50	165.00	94.25	2,576
Nov	104.00	104.00	97.75	97.75	– 8.50	135.00	97.75	895
Dec	105.00	105.00	99.50	99.50	– 10.00	137.00	99.50	388

Actual Mon.; vol 3,904; open int 9,946, –122.

NY GASOLINE, leaded reg. (NYM) 42,000 gal.; $ per gal.

	Open	High	Low	Settle	Change	Lifetime High	Lifetime Low	Open Interest
Aug	.3275	.3285	.3020	.3253	– .0123	.7820	.3020	9,592
Sept	.3220	.3230	.3120	.3224	– .0096	.7350	.3120	6,091
Oct	.3150	.3200	.3055	.3191	– .0046	.4625	.3055	3,291
Nov	.3125	.3160	.3065	.3150	– .0050	.4375	.3065	382

Est vol 5,939; vol Fri 3,929; open int 19,356, +264.

–WOOD–

LUMBER (CME)–130,000 bd. ft.; $ per 1,000 bd. ft.

	Open	High	Low	Settle	Change	Lifetime High	Lifetime Low	Open Interest
July	165.20	165.80	162.00	162.00	– 3.70	190.90	144.00	378
Sept	159.90	160.20	156.60	157.60	– 3.10	182.40	145.50	3,026
Nov	157.40	157.90	155.40	155.60	– 2.60	174.50	146.00	1,413
Jan87	160.70	161.50	159.20	159.80	– 2.70	175.00	150.00	372
Mar	163.00	164.00	162.10	162.50	– 2.00	175.50	153.00	166

Est vol 1,356; vol Fri 1,507; open int 5,419, –150.

–FINANCIAL–

BRITISH POUND (IMM)–25,000 pounds; $ per pound

	Open	High	Low	Settle	Change	Lifetime High	Lifetime Low	Open Interest
Sept	1.4735	1.4820	1.4675	1.4765	– .0125	1.5435	1.3240	28,123
Dec	1.4630	1.4695	1.4560	1.4650	– .0125	1.5360	1.3250	881

Est vol 8,877; vol Fri 16,430; open int 29,024, +329.

CANADIAN DOLLAR (IMM)–100,000 dlrs.; $ per Can $

	Open	High	Low	Settle	Change	Lifetime High	Lifetime Low	Open Interest
Sept	.7244	.7247	.7239	.7246	+.0011	.7305	.6809	8,529
Dec	.7210	.7215	.7205	.7212	+.0011	.7285	.6790	1,675
Mar87	.7175	.7182	.7175	.7178	+.0011	.7256	.6770	393

Est vol 763; vol Fri 1,004; open int 10,670, –41.

JAPANESE YEN (IMM) 12.5 million yen; $ per yen (.00)

	Open	High	Low	Settle	Change	Lifetime High	Lifetime Low	Open Interest
Sept	.6238	.6288	.6230	.6282	+.0072	.6317	.4690	44,512
Dec	.6270	.6321	.6264	.6314	+.0072	.6348	.4720	1,511
Mar87		....	....	.6350	+.0072	.6354	.5850	295

Est vol 16,968; vol Fri 21,955; open int 46,318, –2,247.

SWISS FRANC (IMM)–125,000 francs-$ per franc

	Open	High	Low	Settle	Change	Lifetime High	Lifetime Low	Open Interest
Sept	.5601	.5663	.5593	.5657	+.0084	.5717	.4790	29,502
Dec	.5631	.5688	.5612	.5680	+.0083	.5743	.4878	2,124

Est vol 18,735; vol Fri 26,630; open int 31,660, –1,690.

W. GERMAN MARK (IMM)–125,000 marks; $ per mark

	Open	High	Low	Settle	Change	Lifetime High	Lifetime Low	Open Interest
Sept	.4587	.4632	.4577	.4631	+.0063	.4675	.3762	42,469
Dec	.4610	.4652	.4601	.4654	+.0063	.4703	.4090	1,107

Est vol 19,655; vol Fri 29,266; open int 43,670, –835.

EURODOLLAR (LIFFE)–$1 million; pts of 100%

	Open	High	Low	Settle	Change	Lifetime High	Lifetime Low	Open Interest
Sept	93.56	93.57	93.54	93.56	....	93.78	89.06	9,617
Dec	93.47	93.48	93.45	93.48	+ .01	93.67	90.20	4,843
Mar87	93.29	93.29	93.27	93.30	+ .02	93.46	90.80	2,643
June	93.01	93.04	93.00	93.04	+ .03	93.15	90.85	893
Sept		....	....	92.74	+ .02	92.95	91.65	257
Dec		....	....	92.46	+ .05	92.34	91.96	126

Est vol 1,444; vol Fri 6,154; open int 18,478, +273.

STERLING (LIFFE)–£500,000; pts of 100%

	Open	High	Low	Settle	Change	Lifetime High	Lifetime Low	Open Interest
Sept	90.30	90.31	90.14	90.17	– .25	91.49	87.53	7,543
Dec	90.50	90.51	90.38	90.39	– .24	91.63	87.88	3,862
Mar87	90.42	90.43	90.30	90.31	– .25	91.45	88.00	2,346
June	90.28	90.28	90.15	90.16	– .29	91.45	90.08	1,264
Sept		....	....	90.05	– .25	91.30	90.48	902

Est vol 6,341; vol Fri 3,323; open int 15,989, +338.

LONG GILT (LIFFE)–£50,000; 32nds of 100%

	Open	High	Low	Settle	Change	Lifetime High	Lifetime Low	Open Interest
Sept	120-18	120-18	119-05	119-15	– 1-24	130-10	119-05	14,864
Dec	120-01	120-02	119-09	119-10	– 1-22	125-07	119-09	548
Mar87		....	....	119-04	– 1-22	120-17	120-17	0

Est vol 14,908; vol Fri 7,252; open int 15,412, +101.

EURODOLLAR (IMM)–$1 million; pts of 100%

	Open	High	Low	Settle	Chg	Yield Settle	Yield Chg	Open Interest
Sept	93.56	93.63	93.54	93.61	+ .04	6.39	– .04	76,011
Dec	93.46	93.55	93.43	93.53	+ .06	6.47	– .06	38,366
Mr87	93.26	93.35	93.25	93.34	+ .07	6.66	– .07	19,393
June	93.00	93.08	92.98	93.08	+ .07	6.92	– .07	10,705
Sept	92.71	92.80	92.70	92.79	+ .07	7.21	– .07	6,757
Dec	92.42	92.51	92.42	92.51	+ .07	7.49	– .07	5,110
Mr88	92.15	92.23	92.14	92.24	+ .08	7.76	– .08	4,970
June	91.89	91.96	91.88	91.98	+ .08	8.02	– .08	1,632

Est vol 31,938; vol Fri 40,189; open int 16 2,944, +422.

U.S. DOLLAR INDEX (CTN) 500 times USDX

	Open	High	Low	Settle	Chg	Yield Settle	Yield Chg	Open Interest
Sept	112.53	112.80	111.60	111.86	– .89	129.00	110.71	1,391
Dec	112.92	113.13	112.03	112.23	– .88	129.05	110.72	1,379

Est vol 500; vol Fri 338; open int 2,795, –35.

The index: High 112.09; Low 111.16; Close 111.21 –.79

TREASURY BONDS (CBT)–$100,000; pts. 32nds of 100%

	Open	High	Low	Settle	Chg	Yield Settle	Yield Chg	Open Interest
Sept	99-16	100-17	98-31	100-14	+ 34	7.956	– .107	164,959
Dec	98-23	99-23	98-05	99-20	+ 34	8.038	– .109	23,623
Mr87	97-28	98-28	97-14	98-26	+ 34	8.121	– .110	5,197
June	97-15	98-02	97-15	98-01	+ 34	8.202	– .111	3,372
Sept	96-14	97-11	96-14	97-09	+ 34	8.280	– .113	2,517
Dec	96-13	96-23	96-08	96-20	+ 34	8.350	– .114	1,288
Mr88	95-28	96-03	95-21	96-01	+ 34	8.413	– .116	1,266
June	....	....	....	95-16	+ 34	8.471	– .116	759
Sept	94-24	95-03	94-24	95-01	+ 34	8.522	– .117	304
Dec	....	....	....	94-19	+ 33	8.570	– .114	112

Est vol 200,000; vol Fri 222,906; open int 203,397, +6,152.

TREASURY NOTES (CBT)–$100,000; pts. 32nds of 100%

	Open	High	Low	Settle	Chg	Yield Settle	Yield Chg	Open Interest
Sept	101-19	101-31	101-10	101-27	+ 9	7.732	– .040	58,995
Dec	100-26	101-08	100-21	101-04	+ 9	7.836	– .041	4,188
Mr87	....	....	....	100-14	+ 9	7.936	– .041	267

Est vol 16,000; vol Fri 16,037; open int 63,450, +117.

TREASURY BILLS (IMM)–$1 mil.; pts. of 100%

	Open	High	Low	Settle	Chg	Discount Settle	Discount Chg	Open Interest
Sept	94.47	94.54	94.45	94.53	+ .05	5.47	– .05	27,205
Dec	94.47	94.58	94.47	94.57	+ .08	5.43	– .08	8,994
Mr87	94.32	94.42	94.32	94.42	+ .08	5.58	– .08	1,630
June	94.16	94.20	94.10	94.20	+ .08	5.80	– .08	1,023
Sept	93.87	93.97	93.87	93.96	+ .09	6.04	– .09	442
Dec	....	....	....	93.69	+ .09	6.31	– .09	165
Mr88	....	....	....	93.46	+ .09	6.54	– .09	213

Est vol 4,630; vol Fri 6,335; open int 39,672, –360.

Example 11.8: Long Hedges with Gold Futures

A long hedge is used by a user of a commodity. The objective is to lock into a purchase price of a commodity for delivery in the future. As an example, consider a jeweler who requires 100 troy ounces of gold in five months. To eliminate the risk of gold prices increasing beyond the current five-month futures price, the manufacturer decides to hedge in the futures market. Exhibit 11.6 illustrates the transactions that occur.

EXHIBIT 11.5
Gold Futures Contract Prices

```
GOLD (CMX)—100 troy oz.; $ per troy oz.
July   344.80  345.90  344.80  345.30 −  1.40  349.50  342.50       3
Aug    346.80  347.40  346.00  346.40 −  1.40  427.50  328.00  41,667
Oct    350.10  350.50  349.10  349.40 −  1.50  395.70  331.50   8,264
Dec    353.60  353.80  352.30  352.60 −  1.50  392.00  336.50  19,697
Feb87  356.40  356.40  356.30  355.90 −  1.50  397.50  337.30   7,907
Apr    359.20  359.20  359.20  359.10 −  1.50  405.00  346.30   8,237
June   363.20  363.20  363.20  362.40 −  1.60  409.00  350.50   9,118
Aug     ....    ....    ....   365.90 −  1.60  408.50  356.00   7,144
Oct     ....    ....    ....   369.40 −  1.60  420.00  361.00   5,675
Dec     ....    ....    ....   373.20 −  1.60  399.40  365.00   4,496
Feb88  378.00  378.00  378.00  377.20 −  1.60  389.00  371.50   6,650
Apr     ....    ....    ....   381.30 −  1.60  392.50  378.00   2,947
    Est vol 14,000; vol Fri 13,573; open int 121,805, −3,335.
```

EXHIBIT 11.6
A Long Hedge with Gold Futures

	No Hedge	Hedge
$T = 0$	Anticipate need for gold in November. Current spot price = $336.00.	Buy one 6-month futures contract for $338.00.
$T = 5$	Buy 100 ounces of gold at current spot price of $386.00.	Sell futures contract for current futures price of $389.00.
	Opportunity loss = $50/ounce.	Profit = $57/ounce.

Had the opportunity loss equalled the actual gain, the hedge would have been perfect. In this example, the initial basis was 200 basis points "under" and widened to 300 points "under," resulting in a 100-basis-points net gain. The widening of the basis indicates that the market has a sufficient gold supply and is unwilling to make early storage payments. If the basis had strengthened, the net situation might have been a loss. A strong basis occurs when the spot price is close to or exceeds the futures price and reflects an excess demand level. The effectiveness of this hedge depends on the relationship between the spot and futures market. If the basis weakens (strengthens), the effectiveness increases (decreases). If closed out before maturity, the long hedge results in price uncertainty being replaced with basis uncertainty over the life of the hedge.

Example 11.9: Short Hedges with Gold Futures

Short hedges are used by manufacturers who supply goods to the market. For example, farmers concerned that the price of wheat will fall from its current levels may sell futures contracts to eliminate this risk. A gold mining company may protect itself against gold price declines by selling gold futures. Exhibit 11.7 illustrates the transactions of the latter hedge.

In this example, the basis was initially $4 under and has strengthened to $1 under. The net benefit in this case is $3. A shrinking of the basis in the short hedge results in net gains. Only if the basis remains the same will the position be perfectly hedged. As with long hedges, short hedges replace price risk with basis risk.

EXHIBIT 11.7
A Short Hedge with Gold Futures

	Cash Market	**Futures Market**
$T = 0$	Current spot price = $336.00. Anticipate price falling over the next three months.	Sell one 4-month futures contract for $340.00.
$T = 3$	Sell gold at $325.00.	Buy back futures contract for $326.00.
	Opportunity loss = $11/ounce.	Profit = $14.

Stock Index Futures

Stock index futures were introduced in February 1982 by the Kansas City Board of Trade, which established a futures contract on the Value Line Composite Index. In April 1982 the Chicago Mercantile Exchange introduced a futures contract on the Standard and Poor's 500 and a month later the New York Futures Exchange introduced the New York Stock Exchange Futures Index.

A long (short) position in a stock index futures contract represents a commitment to buy (sell) for a predetermined price an amount of dollars equal to the index value multiplied by a given multiplier. The multiplier for most contracts is $500.

Stock index futures are like stock index options in that their value is established from an index and the deliverable item is cash. Unlike the option contract, however, the futures contract is a firm commitment.

The stock index futures price cannot be established by simple arbitrage arguments. The usual cost-of-carry model is not so straightforward, since the underlying security is an index and settlement is in cash. Nonetheless, in concept, consider an investor who creates a portfolio whose composition and weighting are exactly equal to the index. If this investor sold futures contracts with a face value equal to the market value of the portfolio, all risk would have been eliminated. The return on this portfolio, then, should be the risk-free rate. Using this fact, one could construct the futures price. This type of argument makes several assumptions. First, it assumes forward and futures prices to be the same. Second, it ignores variation margin considerations. Most important, however, it ignores the timing of dividend payments. Holders of the stock portfolio will obtain all dividends. If the dividend stream were continuous and equal to the risk-free rate of return, the futures price and the current index value would be equal. If the dividend stream on the index were continuous (and constant), it could be subtracted from the risk-free rate to obtain the annualized net yield (as in Example 11.2). However, the dividend yields are not continuous. Moreover, the total dividend yields paid out over time form a lumpy sequence. As such, at certain times the futures price may be above the index price, while at other times it may be below the index price. That is, the size of the basis depends on the size and timing of the dividends of the securities on which the index is based.

Exhibit 11.8 illustrates the price quotations of a few index futures contracts including the S & P 500 stock index futures contract, as reported in the *Wall Street Journal*. The first column shows that contracts trade with expiration months of March, June, September, and December. The next four columns give the open, high, low, and settlement quotations. The actual price is obtained by multiplying the quoted value by 500. Minimum futures price increments are 0.05 of the index, or $25. The sixth column gives the change in settlement price since the previous day. The next two columns give the lifetime high and low. The final column gives the amount of contracts outstanding.

EXHIBIT 11.8
Prices of Index Futures

```
        S&P 500 INDEX (CME) 500 times index
Sept    241.15  241.50  238.15  238.30  − 3.95  255.20  187.00  90,806
Dec     243.05  243.10  239.90  240.05  − 4.10  257.25  209.50   3,060
   Est vol 81,359; vol Fri 70,202; open int 93,907, +894.
   The index: High 242.22; Low 238.05; Close 238.11  −4.11
        NYSE COMPOSITE INDEX (NYFE) 500 times index
Sept    139.05  139.05  137.05  137.15  − 2.30  146.80  108.10   9,465
Dec     140.10  140.10  138.15  138.20  − 2.30  148.00  121.10   1,174
Mar87   140.20  140.70  139.80  139.25  − 2.30  148.95  139.80     313
   Est vol 11,783; vol Fri 10,743; open int 10,979, +63.
   The index: High 139.49; Low 137.23; Close 137.27  −2.24
        KC VALUE LINE INDEX (KC) 500 times index
Sept    234.20  234.70  230.90  231.00  − 4.25  250.35  199.45  10,184
Dec     235.40  235.70  232.35  232.35  − 4.10  250.10  232.20     258
   Est vol 2,800; vol Fri 2,427; open int 10,534, − 128.
   The index: High 236.78; Low 233.00; Close 233.09  −3.69
        MAJOR MKT INDEX (CBT) $250 times index
July    346.80  347.10  342.60  342.70  − 4.95  366.10  332.60   4,726
Aug     346.60  347.00  342.70  342.80  − 4.80  366.20  333.75     234
Sept    347.80  347.85  343.50  343.65  − 4.80  366.90  331.00   4,049
   Est vol 7,200; vol Fri 6,227; open int 9,012, .
   The index: High 347.87; Low 342.34; Close 342.38  −5.49
```

The final settlement day is the third Thursday of the contract month. On this day the contract price should equal the closing price of the S & P 500 Index itself.

Suppose an investor wanted to purchase an S & P 500 futures contract. To execute the order, his or her broker would require an initial margin value of, say, $5000 to be placed in the account. Assume the futures price was $153.80. Exhibit 11.9 illustrates the daily cash flows into and out of the account.

EXHIBIT 11.9

Daily Cash Flows Associated with the Futures Transaction
(Initial Futures Price = $153.80)

Day	S & P Futures Closing Price	Daily Change Points	Daily Change $	Account Balance ($5000 Initial)
1	$154.20	.40	200	$5200
2	150.50	−3.70	−1850	3350
3	151.50	+1.00	500	3850
4	149.60	−1.90	−950	2900
5	148.40	−1.20	−600	2300
6	144.85	−3.55	1775	4075
7	140.70	−4.15	2075	2000
8	144.70	+4.00	2000	4000

Equity in excess of the initial margin can be withdrawn. Thus, at the end of day 1, the investor can withdraw $200. If the value of the account declines below the maintenance margin value of, say, $2000, the broker will require that the investor bring the account value up to the initial margin of $5000. If the investor does not comply, the broker will sell the contract. To avoid bringing the equity up to the initial margin, a trader could voluntarily deposit funds if he or she anticipated that the equity could fall below the maintenance margin. For example, in day 7, an investor might deposit additional funds into the account to avoid a margin call should the S & P future closing index drop below $140.70.

Hedging Diversified Portfolios with Stock Index Futures

Stock index futures can be used to hedge diversified portfolios from market volatilities or to protect portfolios against anticipated short-term declines. In addition, spread strategies involving the simultaneous purchase and sale of futures with different contract months can be undertaken in an attempt to take advantage of price discrepancies.

To illustrate how index futures can be used to hedge a diversified portfolio against market-related risk, first consider a portfolio that almost perfectly replicates the payouts of an index on which futures trade. Assuming futures price changes are almost identical to index price changes, an almost perfect hedge can be established by selling index futures against the portfolio. Profits on the stock index futures position obtained from the index declining in value will be partially offset by losses in the portfolio.

As with stock index options, the hedge is not perfect because the portfolio will not replicate the index and because the change in futures prices will not equal changes in the actual index. Typically the futures indices are slightly more volatile than the underlying indices themselves.

If an investor holds a portfolio that has a beta value of 1.5, say, he or she must sell more futures than if the beta value was lower. To establish how many S & P 500 futures to sell, the dollar value of the portfolio must be divided by the dollar value of the S & P 500 futures contract. The procedure is identical to determining the number of index option contracts used in hedges in Chapter 7. This ratio is then multiplied by the beta value of the portfolio.

The decision to use stock index futures or stock index options to hedge against short-term market declines is discussed later.

COMMODITY OPTIONS ON FUTURES

In this section we shall discuss commodity options written on futures contracts. Although such contracts have been in existence in Europe for some time, they have only recently become available in America. In 1982 the Commodity Futures Trading Commission allowed each commodity exchange to trade options on one of its futures contracts. In that year eight exchanges introduced options. These contracts included gold, heating oil, sugar, T-bonds, and three stock market indices.

Options on Futures

Options on futures now trade on every major futures exchange. The underlying spot commodities include financial assets such as bonds, Eurodollars, and stock portfolios, foreign currencies such as British pounds and West German marks, precious metals such as gold and silver, livestock commodities such as hogs and cattle, and agricultural commodities such as corn and soybeans.

An option on a futures contract is like an option on a stock in that it allows the holder to buy or sell the underlying security at the exercise price of the option. Unlike a stock index option, however, a cash exchange equal to the exercise prices does not occur when the futures option is exercised. The *futures call option* allows the owner to assume a long position in the futures contract, whereas the *futures put option* allows the owner to assume a short position. Upon exercise, a futures option holder acquires a long (in the case of a call) or short (in the case of a put) futures position with a futures price equal to the exercise price of the option. When the futures contract is marked to the market at the close of the day's trading, the option holder may withdraw in cash the amount equal to the futures price less the exercise price (for the call) and the exercise price less the futures price (for the put). Thus, exercising a futures option is like receiving in cash the exercisable value or intrinsic value of the option.

The contracts are completely characterized by the name of the underlying futures contract, with its delivery month, and the strike price of the option.

The option contracts cease trading in the month prior to the futures contract delivery month. The exact date of expiration depends on the contract, but usually is no more than one or two weeks before delivery.

Example 11.10

A call option on a gold futures contract has a strike price of $350. The current gold futures price is $360. By exercising the call, the holder will assume a long position in the futures contract, together with $10. (This transaction is actually accomplished by establishing the futures position at the strike price and then immediately marking to market.) Of course, like other option contracts, rather than exercise, it may be more appropriate to sell the contract.

EXAMPLES OF OPTIONS ON FUTURES

In this section two futures options contracts are discussed. The first type is an option contract on stock index futures, while the second is an option on gold futures.

Options on Stock Index Futures

Options trade on stock index futures. For example, there are options on the Value Line Index (Kansas City Board of Trade), on the New York Stock Exchange Index (New York Futures Exchange), and on the Standard and Poor's Index (Chicago Mercantile Exchange). We shall discuss the option contracts on the S & P 500 futures contract.

An option on the stock index futures contract gives the buyer the right to take a position, at a specified price, in the underlying S & P 500 futures contract at any time before the option expires.

Strike prices are set at $5 increments. If the index is 164, for example, strike prices of $160 and $165 will be the most actively traded contracts. New strikes are added as the index price changes unless there are less than 30 days to expiration. As with futures contracts, options contracts trade on a March, June, September, and December rotations. The options expire on the last trading day of the underlying S & P 500 futures contract. The option can be exercised at any point in time. However, if exercised on the last trading day, there is a cash settlement based on the closing level of the S & P 500 Index. The exchange of the option for the futures position is effective on the date the exercise notice is received. Prices of the options are quoted in basis points. The option premium dollar amount is equal to the number of the basis points multiplied by $5. Each minimum fluctuation of 0.05 equals a move of $25 of option value. To calculate the dollar value of the premium, therefore, the quoted price should be multiplied by $500. Thus, an S & P option premium quoted at $9 costs $4500. Exhibit 11.10 illustrates the price quotations of option prices as they appear in the *Wall Street Journal.*

EXHIBIT 11.10

Futures Options Prices from the Wall Street Journal

FUTURES OPTIONS

Monday, July 14, 1986.

-AGRICULTURAL-

CORN (CBT) 5,000 bu.; cents per bu.

Strike	Calls–Settle			Puts–Settle		
Price	Sep-c	Dec-c	Mar-c	Sep-p	Dec-p	Mar-p
150	....	....	....	....	....	....
160	....	....	....	....	....	....
170	....	....	....	....	....	....
180	....	....	....	....	....	....
190	1¼	4½	10¾	18¼	14½	16¾
200	¾	3	7½	27	21½	23½

Est. vol. 2,000; Fri vol. 1,521 calls; 649 puts
Open interest Fri; 37,564 calls; 13,246 puts

SOYBEANS (CBT) 5,000 bu.; cents per bu.

Strike	Calls–Settle			Puts–Settle		
Price	Sep-c	Nov-c	Jan-c	Sep-p	Nov-p	Jan-p
450	....	42	....	1¼	5	6
475	19½	24	....	4	11	13
500	6¼	13½	21½	15½	25½	25½
525	2	7¾	14¼	36½	42½	42½
550	1	4¾	10	59½	64	62½
575	½	3¼	7	84	86½	24

Est. vol. 2,000; Fri vol. 3,067 calls; 607 puts
Open interest Fri; 47,223 calls; 10,840 puts

COTTON (CTN) 50,000 lbs.; cents per lb.

Strike	Calls–Settle			Puts–Settle		
Price	Oct-c	Dec-c	Mar-c	Oct-p	Dec-p	Mar-p
28	2.25	....	....	.25	....	....
29	1.55	2.25	....	.65	.90	....
30	1.00	1.70	2.40	1.00	1.25	1.10
31	.60	1.25	2.10	1.65	1.75	1.55
32	.35	.85	1.50	2.20	2.40	2.05
33	.27	.70	1.10	3.05	3.05	2.70

Est. vol. 100; Fri vol. 318 calls; 83 puts
Open interest Fri; 8,649 calls; 2,516 puts

SUGAR-WORLD (CSCE)-112,000 lbs.; cents per lb.

Strike	Calls–Settle			Puts–Settle		
Price	Oct-c	Mar-c	May-c	Oct-p	Mar-p	May-p
4.00	1.63	....	....	0.06	....	....
5.00	0.91	1.57	1.83	0.30	0.33	0.36
6.00	0.44	1.04	1.22	0.82	0.68	0.70
7.00	0.26	0.72	0.90	1.64	1.38	1.37
8.00	0.13	0.48	0.68	2.52	2.12	2.15
9.00	0.10	0.35	0.53	3.47	2.99	3.00

Est. vol. 1,310; Fri.; vol. 1,242 calls; 682 puts
Open interest Fri.; 19,605 calls; 9,303 puts

CATTLE-LIVE (CME) 40,000 lbs.; cents per lb.

Strike	Calls–Settle			Puts–Settle		
Price	Aug-c	Oct-c	Dec-c	Aug-p	Oct-p	Dec-p
52	3.40	4.45	6.12	0.12	1.25	1.40
54	1.82	3.22	4.85	0.55	2.00	2.10
56	0.77	2.25	3.75	1.50	3.00	2.97
58	0.22	1.52	2.85	2.95	4.22	4.02
60	0.07	1.00	2.12	4.80	5.67	5.27
62	0.02	0.62	1.55	6.75	7.30	6.67

Est. vol. 2,313, Fri vol. 2,248 calls, 2,741 puts
Open interest Friday; 20,146 calls, 19,662 puts

HOGS-LIVE (CME) 30,000 lbs.; cents per lb.

Strike	Calls–Settle			Puts–Settle		
Price	Aug-C	Oct-C	Dec-C	Aug-P	Oct-P	Dec-P
52	4.47	3.30	3.90	0.15	2.70	4.30
54	2.92	2.55	2.60	0.60	3.87	6.00
56	1.30	1.85	1.80	1.10	....	....
58	0.42	1.00	....	2.10	....	....
60	0.17	....	....	3.85	....	....
62	0.05	....	....	....	....	....

Est. vol. 249, Fri vol. 161 calls, 82 puts
Open interest Friday; 2,383 calls, 5,582 puts

-METALS-

COPPER (CMX) 25,000 lbs.; cents per lb.

Strike	Calls–Last			Puts–Last		
Price	Sep-c	Dec-c	Mar-c	Sep-p	Dec-p	Mar-p
54	4.80	5.60	6.25	.05	.40	.55
56	2.90	4.00	4.75	.15	.70	1.00
58	1.30	2.75	3.45	.50	1.35	1.60
60	.40	1.70	2.40	1.60	2.30	2.55
62	.15	1.05	1.65	3.25	3.50	3.65
64	.05	.55	1.05	5.20	5.05	5.00

Est. vol. 400, Fri vol. 781 calls, 33 puts
Open interest Fri 7,286 calls, 3,630 puts

GOLD (CMX) 100 troy ounces; dollars per troy ounce

Strike	Calls–Last			Puts–Last		
Price	Oct-c	Dec-c	Feb-c	Oct-p	Dec-p	Feb-p
330	21.20	25.30	29.70	1.90	3.30	4.70
340	12.50	17.80	22.00	3.30	5.60	6.80
350	6.00	11.50	16.50	6.40	9.00	11.00
360	3.20	7.40	11.50	13.60	14.50	15.30
370	1.70	4.70	7.70	22.10	21.50	21.00
380	1.00	3.10	5.40	31.20	29.50	28.40

Est. vol. 4,000, Fri vol. 5,247 calls, 2,769 puts
Open interest Fri 23,452 calls, 23,142 puts

SILVER (CMX) 5,000 troy ounces; cents per troy ounce

Strike	Calls–Last			Puts–Last		
Price	Sep-c	Dec-c	Mar-c	Sep-p	Dec-p	Mar-p
450	57.0	70.0	83.0	.80	6.0	10.0
475	35.0	50.0	64.0	3.2	11.0	15.5
500	15.0	33.0	48.0	18.5	18.5	23.5
525	4.5	22.0	35.0	22.5	32.0	34.5
550	1.5	14.0	25.5	44.5	49.0	50.0
575	.80	10.0	18.0	68.5	69.0	66.5

Est. vol. 1,300, Fri vol. 590 calls, 139 puts
Open interest Fri 18,232 calls, 8,420 puts

-FINANCIAL-

BRITISH POUND (CME) 25,000 pounds; cents per pound

Strike	Calls–Settle			Puts–Settle		
Price	Sep-c	Dec-c	Mar-c	Sep-p	Dec-p	Mar-p
1425	6.40	7.35	....	1.30	3.50	5.20
1450	4.75	6.00	....	2.10	4.60	6.40
1475	3.35	4.80	5.50	3.20	5.80	7.70
1500	2.25	3.80	4.55	4.60	7.25	9.10
1525	1.50	2.95	....	6.30	8.80	10.70
1550	0.95	2.25	3.05	8.20	10.55	....

Est. vol. 2,078, Fri.; vol. 1,073 calls, 338 puts
Open interest Fri.; 23,645 calls, 11,949 puts

W. GERMAN MARK (CME) 125,000 marks, cents per mark

Strike	Calls–Settle			Puts–Settle		
Price	Sep-c	Dec-c	Mar-c	Sep-p	Dec-p	Mar-p
44	2.54	3.14	....	0.25	0.67	0.94
45	1.79	2.48	2.96	0.49	0.98	1.26
46	1.16	1.91	2.39	0.85	1.37	1.66
47	0.71	1.44	1.95	1.40	1.88	2.16
48	0.41	1.06	1.55	2.09	2.48	....
49	0.25	0.81	....	2.91	....	....

Est. vol. 4,329, Fri.; vol. 4,152 calls, 2,193 puts
Open interest Fri.; 49,122 calls, 38,721 puts

SWISS FRANC (CME) 125,000 francs; cents per franc

Strike	Calls–Settle			Puts–Settle		
Price	Sep-c	Dec-c	Mar-c	Sep-p	Dec-p	Mar-p
55	2.18	3.02	....	0.61	1.26	....
56	1.55	2.46	3.06	0.98	1.66	....
57	1.06	1.95	2.57	1.47	2.13	2.49
58	0.70	1.54	2.14	2.13	2.70	....
59	0.45	1.21	....	2.86	3.28	....
60	....	....	....	....	....	....

Est. vol. 2,419, Fri.; vol. 1,087 calls, 886 puts
Open interest Fri.; 17,936 calls, 17,574 puts

JAPANESE YEN (CME) 12,500,000 yen, cents per 100 yen

Strike	Calls–Settle			Puts–Settle		
Price	Sep-c	Dec-c	Mar-c	Sep-p	Dec-p	Mar-p
61	2.45	3.36	....	0.65	1.26	1.68
62	1.82	2.76	....	1.01	1.65	....
63	1.29	2.24	2.99	1.47	2.10	....
64	0.90	1.80	2.54	2.06	....	....
65	0.61	1.43	....	2.76	....	....
66	....	....	....	....	....	....

Est. vol. 3,797, Fri.; vol. 2,614 calls, 1,221 puts
Open interest Fri.; 25,142 calls, 16,569 puts

STERLING (LIFFE)-b-£25,000; cents per pound

Strike	Calls–Settle			Puts–Settle		
Price	Sep-c	Dec-c	Mar-c	Sep-p	Dec-p	Mar-p
140	8.38	9.06	9.67	0.93	2.81	4.47
145	4.87	6.11	6.98	2.42	4.86	6.78
150	2.43	3.88	4.85	4.98	7.63	9.65
155	1.03	2.32	3.26	8.58	11.07	13.06
160	0.37	1.30	2.11	12.92	15.05	16.91
165	0.11	0.69	....	17.66	19.44	....

Actual Vol. Monday, 798 Calls, 238 Puts.
Open Interest Friday; 3,147, Calls, 4,389 Puts.
b-Option on physical sterling.

EURODOLLAR (LIFFE) $1 million; pts. of 100%

Strike	Calls–Settle			Puts–Settle		
Price	Sep-c	Dec-c	Mar-c	Sep-p	Dec-p	Mar-p
9300	0.58	0.61	0.56	0.02	0.13	0.26
9325	0.37	0.43	0.41	0.06	0.20	0.36
9350	0.21	0.29	0.29	0.15	0.31	0.49
9375	0.09	0.18	0.19	0.28	0.45	0.64
9400	0.03	0.10	....	0.47	0.62	....
9425	0.01	0.05	....	0.70	0.82	....

Actual Vol. Monday, 0 Calls, 0 Puts.
Open Interest Friday; 881, Calls, 1,120 Puts.

EURODOLLAR (CME) $ million; pts. of 100%

Strike	Calls–Settle			Puts–Settle		
Price	Sep-c	Dec-c	Mar-c	Sep-p	Dec-p	Mar-p
9300	0.63	0.64	0.64	0.03	0.13	0.32
9325	0.41	0.48	0.50	0.06	0.22	0.42
9350	0.23	0.33	0.37	0.12	0.30	....
9375	0.12	0.22	0.27	0.26	0.42	....
9400	0.06	0.13	0.19	0.44	....	0.82
9425	0.02	0.08	0.13	0.65	....	....

Est. vol. 3,327, Fri.; vol. 3,913 calls, 10,563 puts
Open interest Fri.; 53,723 calls, 41,282 puts

TREASURY BILLS (IMM)-$1 million; pts. of 100%

Strike	Calls–Settle			Puts–Settle		
Price	Sep-c	Dec-c	Mar-c	Sep-p	Dec-p	Mar-p
94.00	0.56	0.67	....	0.03	....	....
94.25	0.35	0.48	....	0.05	....	....
94.50	0.16	0.33	....	0.13	0.26	....
94.75	0.06	0.22	....	0.27	0.41	....
95.00	0.02	0.14	....	0.49	....	....
95.25	0.01	0.09	....	....	....	....

Est. vol. 754, Fri.; vol. 277 calls, 23 puts
Open interest Fri.; 9,279 calls, 1,533 puts

T-BONDS (CBT) $100,000; points and 64ths of 100%

Strike	Calls–Last			Puts–Last		
Price	Sep-c	Dec-c	Mar-c	Sep-p	Dec-p	Mar-p
96	4-58	5-43	6-17	0-33	2-07	3-38
98	3-25	4-27	5-16	0-63	2-56	4-30
100	2-11	3-25	4-20	1-47	3-52	5-30
102	1-16	2-32	3-30	2-53	4-54	....
104	0-44	1-54	2-48	4-14	6-13	....
106	0-21	1-23	2-15	5-55	7-37	....

Est. vol. 200,000, Fri vol. 42,025 calls, 23,274 puts
Open interest Friday; 210,822 calls, 200,804 puts

T-NOTES (CBT) $100,000; points and 64ths of 100%

Strike	Calls–Last			Puts–Last		
Price	Sep-c	Dec-c	Mar-c	Sep-p	Dec-p	Mar-p
98	3-63	4-00	....	0-14	0-63	....
100	2-19	2-45	....	0-32	1-40	....
102	1-04	1-45	....	1-17	....	....
104	0-27	1-00	....	2-35	....	....
106	0-28	0-37	....	....	....	....
108	0-02	0-19	....	....	....	....

Est. vol. 2,600, Fri vol. 385 calls, 2,130 puts
Open interest Friday; 38,433 calls, 28,278 puts

NYSE COMPOSITE INDEX (NYFE) $500 times premium

Strike	Calls–Settle			Puts–Settle		
Price	Sep-c	Dec-c	Mar-c	Sep-p	Dec-p	Mar-p
136	4.75	7.30	9.35	3.60	5.15	6.20
138	3.75	6.30	8.35	4.60	6.10	7.10
140	2.95	5.40	7.40	5.75	7.15	8.15
142	2.25	4.60	6.55	7.05	8.35	9.25
144	1.65	3.90	5.75	8.50	9.60	10.40
146	1.25	3.25	5.05	10.05	10.95	11.65

Est. vol. 618, Fri vol. 237 calls, 198 puts
Open interest Fri 7,205 calls, 6,610 puts

S&P 500 STOCK INDEX (CME) $500 times premium

Strike	Calls–Settle			Puts–Settle		
Price	Sep-c	Dec-c	Mr-c	Sep-p	Dec-p	Mar-p
230	12.05	16.00	....	3.85	6.25	....
235	9.00	13.20	....	5.75	8.30	....
240	6.55	10.60	....	8.20	10.50	12.20
245	4.55	8.50	....	11.15	13.35	....
250	3.05	6.70	....	14.60	16.35	17.50
255	2.05	5.30	....	18.55	19.75	....

Est. vol. 3,725; Fri.; vol. 1,939 calls; 6,681 puts
Open interest Fri.; 16,336 calls; 24,260 puts

Other Futures Options

Canadian Dollar (CME) 100,000 Can. $, cents per Can. $.

Strike	Sep-c	Dec-c	Mar-c	Sep-p	Dec-p	Mar-p
72	0.94	1.14	1.20	0.49	....	....

Est. vol. 6. Fri vol. 138. Op. Int. 2,466.

Cocoa (CSCE) 10 metric tons; $ per ton

Strike	Sep-c	Dec-c	Mar-c	Sep-p	Dec-p	Mar-p
1900	35	130	185	68	90	107

Est. vol. 0. Fri vol. 4. Op. Int. 231.

There are no margin requirements for the buyer of an option on a stock index futures contract. As with other options, the maximum loss is equal to the size of the investment. Since the seller of an index option has agreed to accept all the risk of the underlying futures position, margin requirements for the writer are similar to those for the writer of the futures contract.

Options on CMX Gold Futures

The Commodity Exchange, New York (CMX) trades call and put options on its gold futures contracts. The options contracts expire on the second Friday of the month prior to delivery. Thus, an April gold futures option will expire on the second Friday of March. Strike prices surrounding the current gold futures price will exist. Options can be exercised until 3 P.M. on any business day.

Exhibit 11.11 illustrates the price quotations of gold futures options as they are reported in the *Wall Street Journal*.

EXHIBIT 11.11
Prices of Gold Futures Options

GOLD (CMX) 100 troy ounces; dollars per troy ounce

Strike Price	Calls–Last			Puts–Last		
	Oct-c	Dec-c	Feb-c	Oct-p	Dec-p	Feb-p
330	21.20	25.30	29.70	1.90	3.30	4.70
340	12.50	17.80	22.00	3.30	5.60	6.80
350	6.00	11.50	16.50	6.40	9.00	11.00
360	3.20	7.40	11.50	13.60	14.50	15.30
370	1.70	4.70	7.70	22.10	21.50	21.00
380	1.00	3.10	5.40	31.20	29.50	28.40

Est. vol. 4,000, Fri vol. 5,247 calls, 2,769 puts
Open interest Fri 23,452 calls, 23,142 puts

Example 11.11

A commercial user of gold wants to avoid the risk of a gold price increase in the next several months. To achieve this goal, he purchases gold futures call options. If gold prices increase, the profit on the calls will offset the higher price the user will have to pay to acquire the gold. If gold prices decline, however, all that is lost is the full premium of the call option. In this case, the gold can be bought at the low market price.

Gold users may benefit by buying call options. Similarly, gold producers can obtain protection against price declines by purchasing put options.

PRICING MODELS FOR OPTIONS ON FORWARD AND FUTURES CONTRACTS

In this section we shall examine how option prices on forward and futures contracts are set. In particular, we shall investigate some pricing relationships between spot options and options on forward and futures contracts. Finally, some put-call parity relationships shall be presented.

A European Futures Option Pricing Model

The development of the original Black-Scholes option pricing model was based on the insight that if a riskless hedge consisting of the stock option and an appropriate position in the underlying asset could be established, its return must be the riskless rate. For options on futures, the riskless hedge consists of a position in the futures option and an opposite position in the underlying futures contract. The critical difference between this portfolio and the stock-option portfolio is that the futures contract requires no initial investment. Following the development of the Black-Scholes model, Black established the following futures option pricing equation:

$$C(T) = \exp(-rT)[F(T)N(d_1^*) - XN(d_2^*)] \qquad (11.24)$$

where $C(T)$ = the call option price with time T to expiration,

       $F(T)$ = the futures price,

       $d_1^* = [\ln(F(T)/X) + \sigma_F^2 T/2]/\sigma_F\sqrt{T}$

       $d_2^* = d_1^* - \sigma_F\sqrt{T}$ and

       σ_F = the volatility of the futures price.

Note that this model does not contain an interest rate term, r, in the definition of d_1^* and d_2^*. This can be explained by the fact that the original investment in the futures contract requires no funds.

The Black model, given by equation (11.24), was really devised for valuing European options on forward contracts. However, the model applies to European futures options if the riskless rate of interest is constant during the life of the futures option. To obtain more insight into the Black model and the pricing of futures options, we shall next consider a binomial approach to valuing European futures options.

The One-Period Binomial Futures Option Pricing Model

Assume the current futures price is F_0 and in each period it can increase to F_{11} or F_{10}, where $F_{11} = uF_0$ and $F_{10} = dF_0$. The futures call option, currently priced at C_0, will either increase to C_{11} or decrease to C_{10}. The riskless rate is $r - 1$, and as usual, to avoid riskless arbitrage, $d < r < u$. The information is summarized below:

$$F_0 \nearrow \begin{matrix} F_{11} = uF_0 \\ \\ F_{10} = dF_0 \end{matrix} \qquad C_0 \nearrow \begin{matrix} C_{11} = \text{Max}(F_{11} - X, 0) \\ \\ C_{10} = \text{Max}(F_{11} - X, 0) \end{matrix} \qquad B_0 \nearrow \begin{matrix} rB_0 \\ \\ rB_0 \end{matrix}$$

A portfolio containing H_0 futures and B_0 dollars in the risk-free asset is constructed to replicate the payouts of the call. No funds are required for the futures contract. The initial portfolio value, B_0, can then appreciate or depreciate to the two values shown below:

$$B_0 \nearrow \begin{matrix} (F_{11} - F_0)H_0 + rB_0 \\ \\ (F_{10} - F_0)H_0 + rB_0 \end{matrix}$$

To replicate the call option we must have

$$C_{11} = (F_{11} - F_0)H_0 + rB_0$$

$$C_{10} = (F_{10} - F_0)H_0 - rB_0$$

Solving these equations yields

$$H_0 = \frac{C_{11} - C_{10}}{F_{11} - F_{10}} \text{ and } B_0 = \frac{C_{11}(F_0 - F_{10}) + C_{10}(F_0 - F_{11})}{(F_{11} - F_{10})r}. \qquad (11.25)$$

To avoid riskless arbitrage, it must follow that the initial value of these two portfolios are the same. Hence,

$$C_0 = B_0 = \frac{C_{11}(F_0 - F_{10}) + C_{10}(F_0 - F_{11})}{(F_{11} - F_{10})r}. \qquad (11.26)$$

The standard recursive procedure can now be used to extend the single model to a multiperiod model.

An American Futures Option Pricing Model

The Black model is not appropriate for valuing American futures options prices. The reasons for this follow from the following property.

Property 11.6

Early exercise of American call futures options may be optimal, regardless of whether the underlying commodity provides a yield.

To see this, note that the value of an American futures option exercised is its intrinsic value, $IV(T)$ say, where $IV(T) = \text{Max}[F(T) - X, 0]$.

Early exercise will be optimal only if the value of the call exercised exceeds the value of the call unexercised. Now under the assumptions of the Black model, the value of a European call is

$$C(T) = \exp(-rT)[F(T)N(d_1^*) - XN(d_2^*)].$$

As the futures price increases, d_1^* and d_2^* increase and $N(d_1^*)$ and $N(d_2^*)$ tend to 1. In the limiting case, the call premium will converge to $\exp(-rT)[F(T) - X]$. Note that this value is smaller than the intrinsic value. Hence, there must exist a futures price above which early exercise is optimal.

The intuition behind this result is that deep-in-the-money options closely replicate the return structure of a futures contract. However, the option requires a substantial commitment of funds that are not necessary for the futures contract. Futures could just as well be substituted into the portfolio without altering the return structure.

A second explanation for early exercise is obtained by recognizing that for a commodity providing no yield, the futures price can be written as $F(T) = S_0\exp(hT)$. *Ceteris paribus,* the value of the futures price should decline as maturity nears (T decreases). In fact, the behavior of the futures price is similar to that of a stock price that pays out a continuous dividend yield. This decline will affect the futures option in the same way that a continuous dividend yield would affect a stock option.

If the underlying commodity provides a future dividend, the *current* futures price will reflect this information. Thus, at the ex-dividend date the futures price will not drop in value as the underlying commodity prices will. While American options on the commodity may be exercised just prior to the ex-dividend date, American options on futures could be exercised at any time.

The binomial futures option model can be adjusted to handle the possibility of early exercise. Specifically, equation (11.26) provides the value of an option unexercised. The value of the option exercised is $\text{Max}[0, F(T) - X]$. Hence, the American call option is the maximum of these two values.

Property 11.7

The price of a European option on a forward contract equals the price of a European option on a futures contract.

To see this, consider a forward and futures contract identical in all terms. Assume options with identical terms trade on the forward and futures contract. The value of the European call options at expiration are

$\text{Max}[0, FO(T) - X]$ for the call option on the forward contract,

$\text{Max}[0, F(T) - X]$ for the call option on the futures.

However, under interest rate certainty, forward prices equal futures prices. Since both contracts are claims on the same value, their current values must be equal.

In reality, the options contract expires just before the delivery date of the futures contract. For example, a February option on a February futures would expire in January and result in delivery of a February futures contract. The basis at expiration, however, should be quite small.

Put-Call Parity Relationships for European Options on Forward Contracts and Futures

---

Property 11.8

The relationship between a European put and call on a futures (or forward) contract is

$$P_0{}^E = C_0{}^E + [X - F(T)]B(0,T). \qquad (11.27)$$

To see this, consider a portfolio, A, that contains a put on a forward contract, a borrowed amount equal to the present value of the option's exercise price, and a long position in the forward contract. A second portfolio, B, contains a call on the forward contract partially financed by borrowing the present value of the forward price. This is represented in Exhibit 11.12.

Note that regardless of the future, the portfolios have equal value. Hence, to prevent riskless arbitrage opportunities from arising, the current values must be equal. Hence,

$$P_0{}^E - XB(0,T) = C_0{}^E - FO(T)B(0,T),$$

from which the result follows.

EXHIBIT 11.12
Relationship Between Put and Call Options on Forward Contracts

Portfolio	Initial Value	Value of Forward Contract at Expiration $FO(0) < X$	$FO(0) \geq X$
A	$P_0{}^E - XB(0,T)$	$X - FO(0) - X +$ $- FO(T) + FO(0)$	$-X + FO(0) - FO(T)$
B	$C_0{}^E - FO(T)B(0,T)$	$-FO(T)$	$FO(0) - X - FO(T)$
		$V_A(T) = V_B(T)$	$V_A(T) = V_B(T)$

For options on forward (and futures) contracts, put-call parity does not hold. Specifically, the value of a put option on a forward contract is not equal to the value of a call on a forward contract plus the present value of the strike price less the current futures price. That is,

$$P_0{}^E \neq C_0{}^E + XB(0,T) - FO(T).$$

Instead, put call parity holds with respect to the implied spot price. That is,

$$P_0{}^E = C_0{}^E + XB(0,T) - S_0$$

where the implied spot price S_0 is given by

$$S_0 = FO(T)B(0,T)$$

The same parity condition holds for futures options, since European put and call futures contracts have the same prices as European put and calls on forward contracts.

Property 11.9

If options on the spot, options on the futures, and futures have the same maturity date, then given the same exercise price, the value of the European option on the spot equals the value of the option on the futures.

This result is quite obvious. At the expiration date the basis shrinks to zero and futures prices equal spot prices. Hence, the European option on the spot and the European option on the futures make claims on the same future value. Hence, their current values must be the same.

Property 11.9 demonstrates that if options exist on the spot commodity, theoretically there are no additional benefits in introducing options on the futures. More will be said about this in the next section.

According to Property 11.9 the price of a European futures option computed by the Black model should equal the price of a commodity option computed by the Black-Scholes equation. To see that these two equations are equivalent, recall that with interest rate certainty the forward price on a commodity, $FO(T)$, equals the futures price, $F(T)$, and both prices are related to the spot price, S_0, by

$$F(T) = FO(T) = S_0 e^{rT}. \tag{11.28}$$

Substituting this equation into the Black model, we obtain the Black-Scholes model.

American Put Futures Options

Property 11.10

Premature exercising of an American put option on a futures contract may be optimal.

The Black model for pricing European put options on futures can be obtained by substituting equation (11.24) into (11.27). Simplifying,

$$P_0^{E}(T) = -\exp(-rT)[-F(T)N(-d_1^*) + XN(-d_2^*)]. \tag{11.29}$$

Note that as the future price tends to zero, equation (11.29) converges to $X\exp(-rT)$, which is less than the intrinsic value of X. Hence, for futures price below a certain value, early exercise is appropriate. Therefore, American put option on futures are worth more than their European counterparts.

American Options on Forward Contracts

Property 11.11

An American call option on a forward contract has the same value as a European call on a forward contract. Equivalently, early exercise of an American option on a forward contract is never optimal.

To see this, we must show that the European call on a forward contract, given by the Black equation, always is worth more than the intrinsic value of the option on the forward contract.

We have seen that the value of the forward contract with price $FO(T)$ at time t is

$$V(T - t) = [FO(T - t) - FO(T)]B(t - T).$$

Therefore, the intrinsic value of an option exercised at time t is

$$[FO(T - t) - X]B(t, T).$$

All that remains to be shown is that this value is always equal to or less than the value of an option unexercised at time t, with time $(T - t)$ remaining. Recall that the price of an option unexercised at time t is

$$C(T - t) = \exp[-r(T - t)][FO(T - t)N(d_1{}^*) - XN(d_2{}^*)]$$
$$= B(t, T)[FO(T - t)N(d_1{}^*) - XN(d_2{}^*)].$$

Hence we must show that

$$FO(T - t)N(d_1{}^*) - XN(d_2{}^*) \geq FO(T - t) - X.$$

The proof that this result is true is provided by Thorp.

Property 11.12

An American put option on a forward contract has the same value as a European put value on a forward contract.

The result follows similarly to the previous result.

In summary, we have seen that the values of European options on spot, forward, and futures contracts are identical, provided the options have the same maturity and exercise. American options on forward contracts are priced as if they were European options. While early exercise of American calls on the spot commodity can occur only if the spot commodity pays out dividends, early exercise of American options on futures may be optimal even if the underlying security provides no yield. Early exercise of American puts on spot and futures markets may always be optimal.

OPTIONS ON CASH MARKETS AND FUTURES MARKETS

There are four possible markets for an instrument: a cash market, a futures market, an option on the cash market, and an option on the futures market. The existence of all four markets for any one instrument may be unnecessary. A cash market, a futures market, and one options market will usually permit all risk-transfer possibilities, since options on the cash market and options on the futures market serve very similar functions.

Commodity and futures options contracts were introduced into organized markets in 1982. Proposals for these contracts were made by management of stock and commodity exchanges two years earlier. However, questions about the division of regulatory responsibilities between the Commodity Futures Trading Commission and the Securities and Exchange Commission delayed the approval process, allowing other exchanges time to prepare similar products. In 1982 President Reagan signed into law an agreement that gave SEC jurisdiction over option contracts traded on physical securities that are traded on organized security and commodity exchanges and options on foreign currencies that are traded on national security exchanges. The CFTC obtained jurisdiction over options on financial futures.

Options on cash instruments and futures currently coexist. For example, there are options on stock indexes and stock index futures, treasury bonds and treasury bond futures, foreign currency and foreign currency futures. In some cases the market participants clearly prefer one option market over the other. In other instances the preferences are not so clear.

The exchange that first brings a new product to market is usually at an advantage because if the product is successful, liquidity develops, making it extremely difficult for a second exchange to compete. Since in this case there were only slight differences between the start-up times of the various products, technical and operational features between the markets made one product more desirable than another. As an example, options on stock indexes (such as the S & P 100 and the Major Market Index) are much more liquid than options on the stock index futures (S & P 500 futures option). One reason for this stems from the fact that the stock index option contracts were much smaller than the futures option contracts, and this attracted more retail interest. Moreover, while the stock index options could be sold by registered stockbrokers, the stock option futures could only be sold through CFTC-registered representatives.

In contrast, options on Treasury bond futures have attracted more business than options on the actual Treasury bonds (such contracts will be discussed in Chapter 13). One reason for this is that the contracts have less retail but more institutional interest. A second reason stems from the design of the contracts. The advantage of the design of options on Treasury bond futures over options on Treasury bonds themselves is discussed in Chapter 13.

Liquidity and existing markets greatly influence the success of any new product. In the case of a commodity like gold or silver, an option on the physical would involve establishing mechanisms for ensuring quality controls at delivery. Consequently, no option market has developed for such commodities. While an option contract on a gold/silver index was introduced, the main market has developed on the gold and silver futures contracts.

In some markets there are several benefits in trading options on the futures rather than options on the cash instrument:

1. The premium of commodity options that trade on cash instruments varies with the price of the commodity. Cash markets are often fragmented, over-the-counter, bid-and-offer markets. They are dominated by major dealers, with little direct public participation. Since quotes on prices may be difficult to obtain or may vary among dealers, and since transaction costs may be high, option premiums may be inflated. Futures trading takes place in centralized markets, where buyers and sellers meet in a freely competitive auction. During the day there are continuous price disclosures. Thus, option premiums will not be inflated because of price uncertainty.

2. Traders in options require the underlying market to be liquid. If the deliverable supply of the commodity is limited, option writers may become concerned. The premiums of options will reflect the liquidity factor. Futures markets do not have problems with limited supplies, as the supply of futures is unlimited.

3. Selling the commodity short may be significantly more difficult than selling a futures contract. Thus, more strategies are available when the underlying commodity is a futures contract.

CONCLUSION

This chapter has investigated forward contracts, futures contracts, and options on futures contracts. By creating a long or short hedge using futures contracts, the investor replaces total price risk with basis risk. Since futures contracts are obligations, they can create significant risk if not used as hedging devices. In this chapter we have investigated forward and futures contracts and their option contracts. Some pricing relationships were investigated, and comparisons between options on cash and options on futures were made.

References

Kolb's textbook provides a broad survey of the futures markets in the United States. Cox, Ingersoll, and Ross, Jarrow and Oldfield, and Richard and Sundaresan provide theoretical discussions of the relationships between forward and futures prices. Empirical studies of futures and cash prices and futures and forward prices have been accomplished by several authors.

 The relationship between spot and futures prices in stock index futures markets and the pricing of stock index futures are discussed by Modest and Sundaresan and Cornell and French. Faboozi and Kipnis have collected a series of articles in *Stock Index Futures*. The use of stock index futures in portfolios is discussed by Figlewski and Kon.

 Black was the first to price commodity contracts. The pricing of options on the spot and options on futures are discussed by Whaley, as well as by Brenner, Courtadon, and Subrahmanyam; Ramaswany and Sundaresan; Wolf; and Asay.

Asay, M. R. "A Note on the Design of Commodity Contracts." *Journal of Futures Markets* 2(Spring 1982): 1-7.

Black, F. "The Pricing of Commodity Contracts." *Journal of Financial Economics* (September 1976): 167-79.

Blau, G. "Some Aspects of the Theory of Futures Trading." *Review of Economic Studies* 12(1944): 1-30.

Brenner, M., G. Courtadon, and M. Subrahmanyam. "Options on the Spot and Options on Futures." *The Journal of Finance* 40(December 1985): 1303-17.

Cornell, B., and K. French. "Taxes and Pricing of Stock Index Future." *Journal of Finance* (June 1983): 675-94.

Cornell, B., and M. Reinganum. "Forward and Futures Prices: Evidence from the Forward Exchange Markets." *Journal of Finance* (December 1981): 1035-46.

Cox, J., J. Ingersoll, and S. Ross. "The Relation Between Forward and Futures Prices." *Journal of Financial Economics* 9(December 1981): 321-46.

Daigler, R. "Futures Bibliography." *Journal of Futures Markets* 5(1985): 131-43.

Faboozi, F., and G. Kipnis. eds. *Stock Index Futures*. Homewood, Ill.: Dow Jones-Irwin, 1984.

Figlewski, S., and S. Kon. "Portfolio Management with Stock Index Futures." *Financial Analysts Journal* (January-February 1982): 52-60.

Grant, D. "How to Optimize with Stock Index Futures." *Journal of Portfolio Management* (Spring 1982): 32-36.

Grauer, F. L. A., and R. Litzenberger. "The Pricing of Commodity Futures Contracts, Nominal Bonds and Other Risky Assets Under Uncertainty." *Journal of Finance* (March 1979): 69-83.

Jarrow, R., and G. Oldfield. "Forward Contracts and Futures Contracts." *Journal of Financial Economics* (December 1981): 373-82.

Kane, E. "Market Incompleteness and Divergence Between Forward and Futures Interest Rates." *Journal of Finance* (May 1980): 221-34.

Khoury, S. *Speculative Markets*. New York: Macmillan, 1984.

Kolb, R. *Understanding Futures Markets*. Glenview, Ill.: Scott, Foresman, 1984.

Kolb, R., G. Gay, and J. Jordan. "Futures Prices and Expected Future Spot Prices." *Review of Research in Futures Markets* 2(1983): 110-23.

Loosigan, A. *Interest Rate Futures*. Princeton, N.J.: Dow Jones Books Inc., 1980.

Modest, D., and M. Sundaresan. "The Relationship Between Spot and Futures Prices in Stock Index Futures Markets: Some Preliminary Evidence." *Journal of Futures Markets* 3(1983): 15-41.

Morgan, G. "Forward and Futures Pricing of Treasury Bills." *Journal of Banking and Finance* (December 1981): 483-96.

Moriarity, E., S. Phillips, and P. Tosini. "A Comparison of Options and Futures in the Management of Portfolio Risk." *Financial Analysts Journal* 37(January–February 1981): 61–67.

Powers, M. *Inside the Financial Futures Markets.* 2nd ed. New York: John Wiley, 1984.

Ramaswany, K., and S. Sundaresan. "The Valuation of Options on Futures Contracts." *Journal of Finance* 60(December 1985): 1319–40.

Rendleman, R., and C. Corabini. "The Efficiency of the Treasury Bill Futures Market." *Journal of Finance* 34(September 1979): 1913–24.

Resnick, B., and E. Hennigar. "The Relationship Between Futures and Cash Prices for U.S. Treasury Bonds." *Review of Research in Futures Markets* 2(1983): 282–99.

Richard, S., and M. Sundaresan. "A Continuous Time Equilibrium Model of Forward Prices and Futures Prices in a Multigood Economy." *Journal of Financial Economics* (December 1981): 321–71.

Schwager, J. *A Complete Guide to the Futures Market.* New York: John Wiley, 1984.

Stevenson, R., and R. Bear. "Commodity Futures: Trends or Random Walks." *Journal of Finance* (March 1970): 65–81.

Stoll, H., and R. Whaley. "The New Options: Arbitrageable Linkages and Valuation." *Advances in Futures and Options Research,* in press.

Thorp, E. "Options on Commodity Forward Contracts." *Management Science* 29(October 1985): 1232–42.

Venkataramanan, L. *The Theory of Futures Trading.* New York: Asia Publishing House, 1965.

Weiner, N. "The Hedging Rationale for a Stock Index Futures Contract." *Journal of Futures Markets* 1: 59–76.

Whaley, R. "On Valuing American Futures Options." *Financial Analysts Journal,* in press, and Working Paper No. 4, Institute for Financial Research, University of Alberta, 1984.

Whaley, R. "Valuation of American Futures Options—Theory and Empirical Tests." *The Journal of Finance* 41(March 1986): 127–50.

Wolf, A. "Fundamentals of Commodity Options on Futures." *Journal of Futures Markets* 2(1982): 391–408.

Working, H. "The Theory of Price of Storage." *American Economic Review* (December 1949): 1262–80.

Exercises

1. What is the difference between a futures contract and a forward contract? Why did organized futures markets develop, rather than organized forward markets?

2. A futures price equals a forward price only if interest rates are deterministic. If interest rates are random, futures prices and forward prices may differ from each other. Assuming interest rates are positively correlated with the spot price, should forward prices be higher or lower than futures prices? Provide intuitive reasons.

3. Program trading involves stock index cash/futures arbitrage. Specifically, if the stock index futures contract is overvalued, it is sold and the portfolio of stocks comprising the index is purchased. What problems can you envision with this arbitrage? In particular discuss the problems of futures valuation, transaction costs, and management of basis risk.

4. Some investors claim that the introduction of stock index futures and options has increased the volatility of the market as a whole. Provide reasons why this

might be. If volatility is increased by the introduction of futures and options, does this mean the market is inefficient? Discuss.

5. The effects of program trading can be dramatic when the market enters the "triple witching hour"—the time when options and futures on stock indexes expire. This happens on the third Fridays of March, June, September, and December. On March 21, 1986, for example, 57 million shares of stock changed hands in the last half hour of trading on the New York Stock Exchange. The Dow Jones Industrial average dropped 36 points. At the same time pandemonium erupted on the floor of the Chicago Mercantile Exchange, where futures contracts on the S & P 500 index were being traded. Explain why this activity took place. If program trading breeds volatility, should the stock index futures and options contracts be banned? If the introduction of stock index futures and options creates new possibilities for investors and serves an economic role, would you expect volatility to increase or decrease? Explain your answer.

6. "Program trading makes bull markets more bullish and bear markets more bearish." "Program trading is dominated by a few large investment houses. These big players are disturbing prices and undermining the work of traditional stock analysts." Discuss these two statements.

7. Explain how a commercial user of gold who is subject to the risk of a gold price increase could obtain price insurance by utilizing gold futures options.

8. The Weatherhead group assesses the probability of winning a sealed bid at 0.04. If the bid is won, the group will require 100 tons of copper. If the bid is lost, no copper is required. Since prices of copper are extremely volatile, the Weatherhead group purchased futures contracts on copper to avoid price increases.
   a. Explain why this strategy is not very effective.
   b. Why would the utilization of options on copper futures have been superior?
   c. Are there any circumstances under which you would advise the Weatherhead group to purchase copper futures?

9. Using hypothetical data, illustrate a short hedge that turns out to be successful. Illustrate how the hedge could turn out to be unsuccessful. Using these two scenarios, show how the hedge replaces price risk with basis risk.

10. Repeat question 9 with a long hedge.

11. Explain why American call options on futures may be exercised early even when the underlying security provides no yield. What circumstances will increase the likelihood of early exercise?

12. Establish a two-period binomial model that prices American options on futures. State the assumptions behind the model.

12

Bond Prices and Interest Rate Risk

As interest rates have become more volatile, investors have become more aware of the need to take interest rate uncertainty into account in designing their bond portfolios. This increased awareness has resulted in the demand for financial mechanisms capable of transferring interest rate risk between parties in a transaction. These mechanisms include interest rate swaps, interest rate options, and financial futures. To understand their role in bond portfolio risk management, one must first understand how bond prices react to interest rate changes. Toward this goal, the primary purpose of this chapter is to describe the problems caused by interest rate uncertainty. Bond valuation and theories of the term structure are reviewed. The sensitivity of bond prices to interest rate changes depends on such factors as bond maturity, coupon values, the current level of rates, and the direction of change. One common measure of bond price sensitivity to interest rate changes is provided by duration. Bond portfolio strategies that use duration are discussed. With this basic understanding, we will describe in later chapters how financial mechanisms, such as interest rate options and futures, allow bond portfolio managers to hedge against interest rate uncertainties.

VALUING A RISKLESS BOND

The value of a fixed-income security is simply the sum of its coupon payments and the principal payment at maturity, discounted back at some rate or series of rates over time. The basic pricing relationship is given by

$$B_0 = \sum_{t=1}^{m} \frac{C_t}{R^t} + \frac{F}{R^m} \tag{12.1}$$

where B_0 = current price of the bond,

C_t = coupon payment in period t, $t = 1, 2, \ldots m$,

F = face value of the bond,

m = number of periods to maturity,

R = discount factor that makes equation (12.1) true.

Example 12.1

A *pure discount bond* pays no coupon and simply returns the face value, F, at maturity in m periods. In this case the bond pricing equation simplifies to

$$B_0 = \frac{F}{R^m}. \tag{12.2}$$

A *consol bond* (or perpetual bond) offers a certain coupon payment, C, forever. In this case the bond pricing equation simplifies to

$$B_0 = \sum_{t=1}^{\infty} \frac{C_t}{R^t} = \frac{C}{(R-1)}. \tag{12.3}$$

If one were to purchase a bond and hold it to maturity, then from equation (12.1) all factors are certain except the discount factor R. In this case the value of R can be computed.

Example 12.2

Consider a one-year-to-maturity discount bond with face value $1000, currently priced at $900. The discount rate for this bond is $R = F/B = 1000/900 = 1.1111$. The effective annual interest rate on this bond is 11.11 percent.

Next consider a two-year-to-maturity discount bond with face value $1000, currently priced at $800. This discount rate for this bond is

$$R^2 = \frac{F}{B} = \frac{1000}{800} = 1.25;$$

$$R = 1.118.$$

The appropriate discount factor for this bond is 11.8 percent.

Finally, consider a bond with face value $1000 and a semiannual coupon rate of 12 percent that matures in two years. The current price of the bond is $900. Using the bond pricing equation, one can compute the six-month discount factor:

$$900 = \frac{60}{R} + \frac{60}{R^2} + \frac{60}{R^3} + \frac{1060}{R^4},$$

from which $R = 1.0912$.

THE YIELD TO MATURITY

The bond pricing equation can be written as

$$B_0 = \sum_{t=1}^{m} \frac{C_t}{(1+r)^t} \tag{12.4}$$

where C_m includes the final coupon payment together with the face value and r, representing the *yield to maturity*, is the value that makes the equation true. The yield provides an alternative method of stating the price of the bond. As the yield rises in value, the bond price must decline.

Interpretations of Yield to Maturity

One way of interpreting yield to maturity corresponds to the interest rate on an equivalent savings account. By *equivalent* we mean that the rate of return on the savings account is the yield, r. Consider an initial deposit to the account of B_0 dollars, where B_0 corresponds to the market value of the bond. If the investor withdraws money from this account in accordance with the bonds coupon payment schedule (usually semiannual), then at maturity the account will be equal to the bond's redemption value.

This analogy provides a basis for comparing bonds with different coupons, maturities, and prices. Since most bonds can be replicated by semiannually compounded savings accounts, the choice between bonds can be based on the semiannual interest rates of their equivalent savings accounts.

However, this simple analogy is far from complete for several reasons:

1. *Schedule of payments.* With savings accounts, investors can schedule withdrawals at any time, whereas bondholders purchase a specific coupon flow and maturity. Two bonds can have the same yield to maturity yet offer significantly different schedules of payments. The differences in size and timing of these payments may provide different investment values to different investors.
2. *Compounding of interest.* Interest in a savings account is usually compounded. Coupon flows from a bond have to be reinvested, usually in another instrument, which may provide a yield different to the yield to maturity. Only if the semiannual interest from the savings account is withdrawn and reinvested in the same way as the coupon payments will the replications be identical.
3. *Account value.* With savings accounts, the amount of principal is well defined at all points in time, regardless of interest rate. However, the value of the bond is not well defined over its lifetime since its value fluctuates in response to interest rate changes. This occurs because a bond paying a fixed rate of interest becomes less attractive to investors in the future if higher riskless rates are offered on alternative investments. The value of the bond declines to a value such that its yield will be competitive with other yields obtained on alternative investments.

Yield to Call

The yield to maturity is based on the assumption that coupon payments will be received up to maturity, at which time the face value payment will also be made. However, this assumption may not be true. Many bonds have call provisions that allow the issuer to buy back the bond at a specific price (the call price) before maturity. The call price is usually set above the face value. In some cases a schedule of call prices exists that decreases over time. The call feature provides the borrower with flexibility, especially when interest rates decline. In such an instance, the borrower can call in the issue and refinance at lower cost. Naturally, this feature is undesirable to bondholders. In fact, any investor who buys a callable bond is buying a straight bond and then granting (writing) a call option to the firm. The strike price of the option corresponds to the call price, and the time to expiration corresponds to the call. Using option pricing theory, the value of this call feature can be established (see Chapter 14). Investors will not purchase callable bonds unless they are compensated by a higher yield for carrying the additional risk. In addition to computing the yield to maturity, investors in callable bonds should compute the yield to call by finding the interest rate that equates the current price of the bond and the assumed cash flows to the call date.

Realized Yield to Maturity

The actual realized yield of a bond depends on the rates at which the coupons received during the life of the bond are reinvested. Given an initial wealth of B_0, we can find the final wealth at maturity, m, by tracing the subsequent reinvestments of the coupons. Let the net wealth of all the subsequent reinvestments together with the final payout and coupon value be B_T. Then the realized compounded yield to maturity, r_y, is given by solving the equation

$$B_0 = \frac{B_T}{(1 + r_y)^m},$$

or

$$r_y = \left(\frac{B_T}{B_0} \right)^{1/m} - 1. \tag{12.5}$$

If all reinvestment rates equal the yield to maturity, r, then the realized yield equals the yield to maturity. However, if the reinvestment rates exceed the yield to maturity, then $r_y > r$.

The realized compounded yield over the life of the bond supplements the yield to maturity in that it includes interest on interest terms over the life of the investment at various assumed reinvestment rates.

SENSITIVITY OF BOND PRICES

Changes in interest rate levels tend to affect the price of some fixed-income securities more than others. The sensitivity of bond prices to interest rate changes depends on many factors, including time to maturity, coupon size, and the riskiness of the bond. At any time the structure of bond prices that differs in these dimensions can be examined and used to predict other bond prices. This analysis is called *yield structure analysis*. Attention is usually focused on differences among bonds along a single dimension. An analysis of yields of similar bonds of different maturities, for example, is called a *term structure analysis*. In this section the factors that influence bond pricing are examined.

Effect of Coupon Size

Consider two bonds alike in all aspects except coupon size. A given change in yields will cause the price of the lower-coupon bond to change more in percentage terms. The reason for this follows from the fact that higher-coupon bonds, having greater cash flows, return a higher proportion of value earlier than lower-coupon bonds. This implies that relatively less of the high-coupon bond faces the higher compounding associated with the new discount factor. Therefore, on a relative basis, less price adjustment is required for the higher-coupon bond.

Example 12.3

Consider two four-year annual coupon bonds, both priced to yield 8 percent. The first bond has a 5 percent coupon, the second a 10 percent. From the bond pricing equation, their prices are $900.92 and $1066.52, respectively.

Assume interest rates change so that each bond is now priced to yield 10 percent. Then the new bond prices are

$$B_1 = \frac{50}{1.10} + \frac{50}{1.10^2} + \frac{50}{1.10^3} + \frac{1050}{1.10^4}$$

$$= \$841.50,$$

and

$$B_2 = \frac{100}{1.10} + \frac{100}{1.10^2} + \frac{100}{1.10^3} + \frac{1100}{1.10^4}$$

$$= \$1000.$$

In percentage terms, the 5 percent coupon bond has changed by

$$\frac{(900.92 - 841.50)}{900.92} = 6.6\%$$

while the 10 percent coupon bond has changed by

$$\frac{(1066.52 - 1000)}{1066.52} = 6.2\%.$$

(continued)

Example 12.3 (cont'd)

Hence, low-coupon bonds are more sensitive to yield changes than high-coupon bonds.

Bonds trading above their face value (premium bonds) usually have higher coupon rates than bonds trading below their face value (discount bonds) and, hence, all things being equal, will be less sensitive to yield changes.

Effect of Maturity

Consider two bonds alike in all aspects except maturity. A given change in yields will cause the longer term bond to change more in percentage terms than the shorter-term bond.

Example 12.4

Consider two 5 percent coupon bonds, both priced to yield 8 percent. One is a four-year bond, the second an eight-year bond. Both bonds pay interest annually. The shorter-term bond is priced at $900.92, while the longer-term bond is priced at $827.60. Assume yields rise to 10 percent. Then, from the bond pricing equation, the four-year bond will be priced at $841.50, while the eight-year bond will be priced at $733.40. In percentage terms, the decline in price of the shorter-term bond is 6.6 percent, compared to 11.4 percent for the longer-term bond.

When rates are rising or expected to rise, potential bond buyers do not want to be locked into a low rate of long-term return or hold a security whose value will decline. In such cases, investors prefer short-term securities. Conversely, if interest rates are expected to drop, potential buyers can lock into high returns by purchasing long-term bonds.

Direction of Yield Change

The percentage price change in bond prices will be greater if the yield change is negative.

Example 12.5

Consider a four-year 8 percent bond with annual coupons sold at par ($1000) to yield 8 percent.

First, assume yields fall to 6 percent. Then the bond price is

$$B_0 = \frac{80}{1.06} + \frac{80}{1.06^2} + \frac{80}{1.06^3} + \frac{1080}{1.06^4} = \$1069.30.$$

(continued)

Example 12.5 (cont'd)

This yield change causes a 6.93 percent change in bond price.

Second, assume yields rise to 10 percent. Then the bond price is

$$B_0 = \frac{80}{1.10} + \frac{80}{1.10^2} + \frac{80}{1.10^3} + \frac{1080}{1.10^4} = \$936.60.$$

This yield change causes a 6.34 percent change in bond price.

Thus, bond prices are more sensitive to yield decreases than yield increases.

THE TERM STRUCTURE OF INTEREST RATES

For ease of exposition, assume riskless discount bonds exist with maturity dates over all periods. Using the bond pricing equation, the yield to maturity for all the discount bonds can be computed.

$$\text{Let } B_0 = \frac{F}{(1 + r_{0j})^j} \qquad j = 1, 2, \ldots n$$

where r_{0j} is the yield to maturity for the discount bond of maturity, j. Hence,

$$r_{0j} = \left(\frac{F}{B_0}\right)^{1/j} - 1 \qquad j = 1, 2, \ldots n. \tag{12.6}$$

A graph of these yields against maturity constitutes the *yield curve*. The yield curve indicates how much additional yield can be obtained in exchange for each extension in maturity. Exhibit 12.1 illustrates two possible yield curves.

EXHIBIT 12.1
Two Possible Term Structures of Interest Rates

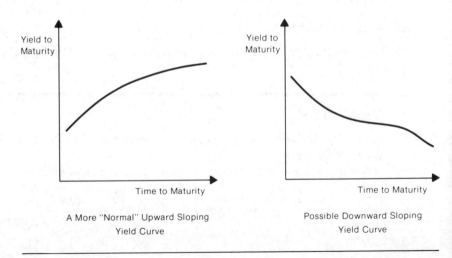

A More "Normal" Upward Sloping
Yield Curve

Possible Downward Sloping
Yield Curve

The relationship that exists between yield and term to maturity is known as the *term structure of interest rates.*

Spot Rates and Forward Rates

Yields obtained from the yield curve are called *spot rates.* The actual spot rate for a one-year bond is r_{01}, whereas the yield to maturity on a two-year bond is r_{02}. If we consider the two-year investment as two consecutive one-year investments yielding r_1^* in the first period and r_2^* in the second period, then we have

$$(1 + r_1^*)(1 + r_2^*) = (1 + r_{02})^2.$$

Since the spot rate for a one period investment is r_{01}, we have $r_1^* = r_{01}$ and hence r_2^* must satisfy the equation

$$(1 + r_{01})(1 + r_2^*) = (1 + r_{02})^2.$$

The forward rate for the second period, r_{12}, is defined as the value r_2^* must take to make the equation true. Hence,

$$r_{12} = \frac{(1 + r_{02})^2}{(1 + r_{01})} - 1. \tag{12.7}$$

This rate represents the riskless rate for an investment starting in period 1 and ending in period 2. It is called the *forward rate,* since it is the rate that must occur in the future to equate the yields on successive purchases of single-period bonds to the yield on the longer-term bond.

Given the current yield curve, we can use the spot rates to compute all single-period forward rates. For example, given the yield on a five-year bond and six-year bond, the forward rate in the sixth year, r_{56}, can be computed. Specifically,

$$r_{56} = \frac{(1 + r_{06})^6}{(1 + r_{05})^5} - 1.$$

More generally, the forward rate in the jth year is

$$r_{j,j+1} = \frac{(1 + r_{0,j+1})^{j+1}}{(1 + r_{0,j})^j} - 1. \tag{12.8}$$

Furthermore, given the single-period forward rates, multiple-period rates can be computed. Specifically, the forward rate from period i to j is given by the value r_{ij}, satisfying

$$(1 + r_{ij}) = (1 + r_{i,i+1})(1 + r_{i+1,i+2}), \ldots (1 + r_{j-1,j}).$$

Example 12.6

Suppose the following spot rates were obtained from the yield curve: $r_{01} = 7\%$, $r_{02} = 8\%$, $r_{03} = 9\%$, $r_{04} = 10\%$, and $r_{05} = 11\%$. Then the forward rates can be computed. Specifically,

$$r_{12} = \frac{1.08^2}{1.07} - 1 = 9\%,$$

$$r_{23} = \frac{1.09^3}{1.08^2} - 1 = 11\%,$$

$$r_{34} = \frac{1.10^4}{1.09^3} - 1 = 13.1\%, \text{ and}$$

$$r_{45} = \frac{1.11^5}{1.11^4} - 1 = 15.1\%.$$

Bond Pricing in a Risk-Neutral Economy

Consider an investor who has a one-period investment horizon and is considering one of two strategies:

Buy a one-year bond and hold it to maturity;
Buy a two-year discount bond and sell it after one year.

The first strategy is a riskless strategy, but the second is not since the bond price in one year's time is uncertain.

Assume the spot one-year rate is 7 percent and the two-year rate 8 percent. Then, as seen earlier, the forward rate, r_{12}, is 9 percent. If the actual rate in the second year is 9 percent, then the actual yield realized by the second strategy would be 7 percent. However, if the future spot rate were higher (lower) than 9 percent, the second strategy would produce lower (higher) yields than the first strategy.

Risk-neutral investors would follow the first (second) strategy if they expected the actual yield in the second year to be higher (lower) than the current forward rate.

Clearly, if the overall consensus in this risk-neutral economy were that next period's rate would be lower than 9 percent, the demand for the one-year discount bond would drop, as investors would prefer the alternative strategy of buying the two-year bond and selling it after one year. This activity would result in a bidding up of prices for the two-year bond and a weakening of prices for the one-year bond. Eventually an equilibrium would be set in which the new forward rate, r_{12}, would represent the market consensus opinion on the expected yield of a one-year discount bond next year. In equilibrium, investors would be indifferent about the maturity of the discount bonds that they purchased.

Example 12.7

Assume the spot rate for a one-year bond is 10 percent and for a two-year bond 12 percent. Assume also that the investor expects the spot rate next year to be 16 percent. Consider an investment of \$1. Over a two-year holding period, the guaranteed yield on the two-year bond is

$$1(1.12)^2 - 1 = 0.254,$$

while the expected yield on the successive investments is

$$1(1.10)(1.16) - 1 = 0.276.$$

Thus, the second alternative will be preferred. Moreover, if the expected future spot rate were 14 percent, the successive investment strategy would yield

$$1(1.10)(1.14) - 1 = 0.254$$

and the investor would be indifferent between the two strategies.

The Expectations Hypothesis of the Term Structure

One version of the expectations hypothesis claims that the term structure of interest rates is established as if all investors were risk neutral. In equilibrium, the forward rates provide unbiased estimators of future spot rates. Since forward rates are equivalent to expected future rates, this version of the pure expectations theory implies that the expected one-year rate in two years, for example, is given by r_{23}.

The pure expectations theory explains all observed shapes of the yield curve solely by reference to expected future rates, which are assumed to be equal to forward rates. If one-year rates are expected to rise, then under the expectations theory, since expected future rates equal forward rates, it must be the case that

$$r_{01} < r_{12} < r_{23} \ldots < r_{n,n+1}$$

These forward rates imply an upward sloping yield curve. Conversely, if one-year rates are expected to fall, the yield curve should be downward sloping.

A second version of the expectations theory is based on the observation that in equilibrium risk-neutral forces will force bonds to be priced in such a way that, regardless of the maturity or sequence of maturities held, the same expected yield will be obtained.

Example 12.8

Suppose the following spot rates prevail:

$$r_{01} = 7\%, r_{02} = 8\%, r_{03} = 9\%, r_{04} = 10\%, r_{05} = 11\%.$$

Then the forward rates are given as

$$r_{12} = 9.0\%, r_{23} = 11\%, r_{34} = 13.1\%, r_{45} = 15.1\%.$$

Consider a four-year holding period and compare the following three strategies:

1. Roll over four successive one-year bonds.
2. Buy a four-year discount bond.
3. Buy a five-year discount bond and sell it after four years.

Under this version of the expectations theory, investors can be viewed as being indifferent to the three strategies, since all provide the same expected yield of 10 percent.

Unfortunately, these two versions of the expectations hypothesis are not perfectly consistent. Forward rates may not be unbiased estimators of expected future spot rates if there is autocorrelation of spot rates. In fact, if the autocorrelation is positive, forward rates will be upwardly biased. This issue is discussed by Cox, Ingersoll, and Ross.

Bond Pricing in a Risk-Averse Economy

In a risk-neutral economy, bond prices are set according to expectations alone. In a risk-averse economy, however, investors will be willing to sacrifice expected returns for a reduction in risk. Thus, an investor with a one-year holding period would prefer to hold a one-year discount bond rather than buy a two-year bond and sell it after one year, even if this strategy provided the same expected return. In fact, even if the latter strategy produced a higher expected return, the investor might still prefer the one-year-bond alternative. To entice the investor away from this bond, the expected return on the risky alternative must provide adequate compensation for the risk borne.

To achieve indifference between the alternatives, the expected one-year yield next year, E_{12}, must be less than the forward rate, r_{12}, by a risk premium. That is, $r_{12} > E_{12}$.

Now consider an investor with a two-year holding period. By purchasing a two-year discount bond and holding it to maturity, the investor creates a riskless strategy. Risk-averse investors will only consider rolling over successive one-year bonds if the expected return in the second year, E_{12}, exceeds the forward rate, r_{12}, by a risk premium. Hence, for this investor, the risky strategy will only be considered if $r_{12} < E_{12}$.

In a risk-averse economy, investors would first attempt to match bond maturity with investment holding period. To entice them away from that strategy, expected returns from alternative strategies must more than compensate for the additional risk borne.

The Liquidity Premium Theory

The liquidity premium theory assumes that lenders have shorter investment horizons than borrowers. As such, investors will view long-term bonds as riskier than short-term bonds, and the former will carry a risk premium. To compensate investors for carrying long-term bonds, forward rates must be set higher than expected future rates.

In contrast to the pure expectations theory, the liquidity premium theory predicts a rising yield curve even when all the expected future one-period rates are equal. Exhibit 12.2 illustrates the effect of the liquidity premium in this case.

EXHIBIT 12.2
The Liquidity Premium

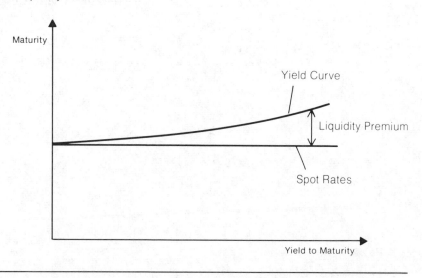

Under the liquidity premium theory, a flat yield curve could be obtained only if rates were expected to drop by exactly the risk premium in each year. Pure expectations proponents claim that if a liquidity premium existed, arbitragers would exploit these premiums and drive them to zero.

The Preferred Habitat Theory

The liquidity premium hypothesis is based on the assumption that lenders typically have short investment horizons and, hence, view long-term bonds as more risky. However, to reduce risk, investors attempt to match the maturity of their bonds with their investment holding periods. Long-term investors would purchase a long-term bond offering a certain return over the investment period. Such investors would view a strategy of sequential reinvestments in short-term bonds as risky over the long horizon. It can readily be argued, then, that if risk premiums exist, they may be positive or negative.

Generally, we can conclude that different investors have different preferred habitats on the term-to-maturity scale, and the distribution and strength of these preferences determine the premiums that exist in market equilibrium.

Coupon Bonds and the Yield Curve

Consider a default-free bond that promises payments of size C_i in period i, $i = 1, 2, \ldots n$. Then, according to the bond pricing equation, we have

$$B_0 = \sum_{i=1}^{n} \frac{C_i}{R^i}.$$

The payouts of this bond can be replicated by a portfolio of n discount bonds of face value $C_1, C_2, \ldots C_n$, which come due in periods $1, 2, 3, \ldots n$, respectively.

Let

$$B_j = \frac{C_j}{(1 + r_{0j})^j} \qquad j = 1, 2, \ldots n.$$

Then

$$B_0 = \sum_{j=1}^{n} B_j$$

$$= \sum_{j=1}^{n} \frac{C_j}{(1 + r_{0j})^j}.$$

Now since

$$(1 + r_{0j})^j = (1 + r_{01})(1 + r_{12})(1 + r_{13}) \ldots (1 + r_{j-1,j}),$$

we have

$$B_0 = \sum_{j=1}^{n} \left[C_j \Big/ \prod_{i=1}^{j} (1 + r_{i-1,i}) \right] \tag{12.9}$$

The equation is the generalized bond pricing equation and can be used to value any default-free coupon bond.

Term Structure and Coupon Bonds

Since coupon bonds pay back their money earlier than discount bonds, the yield on coupon bonds should be higher (lower) than the yield on discount bonds when the yield curve is downward (upward) sloping. Exhibit 12.3 illustrates the term structure of bonds with different coupon sizes under the assumption that the yield curve is upward sloping.

EXHIBIT 12.3
Term Structures Curves

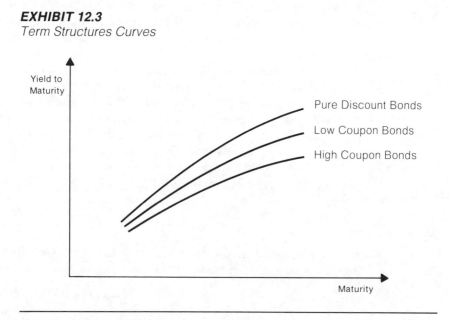

Term Structure and Default Risk

The greater the risk of default of a bond, the higher its expected return must be. Valuation of risky corporate bonds will be discussed in Chapter 15.

IMMUNIZATION

Consider an investor whose goals require that an investment be dedicated to meet a specific liability of nominal amount F that comes due in m periods. If the investor holds a portfolio of discount bonds having face value F and maturity m, then regardless of interest rate behavior, the future value of the portfolio will cover the future liability. This dedicated portfolio is said to be *perfectly immunized* since its value is insensitive to changes in the yield curve.

In some situations discount bonds will not be available to immunize a portfolio against interest rate risk. In such cases coupon bonds must be used. With coupon bonds, two types of risk exist, price risk and coupon reinvestment risk. *Price risk* is the risk that the bond will be sold at a future point in time for a value different from what was expected. *Coupon reinvestment risk* is the risk associated with reinvesting the coupons at rates different from the yield of the bond when it was purchased. If the maturity date coincides with the holding period, then price risk is eliminated. As the maturity date increases, so does price risk.

As interest rates increase (decrease), bond prices decline (increase) while the returns from reinvested coupon receipts increase (decrease). The fact that price risk and reinvestment risk move in opposite directions and are subject to the same influences offers a way to manage interest rate risk. The choice of the appropriate coupon and maturity bond to hold over a given investment holding period is often accommodated by means of a measure called *duration*.

Duration is a mechanism that represents any series of cash flows by an "equivalent" discount bond for purposes of measuring interest rate risk. By comparing the computed duration with the length of the holding period, the investor can determine whether the portfolio possesses net reinvestment risk or net price risk. Immunization of a coupon bond portfolio is achieved by maintaining its duration equal to the remaining length of the holding period. Given assumptions about the yield curve and the nature of yield curve changes, the simple approach ensures that price risk is offset by reinvestment risk.

Duration

Duration is a weighted average number of periods until cash flows are received from the bond, where the weights are the present value factors of each cash flow.

$$D = \left[\sum_{t=1}^{m} \frac{tC_t}{(1 + r)^t} \middle/ B_0 \right]$$
(12.10)

where r = yield to maturity,

   C_t = coupon,

   m = maturity, and

   B_0 = bond price.

The numerator in equation (12.10) is like the bond pricing equation except that each payment is multiplied by t. This means that the greater the time until payments are received, the greater the duration. If the bond is a discount bond, all payment is deferred to maturity and the duration equals the maturity. For bonds making periodic coupon payments, the early payments will reduce the duration value away from the maturity.

Duration is affected by changes in the market yield (the discount rate), the coupon rate, and the time to maturity.

Example 12.9

Exhibit 12.4 illustrates the sensitivity of duration to changes in yield, coupons, and maturity for a five-year bond that pays 12 percent annual coupons and yields 12 percent.

EXHIBIT 12.4

Sensitivity of Duration to Yield, Coupon, and Maturity Changes

Yield	4	8	12	16	20
Duration	4.2	4.1	4.0	3.7	2.9
Coupon	4	8	12	16	20
Duration	4.5	4.2	4.0	3.9	3.8
Maturity	3	5	7	10	30
Duration	2.7	4.0	5.1	6.3	9.0

Duration and Bond Price Sensitivity

Let ΔB_0 be the change in bond price due to an unanticipated change in rates. The instantaneous return due to the change in rates is $\Delta B_0 / B_0$. Under the assumption that the term structure is flat and only parallel shifts in interest rates occur, it can be shown that this instantaneous return divided by the percentage change in interest rates is the negative of duration. Specifically,

$$D = \frac{-\Delta B_0 / B_0}{\dfrac{\Delta(1+r)}{(1+r)}} . \qquad (12.11)$$

Duration thus measures the elasticity of the bond price to changes in the interest rate. From this equation, we have

$$\Delta B = -D \frac{\Delta(1+r)}{(1+r)} B_0. \qquad (12.12)$$

That is, the change in the price of a bond equals the negative of duration, times the percentage change in $(1+r)$, times the original bond price.

Example 12.10

Consider the previous five-year bond that pays 12 percent annual coupons. The duration of the bond, given that it yields 12 percent, is four years. At this rate, the price of the bond is $100. If rates go up to 13 percent, the change in the bond price is

$$\Delta B = -D \frac{\Delta(1+r)}{(1+r)} B_0 = -4 \left(\frac{1}{1.12} \right) 100 = -3.6.$$

Hence, the new bond price = 100 − 3.6 = $96.40. Using the bond pricing equation with $r = 13\%$ yields the same result.

Immunization and Duration

If the term structure is flat and a shift occurs so that the next term structure is flat but at a different level, the interest rate shift is said to be *parallel*. For a flat term structure that experiences a parallel shift in interest rates, it can be shown that a bond investment will be immunized if its duration equals the holding period. That is, the realized yield for the bond will equal its yield to maturity if the investment period equals the bond's duration.

Example 12.11

Consider the previous five-year bond that pays 12 percent annual coupons and yields 12 percent. Assume the investment horizon is four years. Since the duration is four years, the bond is immunized. If rates fall immediately to 8 percent and stay there over the four-year period, the drop from coupon reinvestment returns will be offset exactly by increases in the price of the bond.

The immunization process with coupon bonds, in essence, results in the creation of an "artificial" zero coupon bond with maturity equal to the investment holding period. This artificial security does not last long because the time remaining in the investment period and duration do not decrease at equal rates. Duration, in fact, decreases at a slower rate, a process referred to as *duration drift*. Duration drift necessitates a periodic rebalancing of a portfolio.

Bond Portfolios

Like the beta value of an equity portfolio, the duration of a bond portfolio, D_p, is computed as the weighted average of the durations of the individual bonds:

$$D_p = \sum_{i=1}^{n} W_i D_i, \qquad (12.13)$$

where n is the number of different bonds and W_i is the fraction of portfolio dollar value invested in bond i.

Since in many possible portfolios the duration D_p equals the investment holding period, T, it is not clear which portfolio to select. One possibility would be to select that portfolio that maximized yield. This portfolio could be obtained by solving the following linear program:

$$\text{Maximize}_{\{W_i\}} \quad \sum_{i=1}^{n} W_i r_i$$

$$\text{subject to} \quad \sum_{i=1}^{n} W_i d_i = T \qquad (12.14)$$

$$\sum_{i=1}^{n} W_i = 1$$

$$W_i \geq 0 \qquad i = 1, 2, \ldots n.$$

Alternatively, the immunized portfolio could be constructed from bonds having duration measures close to the investment horizon (a *bullet portfolio*). Another alternative is to choose bonds that are evenly spaced out along a wide range of durations (a *laddered portfolio*). Yet another alternative is to choose some bonds with very short duration while other bonds have very long durations, the weighted average of course satisfying equation (12.14). This is called a *barbell portfolio*. The relative merits of each strategy and their practical implementation is discussed by Granito. In all cases however, as time advances, adjustments in the portfolio must be made to maintain the immunization.

Immunization, using the duration measure defined by equation (12.11), will be perfect only for an instant and only if the term structure is flat and shocks induce parallel changes. Several studies have been made to obtain more robust duration type measures that will apply to more general situations.

CONCLUSION

This chapter has briefly reviewed the risk involved in bond purchases. Bond portfolios suffer from price risk and reinvestment risk caused by shifts in the yield curve. While immunization strategies can often be useful, these strategies are active in the sense that they require frequent readjustments. In the next chapter we shall investigate a few government bonds and discuss the role of futures and options on Treasury securities.

References

Interest rate theory and the pricing of bonds are discussed in several introductory textbooks in investments. Elton and Gruber provide two chapters on this topic. A classic reference is Homer and Liebowitz's *Inside the Yield Book*. Immunization duration and the term structure of interest rates are well presented by Bierwag, Kaufman, and Khang; Reilly and Sidhu, and Ingersoll, Skelton, and Weil. A practitioner's guide to the implementation of bond portfolio immunization methods is provided by Granito.

More advanced theories of the term structure of interest rates are provided by Cox, Ingersoll, and Ross and by Brennan and Schwartz. These continuous time approaches to the pricing of bonds will be briefly discussed in Chapter 16.

Bierwag, G. "Immunization Duration and the Term Structure of Interest Rates." *Journal of Financial and Quantitative Analysis* 12(December 1977): 725–42.
Bierwag, G., and G. Kaufman. "Coping with the Risk of Interest Rate Fluctuations: A Note." *Journal of Business* 50(July 1977): 364–70.

Bierwag, G., G. Kaufman, and C. Khang. "Duration and Bond Portfolio Analysis: An Overview." *Journal of Financial and Quantitative Analysis* 13(November 1978): 671–81.

Brennan, M., and E. Schwartz. "Conditional Predictions of Bond Prices and Returns." *Journal of Finance* 35(1980): 405–17.

Brennan, M., and E. Schwartz. "A Continuous Time Approach to the Pricing of Bonds." *Journal of Banking and Finance* 3(1979): 133–55.

Brennan, M., and E. Schwartz. "Duration, Bond Pricing and Portfolio Management." In G. Kaufman, ed., *Innovations in Bond Portfolio Management: Duration Analysis and Immunization.* Greenwich, Conn.: JAI Press, 1983.

Carleton, W., and I. Cooper. "Estimation and Uses of the Term Structure of Interest Rates." *Journal of Finance* 31(September 1976): 1067–83.

Carr, J., P. Halpern, and J. McCallum. "Correcting the Yield Curve: A Reinterpretation of the Duration Problem." *Journal of Finance* 29(1974): 1287–94.

Conard, J. *Introduction to the Theory of Interest.* Berkeley, Calif.: University of California Press, 1959.

Cox, J., J. Ingersoll, and S. Ross. "Duration and the Measurement of Basis Risk." *Journal of Business* 52(January 1979): 51–61.

Cox, J., J. Ingersoll, and S. Ross. "A Reexamination of Traditional Hypotheses About the Term Structure of Interest Rates." *Journal of Finance* 36(1981): 769–800.

Cox, J., J. Ingersoll, and S. Ross. "A Theory of the Term Structure of Interest Rates." *Econometrica* 53(1985): 385–440.

Culbertson, J. "The Term Structure of Interest Rates." *Quarterly Journal of Economics,* 71(November 1957): 485–517.

Dothan, U. "On the Term Structure of Interest Rates." *Journal of Financial Economics* 6(1978): 59–69.

Elton, E., and M. Gruber. *Modern Portfolio Theory and Investment Analysis.* 2nd ed. New York: John Wiley, 1984.

Fama, E. "Forward Rates as Predictors of Future Spot Rates." *Journal of Financial Economics* 3(October 1976): 361–77.

Granito, M. *Bond Portfolio Immunization.* Lexington, Mass.: Lexington Books, 1984.

Homer, S., and M. Liebowitz. *Inside the Yield Book.* Englewood Cliffs, N.J.: Prentice-Hall, 1972.

Ingersoll, J., J. Skelton, and R. Weil. "Duration Forty Years Later." *Journal of Financial and Quantitative Analysis* (November 1978): 627–50.

Kolb, R. *Interest Rate Futures.* Reston, Va.: Reston Publishing, 1984.

Livingston, M., and J. Caks. "A Duration Fallacy." *Journal of Finance* 32(March 1977): 185–87.

McCulloch, J. "An Estimate of the Liquidity Premium." *Journal of Political Economy* 83(February 1975): 95–119.

McCulloch, J. "Measuring the Term Structure of Interest Rates." *Journal of Business* 44(January 1971): 19–31.

Malkiel, B. "Expectations, Bond Prices and the Term Structure of Interest Rates," *Quarterly Journal of Economics* 71(May 1964): 197–218.

Malkiel, B. *The Term Structure of Interest Rates.* Princeton, N.J.: Princeton University Press, 1966.

Merton, R. "On the Pricing of Corporate Debt: The Risk Structure of Interest Rates." *Journal of Finance* 29(May 1974): 449–70.

Reilly, F., and R. Sidhu. "The Many Uses of Bond Duration." *Financial Analysis Journal* 36(1980): 58–72.

Richard, S. "An Arbitrage Model of the Term Structure of Interest Rates." *Journal of Financial Economics* 6(1978): 33–57.

Roll, R. *The Behavior of Interest Rates.* New York: Basic Books, 1970.

Van Horne, J. *Financial Market Rates and Flows*. Englewood Cliffs, N.J.: Prentice-Hall, 1978.

Van Horne, J. "Interest-Rate Expectations, the Shape of the Yield Curve, and Monetary Policy." *Review of Economics and Statistics* 48(May 1966): 211–15.

Van Horne, J. "Interest-Rate Risk and the Term Structure of Interest Rates." *Journal of Political Economy* 73(August 1965): 344–51.

Exercises

1. Assume a bond has cash flow of $100 each year and a principal payment of $1000 in two years. Compute the yield to maturity.

2. Given the following discount bond prices, compute the spot rates and forward rates.

Bond	Price	Maturity
A	910	1 year
B	830	2 years
C	730	3 years

3. Consider a bond with annual coupon payments of $100, a principal payment of $1000 in five years, and a price of $1000. What is the duration of the bond? What assumptions, if any, have you made?

4. Consider two three-year annual bonds both priced to yield 8 percent. The first bond has a 6 percent coupon, the second a 9 percent coupon.
   a. What are the prices of the bonds?
   b. If interest rates change from 8 percent to 9 percent, what will the new bond prices be?
   c. Which bond is more sensitive to yield changes?

5. A third of an investor's bond portfolio consists of a bond with a duration of two years, while the remaining two thirds of the portfolio is invested in a bond with a duration of ten years. What is the duration of the bond portfolios? Can we compare this portfolio to a single bond that has a duration equal to the portfolio duration? Discuss.

6. Explain why duration may be a good measure of risk for government bonds. What is the weakness of this measure?

7. A call feature on a bond allows the bond issuer to call in a bond if interest rates drop sufficiently. Consider a bond that is sold with a put feature that allowed the investor to return the bond if interest rates rose. Would this feature be viewed positively or negatively by the investor? Why would a bond be issued with such terms?

13

Options on Debt Instruments

The first section of this chapter investigates a few securities issued by the Treasury. Futures and options trading on these securities are then discussed. Options and futures can be used to alter the interest rate risk exposure of debt portfolios. Simple hedging strategies are presented to illustrate the role of these contracts.

Debt option features often are embedded in products or services provided by many institutions. Several examples of such products are presented. These include interest rate caps, floor-ceiling agreements, callable and putable bonds, saving accounts with early withdrawal penalties, and others. As a result, the valuation of debt options is of interest to more investors than just those who trade listed debt option contracts. Valuing debt options, however, is much more complex than valuing stock options. The main reason derives from the fact that the behavior of the bond price fluctuations may vary over the life of the option contract. The problems of debt option valuation are illustrated by the binomial model. A few alternative option pricing models are discussed.

The final section of this chapter investigates bond swaps. Swaps provide useful ways of altering interest rate risk exposure. Several swap contracts contain option features, and options on swaps themselves are available.

GOVERNMENT SECURITIES

Securities issued by the Treasury with maturities of one year or less are issued as discounted securities called *Treasury bills* (T-bills). Securities with maturities greater than a year are *coupon securities*. If the maturity is less (greater) than ten years, the security is called a *Treasury note* (bond).

Treasury securities are issued to finance budget deficits. The securities are issued on a regular schedule. For example, every Monday the Treasury auctions 91-day and 182-day Treasury bills and makes them available the following Thursday. The bids for the Treasury bills are ordered from highest price to lowest and then allocated from the highest price until the total issue is filled. Treasury coupon issues are auctioned on a yield basis. The bids are ranked lowest to highest and then filled, starting from the lowest. The average yield of the allocated bond is used to set the coupon. Usually the coupon is set slightly below the average so that the new bonds trade below par.

The secondary market for Treasury securities is made up of U.S. government dealers who continually provide bids and offers on outstanding Treasuries. These dealers actively compete in auctions and subsequently redistribute the bonds to their customers. They profit by the bid-ask spread and by possible price appreciations in their inventories. Since these inventories are often financed, dealers can experience losses from carrying inventory if the financing charge exceeds the interest return.

Treasury Bills

Treasury bills are issued in multiples of $5,000, with increments of $5,000 above a minimum amount of $10,000. The Treasury bill is the most important money market instrument issued by the Treasury. Over $200 billion are issued per year.

Exhibit 13.1 illustrates the usual reporting of Treasury bill prices as they appear in the *Wall Street Journal*. The maturity date is followed by prices expressed in bank discount yield form, r_y, where

$$r_y = \frac{\dfrac{(F - B_0)}{F}}{\dfrac{360}{m}}$$

(13.1)

where F = face value,
$\quad B_0$ = bond price, and
$\quad m$ = maturity in days.

EXHIBIT 13.1
Price Information on Treasury Bills

U.S. Treas. Bills Mat. date	Bid	Asked	Yield Discount	Mat. date	Bid	Asked	Yield Discount
-1986-				11- 6	5.78	5.74	5.93
7-17	5.65	5.59	5.67	11-13	5.77	5.73	5.92
7-24	5.54	5.50	5.58	11-86	5.76	5.72	5.92
7-31	5.46	5.42	5.51	11-28	5.79	5.75	5.96
8- 7	5.60	5.56	5.66	12- 4	5.79	5.75	5.96
8-14	5.56	5.50	5.60	12-11	5.79	5.75	5.97
8-21	5.54	5.50	5.61	12-18	5.78	5.76	5.99
8-28	5.58	5.56	5.67	12-26	5.80	5.76	5.00
9- 4	5.71	5.67	5.79	-1987-			
9-11	5.67	5.62	5.76	1- 2	5.80	5.78	6.02
9-18	5.70	5.66	5.80	1- 8	5.82	5.78	6.03
9-25	5.70	5.66	5.80	1-22	5.81	5.79	6.05
10- 2	5.80	5.76	5.91	2-19	5.82	5.78	6.04
10- 9	5.77	5.75	5.91	3-19	5.83	5.79	6.06
10-16	5.78	5.76	5.93	4-16	5.88	5.84	6.13
10-23	5.80	5.76	5.93	5-14	5.87	5.83	6.14
10-30	5.80	5.76	5.94	6-11	5.85	5.79	6.12
				7- 9	5.82	5.80	6.15

The difference between the bid and asked discount yield is the profit margin of the dealer. By substituting the asked discount yield into the above equation, the asked bond price, B_0, can be obtained. That is,

$$B_0 = F[1 - \left(\frac{m}{360}\right) r_y].$$

The final column shows the annualized bond equivalent yield, r_A, based on the asked price:

$$r_A = \left[\frac{(F - B_0)}{B_0}\right]\left(\frac{365}{m}\right).$$

Example 13.1

Consider a 13-week $10,000 face value T-bill with an asked discount yield of 8.88 percent. The cost of this bond is given by the bank discount equation:

$$B_0 = F\left[1 - \left(\frac{m}{360}\right) r_y\right] = 10000\left[1 - \left(\frac{91}{360}\right) 0.0888\right] = \$9775.53.$$

The annualized bond equivalent yield, r_A, is

$$r_A = \left[\frac{(F - B_0)}{B_0}\right]\left(\frac{365}{m}\right) = \left[\frac{(10000 - 9775.53)}{9755.53}\right]\left(\frac{365}{91}\right)$$

$$= 9.210\%.$$

The yield to maturity, r, is

$$r = \left(\frac{F}{B_0}\right)^{365/m} - 1 = \left(\frac{10000}{9775.53}\right)^{365/91} - 1 = 9.534\%.$$

This yield is just the annual rate of return corresponding to a quarterly compounded rate of 9.21 percent.

Treasury Bonds

Quotations for Treasury notes and Treasury bonds are usually reported together, ordered by maturity. The bid and ask prices are reported in a special form. For example, a quotation of 86.12 means that the price is 86 12/32 percent of the face value. To actually purchase a bond, the investor must pay the asked price together with accrued interest since the last coupon payment. Exhibit 13.2 illustrates the price quotations as they appear in the *Wall Street Journal*.

EXHIBIT 13.2
Information on Treasury Bonds

TREASURY BONDS, NOTES & BILLS

Monday, July 14, 1986

Representative mid-afternoon Over-the-Counter quotations supplied by the Federal Reserve Bank of New York City, based on transactions of $1 million or more.

Decimals in bid-and-asked and bid changes represent 32nds; 101.1 means 101 1/32. a-Plus 1/64. b-Yield to call date. d-Minus 1/64. k-Nonresident aliens exempt from withholding taxes. n-Treasury notes. p-Treasury note; nonresident aliens exempt from withholding taxes.

Treasury Bonds and Notes

Rate	Mat. Date	Bid	Asked	Bid Chg.	Yld.
12⅝s,	1986 Jul p	100.8	100.12	− .2	3.37
8s,	1986 Aug n	100.4	100.8	.....	4.81
11⅜s,	1986 Aug n	100.13	100.17	− .1	4.72
12⅜s,	1986 Aug p	100.23	100.27	.....	5.33
11⅞s,	1986 Sep p	101.5	101.9	− .1	5.45
12¼s,	1986 Sep n	101.7	101.11	.....	5.51
11⅝s,	1986 Oct p	101.17	101.21	− .1	5.70
6⅛s,	1986 Nov	99.31	100.31	.....	3.14
10⅜s,	1986 Nov p	101.16	101.20	− .1	5.86
11s,	1986 Nov n	101.16	101.20	.....	5.89
13⅞s,	1986 Nov n	102.16	102.20	− .2	5.68
16⅛s,	1986 Nov n	103.6	103.10	− .2	5.78
9⅞s,	1986 Dec p	101.20	101.24	− .1	5.91
10s,	1986 Dec n	101.23	101.27	.....	5.83
9¾s,	1987 Jan p	101.27	101.31	.....	6.00
9s,	1987 Feb n	101.16	101.20	− .1	6.12
10s,	1987 Feb p	102.8	102.12	.....	6.08
10⅞s,	1987 Feb n	102.20	102.24	.....	6.01
12¾s,	1987 Feb n	103.26	103.30	.....	5.79
10¼s,	1987 Mar n	102.23	102.27	.....	6.09
10¾s,	1987 Mar p	103.2	103.6	.....	6.09
9¾s,	1987 Apr p	102.20	102.24	.....	6.14
9⅛s,	1987 May p	102.12	102.16	+ .1	6.15
12s,	1987 May n	104.21	104.25	.....	6.03
12½s,	1987 May n	105	105.4	− .1	6.10
14s,	1987 May n	106.8	106.12	.....	6.04
8½s,	1987 Jun p	102.3	102.7	.....	6.08
10½s,	1987 Jun n	103.30	104.2	.....	6.07
8⅞s,	1987 Jul p	102.18	102.22	+ .2	6.17
8⅞s,	1987 Aug p	102.20	102.24	+ .2	6.31
12⅜s,	1987 Aug p	106.6	106.10	.....	6.26
13¾s,	1987 Aug n	107.22	107.26	+ .1	6.19
9s,	1987 Sep p	102.28	103	+ .1	6.38
11⅛s,	1987 Sep n	105.10	105.14	+ .1	6.38
8⅞s,	1987 Oct p	102.26	102.30	.....	6.47
7⅝s,	1987 Nov n	101.11	101.19	.....	6.36
8½s,	1987 Nov p	102.15	102.19	+ .1	6.50
11s,	1987 Nov p	105.18	105.22	+ .2	6.48
12⅝s,	1987 Nov n	107.21	107.25	− .1	6.44
11¼s,	1987 Dec n	106.12	106.16	.....	6.50
7⅞s,	1987 Dec p	101.23	101.27	.....	6.53
8⅛s,	1988 Jan p	102.4	102.8	.....	6.57
12⅜s,	1988 Jan n	108.9	108.13	− .1	6.40
10⅛s,	1988 Feb n	105.3	105.7	.....	6.60
10⅜s,	1988 Feb p	105.15	105.19	− .1	6.60
8s,	1988 Feb p	102.1	102.5	.....	6.58
12s,	1988 Mar n	108.17	108.21	− .3	6.56
7⅛s,	1988 Mar p	100.23	100.27	.....	6.60
6⅝s,	1988 Apr p	99.29	100.1	.....	6.61
13¼s,	1988 Apr n	110.21	110.25	− .1	6.63
8¼s,	1988 May n	102.25	103.1	.....	6.47
7⅛s,	1988 May p	100.26	100.28	+ .2	6.62
9⅞s,	1988 May n	105.12	105.16	.....	6.64
10s,	1988 May p	105.17	105.21	+ .1	6.67
7s,	1988 Jun p	100.25	100.27	+ .1	6.53
13⅝s,	1988 Jun n	112.14	112.18	.....	6.67
14s,	1988 Jul n	113.15	113.23	+ .1	6.56
9½s,	1988 Aug p	105.8	105.12	+ .2	6.69
10½s,	1988 Aug n	107.4	107.8	+ .1	6.71
15⅜s,	1988 Oct n	117.19	117.27	+ .1	6.70
11⅜s,	1988 Sep p	109.5	109.9	+ .1	6.78
8¾s,	1988 Nov n	104.4	104.12	+ .2	6.69
8⅝s,	1988 Nov p	103.26	103.30	+ .3	6.77
11¾s,	1988 Nov n	110.9	110.13	+ .1	6.85
10⅝s,	1988 Dec p	108.9	108.13	+ .1	6.85
14⅝s,	1989 Jan n	117.7	117.11	− .1	6.94
8s,	1989 Feb p	102.23	102.27	+ .2	6.78
11⅜s,	1989 Feb n	110.9	110.13	+ .2	6.91
11¼s,	1989 Mar p	110.10	110.18	+ .3	6.91
14⅜s,	1989 Apr n	118.2	118.10	+ .4	6.95
6⅞s,	1989 May p	100.9	100.11	+ .2	6.74
9¼s,	1989 May n	105.29	106.5	+ .1	6.82
11¾s,	1989 May n	111.27	111.31	+ .3	7.02
9⅝s,	1989 Jun p	106.30	107.2	+ .4	6.94
14½s,	1989 Jul n	119.18	119.22	+ .3	7.11
13⅞s,	1989 Aug n	118.7	118.11	.....	7.15
9⅜s,	1989 Sep p	106.17	106.21	+ .4	7.02
11⅞s,	1989 Oct n	113.13	113.17	+ .5	7.14
10¾s,	1989 Nov n	110.15	110.19	+ .4	7.12
12¾s,	1989 Nov p	116.4	116.8	+ .4	7.18
8⅜s,	1989 Dec p	103.31	104.3	+ .3	7.17
10½s,	1990 Jan n	110.1	110.5	+ .4	7.17
3½s,	1990 Feb	93.25	94.25	+ .1	5.11
11s,	1990 Feb p	111.22	111.26	+ .6	7.20
7¼s,	1990 Mar p	100.31	101.1	+ .4	6.93
10½s,	1990 Apr n	110.16	110.20	+ .3	7.22
8¼s,	1990 May	104.5	104.21	+ .5	6.85
11⅜s,	1990 May p	113.16	113.20	+ .5	7.24
7¼s,	1990 Jun p	101.8	101.10	+ .5	6.87
10¾s,	1990 Jul n	112.2	112.6	+ .6	7.19
9⅞s,	1990 Aug p	109.7	109.11	+ .3	7.19
10¾s,	1990 Aug n	112.5	112.13	+ .5	7.19
11½s,	1990 Oct n	115.1	115.5	+ .4	7.29
9⅝s,	1990 Nov k	108.22	108.26	+ .6	7.22
13s,	1990 Nov n	120.22	120.26	+ .4	7.31
11¾s,	1991 Jan n	116.16	116.20	+ .2	7.34
9⅛s,	1991 Feb k	107.11	107.15	+ .3	7.18
12⅜s,	1991 Apr	119.25	119.29	+ .5	7.34
8⅛s,	1991 May p	104.2	104.6	+ .4	7.09
14½s,	1991 May n	128.17	129.5	+ .4	7.32
13¾s,	1991 Jul n	126.7	126.11	+ .5	7.36
7½s,	1991 Aug p	102.6	102.8	+ .5	6.96
14⅞s,	1991 Aug n	131.11	131.19	+ .6	7.32
12¼s,	1991 Oct p	120.23	120.31	+ .5	7.36
14¼s,	1991 Nov n	129.26	130.2	+ .7	7.34
11⅝s,	1992 Jan p	118.21	118.29	+ .7	7.38
14⅝s,	1992 Feb n	132.11	132.19	+ .7	7.39
11¾s,	1992 Apr	119.21	119.29	+ .6	7.43
13¾s,	1992 May n	129.3	129.7	+ .7	7.48
10⅜s,	1992 Jul p	113.30	114.2	+ .6	7.43
4¼s,	1987-92 Aug	93.25	94.25	+ .2	5.26
7¼s,	1992 Aug	100.31	101.15	+ .7	6.95
9¾s,	1992 Oct p	111.16	111.20	+ .8	7.39
10½s,	1992 Nov n	115.6	115.14	+ .8	7.40
8¾s,	1993 Jan p	107.2	107.6	+ .8	7.34
4s,	1988-93 Feb	93.29	94.29	+ .2	4.91
6¾s,	1993 Feb	97.31	98.31	+ .11	6.95
7⅞s,	1993 Feb	103.3	103.19	+ .7	7.18
10⅞s,	1993 Feb n	117.14	117.22	+ .8	7.43
7⅜s,	1993 Apr p	100.24	100.28	+ .9	7.21
10⅛s,	1993 May n	113.30	114.6	+ .11	7.44
7¼s,	1993 Jul p	100.16	100.18	+ .12	7.11
7½s,	1988-93 Aug	100.26	101.10	+ .9	6.81
8⅝s,	1993 Aug	106.19	106.27	+ .11	7.37
11⅞s,	1993 Aug n	123.16	123.24	+ .10	7.49
8⅝s,	1993 Nov	106.22	106.30	+ .10	7.38
11¾s,	1993 Nov	123.8	123.16	+ .9	7.52
9s,	1994 Feb	109	109.8	+ .13	7.39
4⅛s,	1989-94 May	93.24	94.24	+ .2	4.94
13⅛s,	1994 May p	132.6	132.14	+ .11	7.56
8¾s,	1994 Aug	107.31	108.7	+ .12	7.38
12⅝s,	1994 Aug p	129.31	130.7	+ .14	7.56
10⅛s,	1994 Nov	115.28	116.4	+ .12	7.49
11⅝s,	1994 Nov	124.24	125	+ .14	7.53
3s,	1995 Feb	93.24	94.24	+ .2	3.72
10½s,	1995 Feb	118.13	118.21	+ .13	7.51
11¼s,	1995 Feb p	122.27	123.3	+ .13	7.55
10⅜s,	1995 May	118.1	118.9	+ .13	7.51
11¼s,	1995 May p	123.6	123.14	+ .11	7.56
12⅝s,	1995 May	131.16	131.24	.....	7.62
10½s,	1995 Aug p	119.6	119.14	+ .14	7.51
9½s,	1995 Nov p	113.11	113.19	+ .12	7.45
11½s,	1995 Nov	126.1	126.9	+ .17	7.53
8⅞s,	1996 Feb p	110.4	110.8	+ .11	7.37
7⅜s,	1996 May p	100.29	101.1	+ .13	7.23
7s,	1993-98 May	97.23	98.7	+ .13	7.23
3½s,	1998 Nov	94.2	95.2	+ .10	4.01
8½s,	1994-99 May	105.16	106	+ .16	7.47
7⅞s,	1995-00 Feb	101.17	102.1	+ .16	7.55
8⅜s,	1995-00 Aug	105.7	105.15	+ .14	7.53
11¾s,	2001 Feb	133.30	134.6	+ .17	7.79
13⅛s,	2001 May	145.12	145.20	+ .19	7.86
8s,	1996-01 Aug	102.20	103.4	+ .14	7.55
13⅜s,	2001 Aug	147.28	148.4	+ .21	7.87
15¾s,	2001 Nov	168.24	169	+ .21	7.91
14¼s,	2002 Feb	155.28	156.4	+ .30	7.92
11⅝s,	2002 Nov	134.3	134.11	+1.5	7.86
10¾s,	2003 Feb	126.15	126.22	+1.3	7.84
10¾s,	2003 May	126.14	126.22	+1.4	7.86
11⅛s,	2003 Aug	130.2	130.10	+ .30	7.87
11⅞s,	2003 Nov	137.2	137.10	+ .24	7.89
12⅜s,	2004 May	142.9	142.17	+ .31	7.89
13¾s,	2004 Aug	155.14	155.22	+ .20	7.91
11⅝s,	2004 Nov k	135.24	136	+1.1	7.88
8¼s,	2000-05 May	104.26	105.10	+ .23	7.62
12s,	2005 May k	140.3	140.11	+ .23	7.86
10¾s,	2005 Aug k	128.9	128.17	+ .24	7.84
9⅜s,	2006 Feb k	116.31	117.7	+ .27	7.66
7⅝s,	2002-07 Feb	99.16	100	+ .24	7.62
7⅞s,	2002-07 Nov	101.23	102.7	+ .30	7.64
8⅜s,	2003-08 Aug	106.12	106.20	+ .19	7.67
8¾s,	2003-08 Nov	109.15	109.23	+ .21	7.72
9⅛s,	2004-09 May	113.10	113.18	+ .20	7.71
10⅜s,	2004-09 Nov	124.10	124.18	+ .21	7.83
11¾s,	2005-10 Feb	137	137.8	+ .21	7.89
10s,	2005-10 May	120.30	121.6	+ .26	7.83
12¾s,	2005-10 Nov	146.30	147.6	+ .26	7.94
13⅞s,	2006-11 May	158.17	158.25	+ .23	7.94

Reprinted by permission from *The Wall Street Journal*, July 15, 1986. Copyright © 1986 Dow Jones & Company, Inc. All Rights Reserved.

FINANCIAL FUTURES FOR FIXED-RATE INSTRUMENTS

Exhibit 13.3 lists a few of the major financial futures contracts that are available for fixed-rate instruments. The largest markets are for Treasury bill, Treasury bond, and Eurodollar futures.

Treasury Bill Futures

Exhibit 13.4 shows the quoted prices of T-bill futures contracts traded by the International Monetary Market (IMM) of the Chicago Mercantile Exchange. The contract calls for delivery of $1 million face value of T-bills having a maturity of 90–92 days. The delivery months are March, June, September, and December. Eight delivery months trade at any point in time. Delivery occurs in the third week of the delivery month.

The price quotations are made according to the IMM index, which is

$$\text{IMM index} = 100 - \text{discounted yield.} \tag{13.2}$$

Example 13.2

Suppose the IMM index for delivery in six months is $89. The market price of the futures contract is

$$\text{Futures price} = \$1m \left[1 - 0.11 \left(\frac{90}{360} \right) \right]$$
$$= \$972,500.$$

If this contract is purchased, a margin of $2,000 is required and the futures contract is marked to the market. Each basis point represents a 0.01 percent change in yield. The basis point has value $(0.01/100)(90/360)(\$1m) = \$25$.

EXHIBIT 13.3
Some Financial Futures for Fixed-Rate Investments

	Contract Size	Underlying Security	Exchanges
Treasury Bills	$1 million	T-bills	ACE, COMEX, CME
Treasury Notes	$100,000	4–6 year T-notes based on 8% coupon	CBOT, CME
Treasury Bonds	$100,000	> 15-year T-bonds based on 8% coupon	ACE, CBOT
Commercial Paper	$3 million 30-day, $1 million 90-day	Prime commercial paper approved by exchange	CBOT
GNMA	$100,000	GNMA based on 8% coupon and 12-year maturity	CME, CBOT, NYFE
Bank CDs	$1 million	3-month CD of prime grade approved by exchange	ACE, CBOT, COMEX
Eurodollars	$1 million	Cash settlement at LIBOR rate for 3-month deposit	COMEX

ACE = Amex Commodities Exchange,
CBOT = Chicago Board of Trade,
CME = Chicago Mercantile Exchange,
NYFE = New York Futures Exchange of the New York Stock Exchange,
COMEX = Commodity Exchange, New York.

EXHIBIT 13.4
Treasury Bill Futures Prices

```
TREASURY BILLS (IMM)—$1 mil.; pts. of 100%
                                        Discount      Open
         Open  High  Low Settle Chg  Settle Chg Interest
Sept    94.47 94.54 94.45 94.53 + .05  5.47 — .05  27,205
Dec     94.47 94.58 94.47 94.57 + .08  5.43 — .08   8,994
Mr87    94.32 94.42 94.32 94.42 + .08  5.58 — .08   1,630
June    94.16 94.20 94.10 94.20 + .08  5.80 — .08   1,023
Sept    93.87 93.97 93.87 93.96 + .09  6.04 — .09     442
Dec     ....  ....  ....  93.69 + .09  6.31 — .09     165
Mr88    ....  ....  ....  93.46 + .09  6.54 — .09     213
   Est vol 4,630; vol Fri 6,335; open int 39,672, —360.

MUNI BOND INDEX(CBT)$1,000; times Bond Buyer MBI
                                                  Open
         Open  High  Low Settle Chg  High  Low Interest
Sept    94-16 95-03 94-04 94-30 + 13 103-01 79-10 12,930
   Est vol 2,600; vol Fri 3,155; open int 13,033, —195.
   The index: Close 94-25; Yield 8.05.
S&P 500 INDEX (CME) 500 times index
Sept   241.15 241.50 238.15 238.30 — 3.95 255.20 187.00 90,806
Dec    243.05 243.10 239.90 240.05 — 4.10 257.25 209.50  3,060
   Est vol 81,359; vol Fri 70,202; open int 93,907, +894.
   The index: High 242.22; Low 238.05; Close 238.11 —4.11
```

Example 13.3

A speculator expecting a decline in interest rates over the next three months decides to purchase a 90-day T-bill futures contract at $87 (13 percent discount). The initial margin in this contract is $2,000. Assume that interest rates declined from 13 percent to 11 percent. The futures price is $89. Ignoring transaction and maintenance margin, the 200 basis point change is worth $5,000.

Hedged Ride on the Yield Curve

Consider an investor who has funds to invest for three months. Rather than invest in three-month T-bills, the investor decides to buy a six-month T-bill and sell it after three months. The strategy of buying and selling the longer maturity is referred to as *riding the yield curve*. The strategy may be superior to purchasing a three-month T-bill if the yield curve is upward sloping and remains stable. If an unexpected upward shift occurs in the yield curve, then the profit could disappear.

To hedge against unexpected changes in rates, an alternative strategy is to buy a six-month T-bill and sell a T-bill futures contract that matures in three months. This strategy is referred to as a *hedged ride on the yield curve*.

Example 13.4

A six-month T-bill trades at a discount of 12.10 percent. The price of the bill is

$$\$1m \left[100 - (0.121)\left(\frac{182}{360}\right)\right] = \$938,827.78.$$

Assume a three-month T-bill future trades at 88.73. Then the delivery price is

$$\$1m \left[100 - 0.1127\left(\frac{91}{360}\right)\right] = \$971,511.94.$$

The three-month return obtained by buying the six-month T-bill and three months later delivering it against the futures contract is

$$\left[\frac{(971511.94 - 938827.78)}{938827.78}\right]\left(\frac{365}{91}\right) = 13.96\%.$$

Since the coupon equivalent yield, r_A, on a three-month T-bill is 12.96 percent, this strategy picks up an additional 100 basis points, or \$2,500. Transaction and margin-related costs may reduce the relative advantage of this strategy. In fact, empirical tests using historical data indicate that in the long run this strategy does not produce significantly greater returns than the strategy of rolling over consecutive T-bills.

Treasury Bill Strips

Consider an investor who plans on investing in short-term government securities. Rather than rolling over maturing three-month T-bills or buying nine-month T-bills, the investor could buy T-bill futures in the nearby month and in each successive month over the investment period. As each T-bill futures contract matures, delivery is taken. This locks in a precise return over the entire period. Essentially, the investor rolls over maturing three-month T-bills on successive futures contracts at prices and yields established today. If this strategy, referred to as a *T-bill strip,* provides a higher yield than the cash Treasury of the same maturity, it will be preferred.

Treasury Bond Futures

The Chicago Board of Trade's (CBT) Treasury bond futures contract is a firm commitment by two parties to make or take delivery of \$100,000 face value of deliverable grade U.S. Treasury bonds during a specific future month. To meet delivery standards, the bond must have at least 15 years to maturity or call. The choice of which bond to deliver is left to the seller. Typically, there are 10 to 20 eligible T-bonds.

The price quotations for T-bond futures are based on a hypothetical 8 percent semiannual coupon-bearing bond with a 20-year maturity. At delivery, cash is exchanged for one of the deliverable bonds. The amount of cash received by the seller is called the *invoice price*. This price depends on the settlement price and the eligible bond and is calculated by multiplying the settlement price by a conversion factor and adding accrued interest measured to the delivery date:

Invoice Price = Futures Settlement Price × Conversion Factor
+ Accrued Interest.

The conversion factor is the price that a one-dollar face value bond with a coupon rate and maturity equal to the delivered bond would have if it were priced to yield 8 percent compounded semiannually. That is,

$$CF = \sum_{i=1}^{m} \frac{C_i}{(1 + 0.04)^i}$$

where CF = conversion factor,

C_i = coupon rate $i = 1, \ldots m - 1$,

C_m = 1 + coupon rate,

m = number of semiannual periods to maturity.

The conversion factors for bonds with coupons less (greater) than 8 percent are less (greater) than one. Using the conversion factor, the future price for all deliverable bonds can be computed. For example, if a particular bond had a factor of 1.5048, then the settlement price for that bond would be 1.5048 times the settlement price of the 20-year 8 percent bond. This means that for each point move in the futures market, the futures price for the particular bond moves 1.5048 points.

During the delivery month, settlement prices for all eligible bonds will not equal spot prices. As a result, the seller may find it advantageous to deliver one bond rather than another. In general, the bond that is the cheapest to deliver is the bond that provides the seller with the maximum advantage. Since the seller buys the bond at the spot price and delivers in the futures market, the bond to be delivered should be the bond that minimizes the difference between the futures and spot prices.

Example 13.5

Suppose the futures price is 70 and two bonds are eligible for delivery. The conversion factors for bond A is 1.4239 and for bond B is 1.616. If bond A is delivered, the futures price is 70(1.4239) = 99.67, whereas if bond B is delivered, the futures price is 70(1.616) = 113.16. Say bond A trades at 100, B at 113.16. Then, clearly, the seller will select to deliver bond B rather than bond A.

(continued)

Example 13.5 (cont'd)

In addition to choosing which bond to deliver, the seller can also choose when to make delivery. Delivery can take place at any time in the delivery month, provided all positions are closed by the end of the month. The delivery process usually takes three days to complete.

Exhibit 13.5 illustrates price quotations as they appear in the *Wall Street Journal*. From the first column it can be seen that contracts mature in March, June, September, and December and are traded for maturities for as long as three years into the future. The next four columns give the open, high, low, and settlement quotations in points and 32nds of a point. Each point is worth $1000 and each 32nd of a point is worth $31.25. The next column gives the change in settlement price since the previous day. The next two columns present the bond-equivalent yield corresponding to the settlement price and the change in that yield. The final column reports the total number of outstanding contracts.

EXHIBIT 13.5
Price Information on Treasury Bond Futures

```
TREASURY BONDS (CBT)-$100,000; pts. 32nds of 100%
Sept   99-16 100-17 98-31 100-14 +  34  7.956 - .107 164,959
Dec    98-23  99-23 98-05  99-20 +  34  8.038 - .109  23,623
Mr87   97-28  98-28 97-14  98-26 +  34  8.121 - .110   5,197
June   97-15  98-02 97-15  98-01 +  34  8.202 - .111   3,372
Sept   96-14  97-11 96-14  97-09 +  34  8.280 - .113   2,517
Dec    96-13  96-23 96-08  96-20 +  34  8.350 - .114   1,288
Mr88   95-28  96-03 95-21  96-01 +  34  8.413 - .116   1,266
June   ....   ....  ....   95-16 +  34  8.471 - .116     759
Sept   94-24  95-03 94-24  95-01 +  34  8.522 - .117     304
Dec    ....   ....  ....   94-19 +  33  8.570 - .114     112
    Est vol 200,000; vol Fri 222,906; open int 203,397, +6,152.
TREASURY NOTES (CBT)-$100,000; pts. 32nds of 100%
Sept  101-19 101-31 101-10 101-27 +  9  7.732 - .040  58,995
Dec   100-26 101-08 100-21 101-04 +  9  7.836 - .041   4,188
Mr87   ....   ....  ....   100-14 +  9  7.936 - .041     267
    Est vol 16,000; vol Fri 16,037; open int 63,450, +117.
TREASURY BILLS (IMM)-$1 mil.; pts. of 100%
                                     Discount   Open
       Open  High  Low Settle Chg  Settle Chg Interest
Sept  94.47 94.54 94.45 94.53 + .05  5.47 - .05 27,205
Dec   94.47 94.58 94.47 94.57 + .08  5.43 - .08  8,994
Mr87  94.32 94.42 94.32 94.42 + .08  5.58 - .08  1,630
June  94.16 94.20 94.10 94.20 + .08  5.80 - .08  1,023
Sept  93.87 93.97 93.87 93.96 + .09  6.04 - .09    442
Dec    ....  ....  ....  93.69 + .09  6.31 - .09    165
Mr88   ....  ....  ....  93.46 + .09  6.54 - .09    213
    Est vol 4,630; vol Fri 6,335; open int 39,672, -360.
```

Example 13.6

Consider an investor who purchased a T-bond futures contract and held it for over a week. Exhibit 13.6 illustrates the cash flows that occurred.

EXHIBIT 13.6
*Daily Cash Flows of a Long Position in a T-Bond Futures Contract
(Initial futures price = 60–20)*

Day	Futures Price	Points Daily Change	Dollar Change	Value of Account
1	60–20	0	0	$5000.00
2	61–15	+ 27/32	843.75	5843.75
3	61–15	0	0	5843.75
4	62–00	+ 17/32	531.25	6375.00
5	61–01	+ 1/32	31.25	6406.25
6	63–20	1 19/32	1593.75	8000.00
7	62–10	–1 10.32	–1312.50	6687.50
8	63–20	+ 10/32	312.50	6999.50
9	64–10	+ 22/32	687.50	7687.00

Short Hedges with T-Bond Futures   A *short hedge* involves the sale of a futures contract to hedge a current position from interest rate increases. For example, a bond dealer with an inventory of bonds could use a short hedge to reduce the risk of rising rates. As a second example of a short hedge, consider a company that needs to borrow funds in the future and is concerned that interest rates will rise. To lock into the prevailing rates, futures contracts could be sold.

Example 13.7

Consider an investor who owns $1 million of 15-year 8 3/4 percent U.S. bonds at 82–15 (value = 82 15/32% or $824,687.50). To protect the investment from unexpected increases in interest rates over the next few months, the investor sells ten four-month bond futures at 80-11. (The basis is 2-4.) Nearly four months later the bonds are at 70-31 and the futures contracts are at 66-31. (The basis has strengthened to 4.) The investor buys back the futures contracts for a gain of (80-11) – (66-31) = 13-12 points per contract. This represents a net profit of $133,750, which more than offsets the loss in the bonds. Specifically, the bonds have depreciated by (82-15) – (70-31) = 11-16 points, which represents $115,000. The net overall gain occurred since the basis moved in the investor's direction. If the basis had weakened, the investor would have incurred net losses. The strategy of selling one futures contract for every $150,000 worth of bonds is referred to as a *naive hedge* or *1-1 strategy* and may not be the most effective hedge.

Long Hedge with T-Bond Futures   A *long hedge* involves buying a futures contract to lock into an interest rate that is believed to be high.

Example 13.8

Consider an investor who wants to buy $1 million of 15-year 8 3/4 percent U.S. bonds. The money for these bonds, however, will only become available in six months' time. The current bond price is 67-29 and the T-bond futures price for six-month delivery is 66-17. The investor believes that interest rates have peaked and would like to buy the bonds before interest rates decline. To lock into a price, the investor buys ten futures contracts that lock the bond prices in at $679,062.50. The current basis is (67-29) – (66-17) = 1-12.

After six months the 8 3/4 percent U.S. T-bonds are trading at 82-14 and the T-bond futures are at 81-18. The basis is (82-14) – (81-18) = 0-28. The investor sells the futures contract for a profit of (81-18) – (66-17) = 15-01 points per contract, or $150,312.50.

The bond prices have increased by (82-14) – (67-29) = 14-17 points, representing an opportunity loss of $145,312.50. The net profit from this transaction is $150,312.50 – $145,312.50 = $5,000. Note that in this case the profit occurred because the basis weakened from +1-12 to +0.28, representing a 0.16 point change ($500) per contract.

DEBT OPTIONS

A call (put) option on a debt instrument gives the holder the right to buy (sell) a fixed amount of debt securities at a given price over a given time period. Debt options trade on physical commodities, as well as on futures. Organized markets, such as the American Stock Exchange and the Chicago Board Options Exchange, trade options on physical securities, while the Chicago Board of Trade trades options on futures. In addition, a significant amount of options are issued in the dealer market.

Options on Physical Securities

The American Stock Exchange trades options on U.S. Treasury bills and notes. The bill contracts are for $1 million in principal value, while the note contracts are for $100,000. The Chicago Board Options Exchange trades options on U.S. Treasury bonds with principal values of $100,000. Debt option contracts are of two types.

Specific security contracts give the call (put) holder the right to buy (sell) a specific number of bonds of a *particular issue* at a predetermined price at any point in time prior to the expiration date. With the passage of time, the maturity of the underlying bonds that can be acquired (sold) changes. For example, a one-year option on a ten-year bond requires the specific ten-year bond to be delivered. At the expiration of the option, the bond will have nine years to maturity. Thus, the maturity date of the bond must be greater than the expiration date of the option.

Fixed deliverable contracts give the call (put) holder the right to purchase (sell) a *bond issue* that satisfies certain criteria at the delivery date. For example, such a contract may require the deliverable bond to have a required maturity (measured from the settlement date) or a required coupon. In this case, there may be more than one debt issue that can be used to satisfy delivery requirements. Furthermore, the actual debt instruments that can be delivered may vary according to the exercise date. Fixed-deliverable option contracts can have a longer lifetime than the maturity of the deliverable item. For example, a nine-month option on a three-month discount bond (Treasury bill) is possible. When the option is exercised, a three-month bill is delivered.

The T-bill options trading on the American Exchange are fixed-deliverable contracts, while the T-note and T-bond contracts trading on the American Exchange and Chicago Board Options Exchange are specific security contracts. Exhibit 13.7 shows the prices of these options as they are reported in the *Wall Street Journal.*

EXHIBIT 13.7
Price Information on Interest Rate Options

INTEREST RATE OPTIONS

Monday, July 14, 1986.

For Notes and Bonds, decimals in closing prices represent 32nds; 1.1 means 1 1/32. For Bills, decimals in closing prices represent basis points; $25 per .01

American Exchange

U.S. TREASURY NOTE—$100,000 principal value

Underlying Issue	Strike Price	Calls—Last Aug	Nov	....	Puts—Last Aug	Nov	....
7⅜ note	100	1.10	....	....	....	....	....
due 5/15/96	102	....	1.05	....	....	....	....

3 p.m. prices of underlying issues supplied by Merrill Lynch: 7⅜% 100 30/32 ; 8⅞% 110 .

Total call vol. 11   Call open int. 1,614
Total put vol. 0   Put open int. 932

Chicago Board Options Exchange

U.S. TREASURY BOND—$100,000 principal value

Underlying Issue	Strike Price	Calls—Last Sep	Dec	Mar	Puts—Last Sep	Dec	Mar
9¼%	114	....	....	....	....	2.04	....
due 2/2016		....	....	....	....	....	....
7¼%	90	....	....	....	0.03	....	....
due 5/2016	98	....	....	....	1.06	....	....
	100	....	3.16	....	1.28	....	....
	102	1.14	....	....	....	....	....

Total call vol. 8   Call open int. 9,888
Total put vol. 71   Put open int. 5,040

3 p.m. prices of underlying issues supplied by Merrill Lynch: T-Bonds—9⅞% 124 8/32; 9¼% 119 23/32; 7¼% 101 7/32. T-Notes—9⅛% 107 11/32; 8⅛% 104 2/32; 7½% 102 6/32.

American Stock Exchange T-Bill Options

The owner of an AMEX T-bill call (put) option has the right to buy (sell) $1 million face value of 91-day T-bills (measured from the settlement date) at a given price. This right exists up to the expiration date.

The price of a T-bill option is quoted in basis points, with each point representing 0.01 percent of the face value in annualized terms. Each basis point has value given by $(0.01/100)(13/52)1,000,000 = \$25$.

The strike price is based on the level of the T-bill index price. Say the current discount on a 13-week bill is 12.02. Then, the index price is $100 - 12.02 = 87.98$, and strike prices surrounding this index value may exist.

The cost of exercising a 13-week T-bill with strike 86 is calculated by computing the actual discount $14(91/360) = 3.559$, and then computing the value $(1 - 0.03559)1,000,000 = \$946,410$.

Exercise notices tendered on any business day are settled on the Thursday of the following week. This exercise process allows the deliverable bills to be purchased on the Thursday auctions scheduled by the Treasury.

Example 13.9

An investor believes that interest rates will rise in the next three months. However, recognizing that this is not certain, he or she decides to construct a hedge position with limited downside risk. The investor creates an interest rate position by buying a 13-week T-bill June 91 put, purchased at a premium of .92 (92 basis points), or $2,300, and selling a 13-week T-bill June 90 put at a premium of .19 (19 basis points), or $475. The profit table at expiration date is shown in Exhibit 13.8.

If the T-bill price is 91 or higher, then the investor's forecast was incorrect. The 91 put expires worthless. If the T-bill price is 90 or higher, the premium from the 90 put is retained. As the T-bill price declines, the losses from the written 90 put are offset by the gains made on the purchased 91 put. The put spread makes money if interest rates rise and T-bill prices fall, and is referred to as a *bearish put spread*.

EXHIBIT 13.8
Profit Table for a Bearish Put Spread

T-Bill Prices	$86	$87	$88	$89	$90	$91	$92
Buy 91 put	47,700	37,700	27,700	17,700	7,700	−2,300	−2,300
Sell 90 put	−39,525	−29,529	−19,525	− 9,525	475	475	475
Total Profit	8,175	8,175	8,175	8,175	8,175	−1,825	−1,875

Treasury Bond (Note) Options

The owner of a T-bond call (put) option has the right to buy (sell) $10,000 face value of a particular bond issue (e.g., 11 3/4 percent bonds due in November 2014) for a given price. This right lasts until an expiration date. No other issue may be delivered unless specific authorization is provided by the Options Clearing Corporation.

Exhibit 13.7 showed the prices of T-bond options as reported in the *Wall Street Journal*. Strike prices bracket the market price. Prices are quoted in points and 32nds of a point, with each point representing 1 percent of the principal value ($1,000). The price paid upon exercise is established by multiplying the strike by the underlying principal and adding accrued interest. For example, the settlement price of an option with strike 90 is simply 100,000(90/100) = $90,000, plus accrued interest.

The following two examples illustrate potential uses of T-bond options.

Example 13.10

A manager expects to receive a significant amount of funds in three months. Currently long-term interest rates are high and the manager expects them to decline. The manager wants to lock in the prevailing high rate for the funds to be received. In order to do this, the manager is considering buying a three-month $96 T-bond call option quoted at 0-20 or $625. This option is written on a 12 percent U.S. Treasury bond, due August 2013, with a principal value of $100,000, currently priced at $95,000. The profit table is as follows:

T-bond prices	$93	$94	$95	$96	$97	$98	$99
Buy 92 call	–625	–625	–625	–625	375	1375	2375

If prices do rise (interest rates drop), the option strategy will produce profits. By purchasing call options, the manager is purchasing protection against interest rate declines or future price increases.

Example 13.11

A corporation is financing a large project by using corporate bonds. However, there is a threat that interest rates will rise before the bonds are issued, which would mean a drop in the bond price. Thus, to lock in to the prevailing low interest rate (high bond price), the company intends to buy a put option on a T-bond. If interest rates do rise and the corporate bond value declines, the put will become valuable and compensate for the loss in corporate bond value. The corporation buys a three-month June 94 put option quoted at 2-16 or $2,500. This option is written on a 12 percent U.S. T-bond, due August 2013, with a principal value of $100,000, currently priced at $95,000. The profit table is as follows:

(continued)

Example 13.11 (cont'd)

T-bond prices	$91	$92	$93	$94	$95	$96	$97
Buy 94 put	1500	500	−500	−1500	−2500	−2500	−2500

Note that if the T-bond prices rise, the put expires worthless. If T-bond prices decrease, then the put moves in the money.

Hedging Strategies

Exhibit 13.9 illustrates the typical option and hedging strategies established according to different interest rate projections. The motivation for these strategies was discussed in Chapter 3.

EXHIBIT 13.9
Some Debt Option Strategies

Rising Rates	Steady to Rising Rates	Flat Rates	Steady to Declining Rates	Decreasing Rates
Declining Prices	Steady to Declining Prices	Flat Prices	Steady to Increasing Prices	Increasing Prices
Buy Puts	Sell Call		Buy Bond	Buy Call
	Horizontal (Time) Spread	Sell Call	Buy Bond/ Sell Put	
Bear Call Spreads			Buy Straddle	Bull Call Spreads
Bear Put Spreads		Sell Straddle		Bull Put Spreads

DEALER OPTIONS

T-bill and T-bond options on physical instruments are not very liquid, and large transactions cannot be easily accommodated. As a result, investors wanting to trade debt options on actual securities often do so on an over-the-counter basis. These markets are maintained by many of the large government securities dealerships. In many cases dealers will establish option contracts tailored to the needs of the institution requesting them. The dealer market is also responsible for introducing specialized option contracts, such as contracts that provide payouts only if the bill-to-bond spread exceeds a particular value. Floor–ceiling agreements, which are discussed later, are particular packages of debt options that dealers may make markets in.

Over-the-counter markets currently have an advantage over the organized option markets in that dealers maintain quotes on a variety of notes and bonds, and liquidity may not be so serious a restriction.

OPTIONS ON TREASURY BOND FUTURES

Options on T-bond futures are traded on the Chicago Board of Trade. Strike prices bracket the current futures price. The interval between strike prices is two basis points (which corresponds to $2,000). Contracts trade on the nearest three futures contracts. The expiration date is the Friday that precedes the first notice day by at least five days. Exhibit 13.10 shows price quotations of options as they appear in the *Wall Street Journal.* The prices are quoted in multiples of 1/64 of 1% of a $100,000 T-bond futures contract Each 1/64 of a point is worth $15.63. The volume of trading in the options contract is about one third the volume of trading in the underlying futures contract.

EXHIBIT 13.10
Prices of Options on T-Bond Futures

EURODOLLAR (CME) $ million; pts. of 100%

Strike	Calls—Settle			Puts—Settle		
Price	Sep-c	Dec-c	Mar-c	Sep-p	Dec-p	Mar-p
9300	0.63	0.64	0.64	0.03	0.13	0.32
9325	0.41	0.48	0.50	0.06	0.22	0.42
9350	0.23	0.33	0.37	0.12	0.30	....
9375	0.12	0.22	0.27	0.26	0.42	....
9400	0.06	0.13	0.19	0.44	....	0.82
9425	0.02	0.08	0.13	0.65	....	....

Est. vol. 3,327, Fri.; vol. 3,913 calls, 10,563 puts
Open interest Fri.; 53,723 calls, 41,282 puts

TREASURY BILLS (IMM)-$1 million; pts. of 100%

Strike	Calls—Settle			Puts—Settle		
Price	Sep-c	Dec-c	Mar-c	Sep-p	Dec-p	Mar-p
94.00	0.56	0.67	....	0.03	....	....
94.25	0.35	0.48	....	0.05	....	....
94.50	0.16	0.33	....	0.13	0.26	....
94.75	0.06	0.22	....	0.27	0.41	....
95.00	0.02	0.14	....	0.49	....	....
95.25	0.01	0.09	....	....	....	....

Est. vol. 754, Fri.; vol. 277 calls, 23 puts
Open interest Fri.; 9,279 calls, 1,533 puts

T-BONDS (CBT) $100,000; points and 64ths of 100%

Strike	Calls—Last			Puts—Last		
Price	Sep-c	Dec-c	Mar-c	Sep-p	Dec-p	Mar-p
96	4-58	5-43	6-17	0-33	2-07	3-38
98	3-25	4-27	5-16	0-63	2-56	4-30
100	2-11	3-25	4-20	1-47	3-52	5-30
102	1-16	2-32	3-30	2-53	4-54	....
104	0-44	1-54	2-48	4-14	6-13	....
106	0-21	1-23	2-15	5-55	7-37	....

Est. vol. 200,000, Fri vol. 42,025 calls, 23,274 puts
Open interest Friday; 210,822 calls, 200,804 puts

T-NOTES (CBT) $100,000; points and 64ths of 100%

Strike	Calls—Last			Puts—Last		
Price	Sep-c	Dec-c	Mar-c	Sep-p	Dec-p	Mar-p
98	3-63	4-00	....	0-14	0-63	....
100	2-19	2-45	....	0-32	1-40	....
102	1-04	1-45	....	1-17	....	....
104	0-27	1-00	....	2-35	....	....
106	0-28	0-37	....	....	....	....
108	0-02	0-19	....	....	....	....

Est. vol. 2,600, Fri vol. 385 calls, 2,130 puts
Open interest Friday; 38,433 calls, 28,278 puts

If an option buyer exercises the call (put), a long (short) position in the futures contract is acquired. The corresponding writer will be assigned a short (long) position. If the strike price equals the futures price, the transaction is complete. However, if the strike price is lower (higher) than the futures price, the call (put) seller must pay the buyer the difference.

The market for options on T-bond futures is more liquid than that for options on T-bonds. There are three main reasons for this. First, options on futures have no coupon payments. In contrast, when exercise of a call (put) option on a bond occurs, the buyer (seller) must compensate the other party for accrued interest. Second, options on bond futures do not suffer from delivery squeezes. In contrast, delivery squeezes on any particular bond issue could occur. Recall that options on bond futures are written on the futures contract, which in turn is written not on one particular bond issue, but rather on a bond having certain properties. Although one bond will always be the cheapest to deliver, if there is a squeeze on that bond, other deliverable bonds would be available. A third reason T-bond option markets have been successful concerns the availability of price information. It is much easier to learn about the price of an underlying bond future than the bond itself. Specifically, the bond futures price is readily available from the last trade, but the actual bond price can only be established by canvassing bond dealers.

USE OF DEBT OPTIONS

Like stock options, debt options provide investors with opportunities to repackage and reallocate risk in ways that were not previously possible. Investors can capitalize on correct market predictions by purchasing calls if they expect rates to decline and purchasing puts if they expect rates to rise. Rather than liquidating bond portfolios when interest rates are projected to increase over the short term, investors can purchase put options as insurance. In general, by meshing interest rate options with the underlying bond, interest rate risk exposure can be altered to fully reflect the preferences of an investor.

Debt options and debt option valuation models have many applications outside the debt option markets. These applications arise because there are a number of interest rate option features embedded in the products and services of many financial institutions. Fixed-income securities with option features include callable and putable bonds, mortgages with prepayment options, installment loans, certificates of deposit with early redemption rights, redeemable insurance contracts, and others. In this section we shall describe a few of these products.

Call and Put Features on Bonds

Bonds are often issued with a call feature, which allows the issuing firm to buy back the bonds at a predetermined price in the future.

Not as common as callable bonds are putable bonds. Such a bond allows the investor to force the company to redeem the bond at a predetermined price at a future date. The value of the call (or put) provision, like any other option, depend on the strike prices, time to expiration, and volatility of interest rates. Reasons for issuing bonds with option features are discussed in Chapter 14.

Savings Accounts with Early Withdrawal Penalties

Consider a bank that provides fixed-interest-rate savings accounts for given time periods. Customers are allowed to withdraw their money early if they are prepared to pay a prestipulated penalty. In the presence of interest rate uncertainty, the early withdrawal feature is a valuable feature to the customer, while the prepayment penalty is a negative feature. The early withdrawal feature provides investors with an option. If interest rates rise above the savings account rate, some investors may choose to exercise their option and withdraw their funds. If one views the savings account as a security that pays coupons, then the holder owns a putable bond. When interest rates rise, the holder will "put" this "bond" on the bank for a strike price equal to the value of the account less a predetermined penalty.

By providing this early withdrawal feature, the bank is essentially writing put options on interest rates. By using an option pricing framework, the bank can establish the cost of providing this service. Moreover, by using the debt option markets to purchase puts, the bank may offset the risk associated with providing this service.

Mortgages

Virtually all mortgages contain provisions that allow homeowners to repay prematurely. This allows homeowners to refinance at better terms or to sell. These options are really call options sold to homeowners by the holders of the mortgages. If interest rates drop substantially, the homeowner will exercise the call to obtain better financing.

Mortgage Origination

Mortgage bankers originate mortgages. During the origination process, a mortgage commitment over a fixed time period is issued to a builder, for example. This commitment is binding to the banker. If interest rates drop in the interim, the builder may go elsewhere for the loan. If interest rates rise, the builder will exercise the option. The mortgage commitment can thus be viewed as a put option. The banker may offset the risk associated with the mortgage commitment by buying a put option.

Interest Rates Caps

In periods of strong economic growth, the yield curve is likely to be upward sloping and some borrowers may choose to load up on cheaper short-term debt. In doing so, however, they take on considerable interest rate risk. In many instances borrowers will be prepared to bear the risk of rising rates, but only if the rates remain below a certain level. Such borrowers may be prepared to pay bankers an upfront fee to place a ceiling on the variable rate. For rates below the ceiling, the loan would remain variable, with the cost of funds fluctuating according to the index on which the loan is priced. However, for rates above the ceiling, the actual rate paid would be treated as the ceiling rate.

Such an agreement splits up the interest rate risk between the two parties, with the borrower retaining the interest rate exposure up to the ceiling and the lender accepting the risk above that level. As the writer of the contract, the bank generates upfront income but bears the risk of lost earnings should the loan rise above the ceiling. In essence, the bank has issued an interest rate put option on the loan. The loan is "put" to the option writer only if the variable interest rate at expiration exceeds the ceiling. The loan is "put" to the option writer only in the sense that it is repriced at expiration and the lender incurs an opportunity cost over the next period equal to the principal times the rate spread.

Example 13.12

Company XYZ has negotiated a five-year, $10 million revolving line of credit. In the first quarter the loan will be priced at the 90-day spot LIBOR, and thereafter repricing will occur in three-, six-, and nine-month intervals at the 90-day LIBOR (London Interbank Offered Rate) then prevailing. Facing a LIBOR yield curve ranging from 9 percent for 90 days to 12 percent for one year, the borrower solicits quotes for an 11 percent cap on the one-year variable rate loan.

In offering this guarantee, the bank has in effect written three consecutive European put options that expire on each of the three repricing dates. At each repricing date the dollar value of the option then expiring is determined by the LIBOR rate prevailing at the time and the cap rate. If after three months LIBOR is 100 basis points above the cap, the value of the option to the borrower will be $5 million $(0.01)(90/360) = \$12,500$.

A European put on a loan priced against LIBOR is equivalent to a European put option on Eurodollar futures. In essence, by providing the cap the bank has issued such options, and so may want to hedge this risk by purchasing put options on Eurodollar futures in the organized market.

Floor–Ceiling Agreements

A floor–ceiling agreement brackets or "collars" the range in which the floating rate instrument can move. If interest rates rise above the ceiling, the borrower effectively obtains financing at the ceiling rate. If interest rates fall below the floor, however, the borrower essentially obtains financing at the floor rate. Floor–ceiling agreements are extensions of cap agreements that allow borrowers and lenders to reallocate the sharing of interest rate risk. The borrower participates in falling rates down to the floor. The lender bears the risk of rates increasing above the ceiling, but is protected from rates dropping below a certain level.

Example 13.13

Firm XYZ has $100 million of five-year debt tied to PRIME, and wants to hedge against interest rate increases. A five-year floor–ceiling agreement has the following terms: the floor is 11.5 percent, the ceiling is 13 percent, and the upfront fee is 3 percent. If the average of PRIME for the previous quarter is greater than the ceiling of 13 percent, the bank will pay the difference between the average PRIME rate and the ceiling. If the average prime rate is between the ceiling and the floor, no payments will be made. Finally, if the average PRIME rate is below the floor, the borrower will pay the bank the difference.

Many large banks will provide a firm with quotes for a specific floor–ceiling agreement drawn up by a potential buyer.

An investor who purchases a floor–ceiling agreement is essentially establishing a put spread. If interest rates drop below the strike price of the written put option, the bank will exercise the option and the investor will be forced to pay at the floor rate, rather than the lower market rate. If interest rates rise high enough, the borrower will exercise the put and pay at the ceiling, rather than the higher market level.

VALUATION OF DEBT OPTIONS

The examples in the previous section have illustrated the importance of being able to value debt options. The dealer of a floor–ceiling arrangement, for example, needs to value the arrangement to set a fee. Moreover, such a dealer needs to know how to effectively hedge the risk incurred by selling such an agreement. This necessitates establishing position delta values for the arrangement. With an option pricing model in hand, the delta values could be computed.

In order to price an option, it is first necessary to specify the statistical process that drives the prices of the underlying security. For stock options this was relatively straightforward because the statistical behavior of stock prices was assumed to remain unchanged over the life of the option. The Black-Scholes model, for example, assumes that the stock price follows a geometric Wiener process with a constant volatility. For debt options, however, the specifications of the statistical process describing bond prices is more complex because the behavior of bond prices may not stay the same over the life of the option. Specifically, as a bond gets closer to maturity, its price becomes more predictable as it converges towards its face value. The volatility of a bond, however, does not depend only on maturity. High-coupon bonds, for example, may be more predictable than low-coupon bonds of the same maturity because high-coupon bonds pay back more of their value earlier, and hence effectively are shorter-term instruments.

In order to analyze bond prices over time, it is necessary to investigate how the entire yield curve changes over time. This analysis is necessary since a coupon bond can be viewed as a portfolio of discount bonds where the value of each discount bond depends on the discount rates drawn from the yield curve.

There are many ways of representing the stochastic process generating bond prices. Some approaches assume that bond prices are affected by movements in the short-term rate. When the short-term rate rises, it not only affects the price of short-term bonds, but also provides a signal that rates are likely to be higher in the future. Therefore, the prices of all maturities are affected. Such models are referred to as *one-state models* since changes in bond prices are assumed to arise solely from the change in the state of short-term rates. The most common model requires that short-term rates have lognormal distributions.

Brennan and Schwartz model bond prices around two interest rates, rather than one. Specifically, they use a short-term rate and a long-term rate. Their model assumes that the short- and long-term rates are bivariate lognormally distributed. In their model, bond prices of all maturities change in response to changes in these two rates. Other two-state variable models have been proposed. For example, Richard has proposed a model that uses an inflation rate as the second variable, while Cox, Ingersoll, and Ross have proposed a model using the market portfolio. Although these models have a richer structure than the one-state model, more empirical research is required to specify and test their detailed structures.

The one-state geometric Wiener process representation of interest rates is not the only one-state process that has been examined. Brennan and Schwartz, Vasicek, and Cox, Ingersoll, and Ross have postulated other representations that include additional parameters. One common assumption is that the short-term interest rate is set up so that it tends to revert back to some natural rate. These processes, called *mean reverting processes,* are characterized by parameters that dictate the speed of adjustment.

In the analysis that follows, we shall assume short-term interest rates follow a binomial process. By suitably defining the up and down parameters together with their probabilities, this model can be made to converge into a variety of interest rate statistical processes. Such a model was first discussed by Rendleman and Bartter. The binomial model will illustrate the problems of debt option valuation.

Binomial Representation of Interest Rates

Assume that in each period the interest rate changes to one of two possible values. To simplify the exposition, we shall assume that the rates of changes are the same for all periods.

Let Z_i = the change in the ith period.
Then

$$Z_i = u \text{ with probability } p$$
$$= d \text{ with probability } q (q = 1 - p).$$

(13.4)

Let r_n be the interest rate after n periods. Then r_n can take on one of $n + 1$ possible values. Let r_{nj} be the actual interest rate in period n, given that j increases and $n - j$ decreases in interest rates have occurred.

Then

$$\tilde{r}_n = \left(\sum_{i=1}^{n} \tilde{Z}_i \right) r_0 \tag{13.5}$$

and

$$r_{nj} = u^j d^{n-j} r_0 \quad \text{for } j = 0, 1, 2, \ldots n. \tag{13.6}$$

Since interest rates follow a binomial process, we have

$$P(\tilde{r}_n = r_{nj}) = \binom{n}{j} p^j q^{n-j}. \tag{13.7}$$

The process can be represented as follows:

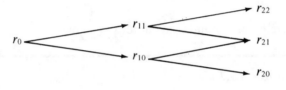

Representation of Bond Prices

Given the interest rate behavior over time, the bond price evolution must be established. In order to achieve this, let B_0 represent the current bond price. As the interest rates change, bond prices adjust. Let B_n be the bond price after n periods. B_n is a random variable that can take on any one of $n + 1$ possible values. Let B_{nj} represent the bond price if the interest rate in period n is r_{nj}. Since bond buyers pay the sellers the accrued coupon interest from the last payment date to the time of purchase, the coupon payment can be divided into equivalent payments per period. For example, if $100 of interest is paid per year and the year is broken into 50 intervals, a coupon payment of $2 per period is appropriate.

The pattern of possible bond prices is illustrated below:

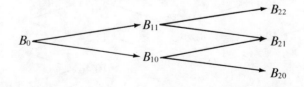

To translate the interest rate tree into a bond price tree requires the specification of a theory of the term structure of interest rates. Two cases are considered.

The Expectations Hypothesis   Under one version of the expectations hypothesis, a bond price is set such that its expected return over the next interval does not depend on maturity or coupon values. That is, in any period the expected return should be the same as that of a default-free discount bond maturing in the next period. To obtain these bond prices, consider period t. The bond price is $B_{t,j}$ and in the next time period can either change in value to $B_{t+1,j+1}$ (if rates rise) or to $B_{t+1,j}$ (if rates fall).

Note that when interest rates rise, bond prices fall. Hence $B_{t+1,j+1}$ is lower than $B_{t+1,j}$. Let p be the probability that rates increase. Then under the expectations hypothesis, the bond price $B_{t,j}$ is related to future bond prices by the equation

$$B_{t,j} = \frac{[pB_{t+1,j+1} + qB_{t+1,j} + c]}{(1 + r_{t,j})} \qquad (13.9)$$

where c is the coupon payout for the period.

Example 13.14

Consider a five-year bond with a face value of $1000 with a 10 percent annual coupon. Let the number of periods = 5, r_0 = 11.25 percent, B_0 = 935.2451, u = 1.076, and d = 0.976. Exhibits 13.11 and 13.12 illustrate the interest rate and bond price trees, respectively.

EXHIBIT 13.11
Interest Rate Tree*

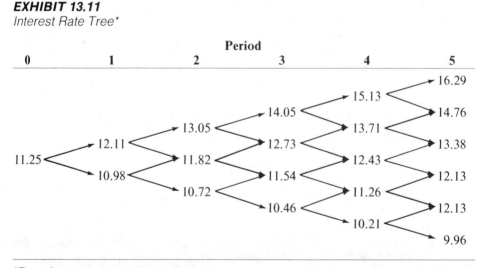

*Data shown represents percentages.

EXHIBIT 13.12
Bond Price Tree

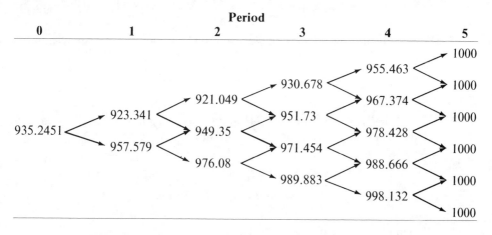

Constant Short-Term Risk Adjusted Return Model   Under the expectations hypothesis, there is no premium for bearing interest rate risk and all
bonds, regardless of maturity, are expected to earn the same return. An
alternative assumption is to price all bonds so that they provide the same
risk-adjusted short-term return. Specifically, let $E(r_B)$ be the expected short-
term return on the bond, and let $\sigma(r_B)$ be the volatility of the return. Under this
assumption, all bonds will be priced such that

$$\frac{[E(r_B) - r]}{\sigma(r_B)} = \lambda \tag{13.10}$$

where λ is a constant across all bonds and is referred to as the market price of
risk.

To understand the idea, reconsider the binomial model, where in period
t we have

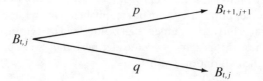

Then

$$E(r_B) = \frac{[(B_{t+1,j+1})p + (B_{t,j})q + c - B_{t,j}]}{B_{t,j}}. \tag{13.11}$$

To compute the variance, recall that

$$\text{Var}(r_B) = E(r_B^2) - E(r_B)^2. \tag{13.12}$$

Now

$$E(r_B^2) = \frac{[(B_{t+1,j+1} + c)^2 p + (B_{t+1,j} + c)^2 q]}{B_{t,j}^2}. \tag{13.13}$$

Substituting (13.11) and (13.13) into (13.12) and simplifying yields

$$\text{Var}(r_B) = \frac{qp(B_{t+1,j+1} - B_{t+1,j})^2}{B_{t,j}^2}. \tag{13.14}$$

Finally, substituting (13.11) and (13.14) into (13.10) and recognizing that the current interest rate r is $r_{t,j}$, we have

$$\frac{[(B_{t+1,j+1})p + (B_{t+1,j})q + c - B_{t,j} - r_{t,j}B_{t,j}]}{\sqrt{pq}(B_{t+1,j+1} - B_{t+1,j})} = \lambda. \tag{13.15}$$

Solving for $B_{t,j}$ we obtain

$$B_{t,j} = \frac{B_{t+1,j+1}(p - \lambda\sqrt{pq}) + B_{t+1,j}(q - \lambda\sqrt{pq}) + c}{(1 + r_{t,j})}. \tag{13.16}$$

Note that if $\lambda = 0$, equation (13.16) reduces to equation (13.9), which is the bond equation derived under the expectations hypothesis. For different values of the price of risk, λ, different bond trees will be obtained.

The example emphasizes the fact that the conversion of an interest rate tree to a bond price tree requires assumptions on investors' behavior. Note, too, that the current bond price is an output of the model. In reality, however, the bond price is observable. Hence, the up and down parameters, together with their probabilities and the price of risk, must be chosen so that the output value equals the deserved price. This issue is discussed later.

Call Pricing

Given the interest rate tree, together with a theory of the term structure, the evolution of bond prices can be established. Given these bond prices, the usual binomial arbitrage argument can be invoked to obtain a price for call options. To see how this is achieved, consider period T. At expiration in the period ($T < M$), the call option is worth

$$C_{T,j} = \text{Max}(0, B_{T,j} - X).$$

Note that if the call is exercised, the buyer receives a bond worth $B_{T,j}$ (for some j) for the exercise price plus a coupon payment, c. This coupon payment is the accrued interest owed to the bond seller.

Now consider an arbitrary period t, when the bond price is $B_{t,j}$, the interest rate $r_{t,j}$, and the unknown price $C_{t,j}$. See Exhibit 13.13. Given that $C_{t+1,j+1}$ and $C_{t+1,j}$ are known, the call price, $C_{t,j}$, can be computed.

EXHIBIT 13.13
Notations for Interest Rates and Bond and Call Prices

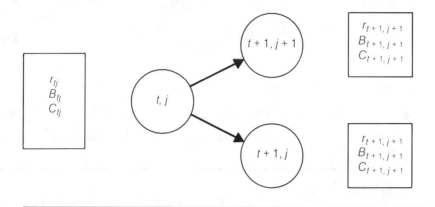

In order to do this, consider a portfolio containing a long position in the bond and a short position in $X_{t,j}$ calls. The current value, $V_{t,j}$, of this portfolio is

$$V_{t,j} = B_{t,j} - X_{t,j}C_{t,j}. \tag{13.17}$$

If the interest rates rise, the portfolio value $V_{t+1,j+1}$ will be given by

$$V_{t+1,j+1} = B_{t+1,j+1} - X_{t,j}C_{t+1,j+1} + c \tag{13.18}$$

whereas, if interest rates fall, the portfolio value $V_{t+1,j}$ will be

$$V_{t+1,j} = B_{t+1,j} - X_{t,j}C_{t+1,j} + c. \tag{13.19}$$

For this portfolio to be riskless, regardless of interest rate movements, the value $V_{t+1,j+1}$ must equal $V_{t+1,j}$. Equating the two expressions and solving for $X_{t,j}$, we obtain

$$X_{t,j} = \frac{B_{t+1,j+1} - B_{t+1,j}}{C_{t+1,j+1} - C_{t+1,j}}. \tag{13.20}$$

Since this portfolio is riskless, to avoid "arbitrage opportunities," it should earn the same return as a full investment in the bond. That is,

$$(1 + r_{t,j})V_{t,j} = V_{t+1,j} = V_{t+1,j+1}$$

or

$$(1 + r_{t,j})(B_{t,j} - X_{t,j}C_{t,j}) = B_{t+1,j} - X_{t,j}C_{t+1,j} + c. \tag{13.21}$$

After substituting for $X_{t,j}$ in this equation and rearranging, we obtain an expression for the call price, $C_{t,j}$, in terms of its future value $C_{t+1,j}$ and $C_{t+1,j+1}$.

Specifically,

$$C_{t,j} = \frac{[\theta C_{t+1,j+1} + (1 - \theta)C_{t+1,j}]}{(1 + r_{t,j})} \qquad (13.22)$$

where

$$\theta = \frac{B_{t+1,j+1} - B_{t,j}(1 + r_{t,j})}{(B_{t+1,j} - B_{t+1,j+1})}. \qquad (13.23)$$

To obtain the call prices, we start at the expiration date, T, at which time the value of the option is

$$C_{T,j} = \text{Max}(0, B_{T,j} - X) \qquad j = 0, 1, 2, \ldots T \qquad (13.24)$$

where X is the strike price of the option, and work backwards using equation (13.22).

Example 13.15

Consider the five-period bond in the previous example. Assume a call option on this bond was available. The option has a strike of 975 and expires after four periods. Exhibit 13.14 illustrates the call and bond price tree.

EXHIBIT 13.14
Call and Bond Price Tree

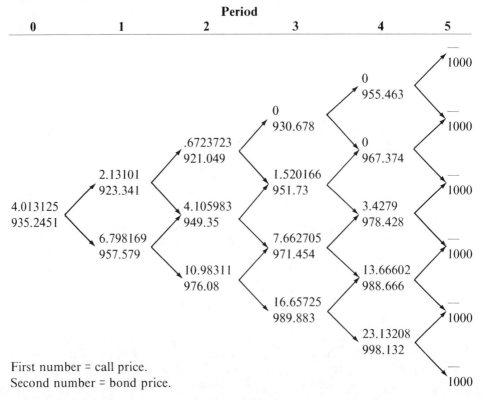

First number = call price.
Second number = bond price.

Unlike the stock option pricing model, the debt binomial option model depends on preferences. These preferences enter the pricing equation because a term structure theory is required to translate rates into bond prices. The option prices developed in the example were based on the expectations theory.

Limiting Behavior of Interest Rates

As the width of each interest rate period is narrowed, the values of the up and down parameters must adjust. We shall assume that the probabilities associated with the up and down movements remain stable through time.

Recall that

$$r_n = \left(\prod_{i=1}^{n} z_i \right) r_0.$$

Hence,

$$\frac{r_n}{r_0} = \prod_{i=1}^{n} z_i.$$

Let ρ_n be the logarithm of the interest rate ratio over n periods. Then

$$\rho_n = \ln\left(\frac{r_n}{r_0}\right) = \sum_{i=1}^{n} \ln(z_i) = \sum_{i=1}^{n} V_i \qquad (13.25)$$

where

$$V_i = a = \ln(u) \text{ with probability } p \qquad (13.26)$$
$$= b = \ln(d) \text{ with probability } q \ (q = 1 - p).$$

Moreover, the expected logarithm of the interest rate ratio, say μ_n, is given by

$$\mu_n = E\left(\sum_{i=1}^{n} V_i\right) = nE(V_i) \qquad (13.27)$$

and the variance, σ_n^2 say, is

$$\sigma_n^2 = \mathrm{Var}\left(\sum_{i=1}^{n} V_i\right) = \sum_{i=1}^{n} \mathrm{Var}(V_i) = n\mathrm{Var}(V_i). \qquad (13.28)$$

Now the expected value and variance of V_i are given by

$$E(V_i) = ap + bq = p(a - b) + b \qquad (13.29)$$

$$\mathrm{Var}(V_i) = E(V_i^2) - E(V_i)^2$$

$$= a^2 p + b^2 q - (ap + bq)^2$$

$$= (a - b)^2 pq. \qquad (13.30)$$

Hence, after n periods,

$$\mu_n = np(a - b) + nb, \tag{13.31}$$

$$\sigma_n^2 = n(a - b)^2 pq. \tag{13.32}$$

As the number of intervals in the time period is increased, the distribution will converge onto a normal distribution. By specifying values for μ_n and σ_n^2 and p, one can solve equations (13.31) and (13.32) for a and b. The solution is

$$a = \frac{\mu_n}{n} + q\left(\frac{\sigma_n^2}{npq}\right)^{1/2} \tag{13.33}$$

$$b = \frac{\mu_n}{n} - p\left(\frac{\sigma_n^2}{npq}\right)^{1/2} \tag{13.34}$$

and hence the up and down parameters are

$$u = \exp(a), d = \exp(b).$$

Example 13.16

Reconsider Example 13.14. Assume equations (13.33) and (13.34) are to be used to set the up and down parameters. By using historical data on short-term rates, estimates of the mean logarithmic ratio and the standard deviation of the logarithmic ratio can be obtained. Specifically, assume the return data consist of the returns constructed from weekly Treasury bill auctions. The mean and standard deviation of the logarithmic ratios are, for example,

$$\hat{\mu}_n = 0.1242, \text{ and } \hat{\sigma}_n^2 = 0.0121.$$

With $p = 0.5$, equations (13.33) and (13.34) yield $u = 1.076$ and $d = 0.976$. In practice, the volatility of interest rates might be more stable than the mean. That is, the estimate $\hat{\sigma}_n^2 = 0.0121$ may be somewhat reasonable, but the estimate $\hat{\mu}_n = 0.1242$ may be a poor predictor of future expectations. By using different values for $\hat{\mu}_n$ in equations (13.33) and (13.34), different interest rates and bond price trees can be established. Indeed, it seems quite reasonable to specify a value for $\hat{\mu}_n$ that equates the theoretical bond price to the actual observed price.

Unlike the stock option pricing model, debt options priced using this approach will depend on means as well as volatilities. As one would expect, bond prices vary inversely with the expected direction of interest rates and the standard deviation. Furthermore, since the prices of bonds are established in accordance with preference assumptions, the option prices generated are not preference free.

In summary, then, the binomial model for debt options is much more problematic than the binomial model for stock options. While the debt binomial option pricing model can be used to price options, these prices will be sensitive to the assumptions placed on investor preferences, and expectation terms as well as the volatility term will enter the pricing equation.

OTHER DEBT OPTION PRICING MODELS*

In this section we briefly describe three debt option pricing models.

The Courtadon Debt Option Pricing Model*

In order to obtain option prices, it is necessary to derive a valuation equation for default-free bonds. According to the one-state model, the market price of a bond can be written as a function of the current short-term rate of interest and time. Several researchers have attempted to value the bond by applying the Black and Scholes arbitrage technique. This technique involves constructing a hedged portfolio of two bonds with different maturities in such a way that the portfolio is instantaneously risk free. Since the hedged portfolio is free of risk, it must earn the current instantaneously risk-free rate of return.

Unfortunately, there is a problem with this approach. Specifically, the differential equations that are obtained depend on preferences. Hence, a further assumption is needed to obtain a solution. One possibility, for example, would be to assume risk neutrality. The assumption that is often used is based on a continuous time version of the capital asset pricing model with logarithmic utility of consumption. According to this model, individuals attempt to maximize an expected time additive utility function of the form

$$\int_t^T x(t)\ell n c(t)dt$$

where $x(t)$ is a continuous function and $c(t)$ is the consumption of goods and services as a function of time. This model essentially identifies the risk premium/standard deviation ratio, λ, as a constant. Depending on the assumptions placed on the behavior of the short-term interest rate, this arbitrage approach can be used to provide specific preference-dependent bond prices.

Using this arbitrage approach. Courtadon obtained a system of equations and boundary conditions for options on default-free bonds. Courtadon assumes the nominal rate of interest obeys the following mean reverting process

$$dr = -\gamma(\alpha - r)dt + \beta r dw.$$

α is defined as the normal rate of interest, γ is the speed of adjustment, and the variance rate of interest is $\beta^2 r^2$.

Although no closed-form solution exists for Courtadon's model, he does present numerical methods for obtaining call prices.

The Courtadon call option price increases with time to expiration and with the rate of variance and decreases as the strike price increases. The price is a nonincreasing function of the instantaneous rate of interest and the average rate of interest over time. To see this property, note that increasing interest rates make bond prices decline and hence should reduce call prices. Thus, unlike stock options, options on bonds depend on means. Finally, the Courtadon option price is a nondecreasing function of the coupon on the underlying bond. At first glance this may appear surprising. Recall that for stock options, increasing the dividend payment could have a negative influence on the call premium. Here increasing the coupon payment has the opposite effect. The reason this occurs stems from the preference assumptions. Specifically, the bond prices were established so that higher coupon bonds would imply higher bond prices. As a result, call prices increase.

The Brennan-Schwartz Model*

Brennan and Schwartz extended the Courtadon model by assuming that the price of any default-free bond depends not only on short-term rates and time to maturity, but also on long-term or consol rates. Using the Black-Scholes argument, they first constructed a hedged portfolio that was instantaneously free of risk. Then by placing assumptions on preferences, they established a differential equation describing the behavior of bond prices over time. This equation, together with appropriate boundary conditions, can be solved numerically to obtain equilibrium prices for bonds. Given this bond pricing equation, option prices could then be established using similar arguments. If the mean and variance of the long-term rates were forced to zero, the model would reduce to the Courtadon model.

The Black-Scholes model can also be obtained as a special case. Specifically, if the short-term rate is assumed constant and the underlying discount bond is of perpetual maturity, then the Brennan-Schwartz model collapses to the Black-Scholes model. From a practical point of view, this suggests that the use of the Black-Scholes model to price options on long-term default-free discount bonds may be valid. Such a result is not surprising since such bonds should display a relatively stable volatility over the life of the option.

The Ball-Torous Debt Option Pricing Model*

Rather than assume the underlying state variable to be the rate of interest, Ball and Torous chose the state variable to be the price of the bond itself. In particular, they considered the statistical process dynamics of a default-free bond price as it converged towards its face value. Specifically, they postulated that this process is a Brownian bridge process. A Brownian bridge process results when the Wiener process is conditioned to take on a particular value at a particular point in time. In this case, the condition is that the price of the bond must equal its face value at maturity. Given this process, Ball and Torous established a preference-free, closed-form solution for an European call option. Preferences no longer are required because the statistical evolution of the bond prices is directly postulated.

INTEREST RATE SWAPS (INTEREST EXCHANGE AGREEMENTS)*

Options and futures on debt instruments are not the only financial instruments that can be used to hedge interest rate risk. Of growing importance are interest rate swaps. Swaps were initially developed in 1981 and have rapidly increased in importance. It is difficult to estimate the volume of swaps, since they are off-balance sheet transactions which, at this time, do not have to be disclosed. Estimates range anywhere from $50 billion to $500 billion of notional principal. In this section we shall briefly discuss interest rate swaps and investigate option contracts that are often associated with them.

An *interest rate swap* is an agreement between two parties to exchange interest payments on a specified amount of principal on agreed payment dates for a specified period of time. The specified amount of principal is referred to as the *notional principal amount*.

There are four major components of a swap: the notional principal amount, the interest rates for each party, the term of the swap, and the timing of the swap payments. A typical swap in swap jargon might be $20 million, two-year, pay fixed, receive variable, semi. Translated, this swap would be for $20 million, where one party would pay a fixed interest rate payment every six months based on $20 million and the counterparty would pay a variable rate payment every six months based on $20 million.

The variable-rate payment is based on a specific short-term interest rate index. The most common variable rate indices used are six-month LIBOR and three-month U.S. Treasury bill bond equivalent yield. Other indices used include New York secondary certificates of deposit, prime, federal funds, and commercial paper. The time period specified by the variable rate index usually dictates the timing of swap payments. For example, a swap that is fixed versus six-month LIBOR would have semiannual interest payments, whereas a swap against three-month Treasury bills would have quarterly exchanges. With most LIBOR rate swaps the rate is set at the beginning of the period and paid at the end. With most T-bill swaps, the variable-rate payment is based on the average of the Treasury auction rates during the period.

The fixed rate for a swap is set on the day the swap agreement is made. The fixed rate is usually quoted as some spread over the U.S. Treasury security yield. The U.S. Treasury security used will have a maturity that corresponds to the terms of the swap. For example, the fixed rate for a three-year swap will be quoted as a spread in basis points over the yield of the current three-year U.S. Treasury note. If the three-year U.S. Treasury note is yielding 10.25 percent and the swap is quoted at three years plus 0.75 percent, then the fixed rate would be 11 percent.

The fixed rate is fixed for the term of the swap. Regardless of where interest rates go during the term of the swap, the size of the fixed-rate payments will not change. In contrast, the variable payments will vary with interest rate behavior. At each payment date, the two parties net out their payments, with one party receiving the difference.

The first interest rate swaps had a minimum notional principal amount of $100 million. Progressively, the average size of swaps have decreased to $50 million, $25 million, and now some as small as $10 million. Indeed, some swap dealers may create swap positions with notional principal amounts of $1 million.

The most common swap maturities are one, two, three, five, seven, or ten years. Interest rate payments can be annual, semiannual, quarterly, or even monthly. In some swaps, interest rate payments may not be swapped simultaneously. For instance, one party may make an interest payment annually, while the counterparty makes interest payments semiannually.

To illustrate the mechanics of a swap, consider two companies, A and B. Suppose A is a high-credit corporation that could issue long-term debt at 11 percent and short-term debt at 25 basis points above LIBOR. Suppose B is a low-credit company that finds it difficult to issue long-term debt but has access to short-term credit facilities. Specifically, B can raise long-term debt at 12 1/2 percent and short-term debt at 50 basis points above LIBOR. We assume that A requires short-term financing and B long-term. Exhibit 13.15 illustrates the situation if no swap exists.

EXHIBIT 13.15
Initial Cost of Funds: No Swap

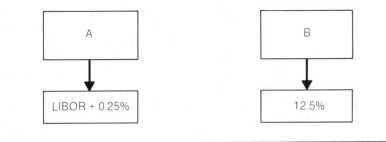

Note that there is a 25-basis-point differential between the two firms' short-term rates and a 150-basis-point spread between the long-term rates. Through a swap, both companies can maximize their relative economic advantage in one market and transfer that advantage to another market. Specifically, to exploit the difference in rates, A could issue bonds at 11 percent. B would then agree to cover the interest rate obligations to the long-term bondholders. Thus, B becomes the fixed-rate payer at 11 percent. Meanwhile, B issues short-term debt at LIBOR + 1/2, and A agrees to cover this obligation by paying B LIBOR – 1/4, say. Exhibit 13.16 illustrates the net effect.

EXHIBIT 13.16
Net Effect of a Swap

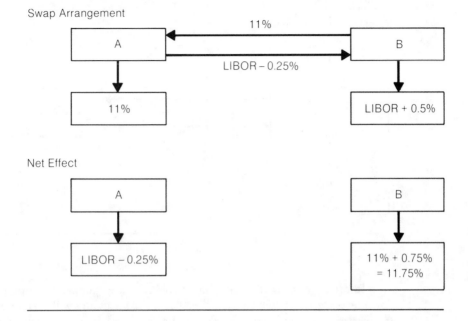

Swap Arrangement

Net Effect

The net effect of this swap is that both A and B are borrowing funds at rates more favorable than they could have obtained otherwise.

Examples of Swaps

We shall consider four examples of swaps.

A thrift institution can convert its short-term liabilities, such as money market accounts, into long-term liabilities to match the maturities of its long-term assets, mortgages, by employing a swap. Exhibit 13.17 illustrates the swap arrangement.

Consider an insurance company that has invested in a short-term instrument that earns six-month LIBOR + 1/8 percent. The company negotiates a swap whereby it receives a fixed interest payment of 12 percent, say, and in turn pays the counterparty six-month LIBOR. Since the insurance company is earning six-month LIBOR + 1/8 percent but paying only six-month LIBOR to its counterparty, it is locking in a return of 12 1/8 percent for the term of the swap. Note that, in order to earn the additional return, the insurance company is taking on some additional risk. This risk is the default risk of the counterparty.

EXHIBIT 13.17
Thrift's Use of a Swap

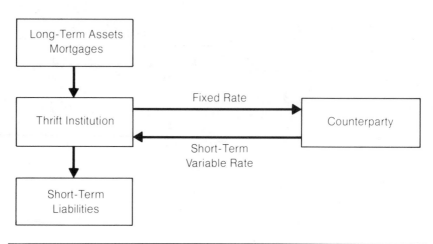

Short-term swaps of less than two years are gaining in popularity. Consider a speculator who anticipates that short-term rates will decline. Such an investor could enter a one-year swap that receives a fixed payment, such as 9.5 percent, in return for three quarterly payments based on a short-term variable index, such as three-month U.S. Treasury bills. Note that in this swap, the fixed payment is made only once, at the maturity date of the swap, while the variable rate is paid quarterly (Exhibit 13.18). Specifically, the speculator may pay the three-month weekly average T-bill bond equivalent yield quarterly in return for a 9.5 percent fixed-interest-rate payment on the maturity date of swap.

Not all swaps involve exchanging fixed with variable rates. Many short-term swaps exchange one variable rate for another. As an example, one party may pay six-month LIBOR semiannually in return for receiving three-month commercial paper quarterly for a year.

EXHIBIT 13.18
Speculator's Use of a Swap

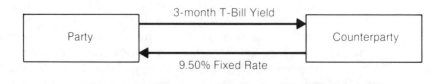

Valuation of Interest Rate Swaps

Since a swap provides the fixed-rate payer with an obligation to receive a stream of variable cash flows in the future for a stream of fixed payments, it can be viewed as a series of forward contracts. The delivery dates of each forward contract coincide with the exchange-of-payment dates. The holder of the forward contract pays a fixed fee in exchange for a variable cash amount. The valuation of the interest rate swap thus may seem similar to the valuation of a portfolio of forward contracts. Unfortunately, this analysis is not completely correct because of default risk. If the counterparty defaults, not only is one forward contract voided, but the entire sequence is voided. Swap agreements must be viewed as an exchange of interest rate risks for credit and basis risks. Indeed, if one evaluated a fixed-versus-variable-rate swap based on interest rate spreads alone, very few swaps would be done. In 1985 five-year fixed-rate swaps against receipt of six-month LIBOR were accomplished at the five-year Treasury yield plus 0.7 percent. At that time it would have been difficult to find a party who felt that six-month rates would exceed the five-year Treasury plus 0.7 percent for the next five years. Obviously there must have been other reasons for doing the swap. Those reasons involve the asset liability structures of the two counterparties. One party may have been willing to pay 0.7 percent over the five-year Treasury because its alternative cost for five-year fixed funds was 1.0 percent over Treasury. The party may have wanted to receive six-month LIBOR payments since its actual short-term financing costs were approximately six-month LIBOR.

Swaps must be evaluated in terms of a party's total financial structure, rather than as isolated transactions. Clearly, the best matches for swaps are firms that face two very different yield curves. In such instances, the interest rate swap can be viewed as an exchange of interest rate risk for credit and basis risk.

Market for Swaps

Unlike futures, which trade on an organized exchange, interest rate swaps are private deals. Most swap participants act through swap dealers or brokers. Brokers merely bring two counterparties together for a fee. A dealer, such as an investment bank or money center commercial bank, may act in a broker role and find a swap counterparty or may act as a principal (counterparty) in the swap.

Swaps began as individualized financial products structured to fit existing assets or liabilities in terms of interest rate indices, maturities, and payment exchange dates. There has been a strong movement to standardize swaps so that they can trade as commodities in a manner similar to government securities. However, it is uncertain whether such a market will develop. Currently a lower-credit company must pay a higher swap spread than it would if it were rated higher. If swaps were standardized, lower-credit companies might have to put up more collateral than higher-credit companies. In this case the net advantage of the swap would disappear. To reiterate, swaps exchange interest rate risk for credit and basis risk.

Hedging Interest Rate Swaps

When a party enters into a swap arrangement to hedge a specific asset or liability, there is always the risk that the counterparty will default leaving the first party with an unmatched asset or liability. The first party must then find a replacement for the counterparty. If interest rates have risen and swap spreads have not narrowed, the newer swap will be at a higher cost. If interest rates have fallen, however, the nondefaulting party will benefit. As a result, the first party would like to purchase insurance only against interest rate increases. Ideally, then, put options on the underlying Treasury bond would provide the appropriate insurance mechanism. In some cases, a dealer may be prepared to sell the party such an option. The alternative would be to use options on Treasury bond futures. One problem with using such options is the underlying Treasury bond corresponds to a longer-term bond. Hence, an analysis must be done to determine the relationship between the futures on the Treasury bond and the Treasury bond corresponding to the maturity of the swap.

Rather than hedge the swap, some swap parties may require that the swaps be "marked to market." That is, the "replacement" swap is repriced periodically. If interest rates rise, the first party can require that the counterparty put up collateral to reflect the additional cost of replacing the swap.

Interest Rate Swap Options

An *initialization interest rate swap option* is an option granted by a dealer that gives the party the right to initiate a swap anytime in the next 90 days with the current Treasury yield locked in. The swap spread that is added will, however, be determined by the market spread that day. A variant of this swap is to lock in the spread during the 90-day period but allow the Treasury yield to fluctuate.

Occasionally a dealer will offer a true swap option. This contract gives the party the right to be the fixed-rate payer (or variable-rate payer) with the fixed rate specified. This option will last for a fixed time period (usually 90 days). Dealers that issue such options bear the risk that the Treasury rate over the next 90 days will increase. To offset this risk, dealers may purchase put options on the specific Treasuries on which the swaps are priced.

CONCLUSION

This chapter has investigated a few financial contracts that can be used to hedge interest rate risk. These contracts include options and futures. While active markets are maintained in some of these markets, some investors may require tailor-made contracts. Such contracts can be negotiated with dealers. A variety of specialized contracts have been issued. Floor–ceiling agreements, for example, allow the borrower and lender to share the interest rate exposures. Other types of contracts, such as interest rate caps, provide borrowers with ceilings on interest rate payments.

Debt option features are embedded in the products and services provided by many institutions. Examples of these products and services have been provided. Valuation of these services is important for institutions. Thus, debt option pricing models are very important. Unfortunately, debt option pricing is complex because the behavior of bond prices over the lifetime of an option may change. Modeling option prices requires a theory of the term structure of interest rates. Given a process describing bond prices, the usual arbitrage approaches are available.

The binomial model illustrates some of the valuation problems. The Courtadon and Brennan-Schwartz models are preference dependent and require numerical methods for obtaining actual prices. Unfortunately, all these models require more inputs (that are not directly observable) than the stock option pricing model. For short-term options on long-term bonds, the use of the Black-Scholes model may be valid because the statistical process describing the bond behavior over the relatively short life of the option may be stable. Moreover, this model is a special case of the Brennan-Schwartz model. For options on short-term bonds, however, the Black-Scholes model is not appropriate and alternative methods must be used.

The final section of this chapter described interest rate swaps and options on interest rate swaps. Such contracts are intended as longer-term hedging devices. Usually swaps have terms of two to seven years, which is much longer than financial contracts such as options and futures. Swaps can be viewed as sequences of forward contracts. Default risk is a possibility and can be partially hedged by using put options on Treasury-bond futures. Dealers of swaps may provide investors with certain option-like terms. The most common feature allows the user to enter a swap at any point in time (prior to 90 days), with the Treasury rate determined but the spread above Treasury set by the market at the time of exercise.

Swaps, floor–ceiling arrangements, caps, futures, and debt options can all help hedge or alter interest rate risks. More products are likely to be introduced in response to the great demand for financial products that alter interest rate exposures.

References

Winning the Interest Rate Game: A Guide to Debt Options consists of a series of articles that explain the fundamentals for understanding debt options and debt options strategies. In addition, it provides applications of debt options for banks and thrifts, life insurance companies, and fixed-income portfolios. The original binomial debt option pricing model was developed by Rendleman and Bartter. Arbitrage models for the term structure of interest rates have been proposed by Brennan and Schwartz; Richard; Vasicek; and Cox, Ingersoll, and Ross. Once the term structure is established, bonds and options can be priced. Option pricing models developed by Courtadon; Cox, Ingersoll, and Ross; Brennan and Schwartz; and Ball and Torous are referenced. Some practical problems in pricing debt options are well discussed by Rendleman and by Madansky. A few applications of option pricing in assessing the risk of bank loan portfolios and pricing loan guarantees are provided. Many more references are provided in Chapter 14. For discussions of interest rate swaps, see Bennett, Cohen, and McNulty; and Arnold and Smith.

Arnold, T. "How to Do Interest Rate Swaps." *Harvard Business Review* (September 1984): 96–102.

Ball, C., and W. Torous. "Bond Price Dynamics and Options." *Journal of Financial and Quantitative Analysis* 18(December 1983): 517–31.

Bartter, B., and R. Rendleman, Jr. "Fee-Based Pricing of Fixed-Rate Bank Loan Commitments." *Financial Management* (Spring 1979): 13–20.

Belongia, M., and T. Gregory. *Are Options on Treasury Bond Futures Priced Efficiently?* St. Louis: Federal Reserve Bank of St. Louis, 1984, pp. 5–13.

Bennett, D., D. Cohen, and J. McNulty. "Interest Rate Swaps and the Management of Interest Rate Risk." Paper presented at the Annual Meeting of the Financial Management Association, Toronto, 1984.

Black, F., and M. Scholes. "The Pricing of Options and Corporate Liabilities." *Journal of Political Economy* (May–June 1973): 399–417.

Brealey, R., S. Hodges, and M. Selby. "The Risk of Bank Loan Portfolios." In *Option Pricing*, edited by M. Brenner. Lexington, Mass.: D. C. Heath, 1983, pp. 153–82.

Brennan, M., and E. Schwartz. "A Continuous Time Approach to the Pricing of Bonds." *Journal of Banking and Finance* 3(1979): 133–55.

Brennan, M., and E. Schwartz. "Alternative Methods for Valuing Debt Options." Working Paper 888, University of British Columbia, Vancouver, B.C., 1982.

Brennan, M., and E. Schwartz. "An Equilibrium Model of Bond Pricing and a Test of Market Efficiency." *Journal of Financial and Quantitative Analysis* 17(September 1982): 301–29.

Brennan, M., and E. Schwartz. "Conditional Predictions of Bond Prices and Returns." *Journal of Finance* (May 1980): 405–17.

Brennan, M., and E. Schwartz. "Savings Bonds, Retractable Bonds and Callable Bonds." *Journal of Financial Economics* (August 1977): 67–88.

Courtadon, G. "The Pricing of Options on Default-Free Bonds." *Journal of Financial and Quantitative Analysis* (March 1982): 75–100.

Cox, J., J. Ingersoll, Jr., and S. Ross. "A Reexamination of Traditional Hypotheses About the Term Structure of Interest Rates." *Journal of Finance* (September 1981): 769–99.

Cox, J., J. Ingersoll, and S. Ross. "An Analysis of Variable Rate Loan Contracts." *Journal of Finance* 35(May 1980): 389–404.

Dothan, U. "On the Term Structure of Interest Rates." *Journal of Financial Economics* (March 1978): 59–69.

Faboozi, F. *Winning the Interest Rate Game: A Guide to Debt Options.* Chicago: Probus, 1985.

Garman, M. "The Duration of Option Portfolios." *Journal of Financial Economics* 14(1985): 309–15.

Jones, P., and S. Mason. "Valuation of Loan Guarantees." *Journal of Banking and Finance* 4(March 1980): 89–107.

Madansky, A. "Debt Options." Paper presented to the Institute for Quantitative Research in Finance, October 1982.

Marsh, T., and E. Rosenfeld, "Stochastic Processes for Interest Rates and Equilibrium Bond Prices." *Journal of Finance* 38(May 1983): 635–50.

Merton, R. "An Analytic Deviation of the Cost of Deposit Insurance and Loan Guarantees: An Application of Modern Option Pricing Theory." *Journal of Banking and Finance* 1(June 1977): 3–11.

Rendleman, R., and B. Bartter. "The Pricing of Options on Debt Securities." *Journal of Financial and Quantitative Analysis* (March 1980): 11–24.

Rendleman., R. "Some Practical Problems in Pricing Debt Options." Working Paper, Fugue School of Business, Duke University, August 1982.

Richard, S. "An Arbitrage Model of the Term Structure of Interest Rates." *Journal of Financial Economics* (March 1978): 33–58.

Smith, C. "Applications of Option Pricing Analysis." In *Handbook of Financial Economics,* edited by J. Bicksler. New York: North Holland Publishing Company, 1979, pp. 79–121.

Smith, D. "Consider an Interest Rate Swap." *Journal of Cash Management* (October 1983): 29–34.

Vasicek, O. "An Equilibrium Characterization of the Term Structure." *Journal of Financial Economics* (November 1977): 177–88.

Exercises

1. Consider a 13-week, $10,000-face-value T-bill with an asked discount yield of 7.5 percent. What is the cost of this bond? What is its annualized bond equivalent yield? What is the yield to maturity?

2. An investor who expects a decline in interest rates over the next three months decides to purchase a 90-day T-bill futures contract at 92. Assuming interest rates decline over the period and the futures price increases to 92, what profit would be made? What assumptions have you made in calculating this profit?

3. A six-month T-bill trades at a discount of 11.5 percent and a three-month T-bill futures trades at 88.5. If possible, construct a portfolio that provides a guaranteed return higher than the current three-month T-bill rate of 11.6 percent. What assumptions have you made?

4. Price quotations for T-bond futures traded by the Chicago Board of Trade are based on a hypothetical 8 percent semiannual coupon-bearing bond with a 20-year maturity. To meet delivery standards, the actual bond delivered must have at least five years to call (or maturity). The actual invoice price is obtained by multiplying the futures settlement price by a conversion factor and adding the interest. Explain the conversion factor and explain how the seller selects which bond to deliver to the buyer.

5. Provide a scenario in which a short hedge with T-bond futures would be an appropriate strategy. Using realistic numbers, illustrate conditions in which the hedge would be profitable and in which it would lose money. Justify the benefits of the hedge.

6. Repeat question 5 for a long hedge using T-bond futures. Using your data, emphasize the fact that total price risk is being replaced by basis risk.

7. Distinguish between specific security options and fixed deliverable options.

8. Compute the actual price of the American Exchange December put option on the 15-week Treasury bill in Exhibit 13.7. The strike price is 936. Explain exactly what an investor obtains if he or she purchases this contract.

9. Compute the actual price of the American Exchange August call option on the 8 7/8 U.S. Treasury note in Exhibit 13.7. The strike price is 106. Explain

exactly what an investor obtains if he or she purchases such a contract. Under what circumstances might one buy such a contract? Describe a situation in which the sale of such a contract would be appropriate.

10. Using the T-bond futures options prices in Exhibit 13.10, price the September call option with strike 90. What does this option contract provide the holder? Using the price of the T-bond futures contract in Exhibit 13.5, compute the intrinsic value of this option and the time premiums.

11. From Exhibit 13.10, the September call with strike 88 is valued at 6–16 while the December call is 6–31. Should the December call always be priced equal to or greater than the September call? If the December call were priced below 6–16, what would this imply?

12. Assume the following price information on CBT Treasury Bond Futures and Futures Options:

Settlement Prices on Treasury Bond Futures (Points 32nds of 100%)

June	69–09
Sept.	68–11
Dec.	67–17

Prices on Options on Treasury Bond Futures (Points 64ths of 100%)

	Calls			Puts		
Strike	June	Sept.	Dec.	June	Sept.	Dec.
66	3–26	3–15	3–10	0–12	1–00	1–45
68	1–54	2–05	2–12	0–36	1–49	2–41
70	0.48	1–15	1–28	1–30	2–55	—
72	0.16	0.44	0.60	2–60	4–17	—

Compute the intrinsic value and time premiums of the options. Explain why the September 66 call trades at a lower price than the June 66, while the reverse is true for the September 68 and June 68 call contracts.

13. How can savings accounts be viewed as putable bonds? Explain how a decision-maker can access the cost of providing the early withdrawal future.

14. What is an interest rate cap, and what is an interest rate collar?

15. Explain why valuation of options on debt instruments is more complex than valuation of options on stocks.

16. Consider a three-year bond with a face value of $1000 and an 8 percent annual coupon. Let the number of periods be 3, $r_0 = 8$ percent, $u = 1.05$, and $d = 0.98$. Compute the binomial interest rate tree and the bond price tree under the expectations hypothesis.

17. Assuming the actual bond price equals the observed bond price computed in problem 16, obtain the value of a call option that expires in two years. Assume the strike price of the call equals the current bond price.

18. Define an interest rate swap and explain why swaps can be beneficial to both parties in the transaction. Explain in detail what the two parties are exchanging. Do these oppportunities exist only because of inefficiencies in the market? Explain.

19. "Swaps are only useful because there are no markets for long-term debt options." Is this statement true? Discuss.

20. Discuss the role of option contracts in swaps. Why should investment banks offer institutions options on swaps? Why would an institution be interested in buying an option on a swap?

14

Valuation of Corporate Securities

The purpose of this chapter is to illustrate how option pricing theory and arbitrage arguments can be used to value or at least obtain pricing bounds on corporate securities. In the first section corporate bonds are discussed. Then option pricing approaches are used to value corporate discount bonds. Within this framework the factors affecting the risk structure of interest rates can be analyzed. The option approach brings into clear focus the conflict of interest between bondholders and shareholders, and this highlights the importance of bond covenants. Subordinated debt is then valued using similar methods.

The analysis becomes more complex when coupon-bearing bonds are introduced. The valuation of such debt requires the concept of compound options. Compound options play an important role in financial economics and more attention is paid to them in Chapter 16.

Many government and corporate bonds have features that give the issuer (or bond owner) the right to redeem them at a particular price at a future date. These option-like features have value that can be easily determined using option pricing methods. After a discussion of such bonds, we consider convertible securities including warrants and convertible bonds.

Warrants can be viewed as call options issued by a firm. Unfortunately, their valuation is complex because their conversion dilutes the outstanding stock. Properties of warrant prices and their similarities to call options are discussed. Convertible bonds are then analyzed. Simple arbitrage arguments are used to establish some boundary pricing relationships. The final section of this chapter investigates compound options and options on the minimum and maximum of two risky assets. Applications of these contracts to several problems are discussed.

CORPORATE BONDS

In order to issue bonds to the public, a firm must establish a legal contract with a third party called a *trustee*. It is the duty of the trustee to ensure that the issuer stands by the provisions of the contract. This contract, or bond indenture, contains the restrictions and promises that back the bond. If the firm does not follow the covenants, the trustee, on behalf of the bondholders, may take legal action.

The indenture sets forth the term to maturity, face value, and coupon payments of the issue. In addition, it states whether the bond is secured or unsecured. A *secured issue* is one for which the firm pledges specific assets that may be used to pay the bondholders if the firm defaults on its payments. For example, the indenture may provide a legal right for the bondholders to receive proceeds from the sale of specific property if the firm defaults. Bonds that are backed by specific real property (land or buildings) are *mortgage bonds.* Many bond issues are unsecured. That is, no specific assets act as collateral. Bondholders are general creditors. Long-term unsecured issues are called *debentures,* while short-term maturities are referred to as *notes.*

If the issuing firm defaults, bondholders who have secured bonds have claims on the collateral. If these assets do not cover the full amount, the secured bondholders join the other creditors as general or unsecured creditors. Since secured bonds receive preferential treatment, debenture holders will often require protection from the firm issuing bonds in the future. In some cases the indenture states that no secured bonds may be issued in the future unless the debentures are secured first. Alternatively, the indenture may require that the firm may issue debentures only if the firm first meets specific earnings conditions and subordinates the new debt to the current issues. That is, the firm cannot service the new (subordinated) debt until it meets its obligations to current bondholders. Finally, debenture holders may require that the indenture contain restrictions on working capital and dividend policies.

Many indentures have special provisions for repaying the loan. For example, the firm may retain the option to call in the bonds prior to maturity at a small premium over the face value. This price is the *call price* or *redemption price* and may vary over time. It is highest in the early years of the loan and gradually decreases until it equals the face value at maturity.

Indentures often provide for *sinking funds* that require the firm to retire a given portion of the bond issue each year. This provision provides evidence of the solvency of the firm and may prevent a crisis at maturity. Some sinking funds commence five to ten years after the bonds' original issue date. The sinking fund requirement may take two forms. The first is for the firm to repurchase the required number of bonds in the open market. The second is for the firm to randomly select the required number of bonds through a lottery system and to call these bonds in for redemption at the sinking fund call price, which usually differs from the call price of the overall issue. The firm will choose the second method if the sinking fund call price is lower than the market price.

An alternative to a sinking fund provision is to issue *serial bonds.* A serial bond issue is divided into a series of different maturities. The issuing firm redeems each part of the series at different dates.

In effect, a firm can issue bonds that have any variety of provisions.

Many firms will bring to market a bond that has a new provision in the hope that the provision will result in a lower interest (higher issue price) expense to the firm. For example, a firm that believes gold prices will remain steady or fall may issue a bond that pays a higher interest rate if gold prices rise. The firm is hoping that the investing public feels gold prices will rise and will, therefore, pay a higher price for the bond. If the firm is right about gold prices and the market's expectations, it may be able to borrow money at a low rate of interest. An interesting issue for the financial management of such a firm is whether the firm should buy options on gold to hedge against possible gold price increases. The point here, however, is that there are an unlimited number of types of bonds. Four of the more common are described below.

Collateral trust bonds are secured by common stocks owned by the borrower. Holding companies often issue such bonds, since most of their assets are stocks of subsidiaries.

Income bonds require interest payments only when it is earned. That is, if the firm incurs losses in one year, no interest is due. These bonds are less valuable to an investor than bonds that require interest payments regardless of a firm's earnings.

Floating rate bonds have an interest rate that varies over the life of the bond and is usually tied to a widely quoted rate, such as a Treasury bill rate.

Index bonds are bonds whose payments are tied to a price index. The gold bonds described above are a type of index bond.

VALUATION OF RISKY DISCOUNT BONDS

We have seen that the value of a default-free, riskless bond is given by

$$B_0 = \exp(-rT)F \qquad (14.1)$$

where r = the instantaneous risk-free rate of return,

T = time to maturity, and

F = face value.

If the bond is not default free, then equation (14.1) cannot be applied. To entice investors into holding risky debt, the bond must offer a higher return. Let r_B denote the required rate of return for a particular bond. Then, for risky discount bonds, we have

$$B_0 = \exp(-r_B T)F \qquad (14.2)$$

where $r_B > r$. The valuation of risky debt (i.e., the determination of r_B) is not simple because the likelihood of default must be considered.

To illustrate how this debt is valued, consider a corporation that has n shares of common stock outstanding and a single issue of discount bonds of total face value F that is due at time T. Let B_0 denote the total current value of the bonds and let S_0 be the current share price. For simplicity, assume the bond indenture prohibits dividend payments during the life of the bond and also prevents the firm from issuing senior debt or repurchasing shares. If the firm cannot pay the face amount F at maturity, then the bondholders take over the company.

The current value of the firm, V_0, is

$$V_0 = B_0 + nS_0. \tag{14.3}$$

At maturity, the value of the firm is V_T and the bondholders have a claim of F dollars. If V_T exceeds F, the debt is paid off and the shareholders are left with the residual value, $V_T - F$. However, if the value of the firm is less than the face amount of the debt, the bondholders take over the firm and the shareholders receive nothing. Exhibits 14.1 and 14.2 illustrate the potential payouts for the bondholders and shareholders at maturity.

By lending to the firm, the bondholders have purchased the firm and sold a call option to the shareholders. To see this more clearly, consider the value of the bond at maturity:

$$B_T = V_T \quad \text{if } V_T < F$$
$$= F \quad \text{if } V_T \geq F.$$

Hence,

$$B_T = \text{Min}(F, V_T).$$

EXHIBIT 14.1
Payout for Bondholders

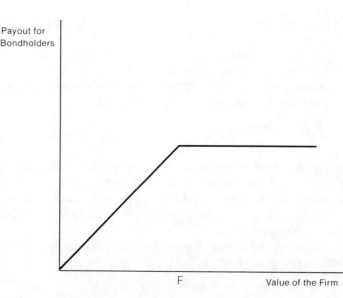

EXHIBIT 14.2
Payout for Shareholders

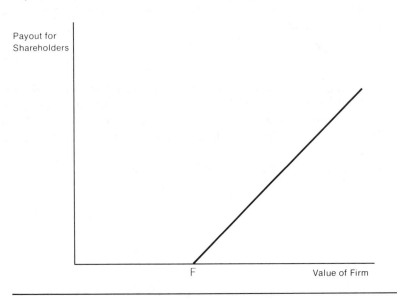

This equation can be rewritten as

$$B_T = V_T - \text{Max}(V_T - F, 0)$$

$$= V_T - C_T$$

where C_T is the terminal value of a call option on the value of the firm with strike price F.

Since the terminal value of the bond is equivalent to the terminal value of the firm less the terminal value of a call on the firm, it must follow, by the law of one price, that the current value of the bond is equivalent to the current value of the firm less the current value of the call.

That is,

$$B_0 = V_0 - C_0. \tag{14.4}$$

Thus, buying a bond issue is equivalent to acquiring a firm and selling a call option on the value of the firm. In effect, by issuing debt, shareholders have surrendered the firm to bondholders and received a call option in exchange. This call option allows shareholders to buy back the firm for the face value of the debt at the maturity date.

Another way of viewing the bond is to establish its value in terms of put options. Again, at maturity the bond value is given by

$$B_T = \text{Min}(V_T, F).$$

This equation can be rewritten as

$$B_T = F - \text{Max}(F - V_T, 0)$$

$$= F - P_T$$

where P_T is the value of a put option on the firm and the strike price equals the face value, F.

The payout of a bond is thus identical to the payout of a portfolio containing a riskless, default-free bond paying out F at time T and a short position in the put. Hence, by the law of one price, it must follow that

$$B_0 = F\exp(-rT) - P_0. \tag{14.5}$$

Within this framework, shareholders can be viewed as owners of the assets of the firm who have borrowed the present value of F and purchased a put. The loan is an obligation that must be met, regardless of what occurs. Without the put option, the shareholders would not have limited liability. That is, at maturity, if the value of the firm was lower than F, the shareholders would be obliged to pay the difference. Fortunately, the put option provides insurance against this event. If the shareholders cannot meet their obligations, they will exercise their in-the-money put option and deliver the firm to the bondholders.

Note that the likelihood of defaulting is exactly equal to the likelihood of exercising the put.

Since $B_0 = F\exp(-rT) - P_0$, we have the result

Bond Price = Default-Free Bond Price − Put Price

or

Bond Price = Default-Free Bond Price − Default Premium.

Risky bonds will thus trade at a discount to default-free bonds. The size of the risk premium can be analyzed by investigating the factors that influence put premiums.

THE RISK STRUCTURE OF BOND PRICES

In order to establish the value of the bond, B_0, it is necessary to value the put premium, P_0. To do this requires assumptions about the stochastic behavior of the value of the firm. If, for example, we assume the Black-Scholes conditions, then from equation (8.30), we have

$$P_0 = F\exp(-rT)N(a_1) - V_0 N(a_2) \tag{14.6}$$

where

$$a_1 = \frac{[-\ln(V_0/F) - (r - \sigma^2/2)T]}{\sigma\sqrt{T}}$$

$$a_2 = a_1 - \sigma\sqrt{T}$$

Substituting equation (14.6) into equation (14.5), we have

$$B_0 = Fexp(-rT)\left[1 - N(a_1) + \frac{V_0 N(a_2)}{Fexp(-rT)}\right]$$

$$= Fexp(-rT)K \tag{14.7}$$

where

$$K = 1 - N(a_1) + \frac{N(a_2)}{\omega}$$

and $\omega = Fexp(-rT)/V_0$ represents a quasi debt-to-value ratio, where the debt is the default-free, discounted value of the face value.

Example 14.1

Consider a firm of value $V_0 = 30$. Assume the face value of the debt is 20 and matures in one year. The riskless rate, r, is 10 percent and the instantaneous volatility, σ, is 0.3.

The value of the bond, B_0, is

$$B_0 = Fexp(-rT) - P_0$$

$$Fexp(-rT) = 20exp(-0.10) = 18.10$$

$$P_0 = Fexp(-rT)N(a_1) - V_0 N(a_2)$$

$$a_1 = \frac{[-ln(V_0/F) - (r - \sigma^2/2)T]}{\sigma\sqrt{T}}$$

$$= \frac{[ln(20/30) - (0.10 - 0.045)]}{0.3} = -1.535$$

$$a_2 = a_1 - \sigma\sqrt{T} = -1.535 - 0.3 = -1.835.$$

Hence,

$$P_0 = Fexp(-rT)N(a_1) - V_0 N(a_2)$$

$$= 18.10(0.0624) - 30(0.033) = 0.13$$

and

$$B_0 = 18.10 - 0.13 = 17.97.$$

Equivalently, from equation (14.7), we have

$$\omega = \frac{Fexp(-rT)}{V_0} = \frac{18.10}{30} = 0.603$$

(continued)

Example 14.1 (cont'd)

and

$$K = 1 - N(a_1) + \frac{N(a_2)}{\omega}$$

$$= 1 - 0.0624 + \frac{0.033}{0.603} = 0.9928.$$

Hence,

$$B_0 = F\exp(-rT)K$$

$$= 18.10(0.9926) = 17.97$$

If the firm had a current value of 25, rather than 30, then the debt would be more risky. In this case $\omega = 0.724$, $K = 0.9652$, and $B_0 = 17.64$. The lower bond price reflects the greater risk.

SENSITIVITY ANALYSIS OF BOND VALUES

The value of the debt B_0 is given by

$$B_0 = F\exp(-rT)K = F\exp(-rT) - P_0$$

and depends on V_0, F, T, σ, and r. That is,

$$B_0 = B_0(V_0, F, T, \sigma, r).$$

By taking the partial derivatives of each of the variables, we can investigate the effects of each variable.

As the value of the firm increases, the probability of default declines. Thus, the chance of exercising the put also declines. As the put moves out the money, its value declines and the bond value increases. Hence, as the value of the firm increases, the bond price increases ($\partial B_0/\partial V_0 > 0$).

As the face value of debt increases, the value of the debt increases ($\partial B_0/\partial F > 0$) because the higher the face value, the higher the default-free portion of the bond's value. Although the bond value increases, the default premium also increases with ω. Thus, the increase in value is not the full increase in the present value of the face value.

As the time to maturity increases, the bond prices decrease ($\partial B/\partial T < 0$) because the present value of the face amount declines and the default premium increases, driving the bond price down.

The maximum payout the bondholders may receive is F. This value does not increase as the variance increases. The variance, however, does affect the default premium. As the variance increases, the value of the put also increases and the value of the bond drops ($\partial B/\partial \sigma^2 < 0$). Exhibit 14.3 summarizes the results.

EXHIBIT 14.3

Sensitivity Analysis of Bond Values

Variable Increases	Direction of Bond Price Change
Value of firm	Increase
Face value	Increase
Maturity	Decrease
Volatility	Decrease

THE RISK STRUCTURE OF INTEREST RATES

From equations (15.2) and (15.7) we have

$$B_0 = F\exp(-r_B T)$$

and

$$B_0 = F\exp(-r T)K.$$

Hence,

$$F\exp(-r_B T) = F\exp(-r T)K$$

and

$$-r_B T = -r T + ln(K)$$

Let the default risk premium be denoted by π. Then

$$\pi = r_B - r = \frac{-ln(K)}{T}. \qquad (14.8)$$

Example 14.2

Using the data from the previous example, we know that

$$r_B = ln\left(\frac{20}{17.97}\right) = 10.7\%$$

Since the risk-free rate is 10%, the default risk premium must be 10.7% − 10% = 0.7%. By using equation (14.8), we can calculate the risk premium directly as $-ln(0.9928)/1 = 0.7\%$.

Those factors that decrease the value of the bond increase the interest rate, r_B. For example, since the volatility of the firm's assets is negatively related with the bond values, it is positively related with the interest rate, r_B.

VALUATION OF STOCK AND THE ROLE OF BOND COVENANTS

In a leveraged firm, the equity holders own a call option on the assets of the firm. Since the value of the call increases with volatility, the shareholders will encourage risky strategies to be adopted. The bondholders, on the other hand, will be adverse to volatility.

Since the shareholders have voting power, the policies of the firm may be directed toward their benefit. With no restrictions, a leveraged firm could invest in risky projects to increase the share price and decrease bond prices. To protect themselves from such actions, bondholders may take certain precautions.

First, bondholders may offer a price for the debt that is low enough to compensate for the most risky actions shareholders could take. If the shareholders do not adopt the most risky projects, then the bondholders will be overcompensated for the risky bond.

Second, bondholders may require that stockholders write a covenant into the bond issue that restricts the kind of projects or assets the firm can acquire.

Third, bondholders may request that stockholders collateralize the bonds. This minimizes uncertainty about the nature of the claim bondholders have over the company.

If the second strategy is adopted, the shareholders are left with a special type of call option when the bond issue is sold. This option gives them the right to buy back the firm for the face value of the debt at maturity. However, this right will be available to the shareholders only if in the interim they have abided by the convenants of the bond. If the covenants are violated prior to expiration, the bondholders can force early exercise. That is, the bondholders can immediately take over the firm, ensure their obligations are met, and then disburse the residual values (if any) to the shareholders. As a result of these restrictions, the call option issued by the bondholders is not as valuable as a European call option. The more restrictive the bond covenants, the lower the value of the call. Call options contracts that can become void if certain events occur are referred to as *down-and-out options*. Down-and-out option contracts can, in some instances, be valued using a modified binomial option pricing approach.

VALUATION OF SUBORDINATED DEBT

Subordinated (or junior) *debt* is debt for which other (senior) debt takes priority. Specifically, in the event of default and subsequent liquidation, subordinated debtholders receive payment only after senior debtholders are paid.

Consider a firm with n shares outstanding and two discount bond issues with the same maturity date. Let F_s and F_j be the face value of the senior debt and junior debt, respectively. Let B_{s0} and B_{j0} be their current values, and let the market price of the shares be S_0. The value of the firm is V_0, where $V_0 = nS_0 + B_{s0} + B_{j0}$.

We shall assume that the firm cannot declare dividends until the debt is paid off. If at the maturity date the value of the firm, V_T, exceeds F_s, then the senior bondholders receive their repayment. If V_T is less than F_s, the senior bondholders receive the assets of the firm while the junior bondholders and shareholders receive nothing. If V_T exceeds $F_s + F_j$, both types of bondholders are paid off and the shareholders receive the residual value. Finally, if V_T exceeds F_s but is less than $F_s + F_j$, the junior bondholders receive the value of the firm less the senior debt, while the shareholders receive nothing. Mathematically, these conditions can be written as follows:

$$nS_T = \text{Max}[0, V_T - (F_s + F_j)]$$

$$B_{sT} = \text{Min}[V_T, F_s]$$

$$B_{jT} = \text{Max}[\text{Min}(V_T - F_s, F_j), 0].$$

Exhibit 14.4 illustrates the payout values to the shareholders, senior debtholders, and junior debtholders at expiration.

EXHIBIT 14.4
Payouts of Stock, Senior Debt, and Junior Debt

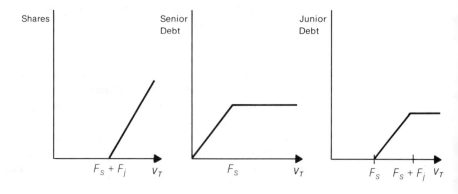

As before, we can represent the payouts of the stock, senior debt, and junior debt by European options. The pricing of senior debt is unchanged. The value of the stock is also unchanged (the strike price is taken as $F = F_s + F_j$). The junior debt can be replicated by a portfolio constructed by buying a call on the firm with strike F_s and selling a call with strike $F_s + F_j$.

Hence,

$$B_{j0} = C_0(F_s) - C_0(F_s + F_j) \qquad (14.9)$$

where $C_0(X)$ is the value of a European call option with strike X and maturity T.

In general, the value of subordinated debt depends on the value of the firm, V_0, the size of the senior debt, F_s, as well as the junior debt, F_j, the volatility of the firm, σ, and the riskless rate, r.

VALUATION OF RISKY COUPON BONDS

As described in Chapter 11, the value of a default-free coupon bond is equivalent to the value of a portfolio of default-free discount bonds. As an example, consider a three-period bond that pays coupons of size k at times t_1, t_2, and t_3. In addition, the face value, F, is due at time t_3.

The value of the bond is equivalent to the value of a portfolio of three discount bonds. The first discount bond has face value $k_1 = k$ and is due at time t_1. The second discount bond has face value $k_2 = k$ and is due at time t_2. The final discount bond has face value $k_3 = F + k$ due at time t_3. Hence,

$$B_0 = \sum_{j=1}^{3} k_j e^{-rt_j} \tag{14.10}$$

Equation (14.10) cannot be extended to risky bonds because the portfolio of discount bonds cannot be assumed to be independent. To see this, note that at time t_2 the shareholders have to determine whether to pay out k_2 or default. If they default, the final payment, k_3, will not be paid.

To understand how coupon bonds are valued, we shall start off at time t_3, then consider time t_2, t_1, and eventually the current time, $t = 0$.

At time t_3, the shareholders must determine whether it is in their interests to pay k_3 and take back possession of the firm. At this time the shareholders own a call option on the firm with strike price k_3. Let C_3 denote this call option.

At time t_2, the shareholders again have to make a decision. By paying k_2, they receive option C_3. If they do not pay k_2, they surrender the company to the debtholders. At this time the shareholders own an option with strike price k_2. Since the underlying security is option C_3, this option contract is really an option on an option and is referred to as a *compound option*. Let C_2 denote this compound option.

Going back to back to time t_1, we can see that the shareholders are in the same situation. They own an option on the compound option C_2. By paying the coupon k_1, the shareholders are exercising their option and receiving C_2. Let C_1 denote this compound option.

Now consider time zero. The stockholders own a European compound option, C_1, that has an exercise price of k_1 and time to maturity of t_1. If exercised, the holders will receive a compound option with strike k_2 and time to expiration $t_2 - t_1$. Finally, if C_2 is exercised at time t_2, the holders will receive a simple European call option with strike price k_3 and time to expiration $t_3 - t_2$.

Exhibit 14.5 illustrates the decision processes. Note that by paying k_1, the shareholders receive more than an option to continue their quest for the firm for another period. At the same time, they receive a promise from the bondholders that if k_2 is met, they will receive a final option on the value of the

EXHIBIT 14.5
Sequence of Compound Options Owned by Shareholders

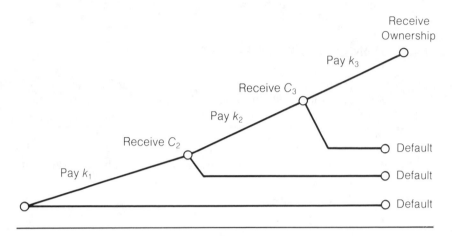

firm. The value of the bond is not equal to the value of a portfolio of simple call options. For example, it is incorrect to assume the shareholders own a portfolio of calls of strike k_1, k_2, and k_3, with times to expiration t_1, t_2, and t_3, respectively. The valuation of compound options is discussed in Chapter 16. Compound options have seen applications in the valuation of insurance products, operating leases, and American options on stocks that pay dividends as well as on risky coupon debt.

CALL AND PUT FEATURES ON BONDS

Bonds are often issued with a call feature, which enables the issuing firm to buy back the bonds at a predetermined price. Bonds are often not immediately callable, and when they are, the call price is initially higher than the face amount but declines over time. For example, a 20-year bond may not be callable until the tenth year. At that time it may have a call price of 110 percent of the face amount, and the call price may decline 1 percent per year.

Not as common as callable bonds are putable bonds. Such bonds allow the investor to force the company to redeem them at a predetermined price. A bond issued with a putable feature will sell at a higher price than one without it. By the same token, a firm will incur lower interest expense if it issues a bond with a putable option. The valuation theory with regard to the put feature is similar to that of the call feature. For this reason, this section concentrates on the call feature.

The call feature has obvious benefits for the issuing firm. It allows the firm to refinance (or pay off) a bond at a date of its choosing. If interest rates decline, the issuing firm may call the outstanding bonds and then refinance the funds at a lower rate of interest. If the call provision did not exist, the firm would have to buy the bonds on the open market.

The call feature can be viewed as an option. When bondholders purchase bonds, they have, in effect, also sold call options to the issuer. If the
bond price rises above the call price, the issuer may exercise the in-the-money
option and redeem the bond. If the bond price does not exceed the call price,
the issuer will not exercise the option.

Exhibit 14.6 shows the difference in value between a bond with a call
provision and a similar bond without the call. The value of the call provision,
like any other option, will depend on the call strike price, time to call, and
volatility of interest rates. Since the call feature cannot be traded separately
from the bond, the value of the call provision affects the value of the bond
itself. This is depicted in Exhibit 14.6, where the potential exercise of the call
provision places a ceiling on the bond price. Since the call feature cannot be
traded separately, the company cannot sell the call alone. The only way the
firm can benefit from an in-the-money call option is by exercising the option
and redeeming the bonds.

EXHIBIT 14.6
Valuation of Callable Bonds

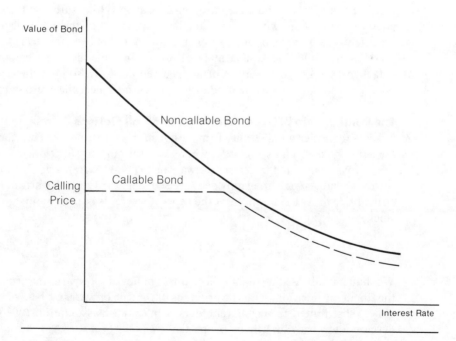

CONVERTIBLE SECURITIES

Convertible securities are securities that can be converted into a different
security of the same firm under given conditions. Within this broad definition,
there are several types, which include warrants, convertible bonds, convertible

preferred stock, and many hybrid securities. In this section, we shall examine a few of them.

Warrants

A *warrant* is an instrument that gives the owner the option of purchasing a specific number of shares of stock at a designated price over a determined time period. When issued, most warrants have a life of between three and five years. However, some have longer terms and there have been instances of perpetual warrants. In most cases the warrants are changeable into common stock, but some companies have issued warrants on their bonds.

Since warrants do not receive dividends or interest, they have no value in their own right. Their sole value derives from the conversion feature. As such, they can be viewed as call options that are issued by the firm. The fact that a firm issues the options makes the valuation of them somewhat complex. The reason is that when warrants are exercised, the firm's equity is diluted. This dilution has an impact on the value of the warrant itself, as will be discussed later.

Firms often issue warrants with other securities to "sweeten" the offering. For example, a bond issue may include warrants to ensure that the bond issue will be sold out with a minimum discount. In effect, the warrants lower the interest rate on the bond. Usually the warrants can be detached from the other security and traded separately. However, in some cases they cannot be detached except upon exercise or at specified dates. In some instances the bond (valued at par) may be used instead of cash to meet the exercise price.

The Relationship Between Warrants and Call Options

To simplify the analysis, consider an all-equity firm with n shares outstanding. The value of the firm, V_0, is given by $V_0 = nS_0$, where S_0 is the current stock price.

Now assume the firm issues k warrants. These warrants are European warrants and, as such, may only be exercised at maturity. Each warrant has a strike price of X. Let q represent the ratio of warrants issued to outstanding stock,

$$q = \frac{k}{n}. \tag{14.11}$$

We shall initially assume that the investment policy of the firm is unaffected by the financing decision, with the proceeds of the sale of warrants being immediately distributed to the shareholders. Under these assumptions, we shall develop a few warrant pricing properties.

Property 14.1

A European warrant will be exercised whenever the value of the firm is sufficiently large to cause call options to be exercised on the stock of an identical firm with no warrants.

To see this, let V_T be the value of the firm at expiration before warrant-holders exercise. If the warrant-holders exercise, the value of the firm increases to V_T^A, where

$$V_T^A = V_T + kX$$

$$= nS_T + nqX \qquad (14.12)$$

where S_T is the stock price of the firm at time T before warrant-holders exercise. Given that the value of the firm adjusts to V_T^A, the stock price will adjust to S_T^A, where

$$S_T^A = \frac{V_T^A}{(k + n)}$$

$$= \frac{(nS_T + nqX)}{(nq + n)}$$

$$= \frac{(S_T + qX)}{(1 + q)} . \qquad (14.13)$$

The warrant-holder will exercise only if the adjusted stock price exceeds the strike price, X. That is, if

$$S_T^A - X \geq 0.$$

Hence, the exercise condition is given by

$$\frac{(S_T + qX)}{(1 + q)} - X \geq 0$$

or

$$\frac{(S_T + qX - X - qX)}{(1 + q)} \geq 0$$

and hence, $S_T \geq X$.

Thus, a warrant-holder will exercise the warrant only if the unadjusted stock price exceeds the strike price. Equivalently, warrants will be exercised only when call options on an identical firm having no warrants would be exercised.

Property 14.2

The value of a European warrant, W_0, is equal to the value of a call option on the stock of an equivalent firm with no warrants multiplied by a term that depends on the dilution factor. Specifically,

$$W_0 = \frac{C_0}{(1 + q)} . \qquad (14.14)$$

To see this, note that at expiration the value of the call option is given by

$$C_T = \text{Max}(S_T - X, 0). \qquad (14.15)$$

If the call is in the money ($S_T > X$), the warrant is in the money and will be exercised. In this case the stock price of the firm will be diluted to S_T^A, where

$$S_T^A = \frac{(V_T + kX)}{(n + k)}. \qquad (14.16)$$

The value of the warrant at expiration will then be

$$
\begin{aligned}
W_T &= \text{Max}(S_T^A - X, 0) \\
&= \text{Max}\left[\frac{(S_T + qX)}{(1 + q)} - X, 0\right] \\
&= \text{Max}\left[\frac{(S_T - X)}{(1 + q)}, 0\right] \\
&= \text{Max}\left[\frac{(0, S_T - X)}{(1 + q)}\right] \\
&= \frac{C_T}{(1 + q)}
\end{aligned}
$$

Furthermore, if the call option expires worthless, the warrant will expire worthless. Thus, regardless of the future, we have

$$W_T = \frac{C_T}{(1 + q)}. \qquad (14.17)$$

Since the warrant is perfectly correlated with the value of the call, their current prices should be proportional. That is,

$$W_0 = \frac{C_0}{(1 + q)}. $$

Property 14.3

The value of a European warrant on a firm is equivalent to the value of the equity on a second firm, identical in all aspects to the first except for financial leverage. This second firm has borrowed a discount bond of amount nX where X is the strike price of the warrant and n is the number of shares outstanding. The firm has no warrants outstanding.

To see this, recall that the price of a warrant at time T is

$$W_T = \text{Max}(0, S_T^A - X) \qquad (14.18)$$

where

$$S_T{}^A = \frac{(V_T + kX)}{(n + k)}. \tag{14.19}$$

Substituting (14.19) into (14.18), we obtain

$$W_T = \text{Max} \left[\frac{(0, V_T - nX)}{(n + k)} \right] \tag{14.20}$$

Now the equity of a firm with debt of size nX due at time T can be viewed as a call option and its value $nS_T{}^*$ at time T is given by

$$nS_T{}^* = \text{Max}(0, V_T - nX). \tag{14.21}$$

Comparing (14.20) and (14.21), we see that

$$W_T(n + k) = nS_T{}^*$$

or

$$W_T = \frac{nS_T{}^*}{(n + k)}. \tag{14.22}$$

Hence,

$$W_T = \frac{S_T{}^*}{(1 + q)}. \tag{14.23}$$

That is, the future value of a warrant is always equal to the future equity of a particular leveraged firm multiplied by the dilution factor. To avoid riskless arbitrage it must follow that $W_0 = S_0{}^*/(1 + q)$.

Note that this result also obtains directly from Property 14.2 if it is recognized that a call option can be viewed as a leveraged position in the stock.

Example 14.3

To illustrate the above three properties, consider an all-equity firm consisting of five shares outstanding. Assume one warrant is issued that is convertible into one share for $18 after two years. The current value of the firm is $100. The value of the firm is assumed to follow a binomial process, as shown below:

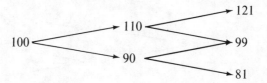

(continued)

Example 14.3 (cont'd)

The stock prices of an equivalent firm with no warrant outstanding is given below:

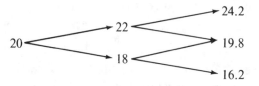

Using the two-period binomial call pricing equation and a risk-free rate of 5 percent, the call price on the stock of the equivalent firm is $C_0 = \$3.78$. Thus, from Property 14.2 we have

$$W_0 = \frac{C_0}{(1 + q)}$$

where

$$q = \frac{k}{n} = \frac{1}{5}.$$

Hence,

$$W_0 = \frac{3.78}{1.20} = \$3.15.$$

Rather than use Property 14.2, the warrant price could be computed by applying the binomial model to stock prices adjusted in period 2 for dilution effects. Specifically, from Property 14.1 we know that at the end of the second period, warrant-holders will exercise if the stock price is above 18. Thus, the after-conversion prices are

$$S_{22}{}^A = \frac{(121 + 18)}{6} = 23.17$$

$$S_{21}{}^A = \frac{(99 + 18)}{6} = 19.50$$

$$S_{20}{}^A = \frac{81}{5} = 16.20.$$

The new stock price tree is given below:

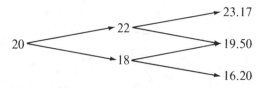

By applying the two-period binomial model to these prices, we obtain the warrant price directly to be $3.15.

(continued)

Example 14.3 (cont'd)

To illustrate Property 14.3, consider a firm with five shareholders, no warrants outstanding but with debt due in two periods with face value equal to $nX = 5 \times 18 = \$90$. The value of the equity of the firm in the second period is

$$S_{22}^* = \frac{\text{Max}(121 - 90,0)}{5} = \frac{31}{5} = 6.2$$

$$S_{21}^* = \frac{\text{Max}(99 - 90,0)}{5} = \frac{9}{5} = 1.8$$

$$S_{20}^* = \frac{\text{Max}(81 - 90,0)}{5} = 0.$$

Since the stock can be viewed as an option on the value of the firm, the two-period binomial model can be used to compute the current stock price. This value is 3.775. Using Property 14.3, the value of the warrant is

$$W_0 = \frac{S_0}{(1 + q)} = (3.775)\left(\frac{5}{6}\right) = \$3.15.$$

Warrant Pricing with Capital Structure Considerations   Thus far we have assumed that the income a firm receives from the sale of a warrant is immediately distributed to the shareholders as a dividend. If this is not the case, then the proceeds increase the value of the firm and alter the stock price. This, in turn, affects the warrant price. To illustrate, assume the \$3.15 was not distributed as a dividend. Then assuming the proceeds were used to expand the scale of existing projects, the value of the firm is given by

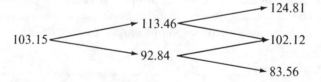

The stock price on an equivalent firm with no warrants is given by

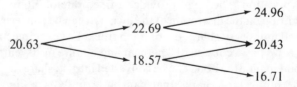

From this $C_0 = 4.38$ and, hence, $W_0 = 4.38/1.2 = 3.65$. If the value of the warrant is \$3.65, not \$3.15, then the initial wealth of the firm is \$103.65, not \$103.15. Using \$103.65 as the initial wealth leads to a new warrant price of \$3.72, which implies the initial wealth is \$103.72, not \$103.65. Exhibit 14.7 illustrates the sequence of warrant prices derived by this iterative argument. Fortunately, after a few iterations the warrant values begin to stabilize. As the exhibit shows, after five iterations the warrant price converges to \$3.73. The example illustrates the complexity of the valuation of a warrant when the value of a firm is not exogenous.

EXHIBIT 14.7
Iterative Valuation of Warrants

	Initial Firm Value	Value of C_0	Value of W_0
Iteration 1	$100.00	$3.78	$3.15
Iteration 2	103.15	4.38	3.65
Iteration 3	103.65	4.47	3.72
Iteration 4	103.72	4.48	3.73
Iteration 5	103.73	4.48	3.73

Dividend Effects and American Warrants   Like call options, warrant prices decline as dividends increase. As a result, the warrant agreement (which serves the same function as an indenture agreement for a bond issue) may impose dividend restrictions. The effect of dividends on the price of the warrant is particularly significant, since the warrant often has a long time to maturity.

The analysis of American warrants is much more complex. With multiple warrants outstanding, early exercise of some of them creates new shares and changes the capital structure of the firm. The value accruing to a particular warrant-holder is therefore not independent of what other warrant-holders do. Indeed, it can be shown that a monopolist who owns all the warrants should not exercise them all at once. However, if the warrants are held by many investors, the assumption that if they are exercised then they are all simultaneously exercised in one block, may not be too severe.

Convertible Bonds

A *convertible bond,* like a conventional bond, is an obligation of the issuing corporation. The bond provides a fixed rate of interest over its lifetime. In addition, at the discretion of the owner, it can be converted (exchanged) into a fixed number of shares of common stock. For example, the convertible bonds of XYZ pay a coupon of 8 percent and mature in 20 years. In addition, at any point in time the bond can be converted into six shares of XYZ common stock. The number of shares that can be acquired via conversion is called the *conversion ratio,* which need not be fixed over time. For example, a bond may be convertible into ten shares during the first three years and six shares thereafter. In addition to surrendering the bond, some convertibles require a cash payment to convert. This additional payment may be fixed or related to the current stock price. For example, conversion of the XYZ convertible bond is accomplished by surrendering the bond and paying an additional $400 or 45 percent of the market value of the common stock, whichever is lower.

Not all convertible bonds are convertible into common stock. Instead, some may be convertible into preferred stock or other securities. Some bonds are convertible into securities of another corporation. This is often done by an issuing corporation that wants to dispose of the securities of another corporation. Many firms issue such securities as a result of a merger. In what follows, we shall discuss the more common convertible bonds that can be exchanged for a fixed number of shares of the stock of the issuing corporation. When such bonds are converted, the firm issues additional stock, which dilutes the shares outstanding. Thus, like the analysis of warrants, the postconversion value of the shares received by the bondholder must be considered.

We shall assume that the indenture specifies that no dividends are allowed prior to the maturity date of the convertible bond. We shall also assume that the bond is noncallable, has a face value of X, provides interest payments of C dollars, and matures in τ years. The total value of the convertible issue is $G(V,\tau)$ where V is the value of the firm. We shall assume that there are n shares outstanding and that the convertible issue can be exchanged for k shares. The stock and convertible issue are the only claims on the capital structure of the firm. As before, the dilution factor, γ, is $\gamma = k/(n+k) = 1/(1+q)$. If the convertible issue is converted, then the value of the firm is $V = (n+k)S^A$ where S^A is the postconversion stock price. The conversion value of this issue is kS^A. Note that $kS^A = kV/(n+k) = \gamma V$. If the bond is not convertible (i.e., is a "straight" bond), then $k = 0$ and $\gamma = 0$. Clearly, the greater k (or γ), the greater the conversion value.

Property 14.4

The convertible issue must sell for at least the conversion value, γV. That is,

$$G(V,\tau) > \gamma V.$$

To see this, note that if this condition were not met, investors would purchase convertibles, exchange them for common stock, and sell the stock to ensure riskless profits.

Property 14.5

At maturity, the value of the convertible issue is given by

$$G(V,0) = \text{Min}[V, \text{Max}(X, \gamma V)].$$

To see this, note that at maturity the value of the firm is either above, below, or equal to the face value of the bond. If it is below the face value, the bondholders receive the value of the firm. If the value of the firm exceeds the face value of the bond, the bondholders can receive the face value or convert their bond. The bondholders will select the strategy that provides them greater wealth.

Property 14.6

Consider two convertible issues identical in all aspects except conversion ratio. Let γ_1 and γ_2 be their two respective dilution values. Then

$$G(V,\tau;\ \gamma_1) \geq G(V,\tau;\ \gamma_2) \qquad \text{for } \gamma_1 \geq \gamma_2.$$

Property 14.6 states that the greater the conversion value, the greater the value of the bond. A bond that converts into four shares, for example, clearly has more value than if the bond could only convert into two shares. If $\gamma = 0$, then the bond is a "straight" bond. Let $F(V, \tau)$ represent such a bond. That is, $F(V,\tau) = G(V,\tau;\ 0)$.

Property 14.7

Convertible bonds with call features that allow the firm to call the bond back for a specific price have less value than identical bonds with no call features.

This property is quite obvious. The conversion feature implies that the bond will increase in price as the stock price appreciates. However, the upside potential is limited by the ceiling created by the redemption price.

Property 14.8

If no dividends occur, then a convertible security will never be converted prior to maturity.

To see this, consider the following two portfolios:

A: Buy the convertible issue $G(V, T)$.

B: Buy the fraction of convertibles and stock where $\gamma = \dfrac{k}{(n+k)}$.

The values of the two portfolios under varying conditions appear in Exhibit 14.8. Portfolio A never produces a payout lower than B. Hence, the current value of Portfolio A must be no less than that of Portfolio B. Therefore, the convertible issue $G(V, T)$ will have a greater value than the "if converted" Portfolio B. Without some additional value such as dividends, there is no reason to convert the bonds prior to their expiration.

EXHIBIT 14.8
Profit Tables for Two Portfolios

		Value at Time T		
Portfolio	Value at Time 0	$V_T \leq X$	$X \leq V_T \leq X/\gamma$	$V_T \geq X/\gamma$
A	$G(V, T)$	V_T	X	γV_T
B	γV	γV_T	γV_T	γV_T
		$P_A(T) > P_B(T)$	$P_A(T) > P_B(T)$	$P_A(T) = P_B(T)$

If the convertible holder wishes to buy the common stock, then selling the bond and purchasing the stock is better than converting. A similar result was obtained for call options on stock. Specifically, call options on nondividend-paying stock should not be exercised prior to expiration.

Property 14.8 can be extended to include callable bonds. For stocks that pay dividends, it can be shown that early conversion of the bond just prior to an ex-dividend date may be optimal.

Property 14.9

The firm's optimal strategy is to call the bond as soon as its value is equal to the call price.

To see this, note that if it is in the best interest of bondholders to delay conversion for as long as possible, it must be in the best interests of the firm to force conversion as soon as possible. By forcing conversion, the firm sacrifices the time premium of the option inherent in the convertible for its intrinsic value. Thus, as soon as the conversion value exceeds the call price, the firm should force conversion.

Exhibit 14.9 depicts the boundary values for a convertible bond having no call provision and a floor value of the face amount (assuming no default risk). The value of the convertible is also bounded by the conversion value of the bond. The slope of this constraint is steeper the higher the conversion rate. Finally, the convertible bond value cannot exceed the value of the firm.

EXHIBIT 14.9
Boundaries for Convertible Bond with No Call Provision

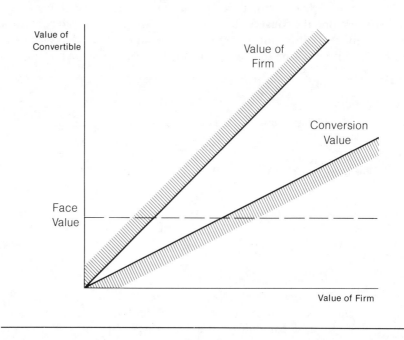

Exhibit 14.10 depicts the boundaries for a convertible bond with a call provision. It is similar to the boundaries for the noncallable convertible, except that there is a ceiling because of the call provision. The value of convertible callable bonds will vary within the bounded region of this exhibit. The exact price will depend on various factors, the most important of which are default risks, interest rates, and volatility of interest rates.

Exhibit 14.11 shows the approximate value functions for issues with different default risks. The greater the chance of default, the lower the bond price. For all firms, the chance of default declines as the firm value increases further and further from the face amount of the bond. In this exhibit firm 1 has less chance of default than firm 2. As interest rates decline, the bond value of a convertible bond increases, as depicted in Exhibit 14.12.

As interest rate volatility increases, the value of a bond decreases. When the value of the firm is close to the face value, the convertible derives most of its value as a bond. In this case, the value of the bond reacts negatively to interest rate volatility. As the value of the firm increases, the convertible acts as equity and reacts favorably to the volatility of the firm. These relationships are shown in Exhibit 14.13.

EXHIBIT 14.10
Boundaries for Convertible Bond with Call Provision

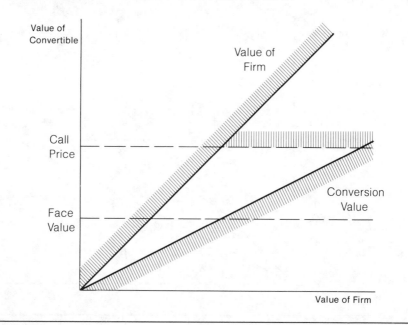

EXHIBIT 14.11
Callable Convertible Bonds and Default Risk

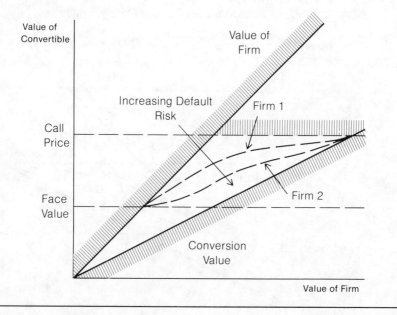

EXHIBIT 14.12
Callable Convertible Bonds and Interest Rates

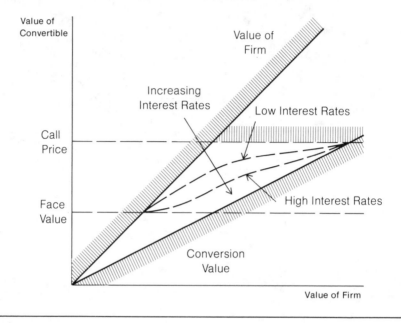

EXHIBIT 14.13
Convertible Callable Bonds and Interest Rate Volatility

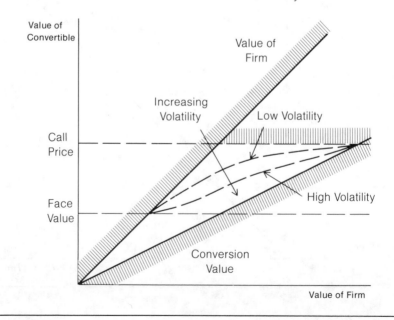

COMPOUND OPTIONS

Earlier in this chapter we saw that risky coupon debt could be viewed as a compound option. We have also seen that the stock of a particular firm can be viewed as a call option. If call options trade on the stock of this firm, then the listed call option could be viewed as an option on an option. Geske has provided a valuation equation for such an option when the underlying value of the firm follows a geometric Wiener process. The model is presented in Chapter 16. In this section we shall provide a few more examples of compound options.

Standard Operating Leases

A *standard operating lease* is a contract that provides the *lessee* with the right to use a specific asset over a specific time period in exchange for periodic rental payments. If the lessee does not make a payment, the lessor can recoup the asset.

Consider an asset that is leased for three periods. The last rental payment, P_3, purchases the right to use the asset for the last period. Payment of P_2 in period 2 purchases the right to use the asset in period 2, as well as an option to make the last rental payment in period 3. Similarly, by paying P_1 the lessee receives the right to use the asset for one period and an option to continue the lease into period 2. The strike price of this option is, of course, P_2. Moreover, if this option is exercised, it will result in the lessee's receiving another option of strike price P_3, which can be exercised in period 3. The lease contract thus provides the lessee with a sequence of options. Using a compound option framework, McConnell and Schallheim have evaluated the worth of such leases.

Life Insurance as Compound Options

Consider an annual premium term insurance contract that offers a renewal guarantee and guaranteed renewal premiums over a fixed number of years. At the end of each year, policyholders will renew their policies if it is in their interest. For example, if an insured becomes ill, renewal of the policy is more likely than if the insured remains healthy. If, on the other hand, interest rates rise, premiums on newly issued policies may fall, in which case healthy policyowners may find it advantageous to let their original policies lapse in favor of new ones.

Such life insurance contracts could be analyzed in an option pricing framework. In each period the insuree pays a premium that provides coverage over the next period and an option to continue coverage over the following period. If this option is exercised, the policyholder receives another option. The contingent claim inherent in the renewal contract clearly has value to the insuree and, equivalently, from the insurer's viewpoint is expensive to provide. This fact suggests that these premiums should be somewhat higher than single-period plans with no renewal terms.

In addition to these problems, compound options have been used extensively to value American options on stocks that pay dividends, and to value securities of firms when stocks pay dividends or when bonds pay coupons.

OPTIONS ON THE MINIMUM OR THE MAXIMUM OF TWO RISKY ASSETS

A wide variety of contingent claims of interest in financial economics have a payoff function that includes the payoff of a put or call option on the minimum or maximum of the prices of two risky assets. In this section we shall provide a few examples of such claims, including the valuation of secured debt, foreign currency bonds, optional bonds, and certain compensation contracts.

Valuation of Secured Debt

Consider a firm that issues a discount bond with face value F_j and maturity T. The bond is secured by a collateral that pays no dividends and is currently priced at S_0. Assume that this debt is junior to another debt of face value F_s, which also matures at time T. According to the indentures, no dividends are allowed before maturity.

Let V_T be the value of the firm at maturity. In the event of default, the bondholders will receive the value of the collateral, S_T. If the residual value of the firm once the senior debt is paid out exceeds S_T, the bondholders will receive additional funds up to a maximum of F_j.

The value of the secured bond at time T, B_T, can be represented as

$$B_T = \text{Min}[F_j, \text{Max}(V_T - F_s, S_T)].$$

This equation can be written as

$$B_T = F_j - \text{Max}[F_j - \text{Max}(V_T - F_s, S_T), 0]. \tag{14.24}$$

Hence, the terminal value of the bond can be represented by the payment of a riskless bond of face value F_j, less the terminal payout of a put option on the maximum of the two risky values. The first risky value is the residual value of the firm once the senior debt is paid out; the second risky value is the value of the secured collateral. The strike price of the option is the face value, F_j.

To avoid riskless arbitrage opportunities, the current value of the bond must equal the value of a riskless bond of face value F_j, less the current value of a European put option on the maximum of the two risky values. The put premium can be interpreted as the additional discount investors must be offered to entice them away from holding riskless bonds.

Foreign Currency Bonds

A simple foreign currency discount bond is a bond whose face value is denominated in a different currency from the currency in which the common stock is traded. Consider a firm of value V_0 that has issued a discount foreign currency bond of face value F^* in foreign currency. Assume the firm has no other debt and does not declare any dividends prior to maturity at time T. Let $x(T)$ be the exchange rate at time T. That is, $x(T)$ is the domestic price of one unit of foreign currency. The payout in domestic currency of the bond at time T is FB_T, where

$$FB_T = \text{Min}[V_T, x(T)F^*].$$ (14.25)

Note that the terms in parentheses in the above equation are uncertain at the current time. Equation (14.25) can be trivially rewritten as

$$FB_T = \text{Max}[0, \text{Min}(V_T, x(T)F^*) - 0].$$ (14.26)

That is, the final payout of the foreign currency bond can be viewed as the payout from a call option on the minimum of two values. The first risky value is the value of the firm; the second risky value is the local currency value of the face price of the bond. The strike price of this option is zero. To avoid riskless arbitrage, the current value of the foreign currency bond must equal the current value of the call option on the minimum of the two risky prices.

Optional Bonds

An *optional discount bond* issued by a firm is a discount bond that promises to pay at maturity either F^* units of foreign currency or F units of domestic currency at the choice of the bearer. Let $B(V_T, x(T), F^*, F)$ be the value of the bond at maturity. As before, we assume the firm has no other debts and pays out no dividends prior to maturity. At maturity, six possible states of nature are possible. Exhibit 14.14 lists these states and gives the value of the bond in each state.

EXHIBIT 14.14
Bond Payouts Under Different States

State	Payout of Bond
$F < x(T)F^* \leq V_T$	$x(T)F^*$
$x(T)F^* < F \leq V_T$	F
$F < V_T \leq x(T)F^*$	V_T
$x(T)F^* < V_T \leq F$	V_T
$V_T < F \leq x(T)F^*$	V_T
$V_T < x(T)F^* \leq F$	V_T

The payouts can be replicated by a portfolio consisting of a riskless discount bond of face value F, a written European put option on the value of the firm with strike F, and a European option on the minimum of two risky values, V_T and H. V_T is the value of the firm and H is the value, in dollars, of a foreign riskless bond of face value F^* and maturity T. That is, at time 0 we have $H_0 = \exp(-r^*T)F^*x(0)$ where r^* is the riskless rate in the foreign currency, and at expiration we have $H_T = F^*x(T)$. The current value of this portfolio, W_0, can be written as

$$W_0 = B_0 + M(V,H; F,T) - P(V; F,T) \qquad (14.27)$$

where

$B_0 = F\exp(-rT)$ is the current value of the discount bond,

$M(V,H; F,T)$ is the value of the option bond on the minimum of V and H, and

$P(V; F,T)$ is the value of the put option on the value of the firm.

The final value of this portfolio, W_T, is given by

$$W_T = F + \text{Max}[\text{Min}(V_T, x(T)F^*) - F,0] - \text{Max}(F - V_T,0).$$

Exhibit 14.15 values this portfolio in each of the six possible states. The exhibit shows that the final payouts of this portfolio are exactly equal to the payouts of the optional bond. Hence, to avoid riskless arbitrage values, the current value of the optional bond, FB_0, must equal the current value of the portfolio, W_0. That is,

$$FB_0 = B_0 + M(V,H; F,T) - P(V; F,T). \qquad (14.28)$$

EXHIBIT 14.15
Payouts of a Replicating Portfolio

State	Bond Value	Value of Option on Minimum	Value of Put	Portfolio Value
$F < x(T)F^* \le V_T$	F	$x(T)F - F$	0	$x(T)F$
$x(T)F^* < F \le V_T$	F	0	0	F
$F < V_T \le x(T)F^*$	F	$V_T - F$	0	V_T
$x(T)F^* < V_T \le F$	F	0	$F - V_T$	V_T
$V_T < F \le x(T)F^*$	F	0	$F - V_T$	V_T
$V_T < x(T)F^* \le F$	F	0	$F - V_T$	V_T

Compensation Contracts

As a final example of options on minimums or maximums, consider a compensation contract that promises the payment at date T of either a fixed fee, F, or a value that depends on the realization of some random variable, Z, at time T, whichever is greater. For example, the incentive variable Z could be sales of a particular product and the contract specifies that compensation would be either \$1 million or 5 percent of sales, whichever is greater.

In general, let CW_T be the compensation at time T. Then this compensation could be written as

$$CW_T = \text{Max}(F,\lambda Z) \qquad (14.29)$$

where λ is the given fraction.

The simplistic representation given by the above equation ignores the fact that the firm is risky and may not be able to pay. For simplicity, we assume the firm has no debt except for the promised payment of F and does not pay dividends before time T. In this case the final payment the creditor receives is at least F or the value of the firm, whichever is smaller. If the value of the firm exceeds F, the creditor may receive additional dollars dependent on the measure λZ. Specifically, we have $CW_T = \text{Min}[V_T, \text{Max}(F, \lambda Z)]$.

In order to value this contract, consider a replicating portfolio. It consists of a discount bond of face value F and maturity T, a written European put option on the value of the firm with strike F and maturity T, and an option on the minimum of V and λZ with strike F and maturity T.

The initial value of the portfolio, W_0, is given by

$$W_0 = B_0 - P(V; F, T) + M(V, \lambda Z; F, T) \qquad (14.30)$$

where $B_0 = F\exp(-rT)$ = the value of the discount bond

$P(V; F, T)$ = the value of the put, and

$M(V, \lambda Z; F, T)$ = the value of the option on the minimum of the two random variables.

To see that this portfolio replicates the payouts of the compensation contract, consider all possible future outcomes.

The value of the portfolio at expiration is given by

$$W_T = F - \text{Max}(F - V_T, 0) + \text{Max}[\text{Min}(V_T, \lambda Z) - F, 0]. \qquad (14.31)$$

Exhibit 14.16 illustrates the final payouts of the portfolio for all possible states. The last column of the exhibit gives the payouts of the compensation contract according to equation (14.31).

Since the final value of the portfolio equals the final value of the compensation contract, it must follow that their current values are the same. That is,

$$CW_0 = B_0 - P(V; F, T) + M(V, \lambda Z; F, T). \qquad (14.32)$$

EXHIBIT 14.16
Payouts of a Replicating Portfolio

State	Bond Value	Value of Option on Minimum	Value of Put	Portfolio Value	CW_T
$F < \lambda Z \leq V$	F	$\lambda Z - F$	0	λZ	λZ
$\lambda Z < F \leq V$	F	0	0	F	F
$F < V \leq \lambda Z$	F	$V - F$	0	V	V
$\lambda Z < V \leq F$	F	0	$F - V$	V	V
$V < F \leq \lambda Z$	F	0	$F - V$	V	V
$V < \lambda Z \leq F$	F	0	$F - V$	V	V

A Pricing Model for European Options on the Minimum or Maximum of Two Risky Assets

All the above examples suggest the need for a pricing model for European options on the minimum or maximum of two risky assets. Stulz has derived such a model under the assumption that the prices of the two risky assets follow a bivariate geometric Wiener process.

Specifically, let μ_v and σ_v^2 and μ_h and σ_h^2 be the instantaneous means and variances of the prices V and H and let ρ_{vh} be the correlation between the two processes. Then we can write

$$\frac{dV}{V} = \mu_v dt + \sigma_v dw_v$$

$$\frac{dH}{H} = \mu_h dt + \sigma_h dw_h$$

$$\text{Cor}(dw_v, dw_h) = \rho_{vh}.$$

Stulz obtains the following European call price for the option on the minimum of V and H:

$$M(V_0, H_0; F, T) = H_0 N_2(\alpha_1, \alpha_2; \rho_c) + V_0 N_2(\beta_1, \beta_2; \rho_c) - F \exp(-rT) N_2(\gamma_1, \gamma_2, \rho_{vh}), \tag{14.33}$$

where V_0 and H_0 are the two risky assets, F is the strike price, T is the time to expiration, $N_2(a, b, \theta)$ is the bivariate cumulative standard normal distribution with upper limits of integration a and b, and the correlation coefficient is θ. In this case,

$$\alpha_1 = \gamma_1 + \sigma_h \sqrt{T}$$

$$\alpha_2 = \frac{\ln(V_0/H_0) - \sigma^2 \sqrt{T}/2}{\sigma \sqrt{T}}$$

$$\beta_1 = \gamma_2 + \sigma_v \sqrt{T}$$

$$\beta_2 = \frac{\ln(H_0/V_0) - \sigma^2 \sqrt{T}/2}{\sigma \sqrt{T}}$$

$$\gamma_1 = \frac{\ln(H_0/F) + (r - \sigma_h^2/2)T}{\sigma_h \sqrt{T}}$$

$$\gamma_2 = \frac{\ln(V_0/F) + (r - \sigma_v^2/2)T}{\sigma_v \sqrt{T}}$$

$$\sigma^2 = \sigma_v^2 + \sigma_h^2 - 2\rho_{vh}\sigma_v\sigma_h$$

$$\rho_c = \frac{(\rho_{vh}\sigma_v - \sigma_h)}{\sigma \sqrt{T}}$$

For further details and applications of the model, the reader should refer to Stulz.

EXCHANGE OPTIONS

An *exchange option* allows the holder to exchange one unit of asset H for one unit of asset V at maturity. The value of such an option at maturity date, T, is given by E_T, where

$$E_T = \text{Max}(V_T - H_T, 0). \tag{14.34}$$

An exchange option is closely related to an option on the minimum of two risky assets when the later strike price is zero. To see this, let W_0 be the present value of a portfolio consisting of one unit of V and a written option that allows the holder to exchange one unit of asset H for one unit of asset V at maturity. The value of this portfolio at maturity, W_T, is

$$W_T = V_T - \text{Max}(V_T - H_T, 0) = H_T \quad \text{if } V_T > H_T$$

$$= V_T \quad \text{if } V_T \leq H_T. \tag{14.35}$$

The value of a call option on the minium of V and H, with an exercise price of zero, at the maturity date T, is given by M_T, where

$$M_T = \text{Max}[0, \text{Min}(V_T, H_T) - 0]$$

$$= H_T \quad \text{if } V_T > H_T$$

$$= V_T \quad \text{if } V_T \leq H_T \tag{14.36}$$

Since the payout of this option equals the payout of the portfolio, it must follow that their current values are the same. That is, $V_0 - E_0 = M_0$, or more precisely,

$$E(H, V; T) = V_0 - M(V, H; 0, T). \tag{14.37}$$

The formula for an option on the minimum of two risky asset prices simplifies if the strike price is zero. As a result, the formula for an exchange option simplifies. Specifically, it can be shown that

$$E(H, V; T) = V_0 N(d_1) - H_0 N(d_2) \tag{14.38}$$

where

$$d_1 = \frac{ln(V_0/H_0) + \sigma^2 T/2}{\sigma\sqrt{T}}$$

$$d_2 = d_1 - \sigma\sqrt{T}$$

where σ is defined earlier.

This model, first developed by Margrabe, can be applied to situations where one large firm tenders for shares of a second smaller firm by offering one of its own shares, currently priced at $100, say, for one of the second firm's shares, currently priced at $80, say. Assume the offer to exchange shares might be good for 60 days. Essentially, shareholders of the second firm have received an option to exchange one of its shares for one share of the other firm's stock.

A sensitivity analysis of the exchange option price reveals that the option price increases as the correlation between the two assets becomes more negative.

An exchange option can also be viewed as a generalization of the Black-Scholes model to the case where the exercise price is now a random variable. Applications of uncertain exercise prices have been given by Fischer.

CONCLUSION

The theory of option pricing as it applies to the valuation of corporate securities is referred to as *contingent claims analysis*. In this chapter, a contingent claims approach has been applied to value a variety of corporate securities. Included in the analyses were valuation of equity, discount bonds, subordinated debt, options on options, lease agreements, optional bonds, incentive contracts, warrants, and convertibles. The examples presented emphasized the fact that these securities could be viewed, and hence valued, as portfolios of contingent claims. The focus of this chapter has been on formulating problems as portfolios of options. Very seldom are simple closed-form equations available for these claims and numerical methods are usually required to obtain solutions. Such procedures are described in Chapter 16.

References

The original Black and Scholes article emphasized the fact that corporate liabilities could be viewed as combinations of simple option contracts. Since then, contingent claims analyses have been used to value all types of corporate securities. The references below list some applications of this theory.

Bartter, B., and R. Rendleman, Jr. "Fee-Based Pricing of Fixed-Rate Bank Loan Commitments." *Financial Management* 8(Spring 1979): 13–20.

Black, F., and J. Cox. "Valuing Corporate Securities: Some Effects of Bond Indenture Provisions." *Journal of Finance* 31(May 1976): 351–68.

Black, F., and M. Scholes. "The Pricing of Options and Corporate Liabilities." *Journal of Political Economy* 81(1973): 637–59.

Boyle, P., and E. Schwartz. "Equilibrium Prices of Guarantees Under Equity-Linked Contracts." *Journal of Risk and Insurance* 44(December 1977): 639–80.

Brennan, M., and E. Schwartz. "The Pricing of Equity-Linked Life Insurance Policies with an Asset Value Guarantee." *Journal of Financial Economics* 3(June 1976): 195–213.

Brennan, M., and E. Schwartz. "Convertible Bonds: Valuation and Optimal Strategies for Call and Conversion." *Journal of Finance* 32(December 1977): 1699–1716.

Brennan, M., and E. Schwartz. "Corporate Income Taxes, Valuation and the Problem of Optimal Capital Structure." *Journal of Business* 51(January 1978): 103–14.

Brennan, M., and E. Schwartz. "Savings Bonds: Valuation and Optimal Redemption Strategies." In *Financial Economics: Essays in Honor of Paul Cootner*, edited by W. Sharpe and C. Cootner. Englewood Cliffs, N.J.: Prentice-Hall, 1982, pp. 202–15.

Brennan, M., and E. Schwartz. "Savings Bonds, Retractable Bonds, and Callable Bonds," *Journal of Financial Economics* 5(August 1977): 67–88.

Brennan, M., and E. Schwartz. "Evaluating Natural Resource Investments." *Journal of Business* 58(1985): 135–57.

Constantinides, G. "Warrant Exercise and Bond Conversion in Competitive Markets." *Journal of Financial Economics* 13(September 1984): 371–97.

Constantinides, G., and R. Rosenthal. "Strategic Analysis of the Competitive Exercise of Certain Financial Options." *Journal of Economic Theory* 32(February 1984): 128–38.

Copeland, T., and J. Weston. "A Note on the Evaluation of Cancellable Operating Leases." *Financial Management* (Summer 1982): 60–67.

Cox, J., J. Ingersoll, Jr., and S. Ross. "An Analysis of Variable Rate Loan Contracts." *Journal of Finance* 35(May 1980): 389–404.

Cox, J., and M. Rubinstein. *Option Markets.* Englewood Cliffs, N.J.: Prentice-Hall, 1985.

Dunn, K., and J. McConnell. "Valuation of GNMA Mortgage-Backed Securities." *Journal of Finance* 35(June 1981): 599–616.

Emanuel, D. "Warrant Valuation and Exercise Strategy." *Journal of Financial Economics* 12(August 1983): 211–36.

Emanuel, D. "A Theoretical Model for Valuing Preferred Stock." *Journal of Finance* 38(September 1983): 1133–55.

Fischer, S. "Call Option Pricing When the Exercise Price Is Uncertain, and the Valuation of Index Bonds." *Journal of Finance* 33(March 1978): 169–76.

Galai, D. "Pricing of Optional Bonds." *Journal of Banking and Finance* 7(September 1983): 323–37.

Galai, D., and R. Masulis. "The Option Pricing Model and the Risk Factor of Stock." *Journal of Financial Economics* 3(January–March 1976): 53–81.

Galai, D., and M. Schneller. "Pricing Warrants and the Value of the Firm." *Journal of Finance* 33(December 1978): 1333–42.

Geske, R. "The Valuation of Corporate Liabilities as Compound Options." *Journal of Financial and Quantitative Analysis* 12(November 1977): 541–52.

Geske, R., and H. Johnson. "The Valuation of Corporate Liabilities as Compound Options: A Correction." *Journal of Financial and Quantitative Analysis* 19(June 1984): 231–32.

Hawkins, G. "An Analysis of Revolving Credit Agreements," *Journal of Financial Economics* 10(March 1982): 529–82.

Ho, T., and R. Singer. "Bond Indenture Provisions and the Risk of Corporate Debt." *Journal of Financial Economics* 10(December 1982): 375–406.

Ho, T., and R. Singer. "The Value of Corporate Debt with a Sinking-Fund Provision." *Journal of Business* 57(July 1984): 315–36.

Hsia, C. "Optimal Debt of a Firm: An Option Pricing Approach." *Journal of Financial Research* 4(Fall 1981): 221–31.

Ingersoll, J., Jr. "A Contingent-Claims Valuation of Convertible Securities." *Journal of Financial Economics* 4(May 1977): 289–322.

Ingersoll, J., Jr. "An Examination of Corporate Call Policies on Convertible Securities." *Journal of Finance* 32(May 1977): 463–78.

Ingersoll, J., Jr. "A Theoretical Model and Empirical Investigation of the Dual Purpose Funds: An Application of Contingent-Claims Analysis." *Journal of Financial Economics* 3(January–March 1976): 83–123.

Jones, E., and S. Mason. "Valuation of Loan Guarantees." *Journal of Banking and Finance* 4(March 1980): 89–107.

Lee, W., M. Martin, and A. Senchack. "An Option Pricing Approach to the Evaluation of Salvage Values in Financial Lease Arrangements." Working Paper, University of Texas at Austin, 1980.

Majd, S., and R. Pindyck. "Time to Build, Option Value, and Investment Decisions." MIT Energy Laboratory Working Paper No. MIT-EL 85-011WP.

Margrabe, W. "The Value of an Option to Exchange One Asset for Another." *Journal of Finance* 33(March 1978): 177–86.

Mason, S., and S. Bhattacharya. "Risky Debt, Jump Processes, and Safety Covenants." *Journal of Financial Economics* 9(September 1981): 281–307.

Mason, S., and R. Merton. "The Role of Contingent Claims Analysis in Corporate Finance." In *Recent Advances in Corporate Finance*, E. Altman and M. Subrahmanyam, eds. Homewood, Ill.: Dow Jones-Irwin, 1985.

McConnell, J., and J. Schallheim. "Valuation of Asset Leasing Contracts." *Journal of Financial Economics* 12(1983): 237–61.

McDonald, R., and D. Siegel. "Investment and the Valuation of Firms When There Is an Option to Shut Down." *International Economic Review* 26(June 1985): 331–49.

Merton, R. "An Analytic Derivation of the Cost of Deposit Insurance and Loan Guarantee: An Application of Modern Option Pricing Theory." *Journal of Banking and Finance* 1(June 1977): 3–11.

Merton, R. "On the Pricing of Corporate Debt: The Risk Structure of Interest Rates." *Journal of Finance* 29(May 1974): 449–70.

Schwartz, E. "The Valuation of Warrants: Implementing a New Approach." *Journal of Financial Economics* 4(January 1977): 79–93.

Smith, C., Jr. "Applications of Option Pricing Analysis." In *Handbook of Financial Economics,* edited by J. Bicksler. New York: North-Holland Publishing, 1979, pp. 79–121.

Smith, C., Jr. "On the Theory of Financial Contracting: The Personal Loan Market." *Journal of Monetary Economics* 6(July 1980): 333–57.

Smith, C., Jr., and J. Zimmerman. "Valuing Employee Stock Option Plans Using Option Pricing Models." *Journal of Accounting Research* 14(Autumn 1976): 357–64.

Sosin, H. "On the Valuation of Federal Loan Guarantees to Corporations." *Journal of Finance* 35(December 1980): 1209–21.

Stapleton, R., and M. Subrahmanyam. "The Valuation of Multivariate Contingent Claims in Discrete Time Models." *Journal of Finance* 39(March 1984): 207–28.

Stulz, R. "Options on the Minimum or the Maximum of Two Risky Assets: Analysis and Applications." *Journal of Financial Economics* 10(July 1982): 161–85.

Exercises

1. Consider a firm of value $40 million. Assume the only debt consists of a discount bond of face value $10 million that matures in one year. The riskless rate is 8 percent, and the annual volatility rate is 0.25.

   a. Compute the value of the corporate discount bond.

   b. State the assumptions you have made.

   c. Compute the default risk premium.

2. Reconsider the previous problem. If the face value of the debt was $20 million, what would the default risk premium be? Explain why the value differs from the risk premium in question 1.

3. A down-and-out option must be exercised if the stock underlying security price drops below a certain value (that may vary over time.)

   a. Using the binomial model, show with an illustration how a down-and-out option price can be computed. Explain why a down-and-out call option will never be worth more than a regular call option with the same strike and time to expiration.

   b. Based on your analysis, explain why strict bond convenants have value to bondholders.

4. "The payout of a subordinated bond is similar to the payout on a bullish European call spread." Under what circumstances, if any, is the above statement true?

5. Explain why a corporate coupon bond cannot be perceived as a portfolio of discount bonds with face values that match the coupon payments.

6. Consider a European warrant, corporate discount bond, and corporate convertible discount bond. Can the payouts of the convertible be replicated by the warrant and convertible bond? If your answer is yes, provide the detailed arbitrage portfolio.

7. Reconsider Example 14.3, assuming six shares were outstanding, rather than five,
   a. What would the value of the warrant be if the firm distributed the warrant income immediately to the shareholders?
   b. What would the warrant value be if the warrant income was returned?

8. Should warrant-holders request in an indenture that the firm pay out no dividends over the lifetime of the warrant? Justify your answer.

9. Construct a binomial model that values a European convertible bond. In order to establish this model, distinguish two cases. In the first case, assume the income from the convertible issue is distributed to the shareholders. In the second case, assume no dividends are declared. In the latter case an iterative algorithm must be developed.

10. Provide two examples that apply the concept of options on the minimum or maximum of two risky assets.

11. In some lease arrangements, the lessee has the right to buy the item for a fixed price at the expiration date of the lease. How could such an option be valued? In particular, how would volatility be estimated?

12. The management of an electric utility faces a choice between building a power plant that burns oil and one that burns either oil or coal. Although the latter plant is costlier, it offers management greater flexibility. In making the choice between the two plants, management must assess the value of this operating option. Using a contingent claims approach, discuss the issues that one may encounter in comparing these two alternatives.

13. A warranty allows the owner to obtain a rebate on an item if the item fails. This right exists over a prespecified lifetime. Can a warranty be viewed as an option? What problems, if any, are encountered when using a contingent claims approach to value a warranty?

15

Foreign Currency Options

Imports and exports can account for a significant percentage of Gross National Product. In the U.S., for example, exports account for over 10 percent of GNP, while in Britain the figure is close to 25 percent. Trades of this magnitude would not be possible without the ability to easily buy and sell foreign currencies. Hedging foreign exchange risk by means of forward, futures, or foreign currency options is becoming an increasingly important feature of treasury management in international corporations and banks.

The bulk of foreign currency transactions take place in the interbank foreign exchange market. This market, which consists of a spot and forward market, is discussed in the next section. Until 1972 the interbank market was the only channel through which foreign exchange transactions took place. Since then, organized markets in foreign currency futures, options on foreign currencies, and options on currency futures have developed. Relative to the interbank foreign exchange market, however, the organized markets are still quite small.

In the next section a brief overview of the interbank and organized exchange markets is presented. Then a brief discussion of forward, futures, and foreign currency options is provided. Examples of a few foreign currency contracts are presented, together with some strategies. Some arbitrage relationships unique to foreign currencies are then presented. The final section looks at a valuation model for foreign currency options.

THE INTERBANK FOREIGN EXCHANGE MARKET

The bulk of foreign exchange transactions are done over the telephone between specialized divisions of the large head offices of the major banks. These banks have rooms equipped with electronic communication devices that allow them to communicate with other banks around the world. The market has no regular trading hours and currencies can be bought or sold somewhere 24 hours a day. The banks are referred to as *market makers* since they trade in the major currencies on a more or less continuous basis. When

366

extremely large transactions occur, *foreign exchange brokers* may be employed as middlemen to find takers for these deals. Unlike specialists at the major banks, these brokers do not trade on their own accounts. Rather, they specialize in large transactions.

The exchange rates quoted in financial newspapers refer to quotes made by banks to other banks for currency deals in excess of $1 million. Exhibit 15.1 shows daily exchange rates as reported in the *Wall Street Journal*. These rates are expressed as the number of units of a particular currency that exchange for one U.S. dollar and the number of U.S. dollars that exchange for one unit of foreign currency.

Regional banks do not deal directly in the interbank foreign exchange

EXHIBIT 15.1
Foreign Exchange Rates

FOREIGN EXCHANGE

Monday, July 14, 1986

The New York foreign exchange selling rates below apply to trading among banks in amounts of $1 million and more, as quoted at 3 p.m. Eastern time by Bankers Trust Co. Retail transactions provide fewer units of foreign currency per dollar.

Country	U.S. $ equiv. Mon.	Fri.	Currency per U.S. $ Mon.	Fri.
Argentina (Austral) ...	1.1223	1.1364	.891	.8800
Australia (Dollar)	.6431	.6387	1.5549	1.5657
Austria (Schilling)	.06523	.06532	15.33	15.31
Belgium (Franc)				
Commercial rate	.02232	.02227	44.80	44.90
Financial rate	.02217	.02215	45.10	45.15
Brazil (Cruzado)	.07225	.07262	13.84	13.77
Britain (Pound)	1.4868	1.5057	.6725	.6641
30-Day Forward ...	1.4820	1.5016	.6747	.6660
90-Day Forward ...	1.4738	1.4934	.6785	.6696
180-Day Forward ...	1.4618	1.4821	.6841	.6747
Canada (Dollar)	.7274	.7259	1.3746	1.3776
30-Day Forward	.7264	.7249	1.3766	1.3795
90-Day Forward ...	.7243	.7228	1.3806	1.3835
180-Day Forward ...	.7212	.7195	1.3866	1.3899
Chile (Official rate) ...	.005225	.005227	191.40	191.30
China (Yuan)	.2708	.2707	3.6920	3.6943
Colombia (Peso)	.005138	.005174	194.61	193.28
Denmark (Krone)	.1226	.1228	8.1550	8.1450
Ecuador (Sucre)				
Official rate	.009153	.009153	109.25	109.25
Floating rate	.005992	.005893	166.90	169.68
Finland (Markka)	.1952	.1963	5.1225	5.0950
France (Franc)	.1435	.1423	6.9700	7.0255
30-Day Forward	.1434	.1423	6.9725	7.0275
90-Day Forward ...	.1433	.1421	6.9805	7.0360
180-Day Forward ...	.1430	.1419	6.99	7.0480
Greece (Drachma)	.007153	.007168	139.80	139.50
Hong Kong (Dollar) ...	.1280	.1280	7.8110	7.8110
India (Rupee)	.07981	.07981	12.53	12.53
Indonesia (Rupiah)	.0008834	.0008834	1132.00	1132.00
Ireland (Punt)	1.3710	1.3815	.7294	.7239
Israel (Shekel)	.6689	.6698	1.495	1.493
Italy (Lira)	.0006689	.0006680	1495.00	1493.00
Japan (Yen)	.006264	.006200	159.65	161.30
30-Day Forward	.006275	.006212	159.35	160.97
90-Day Forward	.006297	.006234	158.80	160.42
180-Day Forward ...	.006329	.006267	158.00	159.56
Jordan (Dinar)	3.0175	3.0175	.3314	.3314
Kuwait (Dinar)	3.4048	3.4048	.2937	.2937
Lebanon (Pound)	.02381	.02203	42.00	45.40
Malaysia (Ringgit)	.3749	.3778	2.6670	2.6670
Malta (Lira)	2.5974	2.5543	.3850	.3915
Netherland(Guilder) .	.4071	.4077	2.4565	2.4530
New Zealand (Dollar)	.5320	.5340	1.8796	1.8727
Norway (Krone)	.1311	.1328	7.6300	7.5325
Pakistan (Rupee)	.06024	.05988	16.60	16.70
Peru (Inti)	.07168	.07168	13.95	13.95
Philippines (Peso)	.04892	.04866	20.44	20.55
Portugal (Escudo)	.006658	.006720	150.20	148.80
Saudi Arabia (Riyal) ..	.2666	.2665	3.7505	3.7520
Singapore (Dollar)	.4597	.4553	2.1750	2.1965
South Africa (Rand)				
Commercial rate	.3815	.3880	2.6212	2.5773
Financial rate	.2140	.2150	4.6728	4.6511
South Korea (Won)	.001130	.001127	884.60	887.70
Spain (Peseta)	.007194	.007245	139.00	138.22
Sweden (Krona)	.1401	.1405	7.1400	7.1175
Switzerland (Franc) ...	.5643	.5599	1.7720	1.7860
30-Day Forward	.5656	.5610	1.7680	1.7826
90-Day Forward	.5668	.5628	1.7600	1.7769
180-Day Forward ...	.5698	.5653	1.7550	1.7690
Taiwan (Dollar)	.02627	.02625	38.07	38.10
Thailand (Baht)	.03818	.03797	26.19	26.34
Turkey (Lira)	.001462	.001480	684.04	689.74
United Arab(Dirham)	.2719	.2719	3.673	3.673
Uruguay (New Peso)				
Financial	.006633	.006633	150.75	150.75
Venezuela (Bolivar)				
Official rate	.1333	.1333	7.50	7.50
Floating rate	.05495	.05495	18.20	18.20
W. Germany (Mark) ..	.4608	.4571	2.1700	2.1875
30-Day Forward	.4680	.4580	2.1650	2.1832
90-Day Forward	.4700	.4596	2.1605	2.1759
180-Day Forward ...	.4750	.4619	2.1550	2.1649
SDR	1.17706	1.18211	0.849571	0.845944
ECU	0.973693	0.979441	....	....

Special Drawing Rights are based on exchange rates for the U.S., West German, British, French and Japanese currencies. Source: International Monetary Fund.

ECU is based on a basket of community currencies. Source: European Community Commission.

z-Not quoted.

market. Usually they have special arrangements with larger banks. Corporations and individuals that require foreign currency engage in such transactions through their own banks. Banks typically charge their customers a higher price for foreign currency than those quoted in the newspapers. The difference in rates partially reflects the bank's profit margin and provides compensation to the bank for holding foreign currency in denominations too small to be sold in the interbank market.

The spot market is not the only foreign currency market that is maintained. For the major currencies, up to four prices will be quoted. One is the spot price. The others are the 30-day forward, 90-day forward, and 180-day forward. The 90-day forward rate, for example, is the rate at which a trader can contract for delivery of some foreign currency in 90 days. The major currencies traded by U.S. banks are the German mark, the British pound sterling, the Canadian dollar, the Swiss franc, the Japanese yen, and the French franc. The annual turnover in currencies exceeds $600 billion. Most of this activity is focused on the spot market. Activity in the forward markets accounts for less then 30 percent of total activity.

Forward markets allow international firms to hedge foreign currency risks. As an example, importers, who must pay for foreign goods in foreign currencies in the future, can eliminate risks of adverse movements in exchange rates by buying forward contracts. Similarly, exporters, who expect to receive foreign currency in the future, can sell these funds forward, thus avoiding the risk of anticipated drops in the foreign currency. In addition to forward contracts, large banks may offer their corporate customers tailor-made foreign exchange option contracts. These over-the-counter contracts offer clients hedging facilities that may be more appropriate to use than forward contracts. These contracts are discussed later in this chapter. While the large U.S. banks issue foreign currency options to their corporate clients, currently there is no interbank option market. For this reason, the premiums for put and call foreign currency options quoted by any bank may depend on other current positions the bank has in the foreign currency. As a result, the premiums may vary significantly among the banks.

In 1984 London banks established an interbank market in foreign currency options. Through this market, banks can offset the risk created by providing options to their clients (by taking opposite positions in the market). Such a market has been quite useful and a similar market will probably emerge in the United States. Indeed, since over-the-counter options issued by banks to their corporate customers are a rapidly growing business, it is surprising that such a market has not already developed.

ORGANIZED FUTURES AND OPTION MARKETS FOR FOREIGN EXCHANGE

In 1972 the International Monetary Market (IMM) of the Chicago Mercantile Exchange (CME) began trading currency futures. Unlike the forward market, in which specific tailor-made deals are struck, contracts in this market are fully standardized and traded by open auction among buyers and sellers in a centralized marketplace (see Chapter 11). Unlike the forward markets, which can only be used by very large customers who deal in foreign trade, the futures market is open to traders who need hedging facilities or speculators with risk capital. This feature is facilitated by the contract sizes, which are much smaller than forward contracts. Examples of specific contracts will be provided in the next section.

In 1982 the Philadelphia Stock Exchange began trading options on some foreign currencies, and in 1984 the IMM began trading foreign options in foreign currency futures. While these markets have been growing at a steady pace, they still account for only a small fraction of foreign exchange transactions.

FOREIGN CURRENCY FORWARD AND FUTURES CONTRACTS

Consider an importer who has to pay for a shipment of goods in foreign currency in three months. To eliminate the risk of an adverse movement in exchange rates, the importer could buy the foreign currency forward. That is, a contract could be constructed that establishes a specific exchange rate of dollars for the relevant foreign currency. Regardless of the future spot exchange rate, the importer knows exactly how many dollars the imports will cost. If the dollar strengthens (weakens), the importer will have regret (no regret). By purchasing forward, however, future exchange rate risks are eliminated.

Note that a buyer of a forward contract on British pounds, say, is committed to buy a certain amount of pounds for each dollar, while the seller is committed to receive a dollar in exchange for the British pounds. The seller of the forward contract can thus be viewed as the buyer of a forward contract that locks in the price of a dollar per British pound.

Differences between forward and futures contracts were discussed in Chapter 11. Exhibit 15.2 summarizes these differences. Exhibit 15.3 summarizes the terms of a few of the foreign currency futures traded on the IMM, and Exhibit 15.4 shows the prices as reported in the *Wall Street Journal.* The exchange quotes all futures as the dollar price of each currency. Investors purchasing foreign currency futures will profit if the dollar price of the currency rises after the position is established. Equivalently, if the dollar weakens (or the other currency strengthens), the buyer profits.

Example 15.1

Consider an investor long in a September Swiss franc position. The buyer has agreed to purchase 125,000 Swiss francs for a given dollar price. Suppose the price is 0.4200 and changes to 0.4220. In this case the investor benefits since the dollar price for the same amount of francs has increased. Specifically, the investor profits by $(0.4220)(125,000) - (0.4200)(125,000) = \$250$.

EXHIBIT 15.2
Comparison of Currency Markets

Futures Market	Spot and Forward Interbank Market
Trading is conducted in a centralized marketplace by "open outcry" of bids, offers, and amounts.	Trading is done by telephone or telex banks primarily dealing with each other.
Participants buy or sell standardized contracts.	Participants quote bid and ask prices.
Nonmember participants deal through brokers who represent them on the trading floor.	Participants deal directly with each other or through brokers.
Market participants usually are unknown to one another.	The participant in each transaction is known by the other trading party.
Prices of futures are available at any point in time.	Indicated bids and offers are available throughout the interbank market.
The credit risk of the opposite side of a transaction is not important since the exchange's clearinghouse becomes the opposite side of each transaction.	The credit risk of the counterparty must be examined.
Settlements are made daily.	Forward contracts are settled on the settlement date.
A small percent (less than 8%) of all contracts result in actual delivery.	The majority of trades result in delivery.
Liquidation of a position is easy.	Forward positions are not as easy to offset or to transfer to other participants.

EXHIBIT 15.3
Some Currency Futures Contract Specifications

	British Pound (BP)	Canadian Dollar (CD)	Deutsche Mark (DM)	French Franc (FR)	Japanese Yen (JY)	Swiss Franc (SF)	European Currency Unit (ECU)
Trading Unit	BP25,000	CD100,000	DM125,000	FR250,000	JY12,500,000	SF125,000	ECU125,000
Quotations	US$ per pound	US$ per Canadian $	US$ per mark	US$ per franc	US$ per yen	US$ per franc	US$ per ECU
Minimum Price Change	.0005 = $12.50	.0001 = $12.50	.0001 = $12.50	.00005 = $12.50	(.00)0001 = $12.50	.0001 = $12.50	.0001 = $12.50
Price Limit	None	None	None	None	None	None	None
Contract Months Actively Traded			March, June, September, December				

SOURCE: *Trading and Hedging with Currency Futures and Options* (Chicago: Chicago Mercantile Exchange, 1985), p. 19.

EXHIBIT 15.4
Prices of Foreign Currency Futures

```
- FINANCIAL -

BRITISH POUND (IMM) - 25,000 pounds; $ per pound
Sept   1.4735 1.4820 1.4675 1.4765 -   .0125 1.5435 1.3240 28,123
Dec    1.4630 1.4695 1.4560 1.4650 -   .0125 1.5360 1.3250    881
   Est vol 8,877; vol Fri 16,430; open int 29,024, +329.

CANADIAN DOLLAR (IMM) - 100,000 dlrs.; $ per Can $
Sept   .7244 .7247 .7239 .7246 +.0011   .7305 .6809 8,529
Dec    .7210 .7215 .7205 .7212 +.0011   .7285 .6790 1,675
Mar87  .7175 .7182 .7175 .7178 +.0011   .7256 .6770  393
   Est vol 763; vol Fri 1,004; open int 10,670, -41.

JAPANESE YEN (IMM) 12.5 million yen; $ per yen (.00)
Sept   .6238 .6288 .6230 .6282 +.0072   .6317 .4690 44,512
Dec    .6270 .6321 .6264 .6314 +.0072   .6348 .4720 1,511
Mar87   ....  .... .6350 +.0072   .6354 .5850  295
   Est vol 16,968; vol Fri 21,955; open int 46,318, -2,247.

SWISS FRANC (IMM) - 125,000 francs-$ per franc
Sept   .5601 .5663 .5593 .5657 +.0084   .5717 .4790 29,502
Dec    .5631 .5688 .5612 .5680 +.0083   .5743 .4878 2,124
   Est vol 18,735; vol Fri 26,630; open int 31,660, -1,690.

W. GERMAN MARK (IMM) - 125,000 marks; $ per mark
Sept   .4587 .4632 .4577 .4631 +.0063   .4675 .3762 42,469
Dec    .4610 .4652 .4601 .4654 +.0063   .4703 .4090 1,107
   Est vol 19,655; vol Fri 29,266; open int 43,670, -835.

EURODOLLAR (LIFFE) - $1 million; pts of 100%
Sept   93.56 93.57 93.54 93.56    ....   93.78 89.06 9,617
Dec    93.47 93.48 93.45 93.48 +  .01  93.67 90.20 4,843
Mar87  93.29 93.29 93.27 93.30 +  .02  93.46 90.80 2,643
June   93.01 93.04 93.00 93.04 +  .03  93.15 90.85  893
Sept    ....  .... 92.74 +  .02  92.95 91.65  257
Dec     ....  .... 92.46 +  .05  92.34 91.96  126
   Est vol 1,444; vol Fri 6,154; open int 18,478, +273.
```

```
STERLING (LIFFE) - £500,000; pts of 100%
Sept   90.30 90.31 90.14 90.17 -   .25  91.49 87.53 7,543
Dec    90.50 90.51 90.38 90.39 -   .24  91.63 87.88 3,862
Mar87  90.42 90.43 90.30 90.31 -   .25  91.45 88.00 2,346
June   90.28 90.28 90.15 90.16 -   .29  91.45 90.08 1,264
Sept    ....  .... 90.05 -   .25  91.30 90.48  902
   Est vol 6,341; vol Fri 3,323; open int 15,989, +338.

LONG GILT (LIFFE) - £50,000; 32nds of 100%
Sept   120-18 120-18 119-05 119-15 -  1-24 130-10 119-05 14,864
Dec    120-01 120-02 119-09 119-10 -  1-22 125-07 119-09  548
Mar87   .... 119-04 -  1-22 120-17 120-17   0
   Est vol 14,908; vol Fri 7,252; open int 15,412, +101.

EURODOLLAR (IMM) - $1 million; pts of 100%
                                           Yield       Open
       Open High Low Settle Chg   Settle Chg Interest
Sept   93.56 93.63 93.54 93.61 + .04   6.39 - .04 76,011
Dec    93.46 93.55 93.43 93.53 + .06   6.47 - .06 38,366
Mr87   93.26 93.35 93.25 93.34 + .07   6.66 - .07 19,393
June   93.00 93.08 92.98 93.08 + .07   6.92 - .07 10,705
Sept   92.71 92.80 92.70 92.79 + .07   7.21 - .07 6,757
Dec    92.42 92.51 92.42 92.51 + .07   7.49 - .07 5,110
Mr88   92.15 92.23 92.14 92.24 + .08   7.76 - .08 4,970
June   91.89 91.96 91.88 91.98 + .08   8.02 - .08 1,632
   Est vol 31,938; vol Fri 40,189; open int 16 2,944, +422.

U.S. DOLLAR INDEX (CTN) 500 times USDX
Sept   112.53 112.80 111.60 111.86 -  .89 129.00 110.71 1,391
Dec    112.92 113.13 112.03 112.23 -  .88 129.05 110.72 1,379
   Est vol 500; vol Fri 338; open int 2,795, -35.
   The index: High 112.09; Low 111.16; Close 111.21 -.79
```

Foreign currency futures markets similar to the IMM exist in other centers, such as London and Singapore. In 1982 the London International Futures exchange began trading foreign currency futures in bundles identical to those sold on the IMM. In 1984 the Singapore International Monetary Exchange began trading in a few foreign currency contracts identical to those offered by the IMM. Contracts traded on this exchange can be offset on the IMM. This arrangement expands the hours of effective trading.

FOREIGN CURRENCY OPTIONS AND OPTIONS ON FOREIGN CURRENCY FUTURES

A call (put) option on a foreign currency gives the holder the right to buy (sell) a certain amount of foreign currency at a given exchange rate. This right exists up to a given expiration date. Listed option contracts can be bought and sold in a secondary market, while dealer options are contracts between the issuing bank and corporate client.

Organized trading in foreign currency options takes place at the Philadelphia Stock Exchange, the Toronto and Montreal Stock Exchanges, and the Amsterdam Stock Exchange. Options on foreign currency futures trade at the IMM. The Philadelphia exchange is the largest exchange-based foreign currency option market. Options are traded on the British pound, German mark, Japanese yen, Swiss franc, and Canadian dollar. Options on these currencies against the U.S. dollar are also traded in Montreal and Toronto. The strike price of each option is the U.S. dollar price of a unit of foreign exchange, and the number of foreign currency units is half the contract size of the futures contract traded at the IMM of the Chicago Mercantile Exchange. The expiration dates of the options correspond to the delivery dates in the futures. Specifically, the last day of trading is the Friday before the third Wednesday of the expiration month. Although the expiration dates are established this way, it should be recognized that the option contracts are options on the spot currency, not on the futures price. Exhibit 15.5 shows the prices of foreign currency options as reported in the *Wall Street Journal*.

EXHIBIT 15.5
Foreign Currency Options

FOREIGN CURRENCY OPTIONS

Philadelphia Exchange

Monday, Jul. 14

Option & Underlying	Strike Price	Calls—Last			Puts—Last		
		Jul	Aug	Sep	Jul	Aug	Sep
12,500 British Pounds-cents per unit.							
BPound	135	r	s	r	r	s	0.30
148.57	.140	r	s	8.70	r	s	0.90
148.57	.145	r	r	5.35	r	1.30	2.70
148.57	.150	r	1.75	2.60	r	3.80	5.20
148.57	.155	r	0.50	1.05	r	r	r
148.57	.160	r	0.15	r	r	r	r
50,000 Canadian Dollars-cents per unit.							
CDollr	...74	r	r	0.19	r	r	r
62,500 West German Marks-cents per unit.							
DMark	..43	r	r	2.95	r	r	0.21
46.06	...44	r	2.25	r	r	r	0.26
46.06	...45	r	1.42	1.78	r	0.30	0.61
46.06	...46	r	0.86	1.23	r	0.78	r
46.06	...47	r	0.41	0.77	r	r	r
46.06	...48	r	0.19	0.42	r	r	r
46.06	...49	r	s	0.26	r	s	r
6,250,000 Japanese Yen-100ths of a cent per unit.							
JYen	... 54	r	s	r	r	s	0.04
62.57	...56	r	r	6.50	r	r	r
62.57	...57	r	r	r	r	r	0.16
62.57	...58	r	r	4.68	r	r	0.19
62.57	...59	r	r	r	r	0.14	r
62.57	...60	r	r	3.16	r	0.21	r
62.57	...61	r	2.46	r	0.43	0.74
62.57	...62	r	1.15	1.77	r	0.70	1.21
62.57	...63	r	0.87	1.32	r	1.16	r
62.57	...64	r	r	0.90	r	r	r
62.57	...65	r	0.35	r	r	r	r

Option & Underlying	Strike Price	Calls—Last			Puts—Last		
		Jul	Aug	Sep	Jul	Aug	Sep
62,500 Swiss Francs-cents per unit.							
SFranc	..53	r	r	r	r	r	0.32
56.39	...54	r	r	r	r	0.22	r
56.39	...55	r	r	r	r	0.42	0.88
56.39	...56	r	r	r	r	1.00	r
56.39	...57	r	0.74	1.10	r	r	r
56.39	...58	r	0.41	0.65	r	r	r
56.39	...60	r	0.14	0.38	r	r	r

Total call vol.   9,885   Call open int.   325,104
Total put vol.   9,966   Put open int.   282,224
r—Not traded. s—No option offered.
Last is premium (purchase price).

Chicago Board Options Exchange

Monday, Jul. 14

Option & Underlying	Strike Price	Calls—Last			Puts—Last		
		Jul	Aug	Sep	Jul	Aug	Sep
25,000 British Pounds-cents per unit.							
BPound	140	r	r	r	r	r	0.95
148.63	.145	r	r	r	r	1.55	2.35
148.63	.150	r	r	r	r	r	r
125,000 West German Marks-cents per unit.							
DMark	..45	r	1.16	1.73	r	r	r
46.07	...47	r	r	0.59	r	r	r
12,500,000 Japanese Yen-100ths of a cent per unit.							
JYen	... 60	r	r	3.17	r	0.32	r
62.58	...62	r	1.37	1.82	r	r	r
62.58	...63	r	0.88	1.26	r	r	r
62.58	...64	r	r	r	r	2.13	r
62.58	...65	r	0.28	r	r	r	r
125,000 Swiss Francs-cents per unit.							
SFranc	...54	r	r	r	r	0.18	r
56.38	...55	r	r	r	r	0.37	0.68
56.38	...56	r	1.10	r	r	0.80	r
56.38	...58	r	0.38	r	r	r	r

Total call volume 2,279   Total call open int. 17,250
Total put volume 804   Total put open int. 12,837
r—Not traded. s—No option offered.
Last is premium (purchase price).

Options on foreign currency futures trade on the IMM. The standardized contracts are characterized by their strike price expiration date and the underlying futures contract. The terms of the contract are almost identical to those of the Philadelphia Stock Exchange options, except that the IMM options are options on the foreign currency futures and the IMM options expire on the Friday prior to the second Wednesday of the futures expiration date.

Exhibit 15.6 lists the currency option contract specifications for options on the German (Deutsche) mark, British pound, and Swiss franc futures. Exhibit 15.7 shows how option premiums are reported in the *Wall Street Journal*.

EXHIBIT 15.6
Options Contract Specifications

	British Pound	Canadian Dollar	Deutsche Mark	Japanese Yen	Swiss Franc
Option Coverage	One BP futures contract (BP25,000)	One CD futures contract (CD100,000)	One DM futures contract (DM125,000)	One JY futures contract (JY12,500,000)	One SF futures contract (SF125,000)
Strike Price Intervals	US 2.5¢	US .5¢	US 1¢	US .01¢	US 1¢
Months Traded	March, June September, December				
Premium Quotations	US ¢ per pound 1.00 = $250 ($.01 × BP25,000)	US ¢ per C. dollar 1.00 = $1000 ($.01 × CD100,000)	US ¢ per mark 1.00 = $1250 ($.01 × DM125,000)	US .01¢ per yen 1.00 = $1250 ($.0001 × JY12,500,000)	US ¢ per franc 1.00 = $1250 ($.01 × SF125,000)
Minimum Price Change	.05 = $12.50	.01 = $10.00	.01 = $12.50	.01 = $12.50	.01 = $12.50
Price Limit	None				
Trading Hours (U.S. Central Time)	7:20 AM to 1:24 PM	7:20 AM to 1:26 PM	7:20 AM to 1:20 PM	7:20 AM to 1:22 PM	7:20 AM to 1:16 PM
Last Day of Trading	Two Fridays before the third Wednesday of the contract month				

SOURCE: *Trading and Hedging with Currency Futures and Options* (Chicago: Chicago Mercantile Exchange, 1985), p. 20.

Suppose the premium of a call option to purchase December Deutsche mark futures at a 35 cent strike price is 29 cents per Deutsche mark, more commonly referred to as 29 points. To calculate the actual dollar premium, the 29 points must be multiplied by $12.50 per point to arrive at a premium of $362.50.

EXHIBIT 15.7
Foreign Currency Options on Futures

– FINANCIAL –

BRITISH POUND (CME) 25,000 pounds; cents per pound

Strike Price	Calls–Settle			Puts–Settle		
	Sep-c	Dec-c	Mar-c	Sep-p	Dec-p	Mar-p
1425	6.40	7.35	....	1.30	3.50	5.20
1450	4.75	6.00	....	2.10	4.60	6.40
1475	3.35	4.80	5.50	3.20	5.80	7.70
1500	2.25	3.80	4.55	4.60	7.25	9.10
1525	1.50	2.95	....	6.30	8.80	10.70
1550	0.95	2.25	3.05	8.20	10.55	....

Est. vol. 2,078, Fri.; vol. 1,073 calls, 338 puts
Open interest Fri.; 23,645 calls, 11,949 puts

W. GERMAN MARK (CME) 125,000 marks, cents per mark

Strike Price	Calls–Settle			Puts–Settle		
	Sep-c	Dec-c	Mar-c	Sep-p	Dec-p	Mar-p
44	2.54	3.14	....	0.25	0.67	0.94
45	1.79	2.48	2.96	0.49	0.98	1.26
46	1.16	1.91	2.39	0.85	1.37	1.66
47	0.71	1.44	1.95	1.40	1.88	2.16
48	0.41	1.06	1.55	2.09	2.48	....
49	0.25	0.81	....	2.91	....	....

Est. vol. 4,329, Fri.; vol. 4,152 calls, 2,193 puts
Open interest Fri.; 49,122 calls, 38,721 puts

SWISS FRANC (CME) 125,000 francs; cents per franc

Strike Price	Calls–Settle			Puts–Settle		
	Sep-c	Dec-c	Mar-c	Sep-p	Dec-p	Mar-p
55	2.18	3.02	....	0.61	1.26	....
56	1.55	2.46	3.06	0.98	1.66	....
57	1.06	1.95	2.57	1.47	2.13	2.49
58	0.70	1.54	2.14	2.13	2.70	....
59	0.45	1.21	....	2.86	3.28	....
60	....	....	....	....	....	....

Est. vol. 2,419, Fri.; vol. 1,087 calls, 886 puts
Open interest Fri.; 17,936 calls, 17,574 puts

JAPANESE YEN (CME) 12,500,000 yen, cents per 100 yen

Strike Price	Calls–Settle			Puts–Settle		
	Sep-c	Dec-c	Mar-c	Sep-p	Dec-p	Mar-p
61	2.45	3.36	....	0.65	1.26	1.68
62	1.82	2.76	....	1.01	1.65	....
63	1.29	2.24	2.99	1.47	2.10	....
64	0.90	1.80	2.54	2.06	....	....
65	0.61	1.43	....	2.76	....	....
66	....	....	....	....	....	....

Est. vol. 3,797, Fri.; vol. 2,614 calls, 1,221 puts
Open interest Fri.; 25,142 calls, 16,569 puts

STERLING (LIFFE) – b-£25,000; cents per pound

Strike Price	Calls–Settle			Puts–Settle		
	Sep-c	Dec-c	Mar-c	Sep-p	Dec-p	Mar-p
140	8.38	9.06	9.67	0.93	2.81	4.47
145	4.87	6.11	6.98	2.42	4.86	6.78
150	2.43	3.88	4.85	4.98	7.63	9.65
155	1.03	2.32	3.26	8.58	11.07	13.06
160	0.37	1.30	2.11	12.92	15.05	16.91
165	0.11	0.69	....	17.66	19.44	....

Actual Vol. Monday, 798 Calls, 238 Puts.
Open Interest Friday; 3,147, Calls, 4,389 Puts.
b-Option on physical sterling.

EURODOLLAR (LIFFE) $1 million; pts. of 100%

Strike Price	Calls–Settle			Puts–Settle		
	Sep-c	Dec-c	Mar-c	Sep-p	Dec-p	Mar-p
9300	0.58	0.61	0.56	0.02	0.13	0.26
9325	0.37	0.43	0.41	0.06	0.20	0.36
9350	0.21	0.29	0.29	0.15	0.31	0.49
9375	0.09	0.18	0.19	0.28	0.45	0.64
9400	0.03	0.10	....	0.47	0.62	....
9425	0.01	0.05	....	0.70	0.82	....

Actual Vol. Monday, 0 Calls, 0 Puts.
Open Interest Friday; 881, Calls, 1,120 Puts.

EURODOLLAR (CME) $ million; pts. of 100%

Strike Price	Calls–Settle			Puts–Settle		
	Sep-c	Dec-c	Mar-c	Sep-p	Dec-p	Mar-p
9300	0.63	0.64	0.64	0.03	0.13	0.32
9325	0.41	0.48	0.50	0.06	0.22	0.42
9350	0.23	0.33	0.37	0.12	0.30	....
9375	0.12	0.22	0.27	0.26	0.42	....
9400	0.06	0.13	0.19	0.44	....	0.82
9425	0.02	0.08	0.13	0.65	....	....

Est. vol. 3,327, Fri.; vol. 3,913 calls, 10,563 puts
Open interest Fri.; 53,723 calls, 41,282 puts

STRATEGIES WITH FOREIGN CURRENCY OPTIONS

Foreign currency option strategies follow the stock option strategies that were discussed in Chapter 3. Investors expecting the futures contracts to rise (fall), for example, could buy call (put) options on those futures. If the futures increase (decrease), the option premiums will increase.

Example 15.2

An American company is to receive yen in three months, and is concerned that the yen may drop in the interim. Since the company wants to sell the yen in exchange for American dollars, it could buy put options. If the yen rises against the dollar, the put option will move into the money. If the yen does not rise against the dollar, the put premium will shrink and the insurance policy (put) will not be exercised.

By purchasing an option, the holder obtains the right, but not the obligation, to buy or sell a currency contract. If a future exchange of currencies is possible but not definite, foreign currency options may prove safer hedges than futures or forward contracts.

As an example, consider the case of a U.S. manufacturer submitting a sealed bid for the sale of a large "turnkey" plant to the Japanese government. The foreign bidder must not only deal with the uncertainty of winning the bid, but also must contend with the exchange rate risk. If, for example, the foreign currency in which the bid is denominated depreciates significantly against the dollar, then the profitability of the bid may be eroded away. To offset this risk, the bidder may use forward, futures, or foreign currency options. If the forward contracts were used and the bid was won, the hedge replaces foreign currency risk with less volatile basis risk. However, if the bid is lost, the bidder has no foreign currency to offset the commitment in the forward contract and significant losses could occur.

Foreign currency options provide a useful alternative hedging mechanism when the future currency exchange is uncertain. If the bid is won, the bidder, having purchased a put option, has limited the exchange rate risk. On the other hand, if the bid is lost, the bidder's losses are limited. Indeed, the bidder is left with a speculative position that could earn speculative rewards. In any case, the bidder is not left with any commitments.

PRICE RELATIONSHIPS WITH FOREIGN CURRENCY OPTIONS

In this section some pricing relationships for currencies are investigated. In particular, geographical (or space) arbitrage, cross-rate (or triangular) arbitrage, and interest rate arbitrage strategies are discussed.

Geographical (Space) Arbitrage

Geographical arbitrage occurs when one currency sells for two prices in two markets. As an example, suppose the following prices are quoted in New York and London for the exchange rate between dollars and pounds:

New York   1.68 dollars per pound.

London   0.60 pounds per dollar.

The New York price implies each pound is worth $1/1.68 = 0.59$ dollars, whereas in London each pound is worth 0.60 dollars. To avoid arbitrage opportunities, these two values should be the same.

Triangular (Cross-Rate) Arbitrage

Given exchange rates between two currencies, such as dollars per pound and dollars per mark, an exchange rate between pounds and marks is implied. This implied rate is referred to as a *cross-rate*. If the actual exchange rate between pounds and marks differs from the cross-rate, arbitrage opportunities exist.

The existence of the cross-rate has resulted in the U.S. dollar's becoming the primary "money" used in foreign exchange markets. Cross-rate markets between many currencies are very thin and forward cross-rate markets may not exist. As an example, the bulk of foreign exchanges between British pounds and Brazilian cruzeiros involve dollar-pound and dollar-cruzeiro transactions, instead of direct pound–cruzeiro trading. In a very liquid market (such as dollar medium market), transaction costs are typically lower. Of course, there are some very liquid markets that do not involve the dollar. These include the currencies of western Europe.

Geographical and cross-rate arbitrage strategies occur if spot or forward prices with the same date are improperly aligned.

Interest Rate Parity

Interest rates are established according to costs of borrowing and lending for specific time periods, and they need not be the same in different currencies. Let r_{us} be the risk-free rate of return for one year in the United States and let r_b be the rate in Britain. Assume an investor has K dollars to invest. If invested in the U.S., the K dollars would grow to $K(1 + r_{us})$ dollars. Let S_0 be the spot exchange rate. That is, K dollars are worth KS_0 British pounds. Invested in Britain, the final value would be $KS_0(1 + r_b)$ British pounds. Unfortunately, at the beginning of the year the investor will not know how much the pound will be worth in one year. Suppose the future spot rate is S_1 pounds per dollar. Then the final dollar value of this investment is $KS_0(1 + r_b)/S_1$. Since S_1 is not certain, the final value of this investment is uncertain. This uncertainty could be removed by selling the $KS_0(1 + r_b)$ pounds forward. Let F_0 be the forward price. That is, F_0 is the amount of dollars an investor can lock into paying for one pound in one year. If such a contract is sold, the future dollar value of the investment is $KS_0(1 + r_b)/F_0$, which is a known quantity. Clearly, to avoid riskless arbitrage, it must follow that

$$K(1 + r_{us}) = \frac{KS_0(1 + r_b)}{F_0}$$

$$\frac{1 + r_{us}}{1 + r_b} = \frac{S_0}{F_0} \tag{15.1}$$

This equation leads to the following important interest rate parity theorem.

Property 15.1
Interest Rate Parity Theorem

Forward and spot exchange rates and relative interest rates in the two currencies are linked together by

$$\frac{F_0}{S_0} = \frac{B(0,T)}{B^*(0,T)} \tag{15.2}$$

where $B(0,T)$ is the riskless discount factor for local currency and $B^*(0,T)$ is the riskless discount factor for foreign currency.

When interest rates are constant, the forward price of a nondividend paying stock must, by arbitrage, command a premium equal to the interest rate (see Chapter 11). In foreign currency markets, however, forward prices can involve forward premiums or discounts. This follows directly from equation (15.2). Specifically, the forward value of a currency is related to the ratio of the prices of riskless bonds traded in each country. From equation (15.2) we have

$$F_0 = S_0 \frac{B(0,T)}{B^*(0,T)} \tag{15.3}$$

and if

$$B(0,T) = \exp(-rT)$$

$$B^*(0,T) = \exp(-r^*T)$$

where r and r^* are the instantaneous risk-free rates in the local and foreign currency, then

$$F_0 = S_0\exp[(r - r^*)T]. \tag{15.4}$$

If r^* exceeds r, then the forward price could be lower than the spot. Note that equation (15.4) is similar to the forward price of a security that pays out a continuous dividend at rate r^*.

ARBITRAGE RELATIONS FOR FOREIGN CURRENCY CALLS AND PUTS

In Chapters 2, 4, and 11, several properties of option prices were developed. Similar properties hold for foreign currency options. In this section a few relationships particular to foreign currency options are discussed.

Property 15.2
International Put-Call Equivalence

The price of a foreign exchange put option in one currency equals that of a call option in the other currency at the same strike price. That is,

$$C(X) = S_0XP^*(1/X), \tag{15.5}$$

$$P(X) = S_0XC^*(1/X). \tag{15.6}$$

To see this, note that an option to buy currency B with currency A at price X is identical to an option to sell currency A in exchange for currency B at price X. Hence, a call option in one currency is just a put option in the other. The price of the call is $C(X)$. In the other currency the price of the put for one unit of foreign currency is $P^*(1/X)$. Hence, the price for a put on X units of foreign currency is $P^*(1/X)$. Since this contract provides the same terms as the call option, they must be priced identically. Hence $C(X) = S_0 X P^*(1/X)$, where S is the spot exchange rate.

A similar argument holds for put options.

Property 15.3
International Options Price Parity

The spot exchange rate, S_0, depends on domestic and foreign call option prices (or put prices) and domestic and foreign interest rates as follows:

$$S_0 = \frac{[C(X) + X B(0,T)]}{X C^*(1/X) + B^*(0,T)}. \tag{15.7}$$

$$S_0 = \frac{[P(X) + X B(0,T)]}{X P^*(1/X) - B^*(0,T)}. \tag{15.8}$$

To see this, we combine Property 15.1 with the interest rate parity theorem and the put-call-forward parity relationship. The link between forward and spot exchange rates and relative interest rates given by the interest rate parity theorem is

$$\frac{F_0}{S_0} = \frac{B^*(0,T)}{B(0,T)}, \tag{15.9}$$

from which

$$F_0 = \frac{S_0 B^*(0,T)}{B(0,T)} \tag{15.10}$$

The put-call forward parity discussed in Chapter 11 is

$$C(X) - P(X) = (F_0 - X) B(0,T). \tag{15.11}$$

Substituting (15.10) into (15.11), we obtain

$$C(X) - P(X) = B^*(0,T) S_0 - B(0,T). \tag{15.12}$$

The put-call forward parity discussed in Chapter 11 is

$$P(X) = S_0 X C^*(1/X). \tag{15.13}$$

Substituting equation (15.12) into (15.13) yields the result.

OPTION PRICING MODELS FOR FOREIGN CURRENCIES

Under the usual Black and Scholes assumptions, a closed-form equation for the price of a foreign currency call option can be derived. If it is assumed that foreign exchange rates follow a geometric Wiener process, that foreign exchange markets are frictionless and provide continuous trading opportunities, and that the instantaneous domestic risk-free rate, r, and foreign risk free rate, r^*, are deterministic over the time to expiration, then the price of a call option is

$$C(X) = S_0 \exp(-rT)N(d_1) - X\exp(-rT)N(d_2)$$

where

$$d_1 = \frac{ln(S_0/X) + r - r^* + \sigma^2/2)T}{\sigma\sqrt{T}}$$

$$d_2 = d_1 - \sigma\sqrt{T}$$

and σ is the instantaneous volatility of the spot rate. Possibly the biggest criticism of this model is the assumption of lognormal distributions of foreign exchange rates. Empirically, Westerfield and McFarland, Pettit, and Sung have found that large deviations from this distribution may occur.

CONCLUSION

Foreign currency risk management is becoming an increasingly important feature of Treasury management in international corporations and banks. In this chapter we have briefly reviewed the interbank market and the organized exchange market. Foreign currency futures, options, and options on futures were discussed and some pricing relationships investigated. Hedging of foreign currency risk using these instruments is not the only way of managing this risk. Designing baskets of currencies in which to pay for foreign goods and negotiating payments in multicurrency units are other ways currency risk can be hedged. Raising funds in designated foreign currencies is also a way of offsetting exchange rate risks.

References

Loosigian provides a survey of the development of foreign exchange dealings from their origins to the present time. He also provides a practical analysis of factors affecting a country's exchange rate, and discusses how companies manage exchange rate risk. For a comprehensive discussion of foreign exchange futures, see Kolb. Giddy summarizes the properties of foreign currency options and provides a more formal treatment to interest rate parity.

For a review of ways U.S. multinationals manage currency risk, see Jacque. For pricing of currency options, see Biger and Hull; Garman and Kohlhagen; and Yang.

For arbitrage tests of the efficiency of foreign currency options markets, see Shastri and Tandon, and for a study of foreign exchange rates, see McFarland, Pettit, and Sung; Rogalski and Vinso; and Westerfield.

Biger, N., and J. Hull. "The Valuation of Currency Options." *Financial Management* (Spring 1983): 24–28.

Bodurtha, J., and G. Courtadon, "Efficiency Tests of the Foreign Currency Options Market." *Journal of Finance* 41(March 1986): 151–62.

Chrystal, K. *A Guide to Foreign Exchange Markets.* St. Louis: Federal Reserve Bank of St. Louis, 1984, 5–18.

Garman, M., and S. Kohlhagen. "Foreign Currency Option Values." *Journal of International Money and Finance* 2(1983): 231–37.

Giddy, I. "An Integrated Theory of Exchange Rate Equilibrium." In *International Finance: Concepts and Issues,* edited by R. Kolb and G. Gay. Richmond, Va.: Robert Dame, Inc., 1982.

Giddy, I. "Foreign Exchange Options." *Journal of Futures Markets* (Summer 1983): 143–66.

Grabbe, J. D. "The Pricing of Call and Put Options on Foreign Exchange." *Journal of International Money and Finance* 2(1983): 239–53.

Grandreau, B. "New Markets in Foreign Currency Options." *Business Review* (July–August 1984): 3–13.

Jacque, L. "Management of Foreign Exchange Risk: A Review Article." In *International Finance: Concepts and Issues,* edited by R. Kolb and G. Gay. Richmond, Va.: Robert Dame, Inc., 1982.

Kolb, R. *Understanding Futures Markets.* Glenview, Ill.: Scott, Foresman, 1985.

Loosigian, A. *Foreign Exchange Futures: A Guide to International Currency Trading.* Homewood, Ill.: Dow Jones-Irwin, 1981.

McFarland, J., R. Pettit, and S. Sung. "The Distribution of Foreign Exchange Price Changes: Trading Day Effects and Risk Measurement." *Journal of Finance* (June 1982): 693–716.

Rogalski, R., and J. Vinso. "Empirical Properties of Foreign Exchange Rates." *Journal of International Business Studies* 9(Fall) 69–79.

Shastri, K., and K. Tandon. "Arbitrage Tests of the Foreign Currency Options Market." Working Paper 571, Graduate School of Business, University of Pittsburgh.

Sweeney, R. "Beating the Foreign Exchange Market." *Journal of Finance* 41(March 1986): 163–82.

Westerfield, J. M. "An Examination of Foreign Exchange Risk Under Fixed and Floating Rate Regimes." *Journal of International Economics* 7(May 1977): 181–200.

Yang, H. "A Note on Currency Option Pricing Models." *Journal of Business Finance and Accounting* 12(Autumn 1985): 429–37.

Exercises

1. Explain why a call option in one currency can be viewed as a put option in another. Using an option contract in Exhibit 15.5, provide an example.

2. Given that an interbank market for foreign currency options exists in London, must such a market exist in the United States? Explain.

3. A company makes a sale for which it will receive DM125,000 (Deutsche marks) in one month. The firm wants to convert this to dollars. Determine the risk the company is bearing. The firm might hedge this risk by selling futures, buying put options, or selling calls. Discuss the advantages and disadvantages of each strategy.

4. At the current time the spot exchange rate for Deutsche marks is $0.3920. The futures price for delivery in 6 weeks is $0.3950. A 40 put option is at $0.0144 and a 40 call option is at $0.0120. After four weeks the spot exchange rate is $0.3540, the futures price is $0.3559, the put option is at $0.0447, and the call is at $0.0001.

   a. If the investor had sold a futures contract, what profit or loss would have occurred?

   b. If the investor had bought a put, what profit or loss would have occurred?

   c. If a call had been sold, what profit or loss would have occurred?

5. If the sale in exercise 3 was conditional on a particular event occurring and the likelihood of the event was only 50 percent, describe alternative ways of hedging the exchange rate risk.

6. If the investor in exercise 3 had not hedged against the declining currency provided in the scenario of problem 4, what losses would have occurred? If the investor had predicted a rising exchange rate scenario, what strategy might he or she have chosen?

7. Assume a bank wants to write a 9-month Deutsche mark call option for a customer on DM 100m. How would the bank price such an option and hedge the transaction?

8. Assume a bank wants to write a 9-month Brazilian cruzeiro call option for a customer. The transaction is large enough that the bank wants to offset the risk, ideally by purchasing a 9-mark call. Since such calls are not readily available, how might the bank establish a hedge?

9. A *currency cocktail* is defined as a portfolio of several currencies. As with a portfolio of securities, the major objective for constructing a cocktail is to reduce exchange rate risk. Consider a multinational corporation based in Saudi Arabia that exports 40 percent of its oil to West Germany, 20 percent to France, and 15 percent to Italy, and keeps the remaining 25 percent in Saudi Arabia. These percentages are stable over time. Moreover, most revenues are returned to be spent in Saudi Arabia. Discuss the exchange rate risks. How could they be reduced by negotiating with all trading partners payments to be made in a multicurrency unit? What multicurrency unit (currency cocktail) would make sense? Defend your answer.

16

An Introduction to
Continuous Time Mathematics

An increasing number of articles in financial economics use continuous time mathematics to value financial claims. This chapter presents a nontechnical treatment of this subject and provides several examples of its applications in finance. The primary purpose is to present the rules of stochastic calculus in such a way that readers of technical papers will be able to follow the literature without being intimidated by the mathematics.

To understand the economic implications of continuous trading, it is necessary to specify the properties of the time series of price changes in this environment. In the first section we briefly restate properties of Wiener and Ito processes and then turn to stochastic calculus. Ito's lemma is presented, together with rules of differentiation. These rules collapse to simple rules of differentiation when uncertainty is removed. Several examples are presented to reinforce the concepts. The second part of the chapter uses the continuous time approach to establish the Black-Scholes equation. Then several other valuation examples are presented. The examples differ according to the hypothesized source of uncertainty. Some of the results discussed in Chapter 14 are derived. For example, the value of stock of the firm and options on the stock are considered.

In most situations no explicit solutions to the resulting differential equations and boundary conditions can be obtained. In this case numerical procedures are often used to obtain approximate solutions.

A STANDARD WIENER PROCESS

A stochastic process $\{w(t), t \geq 0\}$ is a standard Wiener process if
   1. $w(0) = 0$,
   2. $\{w(t), t \geq 0\}$ has stationary and independent increments.   (16.1)
   3. For every $t > 0$, $w(t)$ is normally distributed with mean zero and variance t.

Let Δw be the change in the value of $w(t)$ over a period of length Δt. Then the expected change in value, $E(\Delta w)$, is zero, while the variance, $\text{Var}(\Delta w)$, is equal to the time increment, Δt. Since the variance is given by

$$\text{Var}(\Delta w) = E[(\Delta w)^2] - [E(\Delta w)]^2, \tag{16.2}$$

it follows that the second moment, $E[(\Delta w)^2]$, is given by

$$E[(\Delta w)^2] = \Delta t.$$

The standard Wiener process has the property that all higher moments are of a magnitude smaller than Δt. That is,

$$E[(\Delta w)^n] = O[(\Delta t)^2]. \qquad n > 2.$$

where $O[(\Delta t)^2]$ means the term is of order $(\Delta t)^2$ or smaller.

The Wiener process has the property that, no matter how small Δt is, the properties of the process are still maintained. Furthermore, it can be shown that in the limit, as Δt tends to dt and Δw becomes dw, the second and higher moments of the change, dw, can be viewed as deterministic in the sense that the probabilities of deviations from their means are negligible compared to their means. Indeed, for all practical purposes, only the first two moments play a meaningful role in characterizing the statistical evolution of the process and for all practical purposes we can write

$$E(dw) = 0,$$

$$(dw)^2 = dt + O[(dt)^2],$$

$$dw\,dt = O[(dt)^n] \qquad n > 2.$$

ITO PROCESSES

A stochastic process $\{dx(t), t > 0\}$ is an Ito process if the random variable dx can be represented as

$$dx = \mu(x,t)dt + \sigma(x,t)dw \tag{16.3}$$

where $\mu(x,t)$ is the expected change in x at time t and $\sigma(x,t)dw$ reflects the uncertain term. As an example, x could represent the stock price. The geometric Wiener process would be a special case with

$$\mu(x,t) = \mu x,$$

$$\sigma(x,t) = \sigma x.$$

We shall be interested in a function defined on this type of process. For example, if x represents the stock price, we may be interested in valuing a contingent claim whose value depends on the stock price, x, and on the current time, t (or equivalently on the time to expiration, $T - t$).

Let $F(x,t)$ represent the value of the claim. We shall assume that this function is a twice continuously differentiable function of x and once continuously differentiable function of t.

If $x(t)$ was a deterministic function, then the differential dF is the limit of ΔF, where

$$\Delta F = F(x + \Delta x, t + \Delta t) - F(x,t)$$

and by Taylor's series we have

$$\Delta F = \frac{\partial F}{\partial x} \Delta x + \frac{\partial F}{\partial t} \Delta t + O[(\Delta t)^2].$$

In the limit we obtain

$$dF = \frac{\partial F}{\partial x} dx + \frac{\partial F}{\partial t} dt. \tag{16.4}$$

When $x(t)$ is not certain but instead follows an Ito process, the above differential rule cannot be applied. Ito's lemma is just the stochastic calculus equivalent of this differential rule. In the next section we shall state the lemma, provide a brief sketch of the proof, and then develop some rules for stochastic calculus.

Ito's Lemma

If $F(x,t)$ is a twice continuously differentiable function of x and once continuously differentiable function of t, then the total differential of F is given by

$$dF(t) = \frac{\partial F}{\partial x} dx + \frac{\partial F}{\partial t} dt + \frac{1}{2} \sigma^2(x,t) \frac{\partial^2 F}{\partial x^2} dt \tag{16.5}$$

where

$$dx = \mu(x,t) + \sigma(x,t)dw.$$

Proof: Using Taylor's series, we have

$$\Delta F = \frac{\partial F}{\partial x} \Delta x + \frac{\partial F}{\partial t} \Delta t + \frac{1}{2} \frac{\partial^2 F}{\partial x^2} (\Delta x)^2 + \frac{\partial^2 F}{\partial x \partial t} \Delta x \Delta t + \frac{1}{2} \frac{\partial^2 F}{\partial t^2} (\Delta t)^2 + O[(\Delta t^2)]. \tag{16.6}$$

Now from properties of the Wiener process we have

$$(\Delta x)^2 = [\mu(x,t)\Delta t + \sigma(x,t)\Delta w]^2$$

$$= \mu^2(x,t)(\Delta t)^2 + \sigma^2(x,t)(\Delta w)^2 + 2\mu(x,t)\sigma(x,t)\Delta w \Delta t$$

$$= \sigma^2(x,t)\Delta t + O[(\Delta t)^2] \tag{16.7}$$

$$\Delta x \Delta t = [\mu(x,t) + \sigma(x,t)\Delta w]\Delta t$$

$$= \mu(x,t)\Delta t + O[(\Delta t)^2]. \tag{16.8}$$

Substituting (16.7) and (16.8) into (16.6) and rearranging, we obtain in the limit

$$dF = \frac{\partial F}{\partial x} dx + \frac{\partial F}{\partial t} dt + \frac{1}{2} \sigma^2 \frac{\partial^2 F}{\partial x^2} dt. \tag{16.9}$$

Note that equation (16.9) contains an additional term compared to (16.4). This term arises because, with the Ito process, not all "second order" effects in the Taylor expansion can be ignored.

In order to become familiar with Ito's lemma, consider the following examples.

Example 16.1

Let $F(x,t) = e^x$, where $dx = \mu dt + \sigma dw$. Using Ito's lemma we have

$$dF = \frac{\partial F}{\partial x} dx + \left(\frac{\partial F}{\partial t} + \frac{1}{2} \sigma^2 \frac{\partial^2 F}{\partial x^2} \right) dt$$

$$= e^x dx + \left(0 + \frac{\sigma^2 e^x}{2} \right) dt$$

$$= e^x (\mu dt + \sigma dw) + \left(\frac{\sigma^2 e^x}{2} \right) dt$$

$$= e^x \left[\left(\mu + \frac{\sigma^2}{2} \right) dt + \sigma dw \right].$$

Let $F(x,t) = \ln(x)$ where $dx = \mu dt + \sigma dw$

$$dF = \frac{\partial F}{\partial x} dx + \left(\frac{\partial F}{\partial t} + \frac{1}{2} \sigma^2 \frac{\partial^2 F}{\partial x^2} \right) dt$$

$$= \frac{1}{x} dx + \left(0 - \frac{\sigma^2}{2x^2} \right) dt$$

$$= \frac{dx}{x} - \frac{\sigma^2}{2x^2} dt.$$

Rules for Differentiation

If $F(x,t)$ and $G(x,t)$ are twice continuously differentiable functions of x and once continuously differentiable functions of t, and $x(t)$ is an Ito process, then we have the following rules:

Addition Rule:

$$d(F + G) = dF + dG. \tag{16.10}$$

Multiplication Rule:

$$d(FG) = FdG + GdF + \sigma^2 dt \frac{\partial F}{\partial x} \frac{\partial G}{\partial x} \tag{16.11}$$

Division Rule:

$$d\left(\frac{F}{G} \right) = \frac{(GdF - FdG)}{G^2} - \frac{\sigma^2}{G^3} \frac{\partial G}{\partial x} \left(G \frac{\partial F}{\partial x} - F \frac{\partial G}{\partial x} \right) dt. \tag{16.12}$$

Proof: Let $H = F + G$. Applying Ito's lemma, we have

$$dH = \frac{\partial H}{\partial x} dx + \left(\frac{\partial H}{\partial t} + \frac{\sigma^2}{2} \frac{\partial^2 H}{\partial t^2} \right) dt.$$

Since

$$\frac{\partial H}{\partial x} = \frac{\partial F}{\partial x} + \frac{\partial G}{\partial x}$$

$$\frac{\partial H}{\partial t} = \frac{\partial F}{\partial t} + \frac{\partial G}{\partial t}$$

and

$$\frac{\partial^2 H}{\partial x^2} = \frac{\partial}{\partial x} \left(\frac{\partial H}{\partial x} \right) = \frac{\partial^2 F}{\partial x^2} + \frac{\partial^2 G}{\partial x^2}$$

the equation for dH can be rewritten as

$$dH = \left(\frac{\partial F}{\partial x} + \frac{\partial G}{\partial x} \right) dx + \left[\frac{\partial F}{\partial t} + \frac{\partial G}{\partial t} + \frac{\sigma^2}{2} \left(\frac{\partial^2 F}{\partial x^2} \right) + \frac{\sigma^2}{2} \left(\frac{\partial^2 G}{\partial x^2} \right) \right] dt$$

and hence

$$dH = dF + dG.$$

The multiplication and division rules can be proved by similar methods and are left to the reader. Note that for $\sigma = 0$, the stochastic differentiation rules simplify to the deterministic rules.

Example 16.2

Let $y = xe^x$ with $dx = \mu dt + \sigma dw$.

Let $F(x,t) = x$, $G(x,t) = e^x$, and $H(x,t) = y$. Then $H(x,t) = F(x,t)G(x,t)$, and

$$dH = d(FG) = FdG + GdF + \sigma^2 dt \frac{\partial G}{\partial x} \frac{\partial F}{\partial x}$$

Now

$$dG = \frac{\partial G}{\partial x} dx + \frac{\partial G}{\partial t} dt + \frac{1}{2} \sigma^2 \frac{\partial^2 G}{\partial x^2} dt$$

$$= e^x dx + \frac{1}{2} \sigma^2 e^x dt$$

$$dF = \frac{\partial F}{\partial x} dx + \frac{\partial F}{\partial t} dt + \frac{1}{2} \sigma^2 \frac{\partial F^2}{\partial x^2} dt = dx.$$

Hence,

$$dH = xe^x(dx + \frac{1}{2} \sigma^2 dt) + e^x dx + e^x \sigma^2 dt$$

(continued)

Example 16.2 (cont'd)

which simplifies to

$$dH = e^x(a\,dt + b\,dw)$$

where

$$a = \mu x + \frac{\sigma^2 x}{2} + \sigma^2; \quad b = \sigma x + \sigma.$$

Generalized Ito's Lemma

Ito's lemma can be generalized to take into account valuation of claims on correlated Ito processes. Below we provide the results for two correlated Ito processes. If $F(x_1, x_2, t)$ is a twice continuously differentiable function of x_1 and x_2 and once continuously differentiable function of t, then the total differential of F is given by

$$dF = \frac{\partial F}{\partial x_1}dx_1 + \frac{\partial F}{\partial x_2}dx_2 + \frac{\partial F}{\partial t}dt + \frac{1}{2}\left[\sigma_1{}^2\frac{\partial^2 F}{\partial x_1{}^2} + \sigma_2{}^2\frac{\partial^2 F}{\partial x_2{}^2} + 2\rho\sigma_1\sigma_2\frac{\partial^2 F}{\partial x_1\partial x_2}\right]dt$$

where

(16.13)

$$dx_i = \mu_i dt + \sigma_i dw_i \qquad i = 1, 2$$

$$dw_1 dw_2 = \rho\,dt$$

$$(dw_i)^2 = dt \qquad i = 1, 2.$$

and ρ is the instantaneous correlation between the two processes.

Example 16.3

Let $F(x_1, x_2, t) = x_1 x_2 t$ where

$$dx_1 = \mu_1 dt + \sigma_1 dw_1$$

$$dx_2 = \mu_2 dt + \sigma_2 dw_2.$$

Then

$$dF = \frac{\partial F}{\partial x_1}dx_1 + \frac{\partial F}{\partial x_2}dx_2 + \frac{\partial F}{\partial t}dt + \frac{1}{2}\left[\frac{\partial^2 F}{\partial x_1{}^2}(dx_1)^2 + \frac{2\partial^2 F}{\partial x_1\partial x_2}dx_1 dx_2 + \frac{\partial^2 F}{\partial x_2{}^2}(dx_2)^2\right]$$

$$= tx_2 dx_1 + tx_1 dx_2 + x_1 x_2 dt + \frac{1}{2}(0 + 2t\,dx_1 dx_2 + 0)$$

$$= tx_2(\mu_1 dt + \sigma_1 dw_1) + tx_1(\mu_2 dt + \sigma_2 dw_2) + x_1 x_2 dt$$
$$+ t(\mu_1 dt + \sigma_1 dw_1)(\mu_2 dt + \sigma_2 dw_2)$$

$$= (t\mu_1 x_2 + x_1 x_2 + \rho\sigma_1\sigma_2 + tx_1\mu_2)dt + t\sigma_1 x_2 dw_1 + t\sigma_2 x_1 dw_2$$

Rules for Multivariable Differentiation

If $F(x_1,t)$ and $G(x_2,t)$ are two twice continuously differentiable functions of x_1 and x_2 and once continously differentiable functions of t, and $x_1(t)$ and $x_2(t)$ are Ito processes defined as follows:

$$dx_1 = \mu_1 dt + \sigma_1 dw_1$$

$$dx_2 = \mu_2 dt + \sigma_2 dw_2$$

and $dw_1 dw_2 = \rho dt$, then the following rules hold true:

$$d(F + G) = dF + dG \tag{16.14}$$

$$d(FG) = GdF + FdG + \rho\sigma_1\sigma_2 \frac{\partial F}{\partial x_1} \frac{\partial G}{\partial x_2} \tag{16.15}$$

$$d\left(\frac{F}{G}\right) = \frac{(GdF - FdG)}{G^2} - \frac{\partial G}{\partial x_2}\left(\rho\sigma_1\sigma_2 G \frac{\partial F}{\partial x_1} - \sigma_2{}^2 \frac{\partial G}{\partial x_2}\right)\frac{dt}{G^3} \tag{16.16}$$

Note that when $x_1 = x_2$ these rules reduce to the rules for one variable.

DERIVATION OF THE BLACK-SCHOLES EQUATION

Ito's lemma can be applied to a variety of problems in financial economics. Black and Scholes were the first to apply this lemma to the problem of valuing stock options. In this section we shall provide a derivation of their result.

Assume that the stock price can be represented by a geometric Wiener process,

$$dS = \mu S dt + \sigma S dw. \tag{16.17}$$

Let the call price, C, be a twice continuously differentiable function of the stock price, S, and once continuously differentiable function of time, t, Then using Ito's lemma we have

$$dC = C_s dS + C_t dt + \frac{1}{2}\sigma^2 S^2 C_{ss} dt \tag{16.18}$$

where

$$C_s = \frac{\partial C}{\partial S}, \quad C_t = \frac{\partial C}{\partial t}, \quad \text{and} \quad C_{ss} = \frac{\partial^2 C}{\partial C^2}.$$

Substituting (16.17) into (16.18), we obtain

$$dC = \left[C_s \mu S + C_t + \frac{\sigma^2}{2} S^2 C_{ss}\right] dt + C_s \sigma S dw$$

and hence

$$\frac{dC}{C} = \mu_c dt + \sigma_c dw \tag{16.19}$$

where

$$\mu_c = \frac{C_s\mu S + C_t + \sigma^2 S^2 C_{ss}/2}{C} \qquad (16.20)$$

$$\sigma_c = \frac{C_c\sigma S}{C}. \qquad (16.21)$$

Now consider a portfolio, P, where λ is the fraction of wealth allocated to the option and $1 - \lambda$ is the fraction allocated to the stock. The instantaneous change in the portfolio, dP/P, can be expressed as

$$\frac{dP}{P} = \lambda\left(\frac{dC}{C}\right) + (1 - \lambda)\left(\frac{dS}{S}\right). \qquad (16.22)$$

Now substituting (16.17) and (16.19) into (16.22) and rearranging, we obtain

$$\frac{dP}{P} = [\lambda\mu_c + (1 - \lambda)\mu]dt + [\lambda\sigma_c + (1 - \lambda)\sigma]dw \qquad (16.23)$$

The instantaneous return on this portfolio consists of a deterministic term in conjunction with a stochastic component. If we select a value for λ such that

$$\lambda\sigma_c + (1 - \lambda)\sigma = 0, \qquad (16.24)$$

then the portfolio becomes free of risk. This being the case, the deterministic component must equate to the riskless rate of return, r. That is,

$$\lambda\mu_c + (1 - \lambda)\mu = r. \qquad (16.25)$$

From equation (16.24) we have

$$\lambda = \frac{\sigma}{(\sigma - \sigma_c)} \qquad (16.26)$$

Substituting (16.26) into (16.25), we obtain

$$\frac{(\mu - r)}{\sigma} = \frac{(\mu_c - r)}{\sigma_c} \qquad (16.27)$$

Equation (16.27) says that the net rate of return per unit of risk must be the same for the two assets.

Now substituting for μ_c and σ_c into (16.27), we obtain

$$\frac{(\mu - r)}{\sigma} = \frac{(C_s\mu S + C_t + \dfrac{\sigma^2}{2} S^2 C_{ss})/C - r}{\dfrac{C_s\sigma S}{C}},$$

which simplifies to

$$\frac{\sigma^2}{2} S^2 C_{ss} + rSC_s - Cr + C_t = 0. \qquad (16.28)$$

This nonstochastic equation, together with the following call price boundary conditions, fully characterizes the call price

$$C(S_T, T) = \text{Max}(0, S_T - X) \tag{16.29}$$

$$S_t \geqq 0$$

$$0 \leqq t \leqq T.$$

The solution of this differential equation is the Black-Scholes formula.

A CONTINUOUS TIME APPROACH TO THE PRICING OF SECURITIES

In this section we shall illustrate the use of continuous time mathematics in valuing securities where the source of uncertainty arises from one or two sources. In the initial examples, uncertainty arises from the firm or from interest rates. In later sections, valuation equations are established when there are two sources of uncertainty. For example, a bond pricing model that relies on the assumption that two stochastic factors determine bond prices is discussed.

A Continuous Time Approach to the Pricing of Corporate Liabilities Under Interest Rate Certainty

Consider a firm whose value, V, can be described by the following stochastic differential equation:

$$dV = (\mu V - c)dt + \sigma V dw \tag{16.30}$$

where μ = instantaneous expected rate of return on the firm,

       c = instantaneous dollar payout of the firm,

       σ = instantaneous volatility of the return on the firm.

We shall assume that the firm has common stock and some debt outstanding. This debt could take the form of discount bonds, coupon bonds, or convertibles, for example. We shall assume the face value of the debt is X dollars and the time to maturity is τ. ($\tau = T - t$.) Let $F = F(V, t)$ be the value of a security that depends solely on the value of the firm and the current time, t.

Using Ito's lemma for $F = F(V, t)$, we have

$$dF = F_v dV + F_t dt + \frac{1}{2} F_{vv} \sigma^2 V^2 dt \tag{16.31}$$

$$= F_v[(\mu V - c)dt + \sigma V dw] + \frac{1}{2} F_{vv} \sigma^2 V^2 dt + F_t dt$$

$$= (\mu_f F - c_f)dt + \sigma_f F dw \tag{16.32}$$

where

$$\mu_f = \frac{F_{vv}\sigma^2 V^2/2 + (\mu V - c)F_v + F_t + c_f}{F} \tag{16.33}$$

$$\sigma_f = \frac{\sigma V F_v}{F} \tag{16.34}$$

where μ_f is the instantaneous expected return per unit time on the security, c_f is the instantaneous dollar payout of the security, and σ_f^2 is the instantaneous variance of return per unit time.

Now consider investing x_v dollars in the firm and x_f dollars in the security F. The total dollars $x_v + x_f$ are obtained by borrowing at the riskless rate. If dP is the instantaneous dollar return on the portfolio, then

$$dP = x_v \left[\frac{(dV + cdt)}{V} \right] + x_f \left[\frac{(dF + c_f dt)}{F} \right] - (x_v + x_f)rdt \tag{16.35}$$

where the coefficients of x_v and x_f are the realized yield obtained from price changes and coupon payouts.

Substituting expressions for dV and dF into equation (16.35) and rearranging, we obtain

$$dP = [x_v(\mu - r) + x_f(\mu_f - r)]dt + (x_v\sigma + x_f\sigma_f)dw. \tag{16.36}$$

Now we shall select $x_v = x_v{}^*$, $x_f = x_f{}^*$ such that

$$x_v{}^*\sigma + x_f{}^*\sigma_f = 0. \tag{16.37}$$

Then the dollar return is nonstochastic, and to avoid riskless arbitrage, it follows that

$$x_v{}^*(\mu - r) + x_f{}^*(\mu_f - r) = 0. \tag{16.38}$$

A nontrivial solution to (16.37) and (16.38) exists if and only if

$$\frac{(\mu - r)}{\sigma} = \frac{(\mu_f - r)}{\sigma_f}. \tag{16.39}$$

Now substituting in the expressions for μ_f and σ_f, we obtain, after simplification,

$$\frac{\sigma^2}{2} V^2 F_{vv} + (rV - c)F_v - rF + F_t + c_f = 0. \tag{16.40}$$

Let τ denote the time to maturity. That is $\tau = T - t$, where T is the maturity date and t is the current time. Then $d\tau = -dt$ and $F_\tau = -F_t$. With $F = F(V, \tau)$, we have

$$\frac{\sigma^2}{2} V^2 F_{vv} + (rV - c)F_v - rF - F_\tau + c_f = 0. \tag{16.41}$$

This partial differential equation must be satisfied by any contingent claim whose value can be written solely as a function of the market value V and time to maturity τ. Note that if there is no coupon payout, c_f, and if we assume that the firm does not pay cash dividends, then $c = 0$. In this case the equation reduces to

$$\frac{\sigma^2}{2} V^2 F_{vv} + rVF_v - rF - F_\tau = 0. \tag{16.42}$$

Note, too, that the partial differential equation does not depend on preferences. As a result, a risk-neutral valuation procedure for establishing the fair price of such claims is appropriate.

Valuation of the Equity, Debt, and Options on the Equity of a Firm

Assume the debt takes the form of a discount bond and, following Chapter 14, assume the indenture stipulates that the firm cannot issue any new debt or pay dividends or repurchase shares prior to maturity. Let the face value of the debt be X. The following examples illustrate applications of the above equation.

Valuation of Equity   Let F represent the equity of the firm. Then $F = S(V, \tau)$ and

$$dV = \mu V dt + \sigma V dw$$

$$dS = \mu_s S dt + \sigma_s S dw$$

and from equation (16.42) we have

$$\frac{\sigma^2}{2} V^2 S_{vv} + r V S_v - r S - S_\tau = 0. \tag{16.43}$$

with

$$S(V, \tau) \geqq 0$$

$$S(V, 0) = \mathrm{Max}(V - X, 0).$$

The solution of this equation is the Black-Scholes formula.

Valuation of Debt   The value of the firm is

$$V = S(V, \tau) + B(V, \tau)$$

where $B(V, \tau)$ is the value of the debt. Hence, the value of the debt is

$$B(V, \tau) = V - S(V, \tau). \tag{16.44}$$

The intuition behind this equation is discussed in Chapter 14.

Valuation of Options on Equity of the Firm   We have seen that if the value of the firm follows the process

$$dV = \mu V dt + \sigma V dw$$

then the stock price movements can be represented by

$$dS = \mu_s S dt + \sigma_s S dw$$

where

$$\sigma_s = \frac{V S_v \sigma}{S}.$$

Since the volatility of the stock does not remain constant, a call option on the stock will not be priced by the Black-Scholes equation. Since the stock can be viewed as an option on the value of the firm, the option can be viewed as a compound option.

Let $C(V, \tau_1)$ be the value of the call with strike X_1 and time to expiration τ_1. Then

$$dC = \mu_c C dt + \sigma_c C dw$$

and

$$\frac{\sigma^2}{2} V^2 C_{vv} + rVC_v - rC - C_{\tau_1} = 0.$$

The call must satisfy this equation, together with the following boundary conditions:

$$0 \leq C(V, \tau_1) \leqq C(V, \tau)$$

$$C(V, 0) = \text{Max}[S(V, \tau - \tau_1) - X_1, 0]$$

The solution is made complex because the boundary conditions involve the stock price, which is itself valued by the Black-Scholes equation. The solution is provided by Geske:

$$C_0 = VN_2\left[x, y;\ \left(\frac{\tau_1}{\tau}\right)^{1/2}\right] - X\exp(-rT)N_2\left[x - \sigma\tau_1^{1/2}, y - \sigma\tau^{1/2};\ \left(\frac{\tau_1}{\tau}\right)^{1/2}\right]$$

$$- X_1\exp(-r\tau_1)N(x - \sigma\tau_1^{1/2}) \tag{16.45}$$

where

$$x = \frac{\ln[V/V^*\exp(-r\tau_1)]}{\sigma\sqrt{\tau_1}} + \frac{\sigma}{2}\sqrt{\tau_1}$$

$$y = \frac{\ln[V/X\exp(-r\tau)]}{\sigma\sqrt{\tau}} + \frac{\sigma}{2}\sqrt{\tau}$$

and V^* satisfies

$$V^*N(z) - X\exp[-r(\tau - \tau_1)]N[z - \sigma\sqrt{(\tau - \tau_1)}] - X_1 = 0$$

where

$$z = \frac{\ln(V^*/X\exp[-r(\tau - \tau_1)])}{\sigma\sqrt{(\tau - \tau_1)}} + \frac{\sigma}{2}\sqrt{(\tau - \tau_1)}$$

and $N_2(z_1, z_2; \rho)$ is the probability that V_1 is less than z_1 and V_2 is less than z_2, where V_1 and V_2 are standard normal random variables with correlation ρ.

Geske's compound option formula generalizes the Black-Scholes formula by considering the effects of the capital structure on the volatility of the stock.

VALUATION OF RISK-FREE CLAIMS UNDER INTEREST RATE UNCERTAINTY

In the previous section it was assumed that the only uncertainty concerned the value of the firm. The interest rate, r, was assumed known and constant. This implies that the yield curve is flat and that bonds with no default risk, face value of $1, and time to maturity τ are valued by $B_0 = \exp(-r\tau)$.

In this section we shall examine methods for valuing claims on default-free securities where uncertainty derives from interest rates.

A Single-State Interest Rate Model

Assume interest rates can be described by the following process:

$$dr = \mu(r)dt + \sigma(r)dw \qquad (16.46)$$

where $\mu(r)$ and $\sigma(r)$ are functions that depend solely on the current level of the interest rate, r, and that are defined such that the rate cannot become negative.

Let $B(r,t)$ be the value of a default-free discount bond at time t. The bond has a face value of $1 and maturity τ. Using Ito's lemma, we have

$$dB = B_r dr + B_t dt + \frac{1}{2}\sigma^2(r)B_{rr}dt$$

$$= B_r[\mu(r)dt + \sigma(r)dw] + B_t dt + \frac{1}{2}\sigma^2(r)B_{rr}dt$$

$$= [B_t + B_r\mu(r) + \frac{1}{2}\sigma^2(r)B_{rr}]dt + [\sigma(r)B_r]dw.$$

Hence,

$$\frac{dB}{B} = \mu_B dt + \sigma_B dw$$

where

$$\mu_B = \frac{[B_t + B_r\mu(r) + \frac{1}{2}\sigma^2(r)B_{rr}]}{B}$$

and

$$\sigma_B = \frac{\sigma(r)B_r}{B}.$$

Now if the expected return on the bond, $\mu_B(r)$, was known, then the bond price could be obtained by solving the following differential equation subject to the appropriate boundary conditions

$$\frac{1}{2}\sigma^2(r)B_{rr} + \mu(r)B_r - \mu_B(r)B + B_t = 0 \qquad (16.47)$$

$$B(r,T) = 1$$

$$0 \le t \le T.$$

The problem inherent in (16.47) is that the expected return on the bond, $\mu_B(r)$, must be exogenously determined. Under one form of the expectations hypothesis, for example, it could be postulated that $\mu_B(r) = r$. In this case (16.47) reduces to

$$\frac{1}{2} \sigma^2(r) B_{rr} + \mu(r) B_r - rB + B_t = 0 \qquad (16.48)$$

$$B(r, T) = 1$$

$$0 \le t \le T.$$

The solution to this differential equation can be shown to be the expected discounted value of one dollar obtained at time T.

If the bond to be valued, $B(r,t)$, is one of a class of claims whose value depends on the short term rate, r, then $\mu_B(r)$ can be partially determined. To illustrate how this is achieved consider a hedge portfolio containing two default-free bonds of different maturities (τ_1 and τ_2). Let X_j be the amount of dollars invested in bonds of maturity $\tau_j (j = 1,2)$. The dollars invested in the bonds are financed by borrowing at the instantaneous rate, r. Then the instantaneous dollar return, dP, is given by

$$dP = X_1\left(\frac{dB_1}{B_1}\right) + X_2\left(\frac{dB_2}{B_2}\right) - (X_1 + X_2) r dt$$

$$= [X_1(\mu_{B_1} - r) + X_2(\mu_{B_2} - r)] dt + (X_1\sigma_{B_1} + \sigma_{B_2}) dw \qquad (16.49)$$

Now, if X_1 and X_2 are chosen such that

$$X_1\sigma_{B_1} + X_2\sigma_{B_2} = 0, \qquad (16.50)$$

then the instantaneous return on the portfolio is not random. To avoid riskless arbitrage, it must follow that

$$X_1(\mu_{B_1} - r) + X_2(\mu_{B_2} - r) = 0. \qquad (16.51)$$

For a nontrivial solution to exist for equations (16.50) and (16.51), it follows that

$$\frac{(\mu_{B_1} - r)}{\sigma_{B_1}} = \frac{(\mu_{B_2} - r)}{\sigma_{B_2}} = \lambda(r) \qquad (16.52)$$

where $\lambda(r)$ is the ratio of excess expected return relative to standard deviation and is called the *instantaneous market price* of interest rate risk. This price is common for all bonds, regardless of maturity. Substituting for μ_{B_1} and σ_{B_1} into equation (16.52), we have

$$\frac{[B_t + B_r\mu(r) + \frac{1}{2}\sigma^2(r)B_{rr}]/B - r}{\frac{[\sigma(r)B_r]}{B}} = \lambda(r,t)$$

Rearranging terms, we have

$$\frac{1}{2}\sigma^2(r)B_{rr} + \mu(r)B_r - \lambda(r)\sigma(r)B_r - rB + B_t = 0. \qquad (16.53)$$

By comparing equation (16.53) to equation (16.47) we observe that $\mu_B(\ )$ has been replaced by the risk neutral value r and the problem of estimating $\mu_B(r)$ has been reduced to finding the risk premium, $\lambda(r)$. The risk premium, $\lambda(r)$, could be specified by some equilibrium model or it could be measured empirically. If empirical methods are used, a structure for $\lambda(r)$ must be adopted. Selecting an appropriate structure must be done with care. Note that if the pure expectations theory holds, then $\lambda(r)$ is zero and (16.48) obtains. However, equation (16.53) does contain a preference dependent term. Thus, in order to value contingent claims under interest rate uncertainty, preferences must be considered. For an analysis of such problems see Brennan and Schwartz.

VALUATION OF CLAIMS ON RISKY SECURITIES UNDER INTEREST RATE UNCERTAINTY

The previous analysis can be extended to the pricing of contingent claims whose value depends not only on the level of interest rates, but also on the value of some other security. For example, consider a contingent claim, F, whose value depends on the level of interest rates and on the value of the firm. In this case there are two sources of uncertainty. Assume

$$dV = \mu_v V dt + \sigma_v V dw_1 \qquad (16.54)$$

$$dr = \mu_r dt + \sigma_r dw_2 \qquad (16.55)$$

where dw_1 and dw_2 are correlated Wiener processes, with

$$dw_1 dw_2 = \rho dt \qquad (16.56)$$

Now applying Ito's lemma to $F = F(V,r,t)$, we have

$$dF = F_v dv + F_r dr + F_t dt + \frac{1}{2}(F_{vv}dv^2 + 2F_{vr}dvdr + F_{rr}dr^2). \qquad (16.57)$$

Substituting in the expressions for dr and dV and simplifying, we obtain

$$\frac{dF}{F} = \mu(V,r,t)dt + \sigma_1(V,r,t)dw_1 + \sigma_2(V,r,t)dw_2 \qquad (16.58)$$

where

$$\mu(V,r,t) = \frac{F_v\mu_v V + F_r\mu_r + F_t + \frac{1}{2}F_{vv}\sigma^2 V^2 + F_{vr}\rho V\sigma_v\sigma_r + \frac{1}{2}F_{rr}\sigma_r^2}{F}$$

$$\sigma_1(V,r,t) = \frac{F_v\sigma_v V}{F} \qquad (16.59)$$

$$\sigma_2(V,r,t) = \frac{F_r\sigma_r}{F}.$$

Now consider forming a zero net investment portfolio by investing amounts X_F, X_B, X_v into the contingent claim, default-free bond, and firm, respectively. The dollars $(X_F + X_B + X_v)$ are financed by borrowing at the interest rate, r. The instantaneous return on this portfolio, dP, is given by

$$dP = \frac{X_F dF}{F} + \frac{X_B dB}{B} + \frac{X_v dV}{V} - r(X_F + X_B + X_v)dt. \qquad (16.60)$$

By substituting in expressions for dF/F, dB/B, and dV/V into (16.60) and by requiring the coefficients of both stochastic terms to zero, we obtain the following equation:

$$\frac{1}{2}\sigma_v^2 V^2 F_{vv} + r\sigma_v\sigma_F\rho VF_{vr} + \frac{1}{2}\sigma_r^2 r^2 F_{rr} + rVF_v + rF_r + F_t - rF = 0. \qquad (16.61)$$

Given the boundary conditions that are determined by the specific nature of the contingent claim under consideration, the equation must be solved for the price of the claim. Brennan and Schwartz use this approach to value convertible bonds.

THE BRENNAN-SCHWARTZ TWO-STATE CONTINGENT CLAIM PRICING MODEL

The single-state interest rate model assumed that the only source of uncertainty stemmed from the short-term rate. Indeed, given the behavior of the short-term rate, the entire yield curve could be specified. Clearly, this feature is not desirable. Brennan and Schwartz overcome this problem by allowing interest rates to depend on two sources of uncertainty, the short-term rate and a long-term rate. To establish their model, as before, let the interest rate on immediately maturing riskless bond be r. Let l represent the yield on a perpetuity, or consol, bond. These two values determine the end points of a yield curve. We shall assume that the entire yield curve is determined by the values of these two end points.

Let $B(r,l,\tau)$ denote the price of a default-free discount bond at time t, given that the short-term rate is r, the long-term rate is l, and the time to maturity is τ. The face value of the bond is \$1. From Chapter 12 we have

$$B(r,l,0) = 1$$

$$B(r,l,\infty) = 1/l. \qquad (16.62)$$

In order to model the bond price behavior, we shall assume the short-term and long-term rates, r and l, follow a joint Wiener process, described as follows:

$$dr = \mu_r(r,l,t)dt + \sigma_r(r,l,t)dw_r \qquad (16.63)$$

$$dl = \mu_l(r,l,t)dt + \sigma_l(r,l,t)dw_l$$

where dw_r and dw_l are two correlated Wiener processes, i.e.,

$$dw_r dw_l = \rho dt. \qquad (16.64)$$

$\mu_r()$ and $\mu_\ell()$ are the expected instantaneous rates of change in the short-term and long-term rates of interest, while $\sigma_r^2()$ and $\sigma_\ell^2()$ are their respective variances and ρ is the correlation between the unanticipated changes in the two rates.

Since the bond price depends on r and ℓ, unanticipated changes in these two rates cause unanticipated changes in the bond price. Using Ito's lemma, a stochastic differential equation for the bond price can be derived. Specifically, we have

$$dB = B_r dr + B_\ell d\ell + B_t dt + \frac{1}{2}\sigma_r^2 B_{rr} dt + \frac{1}{2}\sigma_\ell^2 B_{\ell\ell} dt + \rho\sigma_\ell\sigma_r B_{r\ell} dt. \quad (16.65)$$

Substituting in the expressions for dr and $d\ell$ and simplifying, we obtain

$$\frac{dB}{B} = \mu(r,\ell,t)dt + s_1(r,\ell,t)dw_r + s_2(r,\ell,t)dw_\ell \quad (16.66)$$

where

$$\mu(r,\ell,t) = \frac{B_r\mu_r + B_\ell\mu_\ell + \frac{1}{2}B_{rr}\sigma_r^2 + \frac{1}{2}B_{\ell\ell}\sigma_\ell^2 + B_{r\ell}\rho\sigma_r\sigma_\ell - B_\tau}{B}$$

$$s_1(r,\ell,t) = \frac{B_r\mu_r}{B} \quad (16.67)$$

$$s_2(r,\ell,t) = \frac{B_\ell\sigma_\ell}{B}$$

where subscripts on the B denote partial differentiation.

To derive the equilibrium relationship between expected returns of bonds of different maturities, consider forming a portfolio, P, consisting of investing x_1, x_2, and x_3 dollars in bonds of maturities τ_1, τ_2, and τ_3, respectively. The rate of return on this portfolio is

$$\frac{dP}{P} = [x_1\mu(\tau_1) + x_2\mu(\tau_2) + x_3\mu(\tau_3)]dt$$
$$+ [x_1s_1(\tau_1) + x_2s_1(\tau_2) + x_3s_1(\tau_3)]dw_r$$
$$+ [x_1s_2(\tau_1) + x_2s_2(\tau_2) + x_3s_2(\tau_3)]dw_\ell \quad (16.68)$$

where $\mu(\tau_i)$ is the expected term, $\mu(r,\ell,t)$, for the bond with maturity τ_i and $s_1(\tau_i)$ and $s_2(\tau_i)$ are the appropriate $s_1(r,\ell,t)$ and $s_2(r,\ell,t)$ terms.

Now the rate of return will be deterministic if the coefficients of dw_r and dw_ℓ are zero. In this case, to avoid riskless arbitrage opportunities, the coefficient of dt must equal the interest rate, r. Hence, x_1, x_2, and x_3 should be selected such that

$$x_1s_1(\tau_1) + x_2s_1(\tau_2) + x_3s_1(\tau_3) = 0 \quad (16.69)$$

$$x_1s_2(\tau_1) + x_2s_2(\tau_2) + x_3s_2(\tau_3) = 0. \quad (16.70)$$

Then we must require

$$x_1[\mu(\tau_1) - r] + x_2[\mu(\tau_2) - r] + x_3[\mu(\tau_3) - r] = 0. \quad (16.71)$$

We shall assume, without loss of generality, that x_3 is non-zero. Then if we multiply the first equation by an arbitrary value, λ_r, and the second equation by another value, λ_l, and subtract the third equation, we have

$$x_1\Big(\lambda_r s_1(\tau_1) + \lambda_l s_2(\tau_1) - [\mu(\tau_1) - r]\Big)$$
$$+ x_2\Big(\lambda_r s_1(\tau_2) + \lambda_l s_2(\tau_2) - [\mu(\tau_2) - r]\Big)$$
$$+ x_3\Big(\lambda_r s_1(\tau_3) + \lambda_l s_2(\tau_3) - [\mu(\tau_3) - r]\Big) = 0. \tag{16.72}$$

Now since λ_r and λ_l were chosen arbitrarily, we shall choose them such that the coefficients of x_1 and x_2 are zero. That is λ_r and λ_l satisfy the equations

$$\lambda_r s_1(\tau_1) + \lambda_l s_2(\tau_1) = \mu(\tau_1) - r \tag{16.73}$$

$$\lambda_r s_1(\tau_2) + \lambda_l s_2(\tau_2) = \mu(\tau_2) - r. \tag{16.74}$$

Then, since x_3 is not equal to zero, it must follow that

$$\lambda_r s_1(\tau_3) + \lambda_l s_2(\tau_3) = \mu(\tau_3) - r. \tag{16.75}$$

Hence, in order for there to be a nontrivial solution to the three equations, the following equation must be satisfied:

$$\lambda_r s_1(\tau) + \lambda_l s_2(\tau) = \mu(\tau) - r \qquad \text{for all } \tau. \tag{16.76}$$

Equation (16.76) is a partial differential equation that must be satisfied by the prices of all default-free discount bonds. This equilibrium relationship states that the instantaneous risk premium $\mu(\tau) - r$ equals λ_r times a factor sensitive to r plus λ_l times a factor sensitive to l. Unlike the Black-Scholes partial differential equation, this equation contains two preference-dependent values. The first term, λ_r, can be viewed as the market price for bearing short-term rate risk, while the second term, λ_l, can be viewed as the risk premium for the long-term rate. The values λ_r and λ_l are independent of maturity, τ, and depend solely on the utility functions of market participants.

The partial differential equation (16.76) can be simplified further. Specifically, λ_l can be eliminated by making use of the fact that l is a function of the price of an asset, the consol bond, which is assumed to be traded. To see how λ_l can be eliminated, recall that

$$B(r, l, \infty) = 1/l \tag{16.77}$$

Using Ito's lemma for this consol bond, we have

$$dB = B_l \, dl + B_t \, dt + \frac{1}{2}\sigma_l^2 B_{ll} \, dt$$

$$= \frac{-(\mu_l \, dt + \sigma_l \, dw_l)}{l^2} + 0 + \frac{\sigma_l^2}{l^3} \, dt \tag{16.78}$$

Hence,

$$\frac{dB}{B} = \left(\frac{\sigma_l^2}{l^2} - \frac{\mu_l}{l}\right) dt - \left(\frac{\sigma_l}{l}\right) dw_l. \tag{16.79}$$

Recall that, in general, we have

$$\frac{dB}{B} = \mu(r,l,\tau)dt + s_1(r,l,\tau)dw_r + s_2(r,l,\tau)dw_l. \qquad (16.80)$$

Hence, for the consol bond, we have

$$\mu(r,l,\infty) = \frac{\sigma_l{}^2}{l^2} - \frac{\mu_l}{l} \qquad (16.81)$$

$$s_1(r,l,\infty) = 0 \qquad (16.82)$$

$$s_2(r,l,\infty) = -\frac{\sigma_l}{l} \qquad (16.83)$$

Now since

$$\mu(\tau) - r = \lambda_r s_1(\tau) + \lambda_l s_2(\tau)$$

we have

$$\mu(\infty) - r = \lambda_r s_1(\infty) + \lambda_l s_2(\infty) \qquad (16.84)$$

Substituting (16.81), (16.82), and (16.83) into (16.84) we obtain

$$\left(\frac{\sigma_l{}^2}{l^2} - \frac{\mu_l}{l}\right) - r = 0 - \lambda_l \frac{\sigma_l}{l}$$

and hence

$$\lambda_l = \frac{-\sigma_l}{l} + \frac{(\mu_l + rl)}{\sigma_l}. \qquad (16.85)$$

Now substituting λ_l into equation (16.76) together with the expressions for $\mu(r,l,t)$, $s_1(r,l,t)$, and $s_2(r,l,t)$ given by equation (16.67) and simplifying, we obtain the following partial differential equation:

$$\frac{1}{2} B_{rr}\sigma_r{}^2 + B_{rl}\rho\sigma_r\sigma_l + \frac{1}{2} B_{ll}\sigma_l{}^2 + B_r(\mu_r - \lambda_r\sigma_r) + B_l\left(\frac{\sigma_l{}^2}{l} + l^2 - rl\right)$$
$$- B_\tau - Br = 0. \qquad (16.86)$$

This equation is the basic Brennan-Schwartz two-state variable pricing equation.

Note that the equation does not depend on the expected rate of return of the consol bond or on the market price of risk λ_l, associated with the long-term rate. The equation, however, does depend on λ_r, the market price specified exogenously to implement this model. The value λ_r clearly depends on the risk preferences of investors in the economy. Thus, unlike the Black-Scholes model, this Brennan-Schwartz model is preference dependent.

The equilibrium value of all default-free securities whose value depends solely on short rate, r, long rate, l, and maturity, τ, must satisfy equation (16.86). Such securities include default-free pure discount bonds and call options written on these bonds. Let $F(r,l,\tau)$ be the market value of a claim. Then the general pricing relationship is

$$\frac{1}{2} F_{rr}\sigma_r^2 + F_{rl}\rho\sigma_r\sigma_l + \frac{1}{2} F_{ll}\sigma_l^2 + F_r(\mu_r - \lambda_r\sigma_r) + F_l \left(\frac{\sigma_l^2}{l} + l^2 - rl\right) - F_\tau$$
$$- rF + c = 0. \tag{16.87}$$

If the claim represents a default-free pure discount bond, then on the maturity date the boundary condition is

$$F(r,l,0) = B(r,l,0) = 1. \tag{16.88}$$

Alternatively, if the claim is a call option on this default-free pure discount bond, its value on the expiration date, τ_2, say, is given by

$$F(r,l,0) = C(r,l,0) = \text{Max}[B(r,l,\tau_1 - \tau_2) - X,0]. \tag{16.89}$$

$B(r,l,\tau_1 - \tau_2)$ is the value of the bond at the expiration date of the option. $\tau_1 - \tau_2$ is the time from the expiration date of the option to the maturity date of the discount bond, and X is the strike price of the option.

The Brennan-Schwartz Call Option Model

To value the call option, the underlying pure discount bond must first be valued for differing maturities. This is accomplished by solving (16.87) subject to (16.88) and obtaining the equilibrium bond prices for varying maturities. The resulting equilibrium price of a pure discount bond with $\tau_1 - \tau_2$ periods until maturity is then substituted into the boundary condition (16.89) and equation (16.87) is resolved using the new option boundary condition.

The numerical methods used to solve these differential equations are briefly discussed in the Appendix. Implementing the Brennan-Schwartz model for bond and option pricing requires specifying the interest rate process during the short-term and long-term rates. Brennan and Schwartz have postulated and tested models in which the short-term and long-term rates are given as

$$dr = [\alpha_1 + \beta_1(1 - r)]dt + [r\sigma(r)]dw_r$$
$$dl = [\alpha_2 + \beta_2 r + \beta_3 l]dt + [l\sigma(l)]dw_l.$$

Note that the standard deviations of the rates depend solely on their current terms, while the trend terms are interdependent. The short-rate trend term is set such that when r increases, the trend decreases. The long-term rate depends on the short-term rate through β_2.

If other specific functions are specified for the trend terms, $\mu_r()$ and $\mu_l()$ and standard deviation terms, $\sigma_r()$ and $\sigma_l()$, in the Brennan-Schwartz model, simplifications may occur. Two special cases of their model are discussed next.

The Courtadon Option Pricing Model

The Courtadon model is a single-state variable model where the short-term rate, r, characterizes all equilibrium default-free security prices. Consequently, the Courtadon model can be viewed as a special case of the Brennan-Schwartz model, where equilibrium prices are not dependent on l. Hence, we can put $\mu_l() = \sigma_l() = 0$. These restrictions reduce the second-order partial differential equation (16.87) to

$$\frac{1}{2} F_{rr}\sigma_r^2 + F_r(\mu_r - \lambda_r\sigma_r) + F_\tau - rF + c = 0. \tag{16.90}$$

where, as before, λ_r denotes the exogenously specified market price of the short-term interest rate risk. Equilibrium values for the call option are obtained by solving (16.90) subject to the appropriate boundary conditions.

The Black-Scholes Option Pricing Model

The Black-Scholes option pricing model is based on the assumption of constant interest rate, r. If we select $\mu_r = \sigma_r = 0$ and if the underlying pure discount bond is of a perpetual maturity so that its yield is the long-term rate l, then the second-order partial differentiation equation reduces to

$$\frac{1}{2} F_{ll}\sigma_l^2 + F_{ll} \left(\frac{\sigma_l^2}{l} + l^2 - rl \right) - F_\tau - rF = 0. \tag{16.91}$$

Under these assumptions, the value of a call option on a perpetual discount bond is obtained by initially solving (16.91) for the bond price and then for the option price using the appropriate boundary conditions. Note that the coefficients in the differential equation are independent of investors' risk preferences. Hence, the equilibrium call values should also be independent of risk preferences and the Black-Scholes model should result.

In summary, the Brennan-Schwartz model provides a preference-dependent means of valuing options on default-free bonds. The Courtadon model is a special case in which preferences still play a role. Only under quite restrictive assumptions will the Black-Scholes preference-free approach to valuation obtain.

CONCLUSION

This chapter has provided an introduction to the use of continuous time mathematics. The rules of stochastic calculus were presented and a few examples of the pricing methodology were presented. In particular, a proof of the Black-Scholes model was provided and other models were investigated when the number of sources of uncertainty was restricted to one or two.

References

To obtain a meaningful understanding of Ito calculus and continuous time mathematics for finance, the reader is referred to Merton and to Malliaris and the references contained therein.

Brennan, M., and E. Schwartz. "A Continuous Time Approach to the Pricing of Bonds." *Journal of Banking and Finance* 3(1979): 133–55.

Brennan, M., and E. Schwartz. "Finite Difference Methods and Jump Processes Arising in the Pricing of Contingent Claims: A Synthesis." *Journal of Financial and Quantitative Analysis* 13(September 1978): 461–74.

Courtadon, G. "A More Accurate Finite Difference Approximation for the Valuation of Options." *Journal of Financial and Quantitative Analysis* 17(December 1982): 697–705.

Geske, R., and K. Shastri. "Valuation by Approximation: A Comparison of Alternative Option Valuation Techniques." *Journal of Financial and Quantitative Analysis* 20(March 1985): 45–71.

Harrison, J., and S. Pliska. "Martingales and Stochastic Integrals in the Theory of Continuous Trading." *Stochastic Process and Their Applications* 2(1981): 261–71.

Ito, K., and H. McKean. *Diffusion Processes and Their Sample Paths.* New York: Academic Press, 1964.

Jarrow, R., and A. Rudd. *Option Pricing.* Homewood, Ill.: Richard Irwin, 1983.

Malliaris, A. G. *Stochastic Methods in Economics and Finance.* New York: North-Holland Publishing, 1983.

Merton, R. "On the Mathematics and Economic Assumptions of Continuous Time Models." MIT Working Paper 981-83 (1978).

Merton, R. "Theory of Finance from the Perspective of Continuous Time." *Journal of Financial and Quantitative Analysis* 10(1975): 659–74.

Merton, R. "Optimum Consumption and Portfolio Rules in a Continuous Time Model." *Journal of Economic Theory* 3(1971): 373–413.

Appendix

Finite Difference Approximation Methods for Option Valuation

In Chapter 9 the binomial process was used to approximate the stochastic evolution of stock prices over time. With this method, it was possible to develop an option pricing model that could approximate American call and put options. The binomial process approximation is not the only numerical method available for valuing options. Indeed, rather than approximate the stochastic process driving stock prices, methods are available for approximating the resulting partial differential equation. These methods involve splitting up the stock price-time space into a grid of a finite number of points. As the gap between the points, referred to as the *mesh,* gets smaller, the approximations become more precise. Finite difference techniques approximate the partial differential equations by using estimates of the change in option values over stock prices and time points on the grid. Partial derivatives are then approximated by difference equations. While there are many ways to perform the approximations, all of them lead to solutions that can be classified as either *explicit* or *implicit.* In the explicit class, each unknown option price at any node can be solved explicitly in terms of previously calculated option prices, while in the implicit class, a set of simultaneous equations must be solved.

Brennan and Schwartz provide a comprehensive discussion of finite difference methods arising in the pricing of contingent claims. For details of the theory see the references for Chapter 16. Geske and Shastri compare alternative option valuation techniques. They conclude that the binomial method works best for stocks that pay no dividends and is appropriate if only a few options prices need to be computed. However, if a large number of options need to be computed, the finite difference methods are more efficient.

Below is a computer program that prices options using the implicit finite difference method. The theory behind the algorithm is provided in Brennan and Schwartz.

```
1000 '****************************************************************
1010 '    A PROGRAM USED TO CALCULATE OPTION PRICES USING THE
1020 '    IMPLICIT FINITE DIFFERENCE METHOD.
1030 '
1040 '       written by SHYANJAW KUO
1050 '
1060 '    List of variables used in the program
1070 '
1080 '    S     - PRICE OF THE COMMON STOCK
1090 '    X     - STRIKE PRICE
1100 '    R     - SHORT TERM RISK-FREE RATE OF INTEREST
1110 '    U     - ANNUAL EXPECTED RATE OF RETURN
1120 '    SIGMA - THE STANDARD DEVIATION OF THE STOCK
1130 '    T     - MONTHS UNTIL THE OPTION EXPIRES
1140 '    ND    - NUMBER OF DIVIDEND PAYOUTS BEFORE THE EXPIRATION
1150 '    NH    - NUMBER OF STEPS IN PARTITIONING THE STOCK PRICE
1160 '    NK    - NUMBER OF STEPS/MONTH IN PARTITIONING THE TIME
1170 '
1180 '****************************************************************
1190 '**********************
1200 '    INPUT SECTION
1210 '**********************
1220 KEY OFF: CLS: DEFINT I,J,L-N
1230 DIM S(200),W(200),B(200),C(200),D(10),EDD(10)
1240 PRINT "Please Answer the Following Questions.";CHR$(13)
1250 INPUT "ENTER S: the current stock price? $",S
1260 INPUT "ENTER the type of option to be evaluated. (P/C)? ",REPLY$
1270 IF REPLY$="C" OR REPLY$="c" THEN CALLOPTN=1: GOTO 1310
1280 IF REPLY$="P" OR REPLY$="p" THEN CALLOPTN=0: GOTO 1310
1290 PRINT CHR$(7);"INVALID CHOICE. ";
1300 PRINT "PLEASE ENTER P FOR PUT OPTION OR C FOR CALL OPTION.": GOTO 1260
1310 INPUT "ENTER X: the strike price? $",X
1320 INPUT "ENTER R: the continuously compounded riskless rate of interest";R
1330 INPUT "ENTER U: the continuously compounded annual rate of return";U
1340 PRINT "ENTER SIGMA: the standard deviation of the continuously compounde
1350 INPUT "            annual rate of return";SIGMA
1360 INPUT "ENTER T: the time remaining before expiration (in months)";T
1370 INPUT "ENTER the number of dividend payouts before the expiration";ND
1380 IF ND=0 THEN 1440
1390 PRINT CHR$(13);"Please enter the ex-dividend dates and dividend."
1400 FOR J=1 TO ND
1410      INPUT "The ex-dividend date (in month) ";EDD(J)
1420      INPUT "                     Dividend = $",D(J)
1430 NEXT J
1440 INPUT "ENTER the desirable number of steps in stock price";NH
1450 INPUT "ENTER the desirable number of steps/month in time";NK
1460 PRINT CHR$(13);"COMPUTING OPTION PRICE ..."
1470 '***************************
1480 '    INITIALIZATION SECTION
1490 '***************************
1500 SMIN=S/EXP( 3.2*SIGMA*SQR(T/12!)-U*(T/12!))
1510 SMAX=S/EXP(-3.2*SIGMA*SQR(T/12!)-U*(T/12!))
1520 M=NK*T
1530 IF SMIN >= 1 THEN H=(LOG(SMAX)-LOG(SMIN))/NH: GOTO 1550
1540 H=LOG(SMAX)/(NH-2): SMIN=EXP(-2!*H)
1550 Y=LOG(SMIN)
1560 K=T/(12!*M)
1570 D1=(SIGMA/H)^2/2!
1580 D2=(R-SIGMA^2/2!)/(2!*H)
1590 A=(-D1+D2)*K
1600 B=(1!+2!*D1*K)/A
1610 C=(-D1-D2)*K/A
1620 D=(1!-R*K)/A
1630 NH=NH-1
1640 ALPHA=SMIN-X: BETA=SMAX-X
1650 FOR I=1 TO NH: B(I)=B: C(I)=C: Y=Y+H: S(I)=EXP(Y): W(I)=S(I)-X: NEXT I
1660 IF CALLOPTN THEN 1670 ELSE 1730
1670 FOR I=1 TO NH
1680      IF W(I) < 0 THEN W(I)=0
1690      NEXT I
```

```
1700     IF ALPHA < 0 THEN ALPHA = 0
1710     IF BETA  < 0 THEN BETA  = 0
1720     GOTO 1810
1730 FOR I=1 TO NH
1740     IF W(I) < 0 THEN W(I)=-W(I) ELSE W(I)=0
1750     NEXT I
1760     IF ALPHA < 0 THEN ALPHA=-ALPHA ELSE ALPHA=0
1770     IF BETA  < 0 THEN BETA =-BETA  ELSE BETA =0
1780 '*********************************
1790 '   RECURSIVE COMPUTATION SECTION
1800 '*********************************
1810 T1=0
1820 IF ND=0 THEN JE=M ELSE JE=(T-EDD(ND))*NK: T=EDD(ND): M=M-JE
1830 IF CALLOPTN THEN GOSUB 1980 ELSE GOSUB 2110
1840 IF ND=0 THEN 1900 ELSE GOSUB 2290
1850 ND=ND-1
1860 GOTO 1820
1870 '*********************
1880 '    OUTPUT SECTION
1890 '*********************
1900 I=(LOG(S)-LOG(SMIN))/H
1910 PRINT CHR$(7);CHR$(13);"GIVEN TIME TO EXPIRATION =";
1920 PRINT USING "###.##"; T1*12;
1930 IF CALLOPTN THEN OPTN$="CALL" ELSE OPTN$="PUT"
1940 PRINT " MONTHS, THE ";OPTN$;" PRICE IS";
1950 PRINT USING "$$##.##"; W(I)+(W(I+1)-W(I))*(LOG(S)-LOG(SMIN)-H*I)/H
1960 END
1970 '*******************************
1980 '    SUBROUTINE: CALL OPTION
1990 '*******************************
2000 FOR J=1 TO JE: T1=T1+K
2010     FOR I=1 TO NH: B(I)=B: W(I)=D*W(I): NEXT I
2020     W(1)=W(1)-ALPHA: W(NH)=W(NH)-C*BETA
2030     FOR I=2 TO NH
2040         XMULT=1!/B(I-1): B(I)=B(I)-XMULT*C(I-1): W(I)=W(I)-XMULT*W(I-1)
2050     NEXT I
2060     W(NH)=W(NH)/B(NH): N1=NH-1
2070     FOR I=1 TO N1: NI=NH-I: W(NI)=(W(NI)-C(NI)*W(NI+1))/B(NI): NEXT I
2080 NEXT J
2090 RETURN
2100 '*******************************
2110 '    SUBROUTINE: PUT OPTION
2120 '*******************************
2130 FOR J=1 TO JE: T1=T1+K
2140     FOR I=1 TO NH: B(I)=B: W(I)=D*W(I): NEXT I
2150     W(1)=W(1)-ALPHA: W(NH)=W(NH)-C*BETA
2160     FOR I=2 TO NH
2170         XMULT=1!/B(I-1): B(I)=B(I)-XMULT*C(I-1): W(I)=W(I)-XMULT*W(I-1)
2180     NEXT I
2190     W(NH)=W(NH)/B(NH): N1=NH-1
2200     FOR I=1 TO N1: NI=NH-I: W(NI)=(W(NI)-C(NI)*W(NI+1))/B(NI): NEXT I
2210     FOR I=1 TO NH
2220         PREM=X-S(I)
2230         IF PREM > W(I) THEN W(I)=PREM
2240         NEXT I
2250 NEXT J
2260 RETURN
2270 '*****************************
2280 '    SUBROUTINE: EX-DIVIDEND
2290 '*****************************
2300 SBASE=LOG(SMIN): DD=D(ND)
2310 IF CALLOPTN THEN 2320 ELSE 2400
2320 FOR J=NH TO 1 STEP -1
2330     PREM=S(J)-X
2340     DIFF=LOG(S(J)-DD)-SBASE
2350     I=DIFF/H: W(J)=W(I)+(W(I+1)-W(I))*(DIFF-H*I)/H
2360     IF W(J) < PREM THEN W(J)=PREM
2370     IF W(J) <= 0 THEN FOR I=1 TO J: W(I)=0: NEXT I: RETURN
```

```
2380 NEXT J
2390 RETURN
2400 FOR J=NH TO 1 STEP -1
2410     PREM=X-S(J)
2420     DIFF=LOG(S(J)-DD)-SBASE
2430     IF DIFF < 0 THEN FOR I=1 TO J: W(J)=ALPHA: NEXT I: RETURN
2440     I=DIFF/H: W(J)=W(I)+(W(I+1)-W(I))*(DIFF-H*I)/H
2450     IF W(J) < PREM THEN W(J)=PREM
2460     IF W(J) <= 0 THEN W(J)=0
2470 NEXT J
2480 RETURN
```

Index